Peter Bayne

Lessons From My Masters, Carlyle, Tennyson and Ruskin

Peter Bayne

Lessons From My Masters, Carlyle, Tennyson and Ruskin

ISBN/EAN: 9783337057640

Printed in Europe, USA, Canada, Australia, Japan

Cover: Foto ©Thomas Meinert / pixelio.de

More available books at **www.hansebooks.com**

LESSONS FROM MY MASTERS

CARLYLE, TENNYSON

AND

RUSKIN

By PETER BAYNE, M.A., LL.D.

AUTHOR OF "THE CHIEF ACTORS IN THE PURITAN REVOLUTION"
"LIFE AND LETTERS OF HUGH MILLER" ETC.

NEW YORK

HARPER & BROTHERS, PUBLISHERS

FRANKLIN SQUARE

1879

PREFATORY NOTE.

WHEN I began a series of Studies of English Authors in the *Literary World*, of which the first three were devoted to Carlyle, Tennyson, and Ruskin, I stated that it was my intention not to sit in judgment upon them, not to rise from the pleasant place of listener and learner at their feet and assume that of critical censor, but to give such information as might be of use to persons less familiar with their books than myself, and to rehearse, in brief and simple terms, a few of the principal truths they had expounded, facts they had stated, lessons they had taught.

In writing I found it practically impossible to divest myself of the critical function so completely as I had purposed. When I differed in opinion from the eminent men whose works I surveyed, I could not help saying so; and to say so without reason assigned would have seemed unjustifiable assumption. It will, however, I trust, be found that I have in no instance controverted an opinion of "my very noble and approved good masters" without its being evident that my respect and affection for them continued unimpaired. I may be permitted also to say that my own mature opinion upon many questions of the highest importance is necessarily expressed.

The Studies of Carlyle and Tennyson have been carefully revised and considerably extended; that of Ruskin is almost entirely new. I tender my thanks to the Rev. J. Kirkman and other correspondents, who have kindly permitted me to avail myself of their remarks in footnotes.

London, *June*, 1879.

TABLE OF CONTENTS.

THOMAS CARLYLE.

ALFRED TENNYSON.

JOHN RUSKIN.

THOMAS CARLYLE.

1*

CHAPTER I.

THE SCHEME OF HIS LIFE.

I DO not know any word more fitly spoken about Carlyle than that of Professor Masson, that there has been in his life an element of soldierly arrangement. It has not been a life at hap-hazard, but a campaign, planned with reasoning calmness, with comprehensive intelligence, and carried out with adamantine resolution. Finding, as genius has so often found, that he could not adjust himself to the professional pace and dogmatic harness which were ready for him at the close of his college course, he discovered, on the threshold of manhood, that literature was the goal at which he ought to aim, "the haven of expatriated spiritualisms," where shelter and honorable activity might await him. We are not left to conjecture in attempting to realize the spirit and the anticipations with which he entered upon a literary career. Upwards of fifty years ago, in the first book he gave to the world, he described a literary life, its dangers, its temptations, its drawbacks, its advantages; and though the passage is long, we cannot, I think, do better, in commencing our talk about him, than read it over.

THE MAN OF LETTERS.

If to know wisdom were to practise it; if fame brought true dignity and peace of mind; or happiness consisted in nourishing the intellect with its appropriate food, and surrounding the imagination with ideal beauty, a literary life would be the most enviable which the lot of this world affords. But the truth is far otherwise. The Man of Letters has no immutable, all-conquering volition, more than other men; to understand and to perform are two very different things with him as with every one. His fame rarely exerts a favorable influence on his dignity of character, and never on his peace of mind: its glitter is external, for the eyes of others; within, it is but the aliment of unrest, the oil cast upon the ever-gnawing fire of ambition, quickening into fresh vehemence the blaze which it stills for a moment. Moreover, this Man of Letters is not wholly made of spirit, but of clay and spirit mixed: his thinking faculties may be nobly trained and exercised, but he must have affections as well as thoughts to make him happy, and food and raiment must be given him, or he dies. Far from being the most enviable, his way of life is, perhaps, among the many modes by which an ardent mind endeavors to express its activity, the most thickly beset with suffering and degradation. Look at the biography of authors! Except the Newgate Calendar, it is the most sickening chapter in the history of man. The calamities of these people are a fertile topic; and too often their faults and vices have kept pace with their calamities. Nor is it difficult to see how this has happened. Talent of any sort is generally accompanied with a peculiar fineness of sensibility; of genius this is the most essential constituent; and life in any shape has sorrows enough for hearts so formed. The employments of literature sharpen this natural tendency; the vexations that accompany them frequently exasperate it into morbid soreness. The cares and toils of literature are the business of life; its delights are too ethereal and too transient to furnish that perennial flow of satisfaction, coarse, but plenteous and substantial, of which happiness in this world of ours is made. The most finished efforts of the mind give it little pleasure, frequently they give it pain; for men's aims are ever beyond their strength. And the outward recompense of these undertakings, the distinction they confer, is of still smaller value: the desire for it is insatiable even when successful; and, when baffled, it issues in jealousy and envy, and every pitiful and painful feeling. So keen a temperament with so little to restrain or satisfy, so much to distress or tempt it, produces contradictions which few are adequate to reconcile. Hence the unhappiness of literary men, hence their faults and follies. Thus literature is apt to form a dangerous and discontenting occupation even for the amateur. But for him whose rank and worldly comforts depend on it, who does not live to write, but writes to live, its difficulties and perils are fearfully increased. Few spectacles are more afflicting than that of such a man, so gifted and so fated, so jostled and tossed to and fro in the rude bustle of life, the buffetings of which he is so little fitted to endure. Cherishing, it may be, the loftiest thoughts, and clogged with the meanest wants; of pure and holy purposes, yet ever driven from the straight path by the pressure of necessity, or the impulse of passion; thirsting for glory, and frequently in want of daily bread; hovering between the empyrean of his fancy and the squalid desert of reality; cramped and foiled in his most strenuous exertions; dissatisfied with his best performances, disgusted with his fortune, this man of letters too often spends his weary days in conflicts with obscure misery: harassed, chagrined, debased, or maddened; the victim at once of tragedy and farce; the last forlorn outpost in the war of mind against matter. Many are the noble souls that have perished bitterly, with their tasks unfinished, under these corroding woes! Some in utter famine, like Otway; some in dark insanity, like Cowper and Collins; some, like Chatterton, have sought out a more stern quietus, and turning their indignant steps away from a world which refused them welcome, have taken refuge in that strong fortress, where poverty and cold neglect, and the thousand natural shocks which flesh is heir to, could not reach them any more. Yet among these men are to be found the brightest specimens and the chief benefactors of mankind! It is they that keep awake the finer parts of our souls; that give us better aims than power or pleasure, and withstand the total sovereignty of Mammon in this earth. They are the vanguard in the march of mind; the intellectual backwoodsmen, reclaiming from the idle wilderness new territories for the thought and the activity of their happier brethren. Pity that from all their conquests, so rich in benefit to others, themselves should reap so little. But it is vain to murmur. They are volunteers in this cause; they weighed the charms of it against the perils, and they must abide the results of their decision, as all must. The hardships of the course they follow are formidable, but not all inevitable; and to such as pursue it rightly, it is not without its great rewards. If an author's life is more agitated and more painful than that of others, it may also be made more spirit-stirring and exalted; fortune may render him unhappy; it is only himself that can make him despicable. The history of genius has, in fact, its bright side as well as its dark. And if it is distressing to survey the misery, and, what is worse, the debasement, of so many gifted men, it is doubly cheering, on the other hand, to reflect on the few, who, amidst the temptations and sorrows to which life in all its provinces and most in theirs is liable, have travelled through it in calm and virtuous majesty, and are now hallowed in our memories, not less for their conduct than their writings. Such men are the flower of this lower world; to such can the epithet of great be applied with its true emphasis. There is a congruity in their proceedings which one loves to contemplate; he who would write heroic poems should make his whole life a heroic poem! So thought our Milton; and, what was more difficult, he acted so. To Milton, the moral king of authors, a heroic multitude, out of many ages and

countries, might be joined; "a cloud of witnesses" that encompass the
true literary man throughout his pilgrimage, inspiring him to lofty emula-
tion, cheering his solitary thoughts with hope, teaching him to struggle, to
endure, to conquer difficulties, or, in failure and heavy sufferings, to

> Arm th' obdured breast
> With stubborn patience as with triple steel.

We need not hesitate to place Carlyle, along with Milton,
among the moral kings of literature. He has travelled through
life in "calm and virtuous majesty." With the stormful
splendor cast upon Milton's career by his glorious intermeddling in politics, there is indeed nothing in that of Carlyle to
correspond; but in completeness, and what I may call homo-
geneity, as the career of a Man of Letters, that of Carlyle is
superior even to that of Milton. He has known no other
devotion except literature; has done the work of no political
party, has not condescended to a professorship, but has made
it the object of his life to act upon mankind by the pen. As
every peasant that carried a musket in the Grand Army felt
a pride in Napoleon, the little Corporal who had become Emperor of France, so the humblest camp-follower in the huge
army of literature may think with pride of Thomas Carlyle.
Over all the dangers that he foresaw he has regally triumphed;
all the more than princely guerdons, which he declared to be
within the sphere of an author's ambition, he has honorably
earned ; amidst the tumults and changes of a feverish time, and
the quarrels and calamities of petty souls, he has risen above
all jealousy, preserved an absolutely unblemished name, and
never been distracted for an hour from that rest of noble purpose, that peace of serene activity, which is the most substantial happiness attainable on earth. His life has been built
upon realities. With clear discernment and unflinching firmness, he has put aside or trampled on unrealities.

Coming to London in early manhood, he established himself
in an unpretentious house in a quiet street in Chelsea—a house

sufficient, but not more than sufficient, with room for his books and such friends as might visit, not his house, but himself; and there he has remained for forty years, looking with perfect indifference, too profound for conscious scorn, upon the palatial buildings constantly rising to west of him and to north of him, in which successful shopkeepers, stock-jobbers, railway-contractors, bubble company projectors, and other favorites of fortune and the age, had their reward. That small house has been his home and ideal palace, in which, as he had well assured himself, he could partake of all the real joys that flesh is heir to. Thatched in from the wind and rain, paying his way, doing his work, he satisfied all his real wants; and he had within him no raging crew of vanities to appease, such as have tormented Voltaire and other authors, like those dogs that Milton saw at hell-gate yelling in eternal hunger round Sin, their mother. If any Prince Consort, English aristocrat, American humorist, German statesman, or other loyal admirer, wished to see him, the admirer could make his way to Cheyne Row, Chelsea. It was of infinite importance for Carlyle to have the approval of the judge in his own breast; of infinite importance also to have the approval of the Eternal Maker; it was of some importance, but of very little in comparison, what the great body of his countrymen thought of him; it was of no importance at all what the leaders of fashion thought. The impertinence of a cross or a ribbon, offered him in his old age by "him they call Dizzy," he could quietly, not ungraciously, put aside; the more appropriate honor of a place in the Prussian Royal Order for Merit he could graciously accept. He was "king of himself and of his world," as he said of Goethe; able at all times to consume his own smoke; firm in that silent, modest, yet self-sufficing and unconquerable pride, which is as knightly armor to defend and as kingly purple to adorn. His life has been in the plainest sense practical, and yet it has been ideal and sublime.

CHAPTER II.

O F the practicality — perhaps, also, though less obviously,
of the sublimity—of Carlyle's life, the roots are discoverable in his father's house. He came of substantial farmer
people in the Dumfriesshire village of Ecclefechan, where he
was born in 1795. It has been mentioned on good authority
that Carlyle speaks of his father as one of the most remarkable men, if not the most remarkable man, he has ever known.
Intense shrewdness and profound religious fervor were his
characteristics. Among the traditions of young Carlyle's
home, which would come invested with a halo of sacredness
to the child, was that of reverence and affection for the memory of the Covenanters. It is interesting to catch sight of
those threads of connection between memorable characters and
occurrences which nature commonly manages to keep out of
sight. Such a thread is that which connected Oliver Cromwell with Carlyle. It was a man imbued with enthusiasm for
the Covenanters, a man capable, in the nineteenth century, of
sympathetically realizing and reproducing the fire that burned
in their hearts, who could find the key to Cromwell's character, and do justice to him and to the Covenanters alike. But
there was another thread of connection between the strong
Puritanic religion of Carlyle's father's house, and Carlyle's
character as a Man of Letters. The Covenanters are things of
the past. Even in Scotland there are now few or none who,
if a Covenanter of 1638, or a Covenanter of 1643, were to
rise from the dead, would be recognized by either as brethren.

But the fervor of Puritanism passed into the heart of Scotland, into the marrow of the nation's bones, and has lived and throbbed in the moral intensity of a Burns, a Chalmers, a Carlyle. In preaching the gospel of earnestness, in smiting cant and affectation, in tearing to rags, amidst sardonic laughter, all the flimsy sentimentalities which mimic and mock the realities of feeling, Carlyle has been a true Puritan. This has been one of the essential elements in his success. Without earnestness no man is ever great, or does really great things. He may be the cleverest of men; he may be brilliant, entertaining, popular; but he will want weight. No soul-moving picture was ever painted that had not in it depth of shadow. The light must also be there; a gleam on the horizon, if no more, is indispensable; but the light itself is worthless if there is no shadow to give it relief and tenderness.

There is no reason to doubt that some of those touches in which Carlyle describes the childhood and youth of the hero of Sartor Resartus, may be correctly applied to his own biography. His first school-master, "a down-bent, broken-hearted, under-foot martyr, as others of that guild are," pronounced him a genius fit for the learned professions. He took to reading with earnest delight, laying out his coppers on stall literature. That sense of mystery in what, to common observation, are the simplest and most unsuggestive things, which manifests itself in all his books, was early developed. He assigns to Teufelsdröckh's twelfth year the following incident, which I confidently accept as autobiographic: "It struck me much, as I sat by the Kuhbach, one silent noontide, and watched it flowing, gurgling, to think how this same streamlet had flowed and gurgled, through all changes of weather and of fortune, from beyond the earliest date of history. Yes, probably on the morning when Joshua forded Jordan, even as at the mid-day when Cæsar, doubtless with difficulty, swam the Nile, yet kept his Commentaries dry—this little Kuhbach, assiduous as Tiber,

Eurotas, or Siloa, was murmuring on across the wilderness, as yet unnamed, unseen; here, too, as in the Euphrates and the Ganges, is a vein or veinlet of the grand world-circulation of waters, which, with its atmospheric arteries, has lasted and lasts simply with the world. Thou fool! Nature alone is antique, and the oldest Art a mushroom; the idle crag thou sittest on is six thousand years of age." Not only the habit of wondering and pondering in presence of the unfathomable mystery which encompasses us on all sides, but the habit of tracing the connection of one thing with another, and reflecting on the interminable series of consequences flowing from every fact which we meet with in Carlyle's writings, are clearly foreshadowed in the preceding words. "Christ died on the cross," he said once, in conversation with Emerson, as both lay resting on the moorland; "that built the church in the valley yonder, that brought you and me to the moor; all things hang together." I quote from memory, and do not vouch for the words, but this was their sense. In the musings of the boy Teufelsdröckh upon the brook "may there not lie," Carlyle himself significantly asks, "the beginning of those well-nigh unutterable meditations on the grandeur and mystery of time, and its relation to eternity, which play such a part" in the philosophy of that transcendental Professor of Weiss-nicht-wo, who is justly believed to be, in the main, a portrait of Carlyle himself?

He studied at the University of Edinburgh, but he has always and bitterly said that he owes it nothing but the miscellaneous reading afforded by its library. "We boasted ourselves a rational university; in the highest degree hostile to mysticism; thus was the young vacant mind furnished with much talk about progress of the species, dark ages, prejudice, and the like; so that all were quickly enough blown out into a state of windy argumentativeness; whereby the better sort had soon to end in sick, impotent scepticism; the worser sort explode in spiritual self-conceit, and to all spiritual intents become dead." Is this the first declaration of that war against "victorious analysis" and omnipotent "logic-chopping," which Carlyle has carried on for so many years?

From the professors who undertook, apparently with small ability, to instruct him in human science and learning, he passed to other professors, who attempted to instruct him in theology, with a view to his entering the ministry of the Scottish Presbyterian Church. Of them we expressly hear little in his works, but he has always talked freely of the experiences of his youth, and it is no secret that whatever seeds of doubt had been previously sown in his mind germinated vigorously under the gardening of the divines. He experienced "fever-paroxysms of doubt." "In the silent night-watches, still darker in his heart than over sky and earth, he has cast himself before the All-seeing, and with audible prayers cried vehemently for light, for deliverance from death and the grave." The end was that he could not see his way to entering the ministry. Whether his doubts were well-founded or ill-founded, he clearly did right in making no effort to crush them by force, and in abstaining from taking Orders while he continued under their influence. "What the light of your mind," he wrote, long afterward, "which is the direct inspiration of the Almighty, pronounces incredible—that, in God's name, leave uncredited; at your peril, do not try believing that."

He now, for some years, was a school-master, proving to be a stern disciplinarian; but so strong a genius for literature could not fail to assert itself, and his ardent study of German led him gradually into his life-path. He found with unspeakable emotion, in the writings of Goethe, that such doubts as his had been entertained by others, and not only entertained, but triumphed over. Thus commenced a relation to Goethe, which was destined to exert a profound and ineffaceable influence upon his mind. But some time elapsed before he recog-

nized the sovereignty of Goethe in German literature, or, at
least, before he set his throne far above those of all other Germans.   He studied Schiller with ardent enthusiasm, and his
first book was that biography of Schiller, from which I quoted
his description of the Man of Letters.   The work abounds with
beauties, both of thought and style, but is elaborate, polished,
and formal, and has neither the freedom of movement nor the
impetuous force that were to become so characteristic of the
author.   Published originally in the *London Magazine*, it appeared as a book in 1825.   A translation was issued in Germany, with a commendatory preface by Goethe; a correspond-
ence between Goethe and Carlyle ensued; and we find him, in
1828, describing to the great poet the circumstances of his life
at Craigen-Puttoch, a small estate in Dumfriesshire, brought as
a dowry by his wife, to whom he had been married two years
previously.   "Among the granite hills and the black morasses,
which stretch westward through Galloway, almost to the Irish
Sea," the estate stood forth, "a green oasis, a tract of ploughed,
partly enclosed and planted, ground, where corn ripens and
trees afford a shade although surrounded by seamews and
rough-woolled sheep."   Fine descriptive glimpses of the scenery amidst which he lived at the time occur in the famous
book which he wrote amidst its solitudes.   "The rocks are of
that sort called Primitive by the mineralogists, which always
arrange themselves in masses of a rugged, gigantic character;
which ruggedness, however, is here tempered by a singular airi-
ness of form and softness of environment; in a climate favorable to vegetation, the gray cliff, itself covered with lichens,
shoots up through a garment of foliage and verdure; and
white, bright cottages, tree-shaded, cluster round the everlasting granite. . . .   Often, also, could I see the black Tempest
marching in anger through the distance; round some Schreckhorn, as yet grim-blue, would the eddying vapor gather, and
there tumultuously eddy, and flow down like a mad witch's

hair; till, after a space, it vanished, and in the clear sunbeam your Schreckhorn stood smiling grim-white, for the vapor had held snow."

Carlyle had now served his apprenticeship to literature. In addition to the Life of Schiller he had published a translation of Goethe's Wilhelm Meister, and more than one volume of tales from Jean Paul, Tieck, and other German authors. He had begun to write in the *Edinburgh Review*, and produced his memorable essay on Burns. But he had not yet given to the world anything so strongly stamped with his original genius as to mark him out as a great original among living writers. Such a work he produced at Craigen-Puttoch—the name of it Sartor Resartus. It contains the essential facts of his spiritual history, the fundamental principles of his philosophy. I shall give some account of it in the next chapter, and shall close, for the present, with one of those few poems written by Carlyle before he settled finally to prose.

THE SOWER'S SONG.

Now hands to seed-sheet, boys,
We step and we cast; old Time's on wing;
And would ye partake of harvest's joys,
The corn must be sown in spring.
    Fall gently and still, good corn,
    Lie warm in thy earthy bed,
    And stand so yellow some morn,
    That beast and man may be fed.

Old Earth is a pleasure to see
In sunshiny cloak of red and green;
The furrow lies fresh; this year will be
As the years that are past have been.
    Fall gently and still, etc.

Old Mother, receive this corn,
The seed of six thousand golden sires:

All these on thy kindly breast were born;
One more thy poor child requires.
> Fall gently and still, etc.

Now steady and sure again,
And measure of stroke and step we keep;
Thus up and thus down we cast our grain;
Sow well, and you gladly reap.
> Fall gently and still, etc.

There is true melody, as well as exquisite picturesqueness, in this little song. Carlyle was born a poet.

CHAPTER III.

MR. CARLYLE has never pledged himself to any formal system of philosophy, his ineradicable conviction being that it is impossible to sum up truth in any system framed by man, and that, if you train yourself to look at nature through the colored spectacles of any one theory, however comprehensive, you will see falsely, partially, or superficially. One verified fact, he maintains, is worth a score of elaborately-constructed philosophies of the universe. Those men of science who sit in cross-legged complacency, and explain to you how, out of nebulous star-vapors, colliding aerolites, or otherwise, solar systems originate and worlds are formed, call forth his keenest sarcasm. "I would beg to know," he cries, glaring into them with eyes of fiery scorn, "whether an order for a world is likely to come to *your* shop any morning."

Nevertheless his thinking and his writing have from first to last been dominated by a few great thoughts or ideas, and these are discoverable in their purest form in the book composed by him amidst the wilds of Galloway—the world-renowned Sartor Resartus. I look upon this as one of the very few books produced in Great Britain in the present century deserving to be styled a true, original, and important contribution to metaphysics. It connects itself in a very interesting manner with Kant's speculations on space and time, and with Sir William Hamilton's philosophy of the Infinite; but it is distinctively Carlyle's, and cannot be claimed by the disciples either of Kant or of Hamilton.

The thought in this book has an affinity with pantheism,

with which it was identified by John Sterling; but it is not necessarily pantheistic. The thesis, or proposition, which underlies it, from beginning to end, is that all matter and material things are but vesture, clothing, or visual appearance, of spirit. Let us not be startled by the seeming mysticism of this. It is either false, or it is perfectly simple and true. As I hold to be the case with all genuine metaphysics, the proposition carries its own evidence with it, which evidence, if we will but make the effort of patient care necessary to comprehend it—and such an effort is surely worth making, in order to get at the deepest root of thought and belief in a mighty intellectual genius like Carlyle—we can estimate for ourselves, saying at once whether we agree with it or disagree. Matter, as such, he holds to be dead. That is to say, he finds in the universe, as revealed to him by his senses, or conceived by his mind, no matter which itself originates force, or which is a self-originating force. Do you and I, reader, agree with him here? Does a stone sink, or a cork rise, in water, by its own force? Does a magnet originate its own force? For my part, I do not know matter at all—I cannot conceive or think of matter —except as inert, dead. Do we, then, know force at all? Carlyle answers Yes. When he stretches forth his hand, he initiates force. Even Professor Tyndall explicitly allows that his will determines the movement of his arm; and Carlyle, and those who hold with Carlyle that spirit is the only force-originating agency revealed to us either in experience or in consciousness, can challenge all the materialists in the world to name an instance in which mere matter does what Professor Tyndall does when he moves his arm.

"The true, inexplicable, God-revealing miracle," writes Carlyle in Sartor Resartus, "lies in this, that I can stretch forth my hand at all; that I have free force to clutch aught therewith." How should this be a "God-revealing miracle?" I am not sure that Carlyle explicitly answers the question; but we need not have much difficulty in supplying the answer which he suggests. The exertion of force by me reveals to me my own spirit; I am conscious of my own existence when I think, or feel, or act; I cannot do any of these things without, at the same time, becoming aware that I, the indefinable spirit or person who originate force, exist. I never think—I cannot rationally think—that my bones, my blood-vessels, the particles of my brain, in one word, any or all the material instruments, which I set in motion, are the originating force within me. In like manner, seeing the material universe, from star to wave-spray, in motion, I conclude that the only cause known to me as adequate to originate motion, or to use matter as an instrument, is present in the universe, and is a Spirit—God. Strictly, therefore, it is true, as Carlyle says, that the stretching forth of my hand is to me a natural revelation of God; and Professor Tyndall, when he acknowledged to his audience that the exertion of force by his will upon his arm was a primary, indisputable fact, ought, I humbly suggest, to have followed in the steps of Carlyle, and owned that such a fact attests the existence of a Living Spirit who moves the universe. But it requires immense courage in these days to utter and stand to any simple, great, and ancient truth; it is on paradox, extravagance, glittering superficiality, that the plaudits of the crowd are showered.

All is dead save spirit—the spirit, man, the spirit, God: that is the fundamental doctrine of Mr. Carlyle, the kernel and philosophical *open sesame* of all his works. "To the eye of vulgar logic"—these are his words—"what is man? An omnivorous biped that wears breeches. To the eye of pure reason what is he? A soul, a spirit, and divine apparition. Round his mysterious ME, there lies, under all those wool-rags, a garment of flesh (or of senses) contextured in the loom of heaven; whereby he is revealed to his like." That is to say, the body in which the spirit lives is the instrument by which one human

2

spirit can make itself known to another. In this, again, the reader need not be afraid of mysticism or incomprehensibility. It is a plain fact that I know either myself or my brother only through the senses—no man ever saw a soul. But the body, through which spirit communes with spirit, becomes, from that very fact, inexpressibly venerable to Carlyle. It is a garment "sky-woven and worthy of a God." And then he quotes with approval Saint Chrysostom's well-known words, "the true SHEKINAH is man." And thus the *other* half of Carlyle's scheme of things breaks upon us. He reverences common things, attaches worth to all that is visible, because appearance reveals force, and force is fundamentally spirit. "Nothing that he sees"—I piece out my words with Carlyle's own, spoken of Teufelsdröckh—"but has more than a common meaning, but has two meanings: thus, if in the highest imperial sceptre and Charlemagne-mantle, as well as in the poorest ox-goad and gypsy-blanket, he finds prose, decay, contemptibility; there is in each sort poetry also, and a reverend worth. For matter, were it never so despicable, is spirit, the manifestation of spirit; were it never so honorable, can it be more?" Nothing, therefore, is to be looked on with mere hatred and contempt. "What is that we cannot love; since all was created by God?" He "could clasp the whole universe into his bosom and keep it warm." He takes the liberty, however, to greet with sardonic raillery those sniffing gentlemen who deny that there is anything wonderful in the universe, and who pretend to explain everything with their dissecting-knives and their victorious analysis. Wonder is his habitual mood, and aspects and circumstances of human life, which, to ordinary men, would suggest no remark at all, awaken in him the deepest reflections.

Leaving these deep things, let us read that passage in which Teufelsdröckh moralizes on the spectacle of a great modern city by night, as it lies spread below the watch-tower of the solitary student.

A City by Night.

"*Ach, mein Lieber!*" ("Ah, my dear fellow!") said he once, at midnight, when we had returned from the Coffee-house in rather earnest talk, "it is a true sublimity to dwell here. These fringes of lamplight, struggling up through smoke and thousand-fold exhalations, some fathoms into the ancient reign of night, what thinks Boötes of them, as he leads his Hunting-dogs over the Zenith in their leash of sidereal fire? That stifled hum of midnight, when traffic has lain down to rest; and the chariot-wheels of Vanity, still rolling here and there through distant streets, are bearing her to halls roofed in, and lighted to the due pitch for her; and only vice and misery, to prowl or to moan like night-birds, are abroad: that hum, I say, like the stertorous, unquiet slumber of sick life, is heard in heaven! Oh, under that hideous coverlet of vapors and putrefactions and unimaginable gases, what a fermenting-vat lies simmering and hid! The joyful and the sorrowful are there; men are dying there, men are being born: men are praying—on the other side of a brick partition, men are cursing; and around them all is the vast, void night. The proud grandee still lingers in his perfumed saloons, or reposes within damask curtains; wretchedness cowers into truckle-beds, or shivers hunger-stricken into its lair of straw; in obscure cellars, *Rouge-et-Noir* languidly emits its voice-of-destiny to haggard, hungry villains; while Chancellors of State sit plotting, and playing their high chess game, whereof the pawns are men. The lover whispers his mistress that the coach is ready; and she, full of hope and fear, glides down, to fly with him over the borders; the thief, still more silently, sets to his pick-locks and crow-bars, or lurks in wait till the watchmen first snore in their boxes. Gay mansions, with supper-rooms and dancing-rooms, are full of light and music, and high-swelling hearts; but, in the condemned cells, the pulse of life beats tremulous and faint, and bloodshot eyes look out through the darkness, which is around and within, for the light of a stern last morning. Six men are to be hanged on the morrow: comes there no hammering from the *Rabenstein?*—their gallows must even now be o'building. Upwards of five hundred thousand two-legged animals, without feathers, lie around us, in horizontal position; their heads all in nightcaps, and full of the foolishest dreams. Riot cries aloud, and staggers and swaggers in his rank dens of shame; and the mother, with streaming hair, kneels over her pallid dying infant, whose parched lips only her tears now moisten. All these heaped and huddled together, with nothing but a little carpentry and masonry between them; crammed in like salted fish in a barrel; or weltering, shall I say, like an Egyptian pitcher of tamed vipers, each struggling to get its *head above* the other; such work goes on under that smoke-counterpane!—But I, *mein Werther*, sit above it all; I am alone with the stars."

From this and several other passages in Sartor Resartus a penetrating observer might have inferred that a great describer of men and things was about to make his mark in English literature. The warmest sympathy with the activities and the interests of mankind becomes visible here and there in the book. This gloomy picture of a city by night, though evincing a descriptive power which it would be difficult to match in the books of any period, does less, perhaps, to show the writer's heart than his more slight and brief, yet exquisitely clear and tender, sketchings of village life in the daytime. The little town, "all diminished to a toy-box," lies "embosomed among its groves and green natural bulwarks," the hum of its multifarious traffic coming mellowed by distance like music to the ear. "Its white steeple is then truly a starward-pointing finger; the canopy of blue smoke seems like a sort of life-breath: for always, of its own unity, the soul gives unity to whatso it looks on with love; thus does the little dwelling-place of men, in itself a congeries of houses and huts, become for us an individual, almost a person." As a piece of fine imaginative description, and as illustrating that element of humor which abounds in Sartor Resartus, I shall quote the passage in which the hero is represented as having in his wanderings reached the North Cape. The time is midnight in June.

TEUFELSDRÖCKH AT THE NORTH CAPE.

He has a "light blue Spanish cloak" hanging round him, as his "most commodious, principal, indeed sole upper garment;" and stands there on the world-promontory, looking over the infinite brine, like a little blue belfry (as we figure), now motionless indeed, yet ready, if stirred, to ring quaintest changes. "Silence as of death," writes he; "for midnight, even in the Arctic latitudes, has its character: nothing but the granite cliffs ruddy-tinged, the peaceable gurgle of that slow-heaving Polar Ocean, over which in the utmost North the great sun hangs low and lazy, as if he too were slumbering. Yet is his cloud-couch wrought of crimson and cloth-of-gold; yet does his light stream over the mirror of waters, like a tremulous fire-pillar, shooting downward to the abyss, and hide itself under my feet. In such moments solitude also is invaluable; for who would speak, or be looked on, when behind him lies all Europe and Africa fast asleep, except the watchmen: and before him the silent immensity and palace of the Eternal, whereof our sun is but a porch-lamp? Nevertheless, in this solemn moment comes a man, or monster, scrambling from among the rock-hollows; and, shaggy, huge as the Hyperborean Bear, hails me in Russian speech: most probably, therefore, a Russian smuggler. With courteous brevity, I signify my indifference to contraband trade, my humane intentions, yet strong wish to be private. In vain: the monster, counting doubtless on his superior stature, and minded to make sport for himself, or perhaps profit, were it with murder, continues to advance; ever assailing me with his importunate train-oil breath; and now has advanced, till we stand both on the verge of the rock, the deep sea rippling greedily down below. What argument will avail? On the thick Hyperborean, cherubic reasoning, seraphic eloquence were lost. Prepared for such extremity, I, deftly enough, whisk aside one step; draw out, from my interior reservoirs, a sufficient Birmingham horse-pistol, and say, 'Be so obliging as to retire, friend, and with promptitude!' This logic even the Hyperborean understands: fast enough, with apologetic, petitionary growl, he sidles off; and, except for suicidal as well as homicidal purposes, need not return."

The words thrown in, "except the watchmen," are marvellously characteristic of Carlyle's humor. They add just that serio-comic touch to the picture which prevents it from becoming pompous and pedantic. It is notable that our clever friend, M. Taine, for whom Sartor Resartus is a mere piece of Gothic horse-play, entirely omits, in his translation of the passage, this inimitable glimpse of the watchmen stalking about with their eyes placidly on the moon, while all Europe and Africa are slumbering round them. The French have much wit, but little humor.

What is the ethical result—the moral doctrine—of Sartor

Resartus? Teufelsdröckh, whose spiritual history is described, starts with, and is never traitor to, a sovereign desire for truth. "After all the nameless woe that inquiry, which for me, what it is not always, was genuine love of truth, had wrought me, I, nevertheless, still loved truth, and would bate no jot of my allegiance to her. Truth," I cried, "though the heavens crush me for following her; no falsehood! though a whole celestial Lubberland were the price of apostasy!" Though he had been tormented with "motive-grinders and mechanical profit-and-loss philosophies," and lay under "sick ophthalmia and hallucination," he had never ceased to believe in "the infinite nature of duty." His eyes were sealed to God's light, but He was present in his heart, and "His heaven-written law still stood legible and sacred there." The sceptical and mechanical philosophy, however, pressed hard on him with its denial of the spiritual life of the universe. "To me the universe was all void of life, of purpose, of volition, even of hostility; it was one huge, dead, immeasurable steam-engine, rolling on, in its dead indifference, to grind me limb from limb. O, the vast, gloomy, solitary Golgotha, and mill of death!" He "lived in a continual, indefinite, pining fear; tremulous, pusillanimous, apprehensive" of he "knew not what; it seemed as if all things in the heavens above and the earth beneath" would hurt him. But he suddenly put all fear under his feet.

His Victory over Fear.

Full of such humor, and perhaps the miserablest man in the whole French capital or suburbs, was I, one sultry dog-day, after much perambulation, toiling along the dirty little *Rue Saint Thomas de l'Enfer*, among civic rubbish enough, in a close atmosphere, and over pavements hot as Nebuchadnezzar's furnace; whereby, doubtless, my spirits were but little cheered; when, all at once, there rose a thought in me, and I asked myself: "What *art* thou afraid of? Wherefore, like a coward, dost thou forever pip and whimper, and go cowering and trembling? Despicable biped! what is the sum-total of the worst that lies before thee? Death?

Well, death: and say the pangs of Tophet, too, and all that the devil and man will, or can, do against thee! Hast thou a heart; canst thou not suffer whatso it be; and, as a child of freedom, thou outcast, trample Tophet itself under thy feet, while it consumes thee? Let it come, then; I will meet it and defy it!" And, as I so thought, there rushed like a stream of fire over my whole soul; and I shook base fear away from me forever. I was strong, of unknown strength; a spirit, almost a god. From that time the temper of my misery was changed; not fear or whining sorrow was it, but indignation, and grim, fire-eyed defiance.

Things now began to improve. He still, no doubt, lived too much in negation and indifference, but he had at last quelled the spectres of fear, and, being conscious to himself of loyalty to truth and of reverence for moral law, he would not crouch and creep like a dastard, but stand erect like a man. The universe, however, was still, for him, but a machine—the sneering, shallow scepticism of the eighteenth century still held him in its toils. Gradually the deeper and more genial truth, of which we have already heard, dawned upon him. "What," he asks, "is nature? Ha! why do I not name thee God? Art thou not the 'Living Garment of God?' O heavens, is it, in very deed, He then that ever speaks through thee; that lives and loves in thee, that lives and loves in me?" These are the only words in this book which countenance the opinion that Carlyle's main doctrine is pantheistic. But I am not aware that Carlyle has ever owned it to be pantheistic, and he would hardly have met John Sterling's assertion to that effect with a jest if he had seriously accepted pantheism. His doctrine is that the universe is perpetually formed and renewed by the Spirit of God—not that matter is God. In speaking of the universe as the vesture of God, in the sense in which man's body is the vesture of his spirit, he assigns, or may be logically held to assign, to the Spirit, God, that personality, that consciousness, that intelligence, which are the highest attributes of the spirit, man. We found that the body of man was in his view the highest temple. The stern and fruitless sense of

duty, which remained with him while still in doubt, denial, or
indifference, now blooms out into ardor of love, and tenderness of pity, for all mankind.

His New Faith and Love.

Foreshadows, call them rather fore-splendors, of that truth and beginning of truths, fell mysteriously upon my soul. Sweeter than day-spring
to the shipwrecked in Nova Zembla; ah! like the mother's voice to her
little child that strays bewildered, weeping, in unknown tumults; like soft
streamings of celestial music to my too-exasperated heart, came that evangel. The universe is not dead and demoniacal, a charnel-house with spectres; but godlike, and my Father's! With other eyes, too, could I now
look upon my fellow-man; with an infinite love, an infinite pity. Poor,
wandering, wayward man! Art thou not tried, and beaten with stripes,
even as I am? Ever, whether thou bear the Royal mantle or the beggar's
gabardine, art thou not so weary, so heavy-laden; and thy bed of rest is
but a grave. O, my brother, my brother, why cannot I shelter thee in my
bosom, and wipe away all tears from thy eyes!—Truly, the din of many-
voiced life, which, in this solitude, with the mind's organ, I could hear, was
no longer a maddening discord, but a melting one; like inarticulate cries,
and sobbings of a dumb creature, which in the ear of heaven are prayers.
The poor earth, with her poor joys, was now my needy mother, not my
cruel step-dame; man, with his so mad wants and so mean endeavors, had
become the dearer to me; and even for his sufferings and his sins, I now
first named him brother. Thus was I standing in the porch of that "*Sanctuary of sorrow;*" by strange, steep ways, had I too been guided thither;
and ere long its sacred gates would open, and the "*Divine depth of sorrow*" be disclosed to me.

The words quoted by Carlyle in this passage are from
Goethe. To this fathomless depth of affection for men—this
passionate sympathy with his kind—was Carlyle led by him
who is generally represented as a cold-hearted self-worshipper,
a preacher of no Gospel more human or more Divine than
culture. Nearly half a century after this passage was written, Carlyle addressed the students of Edinburgh University as
their lord rector, and then again, after having tested its worth
in a life of heroic labor, he deliberately referred to Goethe's in-

terpretation of the moral significance of Christianity and doctrine of the reverence due by man to his God, to his brethren, and to himself, as what he would rather have written than any other passage in recent literature. "It is only with renunciation," says the great poet and philosopher, who is supposed to have been hewn from ice, and to have had no object in life but to polish himself up, so that the ice might show to advantage—"it is only with renunciation that life, properly speaking, can be said to begin." Such, adopted from Goethe, is the moral teaching of Carlyle in Sartor Resartus.

THE EVERLASTING YEA.

"I see a glimpse of it!" cries he elsewhere; there is in man a higher than love of happiness; he can do without happiness, and instead thereof find blessedness! Was it not to preach forth this same higher that sages and martyrs, the poet and the priest, in all times, have spoken and suffered; bearing testimony, through life and through death, of the godlike that is in man, and how in the godlike only has he strength and freedom? Which God-inspired doctrine art thou honored to be taught; O heavens! and broken with manifold merciful afflictions, even till thou become contrite, and learn it! O thank thy destiny for these; thankfully bear what yet remain; thou hadst need of them; the self in thee needed to be annihilated. By benignant fever-paroxysms is life rooting out the deep-seated chronic disease, and triumphs over death. On the roaring billows of time thou art not ingulfed, but borne aloft into the azure of eternity. Love not pleasure; love God. This is the EVERLASTING YEA, wherein all contradiction is solved; wherein whoso walks and works, it is well with him.

Such is the main purport of this great and glorious book. There is much more in it that might be profitably dwelt upon, but its fundamental ideas have now, I think, been placed before the reader. Sartor Resartus is the grandest counterblast ever blown to the materialism of the age. Its doctrine of spirit is not only essentially and imperishably true, but the fundamental truth of all right religion and all sound philosophy.

2*

CHAPTER IV.

IT is agreed by all judges that the French Revolution, which occupied the last ten years of the eighteenth century, was the most important event in recent history; that it furnished a new point of departure in social and political evolution; that its effects are still everywhere apparent, that its force is unexhausted, and that the conditions of our modern life are largely what it has determined.

This great fact manifestly attracted the attention of Carlyle from his boyish years. The talk of his elders, when he was a child at their knee, would be of that huge convulsion which had reached its central paroxysms three or four years before he was born, and of that soldier of genius who was even then beginning to bind its raging energies within the iron bands of military discipline. From his fifth to his twentieth year he would hear of battles, battles, battles, the air around him never ceasing to vibrate with the thunders of the slowly-retreating storm. The boy of ten was old enough to understand the shrinking of Europe under the fierce blaze of the sun of Austerlitz; the youth of twenty shared the intense joy with which his countrymen saw Napoleon's sun eclipsed at Waterloo. It was natural, therefore, that his imagination should be fired by the French Revolution, and that, when he had attained maturity of manhood, in the sense of having constructed a working theory of life and affairs — come to terms with necessity, as he would himself word it, appeased his doubts and cleared decks for action — a concurrence of motives, from duty down to ambition, should lead him to select the French Revolution as the subject of his first historical work.

He regarded the subject, besides, with a philosophical and religious interest. We saw the transcendent importance which he attached to the principles laid down in Sartor Resartus; and the French Revolution furnished him, from what he styles the Bible of world-history, with an impressive text on which to preach a practical sermon illustrative of those principles. Happily, we are able to state in his own words the general conception he had formed of the French Revolution; after what has been said, the reader can have no difficulty in apprehending their significance. Sans-culottism, I may mention, is a term which has been adopted, both on the Continent and in Great Britain, to indicate the sovereignty of the multitude in its broadest and rudest form.

MEANING OF THE FRENCH REVOLUTION.

The French Revolution means here the open violent rebellion and victory of disimprisoned anarchy against corrupt worn-out authority; how anarchy breaks prison; bursts up from the infinite deep, and rages uncontrollable, immeasurable, enveloping a world; in phasis after phasis of fever-frenzy—till the frenzy burning itself out, and what elements of new order it held (since all force holds such), developing themselves, the uncontrollable be got, if not reimprisoned, yet harnessed, and its mad forces made to work toward their object as sane regulated ones. For as hierarchies and dynasties of all kinds, theocracies, aristocracies, autocracies, strumpetocracies, have ruled over the world; so it was appointed, in the decrees of Providence, that this same victorious anarchy, Jacobinism, Sans-culottism, French Revolution, horrors of French Revolution, or what else mortals name it, should have its turn. The "destructive wrath" of Sans-culottism; this is what we speak, having, unhappily, no voice for singing.

Surely a great phenomenon; nay, it is a *transcendental* one, overstepping all rules and experience; the crowning phenomenon of our modern time. For here again, most unexpectedly, comes antique fanaticism in new and newest vesture; miraculous, as all fanaticism is. Call it the fanaticism of "making away with formulas, *de humer les formules.*" The world of formulas, the *formed* regulated world, which all habitable world is, must needs hate such fanaticism like death; and be at deadly variance with it. The world of formulas must conquer it; or failing that, must die execrating it, anathematizing it;—can nevertheless in nowise prevent its being and its having been. The anathemas are there, and the miraculous Thing is there.

Whence it cometh? Whither it goeth? These are questions! When the age of miracles lay faded into the distance as an incredible tradition, and even the age of conventionalities was now old; and man's existence had for long generations rested on mere formulas which were grown hollow by course of time; and it seemed as if no reality any longer existed, but only phantasms of realities, and God's universe were the work of the tailor and upholsterer mainly, and men were buckram masks that went about becking and grimacing there—on a sudden, the earth yawns asunder, and amidst Tartarean smoke, and glare of fierce brightness, rises SANS-CULOTTISM, many-headed, fire-breathing, and asks: What think ye of me? Well may the buckram masks start together, terror-struck; "into expressive, well-concerted groups!" It is, indeed, friends, a most singular, most fatal thing. Let whosoever is but buckram and a phantasm look to it; ill, verily, may it fare with him; here, methinks, he cannot much longer be. Woe, also, to many a one who is not wholly buckram, but partially real and human! The age of miracles has come back. "Behold the world-phœnix, in fire-consummation and fire-creation: wide are her fanning wings; loud is her death-melody, of battle-thunders and falling towns; skyward lashes the funeral flame, enveloping all things: it is the death-birth of a world!"

Whereby, however, as we often say, shall one unspeakable blessing seem attainable. This mainly: that man and his life rest no more on hollowness and a lie, but on solidity and some kind of truth. Welcome the beggarliest truth, so it be one, in exchange for the royallest sham! Truth of any kind breeds ever new and better truth; thus hard granite rock will crumble down into soil, under the blessed skyey influences; and cover itself with verdure, with fruitage, and umbrage. But, as for falsehood, which, in like contrary manner, grows ever falser—what can it, or what should it do but decease, being ripe; decompose itself, gently or even violently, and return to the father of it—too probably in flames of fire?

Sans-culottism will burn much; but what is incombustible it will not burn. Fear not sans-culottism; recognize it for what it is, the portentous inevitable end of much, the miraculous beginning of much. One other thing thou mayest understand of it: that it, too, came from God; for has it not *been?* From of old, as it is written, are His goings forth; in the great deep of things; fearful and wonderful now as in the beginning: in the whirlwind also he speaks; and the wrath of men is made to praise Him. But to gauge and measure this immeasurable thing, and what is called *account for it,* and reduce it to a dead logic-formula, attempt not! Much less shalt thou shriek thyself hoarse, cursing it; for that, to all needful lengths, has been already done. As an actually existing son of time, *look,* with unspeakable manifold interest, oftenest in silence, at what the time did bring: therewith edify, instruct, nourish thyself, or were it but amuse and gratify thyself, as it is given thee.

These words prove that Carlyle contemplated the French Revolution as a poet or artist, and that he did not profess to trace it to this or that particular cause. He would not attempt "to account for it." Quoting Homer's words, he proposes to describe the "destructive wrath" of the modern democracy, the sans-culottic Achilles of this new Iliad. But he is quite clear as to the fundamental cause of the Revolution. Homer discerned, beneath all the subordinate causes of the terrors and horrors of the Trojan war, the disposing and determining will of Zeus ($\Delta\iota\text{o}\varsigma$ δ' $\dot{\epsilon}\tau\epsilon\lambda\epsilon\acute{\iota}\epsilon\tau\text{o}$ $\beta\text{o}\upsilon\lambda\acute{\eta}$); Carlyle, in the whirlwind of the Revolution, hears the voice of God saying that authority which has become hollow shall be ended; that the old order which has become intolerable shall give place to new. The life of institutions, according to the leading doctrine of Sartor Resartus, is the spirit they contain, and when the spirit is out, the body must die. Such, says Carlyle, in old Calvinistic language, is the decree of God. But that decree is executed in a way which man never surmises, never expects. That other doctrine of Sartor Resartus, that logical theorizing about society is of little avail as a practical power —that the analysis of the man of science, whether his science be social or physical, penetrates but a little way—is also illustrated for him in the French Revolution. There is nothing more characteristic of Carlyle in the book than the irony with which he refers to the fine-spoken, theorizing, analyzing gentle-

men who, having, to their own extreme satisfaction, got rid of
all belief in God, all recognition of the mystery of things—of
the fact of the Infinite and Eternal, on which like a thin film
all the time-world floats—were horror-struck by the Revolution they had evoked, and consumed in the fire they had
kindled. Carlyle does not call these men philosophers, but
philosophes, and their theorizing not philosophy, but philosophism. The promises of their superficial and superfine philosophism he describes in a passage remarkable both for the
breadth of its historical description, and the keenness of its
sarcasm.

The Atheistic Millennium.

How "sweet" are the manners; vice "losing all its deformity;" becoming *decent* (as established things, making regulations for themselves, do);
becoming almost a kind of "sweet" virtue! Intelligence so abounds;
irradiated by wit and the art of conversation. Philosophism sits joyful
in her glittering saloons, the dinner-guest of opulence grown ingenuous,
the very nobles proud to sit by her; and preaches, lifted up over all Bas-
tiles, a coming millennium. From far Ferney, patriarch Voltaire gives
sign; veterans Diderot, D'Alembert have lived to see this day; these with
their younger Marmontels, Morellets, Chamforts, Reynals, make glad the
spicy board of rich ministering dowager, of philosophic farmer-general.
O nights and suppers of the gods! Of a truth the long-demonstrated will
now be done; "the age of revolutions approaches" (as Jean Jacques
wrote), but then of happy blessed ones. Man awakens from his long
somnambulism; chases the phantasms that beleaguered and bewitched
him. Behold the new morning glittering down the eastern steeps; fly,
false phantasms, from its shafts of light; let the absurd fly utterly, aban-
doning this lower earth forever. It is Truth and *Astræa Redux* that (in
the shape of Philosophism) henceforth reign. For what imaginable purpose was man made, if not to be "happy?" By victorious analysis,
and progress of the species, happiness enough now awaits him. Kings
can become philosophers; or else philosophers kings. Let but society
be once rightly constituted by victorious analysis. The stomach that is
empty shall be filled; the throat that is dry shall be wetted with wine.
Labor itself shall be all one as rest; not grievous, but joyous. Wheat-
fields, one would think, cannot come to grow untilled; no man made
clayey, or made weary thereby; unless, indeed, machinery will do it.

Gratuitous tailors and restaurateurs may start up, at fit intervals, one as yet sees not how. But if each will, according to rule of benevolence, have a care for all, then surely no one will be uncared for. Nay, who knows but, by sufficiently victorious analysis, "human life may be indefinitely lengthened," and men get rid of death, as they have already done of the devil? We shall then be happy in spite of death and the devil. So preaches magniloquent Philosophism her *Redeunt Saturnia regna.*

We are next shown, black against this soft brightness, the squalor, misery, and disaffection in which the working millions of France were plunged. These "we," the courtiers and the philosophes, "lump together into a kind of dim, compendious unity, monstrous but dim, far-off as the *canaille;* or, more humanly, as 'the masses.'" "Masses, indeed," says Carlyle; "and yet, singular to say, if, with an effort of imagination, thou follow them, over broad France, into their clay hovels, into their garrets and hutches, the masses consist all of units." Every unit has his own pains and griefs, "and if you prick him, he will bleed." This is one of those touches from Shakspeare by which the language of this book is frequently pointed or enriched. Shakspeare, Homer, and Tacitus appear to have been the masters of literary art whom Carlyle had chiefly before him as models in composition. "Every unit of these masses," he proceeds, "is a miraculous man . . . with a spark of the Divinity, what thou callest an immortal soul, in him!" The chief end of the millions in France seemed to be to keep the privileged hundreds in luxurious ease. On them fell all the taxes. The clergy, the nobility, the *parlements* were exempt. "Untaught, uncomforted, unfed," the people lived in the habitual and angry persuasion that the upper classes, from the Court downward, were their enemies. When the chronic misery and semi-starvation became more than usually acute, they expressed their wretchedness in tumultuary risings, "their voice only an inarticulate cry." In May, 1775, for example, there being a scarcity of bread, "these vast multitudes do here, at Versailles Château, in wide-spread wretchedness, in sallow faces, squalor, winged raggedness, present, as in legible hieroglyphic writing, their petition of grievances. The château-gates must be shut; but the king will appear on the balcony, and speak to them. They have seen the king's face; their petition of grievances has been, if not read, looked at. For answer, two of them are hanged, on a 'new gallows forty feet high;' and the rest driven back to their dens—for a time."

Thus summarily, as if it were a matter of quite subordinate importance, does the Government deal with the masses, and yet Carlyle will have it that the welfare of these is "the sole point and problem of Government," compared with which all other points and problems are "mere accidental crotchets, superficialities, and beatings of the wind." The problem was now to be taken up; and the solution turned out to be such as made the ears of every one hearing it to tingle. The "evangel" of Rousseau had been passionately embraced by the young generation, and the fundamental proposition in Rousseau's system is that governments ought to exist to promote the happiness of the people, or rather that governments have only to set the people free in order to secure their happiness. Carlyle teaches that both Rousseau and the opponents of Rousseau overlook the fact that happiness, whether of one class or of all classes, is not an easy thing to obtain. A "millennium of mere ease and plentiful supply," a "lubberland of happiness, benevolence, and vice cured of its deformity," is in his eyes an imbecile dream. "How, in this wild universe, which storms-in on him, infinite, vague-menacing, shall poor man find, say, not happiness, but existence, and footing to stand on, if it be not by girding himself together for continual endeavor and endurance?" Of all the elements and agencies that produced the French Revolution—of all the forces that, in their volcanic action, tore up the surface of French society, and threw it in fragments into the sky—none was more potent than the per-

suasion which was imbedded in the mind of the nation that
happiness is a natural right and heritage of man, and that it
was the baleful influence of kings, priests, and nobles that
alone prevented the millions of France from being happy.   At
intervals Mr. Carlyle recognizes the nobleness of the aspirations
by which the people were moved; but it cannot be said that
his sympathy with the Patriots of the French Revolution is so
profound as his sympathy with the Puritans of the seventeenth
century. "Great," he once exclaims, "is the moment when
tidings of freedom reach us; when the long-enthralled soul,
from amidst its chains and squalid stagnancy, arises, were it
still only in blindness and bewilderment, and swears by Him
that made it that it will be free! Free? Understand that
well; it is the deep commandment, dimmer or clearer, of our
whole being, to be *free.* Freedom is the one purport, wisely
aimed at or unwisely, of all man's struggles, toilings, and sufferings in this earth." If we admit that the freedom and happiness which the French people desired for themselves were
looked upon by them as a gospel of felicity for Europe and
mankind, we can scarce fail to apprehend that, however sad or
appalling might be the issues of the French Revolution, its
main impulses were noble.

   "The French nation," says Carlyle, treating of that in-
tensely-agitating conjuncture when the Patriots thought that
their Revolution was at last to be consummated—" the French
nation has believed, for several years now, in the possibility,
nay, certainty and near advent, of a universal millennium, or
reign of freedom, equality, fraternity, wherein man should be
the brother of man, and sorrow and sin flee away." Add that
the attainability of all this was a matter of implicit faith.   It
was "enchantment," it was a "devilish legerdemain," it was an
infamous conspiracy of kings, priests, aristocrats, it was at last
the coalesced despots of the North, with Prussian bayonets and
force of cannon-balls, that prevented France from being free

and happy, and making the world free and happy. Wild as
was the hallucination of the French people, there may be a
doubt whether it would not have been as well to leave them to
attempt to realize it in their own way. At all events, if we
would know in any measure what the Revolution meant, and if
we would have any precision and clearness of understanding as
to Carlyle's idea of the secret of its power, we must realize that
the nation which had long sneered, and danced, and laughed,
and taken things, at best or at worst, lightly—the nation which
found its idol in Voltaire—was now intensely in earnest, intensely believing, intensely impressed with a sense of its mission to realize man's kingdom upon earth, and prove Rousseau
a true prophet and apostle. "Yes, reader," says Carlyle once
more, "here is the miracle. Out of that putrescent rubbish
of scepticism, sensualism, sentimentalism, hollow Machiavelism,
such a Faith has verily risen; flaming in the heart of a people.
A whole people, awakening, as it were, to consciousness in deep
misery, believes that it is within reach of a fraternal Heaven-
on-earth. With longing arms it struggles to embrace the unspeakable; cannot embrace it, owing to certain causes. Seldom do we find that a whole people can be said to have any
faith at all, except in things which it can eat and handle.
Whensoever it gets any faith, its history becomes spirit-stirring, noteworthy. . . . Now, behold, once more this French
nation believes! Herein, we say, in that astonishing faith of
theirs, lies the miracle. It is a faith undoubtedly of the more
prodigious sort, even among faiths; and will embody itself in
prodigies. It is the soul of that world-prodigy named French
Revolution; whereat the world still gazes and shudders."

The History of the French Revolution, as treated by Carlyle, is essentially a unity in three parts, each part occupying a
volume, and each having a distinctive title. The subject of
the first is the Bastile; of the second, the Constitution; of the
third, the Guillotine. No single words could be found more

expressive of the various phases through which the Revolution passed. The first volume is divided into seven books, the second into six, the third into seven. These books may be looked upon as cantos in this Epic Poem. They consist of chapters generally brief, the number of chapters in each book varying from four to twelve. The amount of invention displayed in the work, as a whole, and the sustained intensity of the labor undergone in its composition, may be roughly conceived from the fact that every one of those chapters has a heading which assists to produce the general impression aimed at by the author. Look at the names of the chapters in one book—I take it at hap-hazard, and I do not consider the titles as either more characteristic or more felicitous than the average. It is the book in which the Third Estate, or, as we should say in England, the representative Commons, prevail over the two other Estates of nobility and clergy, and in which the Bastile is taken by the Patriots. "Inertia," "Mercury de Brézé," "Broglie the War-God," "To arms!" "Give us Arms!" "Storm and Victory," "Not a Revolt," "Conquering your King," "The Lantérne." It is not possible to devise titles enabling us to realize with more dramatic vividness the essential facts of the situation and the onward march of the Revolution. There is nothing in Homer more stirring than the chapter on the fall of the Bastile. The episode descriptive of Marquis de Bouillé and the military revolt at Nancy has given me—if I may be permitted to supersede the vagueness of eulogistic adjective with a bit of personal experience — more expressly than any other piece of prose I ever read, the feeling of having been present among the events detailed, of having seen Bouillé and the infuriated mutineers face to face, and heard the rattle of the musketry in the streets of Nancy. The description of the flight and capture of the King has also been much and deservedly admired.

In the chapter in which the members of the States-general

defile before the eyes of the reader, the personal appearance and the most prominent characteristics of the leading men are presented with a graphic force with which there is nothing in Gibbon, in Clarendon, or in Macaulay that can be compared. Henceforward we know the personages described. We should recognize them in the highway, if earth were to refuse them shelter in her bosom and they rose from the dead. Let us take five of these likenesses. Sprawling up querulous to see the show, rises Marat, "the man forbid," "squalidest bleared mortal, redolent of soot and horse-drugs," his bleared soul looking through his "bleared, dull-acrid, woe-stricken face." Danton, huge and brawny, "through whose black brows and rude flattened face there looks a waste energy as of Hercules not yet furibund," rolls along. Camille Desmoulins, "with the long curling locks, with the face of dingy blackguardism, wondrously irradiated with genius, as if a naphtha-lamp burned within it," is near Danton. Mirabeau, with thick black hair, "through whose shaggy beetle-brows, and rough-hewn, seamed, carbuncled face, there look natural ugliness, small-pox, incontinence, bankruptcy, and burning fire of genius, like comet fire glaring fuliginous through murkiest confusions," is "the type-Frenchman of this epoch." Robespierre, "anxious, slight, ineffectual-looking, under thirty, in spectacles, his eyes (were the glasses off) troubled, careful, with upturned face, snuffing dimly the uncertain future time, complexion of a multiplex atrabiliar color, the final shade of which may be the pale sea-green," creeps modestly onward. Word-portraits like these are unique in literature; unique, I mean, in respect of the vividness with which the personal appearance is realized. Homer alone, so far as I am aware, can be put into competition with Carlyle in this particular field. Homer certainly liked to *see* his characters as well as to know about them, but I do not think we have so distinct vision of Achilles, Thersites, or even Ulysses, as Carlyle gives us of Mirabeau and Marat. Shakspeare does not throw his power into description of bodily appearance. In taking the whole measure of a man, his mind as well as his body, his moral worth and weight, Carlyle is by no means supreme among writers.

In his word-portraits, and in the History of the French Revolution generally, Mr. Carlyle exhibits to perfection his characteristic style. Critics of a certain order, the purist, the precisian, the grammatical pedant, are much exercised by what they are pleased to call his jargon. It affords amusement to our lively friend, M. Taine. These critics acknowledge his genius, but deplore what they call his irregularities, and wish he were classical and Addisonian. Really this is too absurd. Carlyle is an inventor, a poet, in style. He is a genius of so high an order—such are his powers of expression—that his advent marks a stage in the evolution of our language. In his hands words cease to be fossil; they bloom into life. The spectacle of such a man schooled by grammatical pedants suggests a galaxy of Oxford and Cambridge prize-poets drilling Homer in versification, or an academy of barn-door fowls instructing the eagle how to fly.

In point of fact, however, Carlyle takes no liberty with the English language for which he cannot plead the example of Shakspeare. When he wants to express a shade of meaning for which there is no word in the dictionary, he makes a term by tacking one or two words together. He speaks (in Sartor Resartus) of a " snow-and-rose-bloom maiden ;" a glance into the book before us discovers such adjectives as " rotatory-changeful," " narrow - faithful," " elegiac - applausive," " suppressed - explosive." Carlyle makes these words, as Turner mixed colors, to suit his own pictorial wants. Shakspeare did the same. " Senseless-obstinate," " bitter-searching," " wilful-negligent," " cursed-blessed," and a multitude more of the like, may be culled from Shakspeare. Is it objected that Shakspeare wrote poetry and dramas while Carlyle writes prose ? I answer that, in the old Greek sense of poet—the *maker*—Carlyle is a poet, and further, that there is no reason whatever, in the nature of things, why a prose writer should not avail himself, as well as a poet, of all means to hand for expressing his shades of sentiment or opinion. It may be a question whether both Mr. Carlyle and Mr. Ruskin would not have done well to write in verse; but there is no question that, preferring the liberty of prose, they are entitled to make their prose as expressive as they can.   If Mr. Ruskin and Mr. Carlyle ought to have written in metrical form, it is not because their powers of expression are too great for prose—no powers of expression could be that — but because their intellectual and emotional temperament is that of the poetic seer.

In the History of the French Revolution, the Lectures upon Heroes, and Past and Present, Carlyle's style reached its highest point of development, viewed merely as style.   In the biographies of Cromwell and Frederick, his language was, perhaps, more skilfully adapted to the production of particular effects—more keen, terse, and smiting.   But his florid style—his style with the young man's fondness for color and sound still traceable in it — reached its culmination in those works. During the period when they were written he is understood to have been much influenced by the language of Jean Paul Richter.   Previously he had been more closely under the mastership of Lessing and Goethe, the trenchant vigor of the former delighting him for its strength, the silvery clearness, idiomatic pith, and most expressive, though quiet, intensity of the latter realizing his ideal of what was classic in prose literature. But the exhaustless fancy, hanging, as, Carlyle himself says, a diamond upon every grass-blade, of Jean Paul, had also for him a great charm ; and in Sartor Resartus, the French Revolution, and Past and Present, the fact is abundantly attested. When I mention Richter, however, I must not be supposed to allege that his influence was powerful enough to depress Carlyle's originality. There is not a chapter of the French Revolution which looks in the slightest degree like the work of any man but its author. In reading Jean Paul, it is impossible, I think, not to feel that the color is sometimes more important than the meaning, the embroidery more precious than the stuff; but the intellectual power of Carlyle is great enough to cause his most glowing similitudes to thrill with life. In describing the language of those books, you are forced to fall back on their author's resource of metaphor, and to say that it is now like the gleaming of swords, now like the rustle and glance of jewelled garments, now terrible as the lightning, now tender as the dew, now firm, close, rapid as the tread of armed men, now wildly and grandly vague as the voice of forests or the moaning of the sea.

Mr. Hutton, whose authority on a question of literary criticism I should place as high as that of any living man, observes, respecting a passage he has just quoted from Carlyle, that its style is "crowded with stress, and making the same kind of fatiguing impression on the mind which a handwriting sloped the wrong way makes on the eye—an impression of strain and effort." Such "over-emphasis" is, he holds, "both exhausting and unnatural," being "too crowded for nature," and missing "the neutral tints which are absolutely essential to the harmony of poetry." Mr. Hutton, in making these remarks, is engaged primarily with Mr. Browning's verse, not with Mr. Carlyle's prose, and I am not sure that he would refuse to admit that a degree of emphasis objectionable in poetry, and sometimes objectionable even in prose, might be appropriate in some kinds of prose, and pre-eminently appropriate in the description of a French Revolution. But what I would call attention to is this—that Carlyle, while compelled by his subject to use strong terms in order to reproduce, in literature, an agitation which must have been fatiguing, or indeed agonizing in reality, *was* fully aware, as an artist, that undertones and neutral

tints were necessary to a harmony in which the reigning tone
was that of terror and of tragedy. Accordingly, amidst the
tumult and trampling of his style, he is careful to introduce
touches of tenderness, glimpses of the peace of nature which is
deeper than any raging of man, snatches from that still sad
music of humanity which outlasts the clash of battles and the
frenzied shrieks of revolution. "In the heart of the remotest
mountains rises the little Kirk; the dead all slumbering round
it, under their white memorial stones, 'in the hope of a blessed
resurrection.'" Is not that a tranquillizing tone—a whisper of
peace amidst the storm? "O evening sun of July," he exclaims
at the moment when his reader shudders at the spectacle of
Paris on the evening of the fall of the Bastile, "how, at this
hour, thy beams fall slant on reapers amidst peaceful woody
fields; on old women spinning in cottages; on ships far out
in the silent main,... and also on this roaring hell-porch of a
Hôtel-de-Ville!" I may remark, in passing, that the author of
Philochristus, consciously or unconsciously, follows Mr. Carlyle
in this habit of mingling colors of the dawn with his hues of
earthquake and eclipse. We are taken out by him into the
silence and sunshine of the pastoral hills about Jerusalem, and
shown a shepherd-boy tending his sheep, at the very moment
when the crime of the crucifixion is blackening the earth.

On one other point I must say a word before leaving the
History of the French Revolution, namely, its humor. To
omit mention of this were to neglect to specify one of its
most characteristic features. But it is difficult to describe—
in fact, it is indescribable to any one who has not become acquainted with it in the book itself. To some it may seem
altogether offensive to associate any kind of mirth with such a
subject; and I confess that the mood of scornful pity, of half-
sneering sympathy, of admiration dashed with derision, and
gravity varied with peals of laughter, in which the fearful tale
is told, has sometimes struck me as scarcely human. But we

ought to recollect that never, perhaps, in the history of man were the sublime of anguish and terror, and the ridiculous of imbecility, fanfaronade and pretentious foolery of all kinds, so wildly and inextricably mixed up as in the French Revolution. Some of its incidents, as the Insurrection of Women, were in themselves grotesquely humorous. Into human life in general the absurd enters largely, and no writer who has not an eye for it will truly depict life on the historical scale. It was Professor Wilson, one of the kindest-hearted of men, who said that, if we grant Wordsworth that there are things too deep for tears, we may firmly allege that there is nothing too deep for laughter. The gloom of such occurrences as the French Revolution would become oppressive and intolerable in literary delineation unless relieved by some coruscations of mirth. Mr. Ruskin, commenting on Turner's drawing of soldiers about to begin climbing the hill to their Winchelsea barracks under the lashing rain of a thunder-storm, says that the artist was "partly laughing the strange half-cruel, half-sorrowful laugh that we wonder at, also, so often in Bewick." Few things in art have ever impressed me more painfully than Bewick's apprehension of—for I cannot believe him to have had any sympathy with—that most purely diabolical of all the elements of human nature, pleasure derived from cruelty—apprehension of it, I say, and use of it as a source of interest in his etchings; but I have never discovered even a "half-cruel" laugh in Turner: and grim, almost uncanny, as is the humor of Carlyle in the History of the French Revolution, there is no cruelty in it. I could not say the same of the humor in the Life of Frederick; but as yet Carlyle's mind was thoroughly genial and sunny, full of pity and affection, finding more in the misery of the wicked and the foolish to weep for than in their crimes or errors to curse at.

The humor of the History of the French Revolution is more akin to that of Hamlet when he jests with the ghost—a

humor not inconsistent with earnestness—nay, to all appearance, dependent upon an almost spasmodic, almost maniacal,
tension of brain.   Carlyle's humor recalls Shakspeare's in another aspect.   There is not, so far as I know, any parallel in
literature to the indifference or the unconsciousness with which
these two allow their most pathetic or sublime passages to be
associated with some triviality or absurdity.   Shakspeare is
absolutely incapable of resisting the temptation to pun or otherwise play upon words.   No matter what he has in hand.
He makes Laertes pun upon the water that drowned his sister Ophelia; Edgar upon the "bleeding rings" of his blinded
father's eyes; Lady Macbeth upon the blood-stain with which,
under the fixed eyes of murdered Duncan, she *gilds* the features of the sleeping grooms in proof of their *guilt.*   Carlyle
is not quite so inveterate a punster, but he occasionally perpe-
trates an atrocious pun, and he is equally incapable of resisting
the temptation to make a joke.   He speaks somewhere of a
scapegrace failing to reach the goal of a noble life, and arriving, "by a fatal inversion," at the "Queen's Bench *jail.*"   A
worse pun than that does not fall within the possibilities of
human invention.   In the concluding passage of his Life and
Letters of Cromwell, in the last paragraph of the incomparable
chapter which relates the death of Oliver, he places the England of his own time in contrast with England as portrayed
by Milton in the following words: "The genius of England
no longer soars sunward, world-defiant, like an eagle through
the storms, 'mewing her mighty youth,' as John Milton saw
her do: the genius of England, much liker a greedy ostrich
intent on provender and a whole skin mainly, stands with its
other extremity sunward; with its ostrich-head stuck into the
readiest bush, of old church-tippets, king-cloaks, or what other
'sheltering fallacy' there may be, and *so* awaits the issue.   The
issue has been slow; but it is now seen to have been inevitable.
No ostrich, intent on gross terrene provender, and sticking its

head into fallacies, but will be awakened one day in a terrible *à posteriori* manner, if not otherwise." You see how the idea strikes him, lays hold of him, moves him to peal after peal of wild, sad laughter, will not leave him till he has worked it out from the sticking of the ostrich-head into the bush to the awakening of the bird under the birch-rods of destiny.

I cannot refrain from quoting another example of Carlyle's humor from the History of the French Revolution. "Sovereigns die and sovereignties: how all dies, and is for a time only; is a 'time-phantasm,' yet reckons itself real! The Merovingian kings, slowly wending on their bullock-carts through the streets of Paris, with their long hair flowing, have all wended slowly on—into eternity. Charlemagne sleeps at Salzburg, with truncheon grounded; only fable expecting that he will awaken. Charles the Hammer, Pepin bow-legged, where now is their eye of menace, their voice of command? Rollo and his shaggy Northmen cover not the Seine with ships; but have sailed off on a longer voyage. The hair of Tow-head (*Tête d'étoupes*) now needs no combing; Iron-cutter (*Taillefer*) cannot cut a cobweb; shrill Fredegonda, shrill Brunhilda, have had out their hot life-scold, and lie silent, their hot life-frenzy cooled." Here he starts with the most solemn of all subjects, the great mysteries of time, and death, and eternity. The picture, so intensely real, with its bullock-carts, and streets of Paris, and long-haired kings, and so purely ideal in the "wending on" of these into eternity, is humorous to begin with; and so soon as the odd names of the Merovingians occur to him, the sense of fun gets complete possession of his mind, and he must tell us that Tow-head's hair now "needs no combing," and Iron-cutter "cannot cut a cobweb." Evidently, before he reached this point, his sides were shaking, and there is no reason to doubt that Carlyle writes as he talks, with perpetual dramatic sympathy, and with intermittent bursts of laughter.

In the last extract the sense of mystery is seen associated

with the sense of fun.   The reader of Sartor Resartus need not
be reminded that a feeling of the mystery of things is one of
Mr. Carlyle's deepest characteristics.   Here again, very notably,
he resembles Shakspeare.   It is the mystery of common things,
of facts quite on the surface, that oppresses both these miraculous men.   The old, old tale that we ripe and ripe, and then
rot and rot—that we fat all things to fat ourselves, and fat ourselves for worms—that we are such things as dreams are made
of, and our little life is rounded with a sleep—strikes Shakspeare and Carlyle as inexpressibly wonderful.   Shakspeare, the
greater and perhaps fundamentally the more earnest of the two,
contemplates the mystery oftenest with reference to the future.
He thinks of the undiscovered country from whose bourne no
traveller returns, of the dreams that may come when we have
shuffled off this mortal coil.   Carlyle's sense of wonder dwells
more on the past.   That any man or thing was for a time visible, and then was "swallowed" of darkness, interests him without end.   If Friar Bacon's brass head, in Greene's comedy, had
spoken to him, he certainly would not have let it crack from
want of respectful appreciation of its remarks, "time is" and
"time was."   Most people, however, agree with the simple-
minded watcher that, if the head really had nothing more original or important to say than this, it was not worth while to
waken his overworn master to hear it; and to those who have
not Carlyle's sense of wonder, and are destitute of humor, his
perpetual amazement at, and frequent specification of, the fact
that the Merovingian kings, the builders of Stonehenge, and
our ancestors in general, were once extremely alive, and are
now perfectly dead, is apt to seem sheer ineptitude.   But this
is a shallow account of the matter.   If the obviousness of facts
is to neutralize their wonderfulness, Hamlet's moralizing on the
skull of Yorick will come under the imputation of platitude.

It has been objected to the History of the French Revolution that one may read it without obtaining any definite idea

of the chronological sequence of events—without obtaining, in one word, the kind of acquaintance with the French Revolution which would be useful in a competitive examination. It is, I admit, advisable for one who knows nothing of recent French history to read some other account of the Revolution before taking up Carlyle's. But with careful reading and careful meditating, all the main facts of the business, linked together in chronological and even in organic sequence, are found to be in the book itself. While we read, no doubt, we are apt to overlook dates and other specifications, just as in any exciting crisis we are apt to overlook the lapse of time; but the dates are given; and as we rehearse the whole in memory—Bastile, Constitution, Guillotine—we feel that we have not a less, but a more correct idea of the whole affair than we could have derived from a commonplace history. You do not really learn what kind of thing an eruption of Vesuvius is by being told that at 2 A.M. the lava overflowed the crater, at 1 P.M. it had reached a neighboring valley, at 6 P.M. so many tons of ashes had fallen; you must see it in the work of some painter or some poet, who can show you the mountain's blaze as it reddens the heavens and incarnadines the sea. Statistical history cannot describe a French Revolution. "So soon," says Carlyle, "as history can philosophically delineate the conflagration of a kindled fire-ship, she may try this other task. Here lay the bitumen-stratum, there the brimstone one; so ran the vein of gunpowder, of nitre, terebinth, and foul grease: this, were she inquisitive enough, history might partly know. But how they acted and reacted below decks, one fire-stratum playing into the other, by nature and the art of man, now when all hands ran raging, and the flames lashed high over shrouds and topmast: this let not history attempt. The fire-ship is old France, the old French form of life; her crew a generation of men. Wild are their cries and their ragings there, like spirits tormented in that flame." Still more expressive, if possible, is

the similitude with which Carlyle helps us to realize the paroxysms of the Revolution—that of winds raising the sands of
the desert, and whirling them round and round in Sahara-waltz.
Exactly such an ambient atmosphere of gloom, of heat, of wild
haste, of terror, enveloped the twenty-five millions who whirled
round in the delirium of the Revolution. A grander, more apt,
or more impressive similitude does not exist in literature.

Such is this great and memorable Book. It is not without
its defects; but be they what they may, it is among the Mont
Blancs and Kanchinjingas of the literature of the world.

CHAPTER V.

IN the interval between the French Revolution and Past and Present, Carlyle gave to the world his short treatise on Chartism and his Lectures on Heroes and Hero-worship. The former is remarkable for the bold sympathy it evinces with the working-classes, and the enthusiasm of admiring hope with which it contemplates the industrial outbursts occasioned by the great mechanical inventions and appliances of the early part of the present century. Carlyle seems as yet to have had no serious misgiving as to the effect of mechanical development in depressing the spiritual energy of the nation. The awakening of a great manufacturing city to the industry of a new day, its ten thousand spindles going off "like the boom of an Atlantic tide," was still regarded by him as sublime. The victory of rectitude and excellence over Mammon and brute force he exultingly expected, and to those who shook the head and spoke of the problem of elevating the masses as insoluble, he administered rebukes like this:

THE WORD "IMPOSSIBLE."

It is not a lucky word this same *impossible:* no good comes of those who have it so often in their mouth. Who is he that says always, There is a lion in the way? Sluggard, thou must slay the lion then; the way has to be travelled! In art, in practice, innumerable critics will demonstrate that most things are henceforth impossible; that we are got, once for all, into the region of perennial commonplace, and must contentedly continue there. Let such critics demonstrate; it is the nature of them: what harm is in it? Poetry once demonstrated to be impossible, arises the Burns, arises the Goethe.   Unheroic commonplace being now clearly all we have to look for, comes Napoleon, comes the conquest of the world. It was proved by fluxionary calculus that steamships could never get across from the farthest point of Ireland to the nearest of Newfoundland : impelling force, resisting force, maximum here, minimum there ; by law of nature and geometric demonstration :—What could be done ?   The *Great Western* could weigh anchor from Bristol port ; that could be done. The *Great Western*, bounding safe through the gullets of the Hudson, threw her cable out on the capstan of New York, and left our still moist paper demonstration to dry itself at leisure.   "Impossible," cried Mirabeau ; " *ne me dites jamais ce bête de mot.*"   (Never name to me that blockhead of a word.)

Mr. Carlyle had already lost faith in extension of the suffrage and introduction of the ballot ; but he advocated the universal education of the people, and the encouragement of emigration, proposals which, as has been justly observed, though condemned by the Press at the time as unpractical, have been recognized long since by all rational men as pertinent and wise.

No one of Carlyle's books has been more popular than the Lectures on Heroes and Hero-worship.   Delivered in London to a miscellaneous though brilliant and cultivated audience, they were necessarily clear and easy of comprehension, and do not require to be dwelt upon here.   They contain many admirable passages, as, for example, the descriptions of the old Norse mythology, of Iceland, of the Book of Job, of Luther's Table-talk, and of Dante's Divine Comedy.   These lectures are remarkable for the essentially bright and favorable view they present of human nature.   Carlyle maintains with scornful emphasis that man is no poltroon, no mere greedy egotist and selfish coward, but one whom it is safe to appeal to on his nobler side, one who reverences, and cannot help reverencing, worth and valor when he sees them.   The ethical elevation, the earnest and spiritual religion, the impassioned sympathy with valor, devout self-sacrifice, all that is heroic in man, and the resolute determination to recognize nobleness under all disguises, which pervade this book, render it one of the best that can be put into the hands of young men.

In Past and Present, Carlyle reads a lesson to his generation from an episode in the history of the twelfth century. There exists, in monkish Latin, an account, written by "Jocelin of Brakelond," monk in the convent of St. Edmundsbury, Suffolk, of Samson, who was first monk and then abbot of the convent. This Samson was a highly remarkable man, and Jocelin, who knew him personally for many years, describes his appearance, his mishaps, his election to be abbot, his difficulties and ultimate success in managing the convent. Seen in the watery mirror of Jocelin's Latin, Samson had for ages been known to a few, and but a few. Jocelin's chronicle, edited for the Camden Society, came into Mr. Carlyle's hands, and once more Samson looks forth upon all the world as if in the lineaments of life. We know him henceforward as we do our familiar friends. His dream, at nine years old, of having been saved from Satan by St. Edmund, which caused his mother to take him, like another Samuel, to the convent; his journey to Italy on a mission from Abbot Hugo, which mission he executed with exemplary diligence and fidelity; his punishment by way of thanks when he returned; his wary, sagacious, vigilant conduct while the evil days of Abbot Hugo continued; his election to succeed old Hugo by the St. Edmundsbury monks in presence of King Henry II.; his troubles and consolations and final triumph as Abbot, are all set vividly before us. "A personable man of seven-and-forty," he is first introduced to us; "stout-made, stands erect as a pillar; with bushy eyebrows, the eyes of him beaming into you in a really strange way; the face massive, grave, with 'a very eminent nose;' his head almost bald, its auburn remnants of hair, and the copious ruddy beard, getting slightly streaked with gray. This is Brother Samson; a man worth looking at." The scene in which he

3*

lived, the convent and the town adjoining, are thus made visible by Carlyle:

St. Edmundsbury.

Indisputable, though very dim to modern vision, rests on its hill-slope that same *Bury, stow,* or town of St. Edmund; already a considerable place, not without traffic, nay, manufactures, would Jocelin only tell us what. Jocelin is totally careless of telling: but, through dim fitful apertures, we can see *Fullones,* "Fullers," see cloth-making; looms dimly going, dye-vats, and old women spinning yarn. We have Fairs, too, *Nundinæ,* in due course; and the Londoners give us much trouble, pretending that they, as a metropolitan people, are exempt from toll. Besides there is field-husbandry, with perplexed settlement of Convent rents; corn-ricks pile themselves within burgh, in their season; and cattle depart and enter; and even the poor weaver has his cow—"dung-heaps" lie quietly at most doors (*ante foras,* says the incidental Jocelin), for the town has yet no improved police. Watch and ward, nevertheless, we do keep, and have gates —as what town must not? thieves so abounding; war, *werra,* such a frequent thing! Our thieves, at the Abbot's judgment-bar, deny; claim wager of battle; fight, are beaten, and *then* hanged. "Ketel, the thief," took this course; and it did nothing for him—merely brought us, and indeed himself, new trouble!

Every way a most foreign time. What difficulty, for example, has our *Cellerarius* to collect the *repselver,* "reaping silver," or penny, which each householder is by law bound to pay for cutting down the Convent grain! Richer people pretend that it is commuted, that it is this and the other; that, in short, they will not pay it. Our *Cellerarius* gives up calling on the rich. In the houses of the poor, our Cellerarius finding, in like manner, neither penny nor good promise, snatches, without ceremony, what *vadium* (pledge, *wad*) he can come at: a joint-stool, kettle, nay, the very house-door, "*hostium;*" and old women, thus exposed to the unfeeling gaze of the public, rush out after him with their distaffs and the angriest shrieks: "*vetulæ exibant cum colis suis,*" says Jocelin, "*minantes et exprobrantes.*"

What a historical picture, glowing visible, as St. Edmund's Shrine by night, after seven long centuries or so! *Vetulæ cum colis:* my venerable ancient spinning grandmothers—ah! and ye, too, have to shriek, and rush out with your distaffs; and become female Chartists, and scold all evening with void door-way—and in old Saxon, as we in modern, would fain demand some Five-point Charter, could it be fallen in with, the earth being too tyrannous! Wise Lord Abbots, hearing of such phenomena, did in time abolish or commute the reap-penny, and one nuisance was abated. But the image of these justly offended old women, in their old wool costumes, with their angry features, and spindles brandished, lives forever in the historical memory.

With admirable breadth and marvellous picturesqueness the England of the period is placed before us.

England in the Twelfth Century.

How much is still alive in England; how much has not yet come into life! A Feudal Aristocracy is still alive, in the prime of life; superintending the cultivation of the land, and less consciously, the distribution of the produce of the land; judging, soldiering, adjusting; everywhere governing the people—so that even a Gurth born thrall of Cedric lacks not his due parings of the pigs he tends. Governing;—and, alas! also game-preserving, so that a Robert Hood, a William Scarlet, and others, have, in these days, put on Lincoln coats, and taken to living, in some universal-suffrage manner, under the greenwood tree!

How silent, on the other hand, lie all cotton-trades and such-like; not a steeple-chimney yet got on end from sea to sea! North of the Humber, a stern Wilelmus Conquestor burned the country, finding it unruly, into very stern repose. Wild fowl scream in those ancient silences, wild cattle roam in those ancient solitudes; the scanty sulky Norse-bred population all coerced into silence, feeling that, under these new Norman governors, their history has probably as good as *ended*. Men and Northumbrian Norse populations know little what has ended, what is beginning! The Ribble and the Aire roll down, as yet unpolluted by dyers' chemistry; tenanted by merry trouts and piscatory otters; the sunbeam and the vacant wind's-blast alone traversing those moors. Side by side sleep the coal-strata and the iron-strata for so many ages; no steam-demon has yet risen smoking into being. St. Mungo rules in Glasgow; James Watt still slumbering in the deep of time. Mancunium, Manceaster, what we now call Manchester, spins no cotton—if it be not *wool* "cottons," clipped from the backs of mountain sheep. The Creek of the Mersey gurgles, twice in the four-and-twenty hours, with eddying brine, clangorous with sea-fowl; and is a *Lither*-pool, a *lazy* or sullen pool, no monstrous pitchy city, and sea-haven of the world! The centuries are big; and the birth-hour is coming, not yet come.

The main lesson of Abbot Samson's history, as read by Carlyle, is that the one essential thing, in order that men may be well governed and that institutions may prosper, is the discovery of fit men to rule the one and administer the other. Search out your heroes, he said to his contemporaries, if you have any among you, and set them, as Abbot Samson was set, to do the work of governing. Do not ask how many acres a man has, or how many guineas he has, or how long a pedigree he has, but whether there is heroic manhood, heroic valor, and worth, and insight, and energy in him, and if you find there is, put him in the seat of the governor.

CHAPTER VI.

I HAVE pledged myself to avoid deep discussion in these after-dinner talks, and taken leave to indulge my admiration rather than to assume the strut and sneer of censorship; but we have now arrived at a stage in the literary history of Carlyle at which it is impossible for me to avoid saying that there is much in his teaching on hero-worship to which I cannot assent. To the best of my recollection, I never, at the time of my hottest youthful enthusiasm for Carlyle, had any doubt that on this point he was in serious error; and the first thing in shape of a book that I published contained reasonings against Carlylian hero-worship, the soundness of which has seemed to me to be attested by the observation and experience of every year I have lived since then.

I beg the reader to note that, in objecting to hero-worship, I not only do not disparage great men—I not only admit the supreme importance, in all practical undertakings, of getting the right man into the right place—I not only believe that, unless institutions are souled by earnest and capable men, they have no more chance of prosperous and beneficent activity than dead bodies have of climbing mountains—but I specify, as one essential and weighty part of my contention, that hero-worship *obscures* and *neutralizes* the value of the heroes who are worshipped. Hero-worship a poet, and you make him a fantastic fool. Hero-worship a warrior, and he becomes, in the old Greek sense, a tyrant. Of course I am not imagining that Carlyle proposes actual worship to be rendered by man to man; but it is no imagination that he attaches a mystical

sacredness to the heroic character; and it is this attachment
of mystical sacredness which I hold to be demonstrably and
intensely mischievous. That the tools should be put into the
hands of him who can use them — that every appointment
should be made on grounds of fitness, not of favoritism—that
the foolish have a God-given claim to be ruled by the wise, .
and the wise a God-enjoined duty to rule the foolish—this is
not only true, but is of that order of truth which, to the body
politic, is what good bread and pure water are to the corpo-
real frame. To ascertain how these ends may be attained is
the object of all political science. Constitutional freedom,
electoral privilege, Parliamentary representation, have their *rai-
son d'être* in the vital necessity of sifting out a nation's best
practical capacity and highest worth, in order that thus there
may be provided a national brain, to do, for the nation, what
the head does for the man. Of "hero-worship" thus understood, no one could have a higher appreciation than I have.
But the *other* kind of hero-worship—that which assigns to the
hero a character entitling him to reverence and adoration from
common men—issues naturally in the consecration of despotism. Mr. Carlyle speaks of the man who is to be thus worshipped, sometimes as a hero, sometimes as a man of genius,
but he always commands ordinary men to bow the knee before him. "He is above thee, like a god." Such are Carlyle's words in one of the concluding chapters of Past and
Present. "He is thy born king, thy conqueror and supreme
law-giver." He is apart from the community into which he
is born. "He walks among men; loves men with inexpressible soft pity—as they *cannot* love him; but his soul dwells in
solitude, in the uttermost parts of creation. In green oases by
the palm-tree wells, he rests a space; but anon he has to journey forward, escorted by the Terrors and Splendors, the arch-
demons and archangels. All Heaven, all Pandemonium, are
his escort. The stars, keen-glancing, from the immensities,

send tidings to him; the graves, silent with their dead, from the eternities. Deep calls for him unto deep."

I am perfectly alive to the difficulty of drawing the line between legitimate, nay, imperative and indispensable, respect for great men, and that respect which is idolatrous; but I can precisely state that, when I am required to say of any man, be he a Shakspeare or a Newton, a Julius Cæsar or a Cromwell, that he is above me "like a god," I decline such hero-worship. It is practically and intensely pernicious. In politics it leads, as I said, to the consecration of despotism, to inhuman scorn for the multitude. In ethics it is subtly perversive of equity and righteousness. Ask reason, ask conscience, and they clearly tell you that there is no more merit in being born with the most powerful brain in the planet than there is in being born with the weakest. The sole title to respect is moral excellence; and the sole tenable definition of moral excellence is exertion of the will in unselfish goodness. But the irresistible tendency of hero-worship is to do injustice to the nobleness of common men, to the honest efforts of weak men, to virtues that have no brilliancy in them though they are of sterling quality, and to slur over and make light of the vices or crimes of the gifted. The course pursued ought to be exactly the reverse. The weak ought to be excused rather than the strong. The failings of men of genius—of a Mirabeau, a Danton, a Burns—are more blameworthy on account of their gifts. *Because* a man has been splendidly endowed, the more sacredly incumbent upon him is it to make good use of his gifts, to guard against temptation, to control passion. Mental power is the natural ally of virtue, and ought to re-enforce instead of betraying it; and the man of splendid endowment is a light set on a hill, and therefore more responsible than the crowd.

Under the influence of hero-worship these obvious but infinitely important considerations have been flagrantly set at naught. Every shortcoming of glittering spirits has been

wept over, pitied, condoned, and the comparatively ungifted,
unenlightened crowd have been fiercely reviled because those
bright ones sinned and suffered. Mr. Carlyle, though in his
essay on Burns he justly laid the blame of his misfortunes on
the poet himself, has spoken many times since, and does partly even in that essay speak, as if Burns had been in some sense
the victim of a generation that did not understand hero-worship; and in his delineations of Mirabeau, of Camille Desmoulins, of Danton, and most perhaps of all in his delineation of
Frederick of Prussia, he makes genius cover, or at least palli-
ate, a multitude of sins. Throughout all his later works, Mr.
Carlyle has inveighed against the great body of his countrymen, and in this he has been accurately followed by Mr. Ruskin. On the highest authority, Divine and human, I affirm
that in this they do wrong. "Father, forgive them, *they know
not what they do*," said Jesus Christ, dying upon the cross, the
utterance being no less miraculous and Divine in its exact intellectual apprehension of the nature and extent of the culpa-
bility of the crowd, than in its infinite benevolence. Shakspeare, beyond all comparison the most clear-seeing and sagacious of mere men, discerns with nice precision that the people, if the Coriolanus will but condescend in seeking their
leadership to "ask it kindly"—if the Brutus will but use rational precautions to prevent their being led away by the gleam
of some counterfeit nobleness shown to them by an Antony—
prefer capacity to charlatanism, virtue to vice. But Carlyle
and Ruskin accuse the many and adore the few. "So far as
in it lay," says Mr. Ruskin, "this century has caused every one
of its great men, whose hearts were kindest, and whose spirits
most perceptive of the work of God, to die without hope—
Scott, Keats, Byron, Shelley, Turner. Great England, of the
Iron-heart now, not of the Lion-heart; for these souls of her
children an account may perhaps be one day required of her."
I know not any true sense in which Walter Scott can be said

to have died without hope, nor any conceivable sense in which the author of Waverley and the Lady of the Lake experienced iron-hearted treatment from his contemporaries; but it is quite in accordance with the doctrine and practice of hero-worship, to lay the blame of Byron's frantic profligacy and Turner's avarice and sensuality upon "England." Mr. Ruskin explains that these great men "fell among fiends — took to making bread out of stones at their bidding, and then died, torn and famished; careful England, in her pure, priestly dress, passing by on the other side." The plain fact is, that England all but adored Byron until he infamously treated his wife, and that Turner was not only hailed with acclamation by the constituted art authorities of England, but welcomed with the most considerate friendship to their homes by the English landed gentry. No better illustration than Mr. Ruskin's passage could be found of the saturation of our atmosphere in these times by hero-worship. The brilliant souls are never to be told that *they* are to blame; *sunt superis sua jura;* the laws of honesty, of continence, of simple respect for God and man, are, it seems, for ordinary mortals; and if men of magnificent genius kick against the pricks of God Almighty's buckler, the blame is to be laid not upon them, but upon those who did not sufficiently hero-worship them. It is of course consistent with all that has been said, to add that scrupulous note should be taken of every allowance which can fairly be claimed for men of genius. Plato was certainly correct in alleging that a constitutional unsteadiness has been associated with many forms of genius. Perilous excitability, subtle disease, often attend it. Let men of genius be considerately, tenderly, delicately treated — only not worshipped.

I have been thus explicit on the subject of hero-worship because it is to his great mistake on this point that I trace everything to which I most seriously object in Mr. Carlyle's later writings. In some respects these are superior to his earlier;

but, on the whole, the canker of hero-worship eats into them more deeply; and though I should hesitate to say that his book on Cromwell reveals any trace of failing power, or is not, all things considered, his greatest achievement, I regard it as marred by the evil influence. Hero-worship bears therein its natural fruit of injustice toward such men as Hampden, Pym, Vane, and others, who toiled as faithfully in the cause of Puritanism and of England as Cromwell himself. Historically also the same influence depresses the value of the book; for the constitutional aspects of the struggle are slightly, almost scornfully, treated, and a certain amount of obscurity is thus inevitably thrown over the relation of the Puritan Revolution to the course of political development, since the seventeenth century, in England and America. Cromwell being viewed from the first as a hero, to be worshipped, an exaggerated idea is presented of the injustice that had been previously done him. This remark applies more particularly to the preliminary vindication of Cromwell in the Lectures on Heroes than to the Life and Letters; but the reference to preceding writers on Cromwell in the Lectures on Heroes remains to this day unaltered. "Few Puritans of note," it is there written, "but find their apologists somewhere, and have a certain reverence paid them by earnest men. One Puritan, I think, and almost he alone, our poor Cromwell, seems to hang yet on the gibbet, and finds no hearty apologist anywhere. Him neither saint nor sinner will acquit of great wickedness. A man of ability, infinite talent, courage, and so forth: but he betrayed the cause. Selfish ambition, dishonesty, duplicity; a fierce, coarse, hypocritical *Tartufe;* turning all that noble struggle for, constitutional liberty into a farce played for his own benefit: this and worse is the character they give of Cromwell." I shall not say that any author of European reputation, at the time when this was written, had accurately stated in how far Cromwell could justly be charged with the "wickedness" of erecting a military despotism on the ruins of that liberty for which he and his fellows had fought. It is more than doubtful whether a majority of competent judges would decide, at this hour, that Mr. Carlyle's own vindication on this point is complete. Such judges would not accept Mr. Carlyle's doctrine of the partial irresponsibility of the hero, and the Divine right of men of transcendent genius to dismiss parliaments and supersede laws. But the terms in which Macaulay, writing in the *Edinburgh Review*, and, therefore, expressing an opinion in which he reckoned on the concurrence of Liberal Europe, had previously characterized Cromwell, prove that the theory of his being a Tartufe, who turned the struggle for constitutional liberty into a farce, had been thoroughly discarded. Comparing him with Cæsar and Napoleon, Macaulay placed Cromwell above the latter. He expressly denied that the Protector's ambition was of "an impure or selfish kind," which it must have been if it was like the ambition of Tartufe. "No sovereign," wrote Macaulay in the *Edinburgh Review*, so early as 1828, "ever carried to the throne so large a portion of the best qualities of the middling orders, so strong a sympathy with the feelings and interests of his people. He was sometimes driven to arbitrary measures; but he had a high, stout, honest, English heart. Hence it was that he loved to surround his throne with such men as Hale and Blake. Hence it was that he allowed so large a share of political liberty to his subjects, and that, even when an opposition dangerous to his power and to his person almost compelled him to govern by the sword, he was still anxious to leave a germ from which, at a more favorable season, free institutions might spring. We firmly believe that, if his first Parliament had not commenced its debates by disputing his title, his government would have been as mild at home as it was energetic and able abroad." This is the language of cordial and proud appreciation; and it was surely too much, after this had appeared in the most influential of European periodicals, from the pen of one of the most brilliant of European writers, to say that "selfish ambition, dishonesty, duplicity" were the characteristics universally attributed to the great Protector.

THE exceptions taken in the preceding chapter to Carlyle's Life and Letters of Oliver Cromwell are nowise incompatible with an almost reverential admiration for the book. Whatever had been done for Cromwell before its appearance, much remained to be done. Carlyle afforded him what, most certainly, no previous writer had been able to afford him—the sympathetic interpretation of a kindred spirit. "There may still be discussion," I have recently had occasion to write, "long and searching, about Cromwell; but until Mr. Carlyle wrote, his life was unintelligible. Carlyle raised him from the dead."

It was not, however, by sympathy of kindred genius alone that Carlyle could enable his contemporaries to understand Cromwell. Hard work was to be done, work of a peculiarly tedious and wearing kind, work requiring immense patience and the most sustained attention, work to which men of high literary genius are seldom willing to stoop. The history of literature affords no richer treat than may be derived from a comparison of Cromwell as painted by Hume, with Cromwell as painted by Carlyle. Cautious David Hume was so sure of his judgment, and that of his knowing contemporaries in the sceptical eighteenth century, respecting the great Puritan, that he ventured to utter a kind of prophecy upon the subject.

"The great defect in Oliver's speeches," says Hume, in a note to the sixty-first chapter of his History of England, "consists not in his want of elocution, but in his want of ideas. The sagacity of his actions, and the absurdity of his

discourse, form the most prodigious contrast that ever was
known. *The collection of all his speeches, letters,* sermons (for
he also wrote sermons), *would make a great curiosity, and, with
a few exceptions, might justly pass for one of the most nonsensical books in the world.*" Cromwell preached sermons, but
Hume was letting fly an arrow into the air when he spoke
of Cromwell writing sermons, nor did the rough troopers to
whom he preached take reports of his sermons. But the
letters and speeches of Cromwell, Hume's prophecy respecting
which I put into italics, *have* been collected by Carlyle; and
the collection forms, by universal consent, one of the noblest
books within the whole range of literature. Hume quotes a
passage from one of Cromwell's speeches, and, as Hume gives
it, no mortal can make sense of it. The subject to which it
relates is the offer of the title of king to Cromwell. Turning
from the coil and welter of unintelligible words, presented to
us as Cromwell's by Hume, we take up Carlyle and read the
passage. The artist-biographer, basing his art, as all true art
is based, on honest labor, realizes for us, to begin with, the
exact position in which Oliver stood at the time. The Parliament was offering him the Crown; the Ironsides could not
be got to tolerate his assumption of kingship; and Cromwell
had to solve the very ticklish problem of letting the Parliament know, without inflicting any insult, that the will of the
Ironsides, not the will of the Parliament, must, in this instance,
be done. Having thus, by accurate knowledge, made the past
present, Carlyle takes up the unpunctuated jumble of words
that had contented Hume; fits clause to clause; and traces
the frontier line between the sentences. The change is magical or more. *Fiat lux,* says Carlyle, and the chaos beams into
order.

What Carlyle did for that passage he did, more or less, for
all the extant letters and speeches of Cromwell. The toil of
brain, and even of body, involved in the enterprise was enor-

mous, but the reward was great—a consciousness, namely, of having made the voice of one of the most remarkable men that ever lived, after it had been all but dumb for two hundred years, once more, and now for evermore, audible to mankind. Any reward in the way of fame and reputation, compared with this consciousness, was as the fine dust of the balance; but if anything could add piquancy to such a triumph, if any splendor of blazoning could enhance such a victory, it would be the prediction by Hume that Cromwell's letters and speeches would form one of the most nonsensical books in the world.

There were some indications in the History of the French Revolution that Carlyle had a special gift for military description, but it was in this book on Cromwell that he fairly proved himself the rival of Homer in delineating battles. I shall quote part of his picture of the Battle of Dunbar. The moment at which the extract commences is when, on the night of the 2d of September, 1650, David Lesley, commander of the Scots, is bringing his men down from their unassailable position on the heights above Dunbar, to the level ground on which they will be exposed to the attack of Cromwell.

THE BATTLE OF DUNBAR.

At sight of this movement, Oliver suggests to Lambert standing by him, Does it not give *us* an advantage, if we, instead of him, like to begin the attack? Here is the enemy's right wing coming out to the open space, free to be attacked on any side; and the main-battle hampered in narrow sloping ground between Doon Hill and the brook, has no room to manœuvre or assist: beat this right wing where it now stands; take it in flank and front with an overpowering force—it is driven upon its own main-battle, the whole army is beaten? Lambert eagerly assents, "had meant to say the same thing." Monk, who comes up at the moment, likewise assents; as the other officers do, when the case is set before them. It is the plan resolved upon for battle. The attack shall begin to-morrow before dawn. And so the soldiers stand to their arms, or lie within instant reach of their arms, all night; being upon an engagement very difficult indeed. The night is wild and wet;—2d of September means 12th by our calendar; the harvest-moon wades deep among clouds of sleet and hail. Whoever has a heart for prayer, let him pray now, for the wrestle of death is at hand. Pray—and withal keep his powder dry! And be ready for ex- tremities, and quit himself like a man! Thus they pass the night, making that Dunbar Peninsula and Brock rivulet long memorable to me. We English have some tents; the Scots have none. The hoarse sea moans bodeful, swinging low and heavy against those whinstone bays; the sea and the tempests are abroad, all else asleep but we, and there is One that rides on the wings of the wind.

Toward three in the morning, the Scotch foot, by order of a major-gen- eral, say some, extinguish their matches, all but two in a company: cower under the corn-shocks, seeking some imperfect shelter and sleep. Be wake- ful, ye English; watch, and pray, and keep your powder dry. About four o'clock comes order to my pudding-headed Yorkshire friend that his regi- ment must mount and march straightway; his and various other regiments march, pouring swiftly to the left to Brocksmouth House, to the Pass over the Brock. With overpowering force let us storm the Scots' right wing there; beat that, and all is beaten. Major Hodgson, giving his charge to a brother officer, turned aside to listen for a minute, and worship and pray along with them; haply his last prayer on this earth, as it might prove to be. But no: this cornet prayed with such effusion as was wonderful; and imparted strength to my Yorkshire friend, who strengthened his men by telling them of it. And the heavens, in their mercy, I think, have opened us a way of deliverance!—The moon gleams out, hard and blue, riding among hail-clouds; and over St. Abb's Head a streak of dawn is rising.

And now is the hour when the attack should be, and no Lambert is yet here, he is ordering the line far to the right yet; and Oliver occasionally, in Hodgson's hearing, is impatient for him. The Scots, too, on this wing are awake, thinking to surprise us; there is their trumpet sounding, we heard it once; and Lambert, who is to lead the attack, is not here. The Lord General is impatient;—behold Lambert at last! The trumpets peal, shattering with fierce clangor night's silence; the cannons awaken along all the line: "The Lord of Hosts! the Lord of Hosts!" On, my brave ones, on!

The dispute on this right wing was hot and stiff for three-quarters of an hour! Plenty of fire from field-pieces, snaphances, match-locks, enter- tains the Scotch main-battle across the Brock;—poor stiffened men, roused from the corn-shocks with their matches all out! But here on the right, their horse, " with lancers in the front rank," charge desperately; drive us back across the hollow of the rivulet; back a little; but the Lord gives us courage, and we storm home again, horse and foot, upon them, with a shock like tornado tempests; break them, beat them, drive them all adrift. "Some fled across Copperspath, but most across their own foot." Their own poor foot, whose matches were hardly well alight yet! Poor men, it was a terrible awakening for them: field-pieces and charge of foot across the Brocksburn; and now here is their own horse in mad panic trampling them to death. Above three thousand killed upon the place: "I never saw such a charge of foot and horse," says one; nor did I. Oliver was still near to Yorkshire Hodgson when the shock succeeded; Hodgson heard him say, "They run! I profess they run!" And over St. Abb's Head and the German Ocean, just then, bursts the first gleam of the level sun upon us, and I heard Noll say, in the words of the Psalmist, "Let God arise, let His enemies be scattered"—or in Rous's metre—

> Let God arise, and scattered
> Let all His enemies be;
> And let all those that do Him hate
> Before His presence flee!

Even so. The Scotch army is shivered to utter ruin; rushes in tumultuous wreck, hither, thither; to Belhaven, or, in their distraction, even to Dunbar; the chase goes as far as Haddington; led by Hacker. "The Lord General made a halt," says Hodgson, "and sang the hundred-and-seventeenth psalm," till our horse could gather for the chase. Hundred-and-seventeenth psalm, at the foot of the Doon Hill; there we uplift it to the tune of Bangor, or some still higher score, and roll it strong and great against the sky:

> O give ye praise unto the Lord,
> All nati-ons that be:
> Likewise ye people all, accord
> His name to magnify!
>
> For great to-us-ward ever are
> His loving-kindnesses;
> His truth endures for evermore:
> The Lord O do ye bless.

And now to the chase again.

Carlyle regards universal history as, in the widest and deepest sense, a Bible—the record of *what has been* in God's world; and as we read a passage like this, we cannot refuse to acknowledge that he has made his contribution to the Bible of

4

England's history with the earnestness of a Hebrew seer.   The
sublime chapter on the death of Oliver is, if possible, still more
Biblical in its tone; and I must confess that it seems to me
sheer superstition to impute infallible inspiration to every page
in the annals and chronicles of the kings of Israel and Judah,
and to refuse to admit the existence of any inspiration at all
in that soul-thrilling account of the last hours of the greatest
and godliest Prince that ever reigned in England.   If any man
tells me that he can read that chapter with sneering indifference, I shall be unable to believe him if he adds that he feels
his heart glow within him while he reads the prophecies of
Isaiah or the letters of Paul.

CHAPTER VIII.

RETROSPECT.—IIIS WORK BEFORE FIFTY.—CHANGE IN IIIS MOOD.—THE LATTER-DAY PAMPHLETS.

WE are now in a position to appreciate the justice of Professor Masson's remark, referred to in the outset, that there has been an element of military arrangement in the life of Carlyle. As a general plans a great campaign—as a true man, to use Milton's image, makes his whole life an epic poem—so did Carlyle lay out his life, so, at least, are we, as we look along it, almost constrained to believe that he arranged and planned it. Of course any express or literal planning is out of the question, and all the unity of his life has been derived from elevation of principle and fortitude of will. His career has been an exact antithesis to what he declares that of the German literary man, Hoffmann, to have been. "Hoffmann belongs to that too numerous class of vivid and gifted literary men, whose genius, never cultured or elaborated into purity, finds loud and sudden, rather than judicious or permanent admiration; and whose history, full of error and perplexed vicissitude, excites sympathizing regret in a few, and unwise wonder in many."

It has been a prevailing and most pernicious idea that this character belongs by some natural fitness to the man of letters. IIe has from time immemorial been regarded as a kind of privileged yet, on the whole, pitiable outcast from the regular professions, one who, unless he choose to expose himself to the reproach of dulness, must indulge in more or less of Bohemianism. There has been nothing "disjointed" in Carlyle's life, no solution of moral and intellectual continuity; and yet no life could have been less formal or pedantic, less bound in the trammels of clock-work regularity and routine. "A man," he says, "should withal be king of his habitudes." This he can be in a kingly fashion only when he is sure of his principles.

It was in 1845 that the Letters and Speeches of Oliver Cromwell appeared. Carlyle was still under fifty, and yet consider what a spell of work he had done. Sartor Resartus, exquisite in the best and highest order of idyllic description, profound in philosophy, original in character-painting; three or four volumes of the finest Review essays ever written, many of them complete and masterly biographies; Chartism, an eloquent and suggestive comment upon certain incidents and characteristics of the time, probably imperishable, notwithstanding the ephemeral nature of much of what suggested it; Past and Present, a reproduction, in all the warmth of living color, of an instructive and charming episode in the history of England in the twelfth century, with brilliant, and, on the whole, sagacious application of its main lessons to modern requirements; Lectures on Heroes and Hero-worship, which, whatever their merits or demerits, set Thomas Carlyle at the head of all hitherto known platform lecturers; the History of the French Revolution, one of the glories of English Literature; and the Letters and Speeches of Oliver Cromwell, with historical reproduction of Oliver's environment, in which, dug from beneath a mountain of rubbish, the real Cromwell, in his fashion as he lived, was set upon a pedestal from which detraction rude will never cast him down. Such is the magnificent roll of Carlyle's achievements before he was fifty years old. How much grander it is than the roll of Frederick's or Napoleon's battles! It seems to me to justify an ardor of enthusiastic admiration, stronger than any words of mine can express; and if we studiously and conscientiously divest ourselves of hero-worship, we may indulge our admiration without risk to our judgment, and feel that we are sane and self-respecting men in saying "honor, honor, honor to Thomas Carlyle," as well as in frankly challenging those errors in his works into which all men are liable to fall.

"They are going to make Rhadamanthus of you," said John Sterling to Carlyle, at one of their last interviews. The prediction was uttered not without sadness, and may, perhaps, be taken as an indication that the hopeful and happy-thoughted Sterling perceived the tendency to fault-finding to be growing upon his friend, and threatening to overshadow his brain. Fault-finding in excess is the besetting sin of those men in whom the keen sensibilities of genius combine with impassioned moral fervor to produce what we may call the prophetic temperament. They do not see the bright side of things; instead of working side by side with the seven thousand who serve God and man as honestly as themselves, they ignore their existence. I think it likely that absorbing study of the words and deeds of Cromwell, vehemence of sympathy with the Hebraic rigor of militant and triumphant Puritanism, contributed to deepen Carlyle's gloom, and to darken still more those unfavorable views of men and affairs which are natural to the afternoon and evening rather than to the morning of life. In resuscitating Cromwell, he had not only, as biographers commonly have, to glance over his hero's letters and speeches, but to read "every fibre" of them "with magnifying-glasses." By force of dramatic sympathy, he lived Cromwell's life over again. That was dangerous. A man of his temperament was not in safe company with Cromwell at the siege of Drogheda. In the latter half of his literary activity, the hope, the joyousness, the calm which he learned from Goethe, have been replaced by less melodious moods of mind. The first book which he published after the Letters and Speeches of Cromwell was the Latter-day Pamphlets. There is less of music in it than in any of his books.

A glance into the far-famed Pamphlets proves two things:
that their general power is not less than that of Carlyle's earlier works, and that their literary form is defective. The power
is seen everywhere. "The present time," I quote from the first
paragraph of the first pamphlet, "youngest born of eternity,
child and heir of all the past times with their good and evil,
and parent of all the future, is ever a 'new era' to the thinking man, and comes with new questions and significance, however commonplace it look; ... nor is there any sin more fearfully avenged on men and nations than that same, which, indeed, includes and presupposes all manner of sins: the sin
which our old, pious fathers called 'judicial blindness;' which
we, with our light habits, may still call misinterpretation of
the time that now is." That is a weighty commencement.
Published in 1849, the Pamphlets were written while Europe
was still tormented with the din and tumult of the revolutions
of 1848. "Few of the generations," says Carlyle, a few lines
farther on, "have seen more impressive days. Days of endless
calamity, disruption, dislocation, confusion worse confounded;
if they are not days of endless hope, too, then they are days of
utter despair." Sketching with a few strokes of graphic and
grimly humorous delineation, the attempt made to reform the
Papacy, and pronouncing it hopeless and suicidal, he points out
that, by the reforming Pope, "the sleeping elements, mothers
of the whirlwinds, conflagrations, earthquakes," were awakened,
and the general overturn of 1848 brought about. In the thirty
years which have passed since then a new generation has arisen,
and as the commotions of 1848 have left very little mark in
history, our new generation may have difficulty in realizing
that singular year. It was a year of revolutions, but of paltry
anarchic revolutions, without heroism either in the attack or
the resistance. The mob, led by chattering attorneys and
crack-brained professors, assailed the constituted authorities;
and the kings and ducal eminences, and serene dignitaries in

general, instead of showing fight, caught up their carpet-bags, announced that they were scions of the family of Smith, and ran for their lives. This state of things is brilliantly, and with graphic selection of the characteristic features and salient points, touched off in the following passage :

The Year 1848.

As if by sympathetic subterranean electricities, all Europe exploded, boundless, uncontrollable; and we had the year 1848, one of the most singular, disastrous, amazing, and, on the whole, humiliating years the European world ever saw. Not since the irruption of the Northern Barbarians has there been the like. Everywhere immeasurable democracy rose monstrous, loud, blatant, inarticulate as the voice of Chaos. Everywhere the official holy-of-holies was scandalously laid bare to dogs and the profane :—enter, all the world, see what kind of official holy it is. Kings everywhere, and reigning persons, stared in sudden horror, the voice of the whole world bellowing in their ear, "Begone, ye imbecile hypocrites, histrios not heroes! Off with you, off !"—and, what was peculiar and notable in this year for the first time, the kings all made haste to go, as if exclaiming, "We *are* poor histrios, we, sure enough ; did you want heroes? Don't kill us; we couldn't help it !" Not one of them turned round and stood upon his kingship, as upon a right he could afford to die for, or to risk his skin upon ; by no manner of means. That, I say, is the alarming peculiarity at present. Democracy, on this new occasion, finds all kings *conscious* that they are but play-actors. The miserable mortals, enacting their High Life Below Stairs, with faith only that this universe may, perhaps, be all a phantasm and hypocrisis—the truculent Constable of the Destinies suddenly enters : "Scandalous phantasms, what do *you* here? Are 'solemnly-constituted impostors' the proper kings of men? Did you think the life of man was a grimacing dance of apes? To be led away by the squeak of your paltry fiddle? Ye miserable, this universe is not an upholstery puppet-play, but a terrible God's fact; and you, I think—had not you better be gone !" They fled precipitately, some of them with what we may call an exquisite ignominy, in terror of the tread-mill or worse. And everywhere the people, or the populace, take their own government upon themselves; and open "kinglessness," what we call *anarchy*—how happy if it be anarchy *plus* a street-constable !—is everywhere the order of the day. Such was the history, from Baltic to Mediterranean, in Italy, France,

Prussia, Austria, from end to end of Europe, in those March days of 1848. Since the destruction of the old Roman Empire by inroad of the Northern Barbarians, I have known nothing similar.

A curious interest attaches at this moment to Carlyle's speci-fication, as one notable characteristic of the undivine comedy or tragi-comedy of 1848, that it was, in a quite unprecedented degree, the work of young men. "Students, young men of letters, advocates, editors, hot inexperienced enthusiasts, or fierce and justly bankrupt desperadoes, acting everywhere on the dis-content of the millions," blew the European nations into flame. "Never," says Carlyle, "till now did young men, and almost children, take such a command in human affairs. A changed time since the word *Senior* (Seigneur, or *Elder*) was first de-vised to signify 'lord,' or superior; as in all languages of men we find it to have been! In times when men love wisdom, the old man will ever be venerable, and be venerated, and reck-oned noble." All who are acquainted with the writings of Lord Beaconsfield will recollect his theory that it is to young men the progress of the world is due; and the intense and radi-cal diversity of nature between Lord Beaconsfield and Thomas Carlyle could hardly, perhaps, be more pertinently illustrated than in the preference of the one for the flashy virtues of youth, and of the other for the experienced wisdom of age. In times of wide-spread folly, however, old men, Carlyle goes on to say, are apt to be mere superannuated boys, with the foolishness of boys, yet "without the graces, generosities, and opulent strength of young boys." Therefore, in our time we must after all look for leadership to young men; "the mature man, hardened into sceptical egoism, knows no monition but that of his own frigid cautions, avarices, mean timidities." That Carlyle is here in the right as to the general rule and law that the elders of the people are their natural leaders, whether in court, camp, or congregation, I have no doubt. There may be more question as to the alleged apathy and prudential cowardice of mature or aged men in this, as distinguished from other times.

In literary form, the Latter-day Pamphlets are inferior to Carlyle's earlier writings. His mannerism is now too obvious, too strongly obtruded. His humor becomes harsher, and sometimes borders upon coarseness. Heavyside, Flimnap, MacCrowdy, Crabbe with his *Radiator*, Smelfungus, Sauerteig, Peter, Bobus of Houndsditch, Phantasm Captains, and the rest of the *dramatis personæ*, cease to be amusing from the frequency of their appearance on the boards. The vehemence has now become almost spasmodic, and the " green oases by the palm-tree wells," the spaces of repose and chastened and genial beauty, have become far less frequent than formerly.

4*

CHAPTER IX.

ON DEMOCRACY.

THE good and the bad in the Latter-day Pamphlets are almost inextricably coiled and twisted together. Having read each Pamphlet when it came out, being then a lad of nineteen, and having had the volume often in my hand, and always, more or less, in my head since then, I ought to have some skill in separating its good from its evil; and it is upon the strength of my performance of this problem, and the inferences drawn therefrom, that, Liberal as I am, I pretend to be a more legitimate pupil and disciple of Carlyle in the political department than those Conservative persons for whom the Latter-day Pamphlets are a fountain of speculative and practical Toryism. I find certain of those fundamental facts recognized in them, certain of those fundamental principles laid down in them, on which rational and constructive Liberalism rests.

The first fact recognized by Carlyle is that sovereignty has in these times passed into the hands of the whole people. "Universal *democracy*," he says, "whatever we may think of it, has declared itself as an inevitable fact of the days in which we live; and he who has any chance to instruct, or lead, in his days must begin by admitting that: new street barricades, and new anarchies, still more scandalous if less sanguinary, must return and again return, till governing persons everywhere know and admit that." Even in Russia democracy is working underground, and may soon come above ground; "and here in England, though we object to it resolutely in the form of street-barricades and insurrectionary pikes, and decidedly will not open doors to it on those terms, the tramp of its million feet is on all streets and thoroughfares, the sound of its bewildered thousand-fold voice is in all writings and speakings, in all thinkings, and modes, and activities of men: the soul that does not now, with hope or terror, discern *it*, is not the one we address on this occasion." No acceptance of democracy as an inexorable fact could be more explicit than this; and I am unable to attach any coherent sense to the words, "acceptance of democracy," unless they imply . that government is to take place, not in opposition to the national will, not in scornful indifference to the national will, but with the assent and by the authority of the national will.

Mr. Carlyle next lays down the principle that what is essential to prosperous governing is that "the man or nation can discern what the true regulations of the universe are in regard to him and his pursuit, and can faithfully and steadfastly follow these." The form of expression may here be vague, but the meaning is incontrovertible. You want good government. Will democracy ensure that? Self-government by fools is ruin. So much importance does Carlyle attach to the fact that government by the people's will is not necessarily right government, that we shall not do him justice unless we quote at least one of those passages in which he impales the idiotic notion, possibly entertained by a brainless mobocrat here and there, that, if you only perfect your voting apparatus, you are absolutely certain of good government.

Rounding the Political Cape Horn.

Your ship cannot double Cape Horn by its excellent plans of voting. The ship may vote this and that, above decks and below, in the most harmonious, exquisitely constitutional manner; the ship, to get round Cape Horn, will find a set of conditions already voted for, and fixed with adamantine rigor, by the ancient elemental powers, who are entirely careless how you vote. If you can, by voting or without voting, ascertain these conditions, and valiantly conform to them, you will get round the Cape; if you cannot—the ruffian winds will blow you ever back again; the inexorable icebergs, dumb privy councillors from chaos, will nudge you with most chaotic "admonition;" you will be flung, half-frozen, on the Patagonian cliffs, or admonished into shivers by your iceberg councillors, and sent sheer down to Davy Jones, and will never get round Cape Horn at all! Unanimity on board ship; yes, indeed, the ship's crew may be very unanimous, which doubtless, for the time being, will be very comfortable to the ship's crew, and to their Phantasm Captain, if they have one; but if the tack they unanimously steer upon is guiding them into the belly of the abyss, it will not profit them much! Ships accordingly do not use the ballot-box at all; and they reject the Phantasm species of captains; one wishes much some other entities—since all entities lie under the same rigorous set of laws—could be brought to show as much wisdom and sense at least of self-preservation, the *first* command of nature. Phantasm captains with unanimous votings: this is considered to be all the law and all the prophets, at present.

Into the vagaries of political lunacy it were bootless to inquire, but I am not aware that I ever met with any one foolish enough to dispute in terms the principle thus picturesquely stated. Dazzling imagery, however, may interfere with, rather than promote, the investigation of many-sided truth, and we must look into this case of the Cape Horn voyagers somewhat closely.

The safety of the ship, in doubling Cape Horn, depends primarily upon whether the captain understands his business, or does not; and secondarily, though in an important degree, upon the loyalty and promptitude of the crew in rendering him obedience. This loyalty and promptitude may depend considerably upon the way in which the captain has been appointed; and if any gross jobbery or flagrant injustice has been perpetrated in his appointment, the circumstance may materially affect that energetic obedience to his commands, on the part of the crew, which he will want in the Straits of Magellan.

One thing also is pretty sure, though it may look surprising, that, if the captain were appointed by vote of the crew, he would be a good seaman. Nothing seems much more absurd on paper than almost all kinds of popular election, and yet it has been proved in countless instances to be practically superior to any other that has been devised. The professors whose genius spread the fame of Edinburgh University throughout the world were elected by a parcel of shopkeepers, who could give no other guarantee of choosing rightly, except that they sincerely wished to get the best man. David Hume makes a note in his Memorandum-book, referring to Livy as his authority, that many of the chief officers of the army were named by the people in old Rome. Lord Advocate Young told the Social Science Congress at Aberdeen, in 1877, that he would back the verdict of a jury taken from all grades of society, "and most of them uneducated men," against the verdict of fifteen of the best trained lawyers in Scotland. Who has not heard "fellows in buckram" descanting on the absurdity of election of pastors by their congregations? But the Duke of Argyll, having some twenty-five livings in his gift, made it a rule of appointing men who were chosen by the people; and he publicly stated that, in many years' experience, he had never found the people err in their choice. On the other hand, the Bishop of Peterborough, appointing pastors, with all the formalities and precautions that the buckram fellows could desire, declared, in 1875, that, since entering on the duties of his diocese, he had been called upon to institute one clergyman who was paralytic, one who was hopelessly aged and infirm, one reclaimed drunkard, who had been intemperate in a parish adjoining that in which he was to minister, and one who had resigned a public office rather than face a charge of "the most horrible immorality." The facts were notorious, but the Bishop was advised that he had no legal power to refuse institution. Whether St. Paul would have granted institution, even when the law of England told him to make a laughing-stock of the law of Christ ("Feed my lambs"), may be doubted; but that is not our present affair.

Popular election is not infallible; but no infallible form of election is to be had; and the question before us is whether the ship of Government is less likely to be got round Cape Horn by a parliament elected by the many, than by a king, with a council named by himself. Mr. Carlyle vehemently repudiates the popular method, and proposes—by way of performing what I unreservedly acknowledge to be the essential operation of sifting out the ablest and noblest men in the nation to do the governing—that the Crown should name a certain proportion of the members of Parliament, and that it should cease to be incumbent upon the members of the Cabinet to have seats in either House. Thus and thus only does Carlyle hope that political salvation may gradually be found for England. The *other* hypothesis—namely, that the people may learn to choose those who, by natural fitness, are proved to have a divine right to govern—he impatiently rejects. And yet it seems to me irresistibly clear that, by accepting the fact of democracy, he practically bound himself to choose this last hypothesis. If democracy is the inexorable ordinance of Heaven, it is too late to fall back upon any scheme of strengthening the influence of the Crown, whether that scheme be Temple's, Bolingbroke's, Beaconsfield's, or Carlyle's. I shall endeavor to show in a few words that it is unnecessary to have recourse to any such expedient.

Even from the book before me, set in the light of the subsequent history of the country, I derive most encouraging evidence that the people of Great Britain are not so wedded to folly as to preclude the possibility of their sending good men to Parliament. Mr. Carlyle suggests in these Pamphlets many admirable reforms, which Sir Robert Peel—for he was the man whom Carlyle fixed upon as the Premier of the new era—assisted by a cabinet placed beyond influence by the popular gale, might carry through. These embraced the education of the people, the relief of the labor market by systematic emigration, the employment of our soldiers in works of industry, the introduction of order and efficiency into all departments of the public service. Well, what do we now behold? The Crown names no members of Parliament, the Ministers are still directly responsible to the House; but the impartation of the elements of knowledge to the whole people has been assumed as a duty by Government. Our soldiers are not employed, during peace, in building harbors of refuge or draining morasses, but the stagnation and idleness of the olden times have been broken up, and the autumn manœuvres give our soldiers something to do. The whole Volunteer movement might, with not much straining, be represented as the carrying out of a suggestion thrown out in these pamphlets; for the Volunteers are soldiers who do their work as well as their soldiering; but it has been carried out by popular impulse, not by Government orders. Our ships of war have not, as Carlyle proposed, been employed in carrying emigrants to the colonies, but emigration has proceeded on a large scale, and has been placed under Government superintendence, and partially assisted, if not by the Home Government, then by the Colonial authorities. There is still, we may be pretty sure, in the departments of the Civil Service less efficiency than would have satisfied Cromwell; but something has been done in the way of balking favoritism, declining "the Queen's bad bargains," and securing that those who prove themselves, on terms as fair as can be arranged, better men than those whom they vanquish in open competition, shall become servants of the State. While these and a multitude of other reforms have been taking place, the great fact of democracy, signalized by Carlyle, has been so far recognized and accepted that immense additions have been made to the national constituency, and that the property qualification for members of Parliament has been abolished. The general result has been that the pauperism, which appalled Carlyle in 1849, has dwindled into compara-

tive insignificance; that political sedition has become a reminiscence of middle-aged gentlemen, who require to explain to
their sons and daughters what the Five Points of the Charter
meant; that, as Macaulay said, there is no more fear of a
revolution in England than of the falling of the moon; and
that two working-class members of Parliament receive defer-
ential audience from the House when they explain to it the
wants and claims of the multitude. Is not this better than
if an attempt of a highly artificial kind had been made to
turn the history of England into a new channel, and to have
recourse to the traditions and habitudes of more or less des-
potic monarchy?

Even if the deliberate acceptance and resolute, though gradual, effectuation of the democratic principle in our Government
had been attended with far different and less favorable results,
we should still have to inquire whether the failure had or had
not been due to the inadequate performance of political duty
by men who ought to have been the guides of the people.
Mr. Carlyle sneers, and all Carlylian anti-Liberals join him in
sneering, at the privilege of sending the ten-thousandth part
of a member to Parliament. Can anything, they ask, be done
by so small a power as that? I answer, Yes. How many
million rootlets suck in the moisture from the ground that
goes to support the oak whose shadow has been widening for
a thousand years? Can you measure with your finest instruments the infinitesimal part of the work done by each of those
million rootlets? Yet if *each* of these rootlets thought its
part too small to be performed, would the shadow have grown
for a thousand years? When every unit in the millions of
free men constituting a great free State does his political duty,
there will be no danger in democracy. Mr. Ruskin, the most
brilliant of all the Carlylian anti-Liberals, announces, in what
seems a boastful tone, that he never in his life voted for a
member of Parliament. If that had been the habit of Eng-

lishmen when John Hampden rode from county to county addressing the electors of the Long Parliament, would not the old oak of England's greatness have long since withered away? I am sure I shall reflect with satisfaction on my death-bed that I did my poor best, in the cold spring of 1874, to put a good member into the House of Commons and to keep a less good out.`

CHAPTER X.

NOTHING in the Latter-day Pamphlets; nothing perhaps in Carlyle's writings, has occasioned more discussion than his depreciatory notice of John Howard, his scornful denunciation of what may be vaguely but intelligibly styled the philanthropic movement, and his insistence upon severe methods in the treatment of criminals. Here, again, there is vital and vivid truth in what he says, but here also that truth can be discerned, and can be made practically useful, only when it is separated from the un-truth with which it is associated.

Bitter as is the contempt with which he ultimately dismisses philanthropists—"You may go down!"—he begins with what seems an important act of fairness. He distinguishes between them and a still more culpable and contemptible class of persons. "One large body," he says, "of the intelligent and influential accepts the social iniquities, or whatever you may call them, and the miseries consequent thereupon; accepts them, admits them to be extremely miserable, pronounces them entirely inevitable, incurable except by Heaven, and eats its pudding with as little thought of them as possible." This indifferent, do-nothing class he dismisses as incorrigible and ignoble. Philanthropists form "the select small minority," in whom public spirit and human pity survive. Among them it is that soldiers for "the Good Cause" are to be found. This fact, one would think, entitles them to considerable respect. But Mr. Carlyle has no respect for them whatever. Instead of treating them as soldiers of the good cause who wish to be shown how to fight, he permits his anger to master him to such an extent

that he positively, though, to all appearance, unconsciously, can-
cels his own distinct concession as to their human pity and
public spirit. Unless he has been meaning that these sentiments are genuine, he virtually affirms that the "select minority" are more blameworthy and despicable than the apathetic
majority; for the latter are unimpeachably sincere in their indifference; and sincere apathy is better than hypocritic philanthropy. It follows, therefore, that he explicitly contradicts
himself when, after a few pages of fierce reprimand, he thus
addresses philanthropists: "You mistake in every way, my
friends. The fact is, you fancy yourselves men of virtue, benevolence, what not; and you are not even men of sincerity
and honest sense." This may, however, be treated as a slip of
the pen or the memory—a thing to which prophets are liable;
or, at lowest, we may grant to Carlyle that there are degrees of
honesty and sincerity, that the motives of good men are mixed,
and that even select minorities and soldiers of the good cause
are not absolutely sincere.

The point on which it is essential to insist is that a "sentiment of public spirit," energetic enough to look for employment in works of beneficence, and a pity vivacious enough to
seek relief in helping the wretched, are so precious, and, indeed, so rare, that it is thriftless to sneer at them. Mr. Carlyle admits the minority in whom these things are found to be
small, and it is a minority that has all the powers of the world,
the flesh, and the devil in league against it. The instinct of
society is to let things alone, to permit nothing to ruffle the
cruel serenity of its pleasures, to vote every one a bore who
dwells upon any scheme for human improvement one moment
longer than is necessary for the purposes of small talk. The
force which drags us ever down toward lethargy and indifference is, in its colossal potency, like that force of the earth's
gravitation, against which the thin spear-points of a million
blades as they pierce the ground in spring, and the leaves and

aspiring stems of forest trees, and all that is most finely and
vitally beautiful in our planet, make resistance.   Philanthropy
bears up in the teeth of that mighty ebb-tide, to move with
which, like drift-wood, "hereditary sloth"* instructs us.   Those
in whom there is any true enthusiasm of humanity—those in
whom the sting of anger against wrong, or the sympathetic
pang of tenderness in presence of anguish, are strong enough
to induce the sacrifice of an hour or a guinea—are so few that
they ought to encourage each other, and not countenance the
cynics in their sneers or the sluggards in their folding of the
hands.

The sin and blunder with which Carlyle charges philanthropists is that of trying "to cure a world's woes by rose-water."
They will have none but mild methods.   "It seems not," he
says, "to have struck these good men that no world, or thing
here below, ever fell into misery, without having first fallen
into folly, into sin against the Supreme Ruler of it, by adopting as a law of conduct what was not a law, but the reverse of
one; and that, till its folly, till its sin be cast out of it, there is
not the smallest hope of its misery going—that not for all the
charity and rose-water in the world, will its misery try to go
till then."

This sentence is curiously interesting in a biographic point
of view, for it proves that, when well past fifty years of age,
Carlyle was still fundamentally an optimist.   That he could
have written down the words, read them over, sent them to the
printer, seen them in the proof-sheets, and given them to the
public, is to me a wonder of wonders.   Why, if the truth be
indeed as he puts it, the riddle of the world is an asses' bridge
over which every frolicsome donkey may go at a canter.   If

---

* *Antonio.* I'll teach you how to flow.
  Sebastian.   Do so: to ebb,
  Hereditary sloth instructs me.—*The Tempest.*

all sorrow is punishment for crime, then Job was a teasing hair-splitter and Solomon a fantastic grumbler. If misery were always apportioned to sin, or to sinful folly, there would, indeed, be no call for hesitation on the part of priest or Pharisee in taking up stones to cast at offenders. Literally, obviously, triumphantly, the ways of God would be justified to man; every one would have his desires; no knave would escape whipping; the barns of the righteous would always be filled with plenty, and their presses burst with new wine. But science, with the assent now, tacit or declared, of all the Churches, announces that if pain and anguish constitute misery, then misery existed in the world myriads of ages before man or man's sin appeared; and whosoever looks candidly over society will find that to-day, as in the time of Solomon and Job, the good are often exposed to suffering, the wicked are often successful, misery is often the child of misfortune as well as of guilt, and the ascertainment of merit and demerit is so subtly difficult that, except in the way of rough approximation, the Infinite Wisdom alone can achieve it.

One thing, and one only, can be said with clearest affirmation of reason and conscience, as to the connection between sin and misery—that, where guilt is deliberate, undoubted, and wilful, punishment ought to be inflicted. This is the first principle of all moral government; and Mr. Carlyle does service worthy of himself when he rests this pillar of the moral universe, not upon mere social expediency, but upon those authoritative instincts of our spiritual nature in which we hear the voice of God. If there are any who propose to heal the wounds of society by "indiscriminate contributions of philanthropy," no words can be too strong to express the greatness of their mistake. The persuasion has been general, and I am not prepared to say that it has been wholly erroneous, that, in the period immediately preceding the publication of the Latter-day Pamphlets, the mild method in the treatment of criminals was carried to ex-

cess. Any softening of moral indignation against deliberate
wickedness would be fatal to the spiritual health of the community, and if the malady is baneful, we need not quarrel with
Carlyle for some display of vehemence in applying the cure.
Let us, therefore, have the state of things to which he objected, and which he proposed to amend, set before us in his own
words.

A PRISON THIRTY YEARS AGO.

Several months ago some friends took me with them to see one of the
London prisons—a prison of the exemplary or model kind. An immense
circuit of buildings; cut out, girt with a high ring wall from the lanes
and streets of the quarter, which is a dim and crowded one. Gate-way as
to a fortified place; then a spacious court, like the square of a city; broad
staircases, passages to interior courts; fronts of stately architecture all
around. It lodges some thousand or twelve hundred prisoners, besides
the officers of the establishment. Surely one of the most perfect buildings within the compass of London. We looked at the apartments, sleep-
ing-cells, dining-rooms, working-rooms, general courts, or special and private: excellent all, the *ne plus ultra* of human care and ingenuity; in my
life I never saw so clean a building; probably no Duke in England lives
in a mansion of such perfect and thorough cleanness.

The bread, the cocoa, soup, meat, all the various sorts of food, in their
respective cooking-places, we tasted; found them of excellence superlative. The prisoners sat at work, light work, picking oakum, and the like,
in airy apartments with glass-roofs, of agreeable temperature and perfect
ventilation; silent, or, at least, conversing only by secret signs; others
were out, taking their hour of promenade in clean flagged courts; methodic composure, cleanliness, peace, substantial, wholesome comfort reigned
everywhere supreme. The women in other apartments, some notable murderesses among them, all in the like state of methodic composure and
substantial wholesome comfort, sat sewing: in long ranges of wash-houses,
drying-houses, and whatever pertains to the getting-up of clean linen, were
certain others, with all conceivable mechanical furtherances, not too ardu-
ously working. The notable murderesses were, though with great precautions of privacy, pointed out to us; and we were requested not to look
openly at them, or seem to notice them at all, as it was found to "cherish
their vanity" when visitors looked at them. Schools, too, were there; intelligent teachers of both sexes, studiously instructing the still ignorant of
these thieves. . . .

The captain of the place, a gentleman of ancient military or Royal navy habits, was one of the most perfect governors: professionally and by nature zealous for cleanliness, punctuality, good order of every kind; a humane heart and yet a strong one; soft of speech and manner, yet with an inflexible rigor of command, so far as his limits went: iron hand in velvet glove, as Napoleon defined it. . . . This excellent captain was too old a commander to complain of anything; indeed he struggled visibly the other way, to find in his own mind that all here was best; but I could sufficiently discern that, in his natural instincts, if not mounting up to the region of his thoughts, there was a continual protest going on against much of it; that nature and all his inarticulate persuasion (however much forbidden to articulate itself) taught him the futility and unfeasibility of the system followed here. The visiting magistrates, he gently regretted rather than complained, had lately taken his tread-wheel from him, men were just now pulling it down; and how he was henceforth to enforce discipline on these bad subjects, was much a difficulty with him. "They cared for nothing but the tread-wheel, and for having their rations cut short:" of the two sole penalties, hard work and occasional hunger, there remained now only one, and that by no means the better one, as he thought. . . . To drill twelve hundred scoundrels by "the method of kindness," and of abolishing your very tread-wheel—how could any commander rejoice to have such a work cut out for him? You had but to look in the faces of these twelve hundred and despair, for the most part, of ever commanding them at all. Miserable distorted blockheads, the generality: ape-faces, imp-faces, angry dog-faces, heavy sullen ox-faces; degraded underfoot perverse creatures, sons of *in*docility, greedy mutinous darkness, and, in one word, of STUPIDITY, which is the general mother of such. Stupidity intellectual and stupidity moral (for the one always means the other, as you will, with surprise or not, discover if you look) had borne this progeny: base-natured beings, on whom in the course of a maleficent subterranean life of London scoundrelism, the genius of darkness (called Satan, Devil, and other names) had now visibly impressed his seal, and had marked them out as soldiers of chaos and of him—appointed to serve in *his* regiments, first of the line, second ditto, and so on in their order. Him, you could perceive, they would serve; but not easily another than him. These were the subjects which our brave captain and prison-governor was appointed to command, and reclaim to *other* service, by "the method of love," with a tread-wheel abolished.

Hopeless for evermore such a project. These abject, ape, wolf, ox, imp, and other diabolic animal specimens of humanity, who of the very gods could ever have commanded them by love? A collar round the neck, and a cart-whip flourished over the back; these, in a just and steady human hand, were what the gods would have appointed them; and now when, by long misconduct and neglect, they had sworn themselves into the Devil's regiments of the line, and got the seal of chaos impressed on their visage, it was very doubtful whether even these would be of avail for the unfortunate commander of twelve hundred men.

Management of criminals, whether with a view to their reformation or merely in order that their punishment may be pacifically undergone, without means for the application of discipline, is a hopeless enterprise. The abolition of the tread-wheel, therefore, in this model prison, was a highly questionable measure. But before we condemn the whole scheme and method of the place, a point or two will require to be taken into consideration.

The perfect cleanness of everything, though promotive of comfort to Mr. Carlyle, would probably be irksome rather than otherwise to the criminal inmates, and would, at all events, be practically educational in the best possible way. The food was found good in quality, but we are not informed as to the quantity allowed to each prisoner, and whatever might be the case when this pamphlet was written, the food of prisoners is now of the plainest character, and regulated, as to amount, by the rigorous demands of health. The work was oakum-picking, in silence, in rooms with glass roofs. The labor exacted from criminals sentenced to penal servitude is so hard that death is commonly considered a less grievous punishment; and though the oakum-picking, when looked at for a few minutes, might seem light, yet compulsorily persisted in, hour by hour and week by week, between dead walls, without one word of talk to relieve the tedium, it might be inexpressibly vexing.

It is obviously unfair, however, to estimate the severity of imprisonment as a punishment by the actual pain inflicted at any particular moment. In the forfeiture of all that makes life valuable, in the exchange of freedom for the most degrading form of slavery, in the total extinction for the present of that hope of "bettering" which man, according to Schiller, never ceases to cherish, and in the all but total extinction of hope even when liberty shall be regained, do the wormwood and the gall of convict life consist. Moved about in that grave-like silence, every spark of spontaneity quenched in your existence, conscious of being converted from a man into a thing, and made the part of a huge clock-work mechanism, must you not feel the sands of life drag themselves along with unutterable weariness? The minuteness of the precautions necessary to prevent suicide in prisons demonstrates the agonizing nature of imprisonment as a punishment.

We should try, says Mr. Carlyle, "to do justice" to our criminals. Assuredly; but it is really impossible, at whatever cost in the way of obstruction to the flow of discourse, to proceed practically, without asking what is meant by justice. "I have no pocket definition of justice," angrily replies Mr. Carlyle. The law of England, in respect of criminals, must "correspond to the law of the universe." We are to do toward them "approximately as God Almighty does toward them." The "official person, a polite man otherwise," to whom Mr. Carlyle offered this definition of justice to criminals, "grinned as he best could some semblance of a laugh, mirthful as that of an ass eating thistles, and ended in ' Hah, oh, ah !' " The official person could not, without violation of colloquial courtesy, have told his eloquent rebuker that there is no way of extracting rules for practical guidance out of propositions to which a score of persons may attach a score of different meanings. We are forced, however, to pause for a moment in presence of the question, What is justice?

Kant wondered that there is so much kindness and so little justice in the world. John Stuart Mill expresses in his Posthumous Essays the opinion that there is a trace of kindness

5

discoverable in nature, but no trace whatever of justice. These are weighty authorities; yet, if justice is the doing or giving something for an equivalent, and kindness the doing or giving something without money and without price, then it seems to me that, in the arrangements of nature, there is more of justice than of kindness. Nature, in a rather vague but, on the whole, trustworthy fashion, does give a *quid pro quo*. If you plough the ground, sow the seed, hoe out the weeds, and reap the corn, you may count upon having a return for your labor. But nature gives nothing for nothing. No fruit drops into the mouth. All life, from its first quiverings in protoplasmic jelly, to its manifestation in the highest activities of civilized man, is sustained by what we may figure either as a struggle with nature, or as a paying to nature, in labor, of nature's price. When this price is not paid, nature shows no mercy; and it is not always through wickedness, it is very often through weakness, that nature's price is not paid. Nature's justice is to punish weakness with death. Is this, then, the justice we are to follow in dealing with human criminals?

Within the provinces of life there is kindness; animals are tender to their young, more or less gentle or tolerant to each other, when not raging with hunger; and in human society a great part is played by kindness. But it is only from associating nature, in idea, with sentient, rational, and benevolent beings, that nature can be called kind. The dew-drop is tender, only because it is like a human tear. As we rise from stage to stage of life, from stage to stage of civilization, we find nature's merciless justice more and more softened. And is there not the very highest authority, human and Divine, for asserting that

> Earthly power doth then show likest God's
> When mercy seasons justice?

To season justice with mercy is indeed a delicate and difficult problem, and intensest care must be taken that the mercy does not corrupt the justice; but the mood of burning anger is not that in which this problem is likely to be rightly solved. "Mark it," says Mr. Carlyle, "my diabolical friends, I mean to lay leather on the backs of you, collars round the necks of you; and will teach you, after the example of the gods, that this world is *not* your inheritance, or glad to see you in it. You, ye diabolical canaille, what has a governor much to do with you? You, I think, he will rather swiftly dismiss from his thoughts—which have the whole celestial and terrestrial for their scope, and not the subterranean of scoundreldom alone. You, I consider, he will sweep pretty rapidly into some special Convict Colony or remote domestic moorland, into some stone-walled silent system, under hard drill-sergeants, just as Rhada-manthus, and inflexible as he, and there leave you to reap what you have sown; he meanwhile turning his endeavors to the thousand-fold immeasurable interests of men and gods—dismissing the one extremely contemptible interest of scoundrels; sweeping that into the cesspool, tumbling that over London Bridge, in a very brief manner, if needful."

The still small voice of mercy, venturing to season this Draconian justice with the accurate information of science, pauses to inquire who the criminals, thus destined for the cesspool, are. Science finds that there is a too literal truth in Carlyle's description of the dog-faces, ox-faces, and so on, for which he would appoint the whip and the collar. Professor Benedict, of Vienna, having instituted researches into the brains and skulls of criminals, found that, out of sixteen brains examined, not one was normal, all approached the types of brain found among animals. Medical men have discovered that an enormous proportion of criminals possess a naturally defective constitution. Such persons are born to a heritage of woe, placed under fearful disadvantage in the battle of life.

Convicts have been divided by careful and calm observers into (1) those who, by evil propensity and inveterate bent of

nature, are incorrigibly bad; (2) those who, not through volun-
tary badness, but from irremediable infirmity of will, or confusion of mental perceptions, cannot keep up in the march of
life, or hold their own in the universal competitive battle, or
resist temptation; and (3) those who are, in no deep sense,
criminals at all, but have, either through erroneous judgment
of the tribunals, or some quite exceptional act of criminality,
become convicts.   As an illustration of the kind of justice
which may overtake criminals of the third class, I would refer
to a case stated by Lord Advocate Young to the Social Science
Congress in 1877.   A youth, having been respectable, fell into
crime, was convicted, conducted himself excellently in prison,
and was released with a certificate.   Getting employment as a
railway porter, he rose to be stoker, and was on the eve of being promoted to be engine-driver, when he was discovered to
be a returned convict, and was discharged.   Three times he
procured a situation, and three times he was turned adrift, because either his employers or his fellow-workmen heard that he
had been a ticket-of-leave man.   Driven to despair and drink,
he fell again into crime, and, when the Lord Advocate spoke,
he was awaiting his trial.   To such an extent had utter hope-
lessness racked his brain that his reason was in danger.

Justice and mercy both would decline to put the second and
third of the above classes of convicts into the same category
with the first; and even for the first, who may have inherited
criminal propensities of demon-like strength, justice and mercy
both would prescribe, after due trial made, swift death rather
than the chronic death-in-life of hopeless captivity.   He who
would lay on the scourge with the heaviness of God's hand
would need the omniscience of God's eye.

Mr. Carlyle will have it that intellectual stupidity is equivalent to moral delinquency.   "The one always means the other."   But this, with the utmost deference consistent with absolute disagreement, I hold to be one of the worst of those

errors which flaw the rock of Carlyle's mountain-ranges. I cannot imagine any one who has seen the tear gather in the eye of an honest, ingenuous, good child, while it resolutely but vainly attempted to remember the stanza or to do the sum which, to the brighter sister or brother, presented no difficulty whatever, continuing to doubt that a golden heart may beat below a brain of lead. Here again, strangely but indubitably, amidst his Draconian utterances, crops out Mr. Carlyle's optimistic vein. He cannot bring himself to believe that nature could ever treat weakness as vice, unless weakness were necessarily vicious; but those who believe that, at this point precisely, the universal imperfection of created things reaches its climax of imperfection, are under no temptation to paint the shadows out of nature's landscape. It is because nature's justice is blind and hard, and because man is weak, that the religion of Divine Pity was taught at Bethlehem and on Calvary.

Mercy, at all events, has been justified of her children. While the Draconian method was pursued with criminals—before the reforms instituted by Howard, and carried out by a large succession of men worthy to walk in his steps, were dreamed of — while little boys were hanged with stones in their pockets to make them heavy enough, and criminals of all ages were treated as a "diabolic canaille"—the criminal classes did not diminish, and society was warred upon with a defiant ruthlessness correspondent to its own. But the tempering of justice with mercy, the mingling of hope with the anguish of criminal suffering, the consideration of all those circumstances which mitigate the guilt of convicts, the persevering attempt to awaken within them the reminiscence of a nobler manhood, have proved their efficacy by the gradual but sure curtailment of the criminal class. Crime being found to be, in very many cases, the offspring as well as the parent of misery and misfortune, some progress has been made toward the application to the criminal problem, on a far wider scale than had been attempted previously, of the hygienic method. What, to the eye of God, reveals itself as guilt—*i. e.*, wilful and chosen badness, deliberate cruelty, inhuman selfishness—will never, I believe, be identified with disease; but in a vast proportion of cases, the patient investigation of science, Christian and kind, discovers that what seemed guilt has been rooted in disease; and my own profound conviction, fixed in me now for a good many years, is that, in a society approximately Christian and scientific, the prison would, to a very great extent, be turned into an asylum. Entire provisional forfeiture of freedom, with subjection to hygienic treatment, physical and moral, would practically have all the severity required, for purposes of punishment, except in extreme cases. And for extreme cases, the kindest as well as the justest treatment would be death.

THE Latter-day Pamphlets, issued singly in the second half of 1849, appeared collectively in 1850, and in the year following—the year of the first International Exhibition—we find Carlyle employed in writing the biography of John Sterling. The interest of that book lies chiefly, in fact almost solely, in this—that in it we learn what is Carlyle's practical solution of the religious problem of his time. That problem comes up in the Latter-day Pamphlets, and no criticism of the Pamphlets can have a pretence to completeness if it omits consideration of the views therein presented on the religious question; but the Life of Sterling is an illustrative comment of the most pertinent and instructive kind on the religious principles advocated in the Pamphlets, enabling us to translate the abstract into the concrete, to mate principles with facts, to say specifically how, in a given example, Carlyle proposed that religious doubts and difficulties should be dealt with. What, then, are the religious principles enunciated in the Latter-day Pamphlets?

The type and embodiment of what, in connection with religion, he regards as supremely wrong, Carlyle finds in Ignatius Loyola. Let no Protestant, however, lay the flattering unction to his soul that it is on Jesuits and Roman Catholics alone that Carlyle pours his fiery indignation. "For some two centuries," he says, "the genius of mankind has been dominated by the Gospel of Ignatius, perhaps the strangest and certainly among the fatalest ever preached hitherto under the sun." Two centuries ago, when Oliver Cromwell sank, and Charles II. rose, we

Protestants of Great Britain, "deeply detesting the *name* of Saint Ignatius, did nevertheless gradually adopt his Gospel as the real revelation of God's will, and the solid rule of living in this world." The essential purport of this Gospel he sums up in two sentences. "That to please the supreme Fountain of Truth your readiest method, now and then, was to persist in believing what your whole soul found to be doubtful or incredible. That poor human symbols were higher than the God Almighty's facts they symbolized; that formulas, with or without the facts symbolized by them, were sacred and salutary; that formulas, well persisted in, could still save us when the facts were all fled."

Two heads and fronts of offending are to be distinguished here. Our first offence is that we. do not dare to disbelieve what is incredible. We think it prudent and virtuous to shilly-shally between truth and falsehood; we try to hush up inquiry; we strangle our doubts, and seek to persuade ourselves that reverence and piety are our motives for so doing. "'Be careful how you believe truth,'" cries the good man everywhere: "'composure and a whole skin are very valuable. Truth—who knows?—many things are not true; most things are uncertainties, very prosperous things .are even open falsities that have been agreed upon. There is little certain truth going. If it isn't orthodox truth, it will play the very devil with you.'" The principle on which these pseudo-virtuous persons proceed is "that God can be served by believing what is not true;" that it is a duty "to put out the sacred lamp of intellect within you; to decide on maiming yourself of that higher Godlike gift, which God himself has given you with a silent. but awful charge in regard to it." This cowardly prudence, this willingness to make shift with half-truths, or even to make believe that incredibilities are truths, this distrust and suspicion of the aggressive intellect, associated with a mawkish and maudlin sanctimoniousness of phrase, go to form what Carlyle names cant. Against cant he has always inveighed with a vehemence that would have been frantic, if any degree of vehemence in adjuring your friends not to drink what you believe to be deadliest poison could deserve the term.

The second point in Carlyle's general accusation is that we cling to symbols after they have become obsolete, that we make more of the symbols than of "the God Almighty's facts they symbolized." In Sartor Resartus, he teaches that political institutions are but the form and embodiment of truths, ideas, spiritual facts, and that, when the spirit has departed, the material form ought to disappear. All religions, in like manner, are represented by symbols, and it is the inevitable and universal law that the symbols grow old and perish. To try to perpetuate them when they have lost vitality is a criminal error, fraught with baleful consequences. These two charges—sham-belief and worship of dead symbols—are intimately connected with each other, and both may be included in the central, all comprehending iniquity of cant.

The symbols must go. They wax old as doth a garment, and it becomes an imperative duty to fold them up and change them. The truth embodied in the symbols, if really true, is, he admits, imperishable; he grants, also, that man must have his symbols, that the soul cannot feed on abstractions, that religion in the sense of felt and owned relationship to the Infinite is essential to national health. To the knowing sceptics of an irreverent age he frankly announces that their reduction of man to a mere intellectual animal or a machine is preposterous. " My enlightened friends of this present supreme age, what shall I say to you? That time does rest on eternity; that he who has no vision of eternity will never get a true hold of time, or its affairs. Time is so constructed; that is the *fact* of the construction of this world. And no class of mortals who have not—through Nazareth or otherwise—come to get heartily acquainted with such fact, perpetually familiar

with it in all the outs and ins of their existence, have ever
found this universe habitable long." In all Carlyle's writings,
there are, perhaps, no words more important than these. He
proceeds to refer to certain lessons of history which are so
well-known that it is trite to quote them, but whose triteness
does not in the slightest degree impair their validity or importance. There had been no heroic old Rome, there had been
no early Greece, resplendent to all time, if those fathers of
modern Europe had not known "that in man's life there did
lie a Godlike, and that his time-history was verily but an emblem of some Eternal." Generations without faith, such as he
declares ours to be, have ceased to believe in the old symbols,
and yet cannot provide new ones. "They sit as apes do round
a fire in the woods, but know not how to feed it with fresh
sticks." Deeply significant in this connection is his judgment on

THE CHURCH.

Church, do you say? Look eighteen hundred years ago, in the stable
at Bethlehem: an infant laid in a manger! Look, thou ass, and behold
it; it is a fact—the most indubitable of facts; thou wilt thereby learn
innumerable things. Jesus of Nazareth, and the life He led, and the
death He died, does it teach thee nothing? Through this, as through a
miraculous window, the heaven of martyr heroism, the "Divine depths
of sorrow," of noble labor, and the unspeakable silent expanses of eternity, first in man's history disclose themselves. The admiration of all nobleness, Divine *worship* of Godlike nobleness, how universal it is in the
history of man!

But mankind, that singular entity mankind, is like the fertilest, fluidest,
most wondrous element, an element in which the strangest things crystal-
lize themselves, and spread out in the most astounding growths. The
event at Bethlehem was of the year one; but all years since that, eighteen
hundred of them now, have been contributing new growth to it, and see,
there it stands: the Church! Touching the earth with one small point;
springing out of one small seed-grain, rising out therefrom, ever higher,
ever broader, high as the heaven itself, broad till it overshadow the whole
visible heaven and earth, and no star can be seen but through *it*. From
such a seed-grain so has it grown: planted in the reverences and sacred

opulences of the soul of mankind; fed continually by all the nobleness of some forty generations of men. The world-tree of the nations for so long!

Alas! if its roots are now dead, and it have lost hold of the firm earth, or clear belief of mankind, what, great as it is, can by possibility become of it? Shaken to and fro, in Jesuitisms, Gorham controversies, and the storms of inevitable fate, it must sway hither and thither; nod ever farther from the perpendicular: nod at last too far; and—sweeping the eternal heavens clear of its old brown foliage and multitudinous rooks' nests—come to the ground with much confused crashing, and *disclose* the diurnal and nocturnal upper lights again! The dead world-tree will have declared itself dead. It will lie there an imbroglio of torn boughs and ruined fragments, of bewildered splittings and wide-spread shivers, out of which the poor inhabitants must make what they can!

I said that Carlyle by no means exempts his Protestant countrymen from the application of his censures, but it is nevertheless true that this passage bears with peculiar emphasis upon the Church of Rome. It is a speciality of Carlyle to hate the Papacy with all the fervor of an old Puritan. In this he stands alone among men of anything like his own intellectual order, and differs pointedly from his enthusiastic disciple, Mr. Ruskin. In his late writings Mr. Ruskin has betrayed a growing fondness for the monastic virtues, a growing tendency to recur to that early phase of his æsthetic development in which he looked upon all European art, subsequently to Giotto, Angelico, and John Bellini, as mere decadent recklessness and rebellion. Macaulay, strong as were his Protestant sympathies, could reason with entire calmness on the possibility that the Church of Rome might still flourish when London was in ruins. Goethe had that perfect tolerance for Roman Catholics which he extended to sincere professors of every religion. Even Scott, with whom, as seems to have been the case with Carlyle, detestation of Popery might have been an inherited instinct, spoke with beautiful pathos in his old age of the redeeming gentleness of a faith which found its chief symbolism in a Mother and a Child. But in the eyes of Carlyle, "the so-called throne of St. Peter" is "a falsity, a huge mistake, a pestilent dead carcass." At the time of the Reformation it was condemned by Heaven, and by all intelligently reverent men, and its duty since then has been "to begone, and let us have no more to do with *it* and its delusions and impious deliriums."

Roman Catholics and Protestants alike have a right to ask this austere prophet what they are to believe. Even "across this black deluge" of Jesuitism and cant, he sees "the world ripening toward glorious new developments, unimagined hitherto." The miserable apes to which he likens us, squatted with blinking eyes round their dying fire, are contemptible above all in that they cannot feed their fire with new fuel. How, then, are we to get a glimpse of those "glorious developments?" How are we to find fuel for that fire without which, our censor himself being witness, we must become spiritually and morally dead? To answer these questions with precision is most difficult.

Fundamentally the meaning of a great variety of expressions made use of by Carlyle must be that we are to fall back upon natural religion. "The first heroic soul," he says, "sent down into this world, he, looking up into the sea of stars, around into the moaning forests and big oceans, into life and death, love and hate, and joy and sorrow, and the illimitable loud-thundering loom of time, was struck dumb by it (as the thought of every earnest soul still is); and fell on his face, and with his heart cried for salvation in the world-whirlpool: to him the 'open secret of this universe' was no longer quite a secret, but he had caught a glimpse of it—much hidden from the like of us in these times: 'Do nobly, thou shalt resemble the Maker of all this; do ignobly, the Enemy of the Maker.' This is the 'Divine sense of right and wrong in man;' true reading of his position in this universe for evermore; the indisputable God's-message still legible in every created heart—though speedily erased and painted over, under 'articles,' and cants and empty ceremonials, in so many hearts; making the 'open secret' a very shut one indeed!"

Shall we say, then, that the essential truth, symbolized in all religions, is responsibility to God? If we do, we shall probably not be far from what Carlyle really means. To the primitive man, sincere and unsophisticated, "this visible universe was wholly the vesture of an Invisible Infinite; every event that occurred in it a symbol of the immediate presence of God. Which it intrinsically *is*, and forever will be, let poor stupid mortals remember or forget it!" To the railway, scrip, and cotton millionnaires of England, boasting of their mechanical achievements, Carlyle puts the question, "Will you teach me the winged flight through immensity, up to the Throne dark with excess of bright?" He tells them that, unless they "*can* reach thither in some effectual, most veritable sense," they are "doomed to Hela's death-realm, and the abyss where mere brutes are buried." He wants, not cheaper cotton, swifter railways, but "what Novalis calls 'God, Freedom, Immortality.'"

Novalis, though his teaching is obscured by a kind of scientific mysticism, must be classed among the explicit defenders of the Christian revelation against its modern assailants; and no words could more comprehensively indicate those truths which the Christian seeks to make good against the sceptic than the words "God, Freedom, Immortality." Carlyle, then, appears to accept all three. Nay, he seems to go one step farther in the way of pointing out ground common to him and to those who accept Christianity. "As propitiation," he says, "or as admiration, 'worship' still continues among men, will always continue." Such an expression, standing, as it does, alone, is bitterly tantalizing; but I submit that its natural and obvious meaning is that propitiation or atonement, in some sense, is part of that kernel of religious truth which Mr. Carlyle regards as imperishable. Our Christianity, in fact, viewed as a body of belief, is not so much in fault as our practical failure to realize what we profess. Superstition is not the deepest accusation he brings against us. "The worst of some epochs is, they have along with their real worship an imaginary, and are conscious only of the latter as worship. They keep a set of gods or fetiches, reckoned respectable, to which they mumble prayers, asking themselves and others, triumphantly, 'Are not these respectable gods?' and all the while their real worship, or heart's love and admiration, which alone is worship, concentrates itself on quite other gods and fetiches—on Hudsons and scrips, for instance." There is thus added to our idolatry the guilt of hypocrisy, "which is the quintessence of all idolatries and misbeliefs and unbeliefs."

The real religion of a man "is his *practical Hero-worship*." The italics are Carlyle's. If in his heart he honors and admires the good and great man, "God's servant," then he truly worships God: if in his inmost soul he bows down to the man who has made money, and who may teach him how to make money, then it is the devil's servant, and that servant's master, whom he truly worships. "All conceivable evangels, Bibles, homiletics, liturgies and litanies, and temporal and spiritual law-books for a man or a people, issue practically there. Be right in that, essentially you are not wrong in anything; you read this universe tolerably aright, and are in the way to interpret well what the will of its Maker is."

CHAPTER XII.

AND who is the interpreter of the will of the Maker to our generation? Carlyle emphatically replies that it is *not* the priesthood of any Church. "The so-called Christian *clerus*," he describes in these fiercely contemptuous terms: "Legions of them, in their black or other gowns, I still meet in every country; masquerading in strange costume of body, and still stranger of soul; mumming, primming, grimacing— poor devils, shamming, and endeavoring not to sham: that is the sad fact. Brave men many of them, after their sort; and in a position which we may admit to be wonderful and dreadful! On the outside of their heads some singular head-gear, tulip mitre, felt coal-scuttle, purple hat; and in the inside—I must say, such a theory of God Almighty's universe as I, for my share, am right thankful to have no concern with at all." Such is his negative answer to our question—clear enough, at all events. Now for the positive answer. "The poet in the fine arts, especially the poet in speech, what Fichte calls the 'Scholar' or the 'Literary Man,' is defined by Fichte as the 'Priest' of these modern epochs — all the priest they have. And indeed nature herself will teach us that the man born with what we call 'genius,' which will mean, born with better and larger understanding than others; the man in whom 'the inspiration of the Almighty,' given to all men, has a higher potentiality—that he, and properly he only, is the perpetual priest of men; ordained to the office by God himself, whether men can be so lucky as to get him ordained to it or not; nay, he does the office, too, after a sort, in this and in all epochs." In our time and country the office of the literary priesthood is to write the Bible of our past and present history—to extract from the doings and sayings of Englishmen in the past, as well as from current events, what perennial truth they may contain.

Carlyle's views on religion and literature are exemplified and maintained in the Life of John Sterling. Here was an ardent, noble-minded young man, who sought earnestly to lead a noble life in England. He encountered the doubts and difficulties of the time, ran hither and thither in search of knowledge, visited this and that oracle of wisdom. Carlyle details what may be described as his voyage of discovery in quest of a religion, and of an honorable vocation. At first he was a speculative Radical, uttering fierce words against the clergy which ravish the heart of Carlyle, content with negation and destruction, or what his biographer calls "the work of blasting into merited annihilation the innumerable and immeasurable recognized deliriums, and extirpating or coercing to the due pitch those legions of 'black dragoons,' of all varieties and purposes, who patrol, with horse-meat and man's-meat, this afflicted earth, so hugely to the detriment of it." He tried law a little, but did not take to it. His religion at this time Carlyle describes as "altogether Ethnic, Greekish, what Goethe calls the Heathen form of religion." But such religion did not satisfy him, and among those to whom he turned for guidance to a better faith was the renowned poet and thinker, Samuel Taylor Coleridge. Understood to be familiar with the latest results of German speculation, and to be himself a man of original and powerful genius, Coleridge nevertheless "could still, after Hume and Voltaire had done their best and worst with him, profess himself an orthodox Christian." Carlyle's chapter on Coleridge is, in literary form, as I may remark in passing, one of the finest things in the English language. The satire is very keen, but it is now of a far more quiet and polished kind than we had in the Pamphlets. I quote a passage.

COLERIDGE.

The good man, he was now getting old, toward sixty, perhaps; and gave you the idea of a life that had been full of sufferings; a life heavy-laden, half-vanquished, still swimming painfully in seas of manifold physical and other bewilderment. Brow and head were round, and of massive weight, but the face was flabby and irresolute. The deep eyes, of a light hazel, were as full of sorrow as of inspiration; confused pain looked mildly from them, as in a kind of mild astonishment. The whole figure and air. good and amiable otherwise, might be called flabby and irresolute; expressive of weakness under possibility of strength. He hung loosely on his limbs, with knees bent, and stooping attitude; in walking, he rather shuffled than decisively stepped; and a lady once remarked he never could fix which side of the garden-walk would suit him best, but continually shifted, in corkscrew fashion, and kept trying both. A heavy-laden, high-aspiring, and surely much-suffering man. His voice, naturally soft and good, had contracted itself into a plaintive snuffle and sing-song; he spoke as if preaching—you would have said, preaching earnestly and also hopelessly the weightiest things. I still recollect his "object" and "subject," terms of continual recurrence in the Kantean province; and how he sung and snuffled them into "om-m-mject" and "sum-m-mject," with a kind of solemn shake or quaver, as he rolled along. No talk, in this century or in any other, could be more surprising.

Sterling, who assiduously attended him, with profound reverence, and was often with him by himself, for a good many months, gives a record of their first colloquy. Their colloquies were numerous, and he had taken note of many; but they are all gone to the fire, except this first, which Mr. Hare has printed—unluckily without date. It contains a number of ingenious, true, and half-true observations, and is, of course, a faithful epitome of the things said; but it gives small idea of Coleridge's way of talking;—this one feature is, perhaps, the most recognizable, "Our interview lasted for three hours, during which he talked two hours and three-quarters." Nothing could be more copious than his talk; and furthermore, it was always, virtually or literally, of the nature of a monologue; suffering no interruption, however reverent; hastily putting aside all foreign additions, annotations, or most ingenuous desires for elucidation, as well-meant superfluities which would never do. Besides, it was talk not flowing any-whither, like a river; but spreading everywhither in inextricable currents and regurgitations, like a lake or sea; terribly deficient in definite goal or aim—nay, often in logical intelligibility; *what* you were to believe or do, on any earthly or heavenly thing, obstinately refusing to appear from it. So that, most times, you felt logically lost; swamped near to drowning in this tide of ingenious vocables, spreading out boundless, as if to submerge the world.

To sit as a passive bucket, and be pumped into, whether you consent or not, can in the long run be exhilarating to no creature; how eloquent so-ever the flood of utterance that is descending. But if it be withal a confused, unintelligible flood of utterance, threatening to submerge all known landmarks of thought, and drown the world and you! I have heard Coleridge talk, with eager musical energy, two stricken hours, his face radiant and moist, and communicate no meaning whatsoever to any individual of his hearers—certain of whom, I for one, still kept eagerly listening in hope; the most had long before given up, and formed (if the room were large enough) secondary humming groups of their own. He began anywhere; you put some question to him, made some suggestive observation. Instead of answering this, or decidedly setting out toward answer of it, he would accumulate formidable apparatus, logical swim-bladders, transcendental life-preservers, and other precautionary and vehiculatory gear for setting out; perhaps did at last get under way, but was swiftly solicited, turned aside by the glance of some radiant new game on this hand or that, into new courses, and ever into new, and before long into all the Universe, where it was uncertain what game you would catch, or whether any. His talk, alas! was distinguished, like himself, by irresolution; it disliked to be troubled with conditions, abstinences, definite fulfilments; loved to wander at its own sweet will, and make its auditor and his claims and humble wishes a mere passive bucket for itself! He had knowledge about many things and topics, much curious reading; but generally all topics led him, after a pass or two, into the high seas of theosophic philosophy, the hazy infinitude of Kantean transcendentalism, with its " sum-m-mjects" and "om-m-mjects." Sad enough; for with such indolent impatience of the claims and ignorances of others, he had not the least talent for explaining this or anything unknown to them; and you swam and fluttered in the mistiest, wide, unintelligible deluge of things, for most part in a rather profitless, uncomfortable manner. Glorious islets, too, I have seen rise out of the haze; but they were few, and soon swallowed in the general element again. Balmy, sunny islets, islets of the blessed and intelligible— on which occasions those secondary humming groups would all cease humming. Eloquent artistically expressive words you always had; piercing radiances of a most subtle insight came at intervals; tones of noble pious sympathy, recognizable as pious, though strangely colored, were never wanting long; but in general you could not call this aimless, cloud-capped, cloud-based, lawlessly meandering human discourse of reason by the name of excellent talk; but only of "surprising," and were reminded bitterly of Hazlitt's account of it; Excellent talker, very—if you let him start from no premises, and come to no conclusion.

The irresolution which foiled the possibilities of Coleridge's life, and showed itself in his aimless, interminable talk, is represented by Carlyle as producing its worst result in his theory that the Christian Churches, though they "had died away into a godless mechanical condition," and though their theology had been refuted by Hume and Voltaire, could be "revivified into pristine florid vigor," by listening to man's "reason," and "duly chaining up" man's "understanding." The reference is to Coleridge's celebrated doctrine that the reason alone discerns spiritual truth, and that the understanding is authoritative only when it deals with the facts revealed by our senses, and with the inferences drawn from them. Carlyle laughs at this doctrine, declaring that "it all turned on the *Vernunft* (Reason) and *Verstand* (Understanding) of the Germans, if you could well understand them, which you couldn't." At one period of his life, however, he himself attached supreme importance to this distinction. In his essay on Voltaire he writes as a disciple of Coleridge, and supremely honors the particular doctrine which, in his Life of Sterling, he derides. "Religion," he says in the essay, "is not of sense, but of faith; not of understanding, but of reason. He who finds himself without the latter, who by all his studying has failed to unfold it in himself, may have studied to great or to small purpose, we say not which; but of the Christian Religion, as of many other things, he has and can have no knowledge."

Why did Carlyle, having at one time agreed with Coleridge

as to the supreme importance, in judging spiritual things, of having recourse to reason and faith, not to the senses and the logical understanding, afterward sneer at Coleridge's position? In the first place, the disciple of Carlyle might reply, he had, in 1851, the amplest right to discard an opinion expressed by himself in 1828, he having, in the intervening years, outgrown and passed beyond it. In the second place, his apologist might urge, though Carlyle rejects Coleridge's attempt to prove, by means of the distinction between reason and understanding, that the Church of England, or any extant Church whatever, is a true and living oracle of God, he does not disallow the doctrine that spiritual things are to be spiritually discerned, but only this particular application of it. In the same chapter in which Carlyle laughs at Coleridge as "an artist who could burn you up an old Church, root and branch, and then, as the alchemists profess to do with organic substances in general, distil you an 'astral spirit' from the ashes, which was the very image of the old burned article, its air-drawn counterpart," he says that there is, in Coleridge's doctrine, "a precious truth, or prefigurement of truth." In the Life of Sterling, as well as in the Pamphlets, he asserts that "man and his universe" are "eternally divine," and that "no past nobleness, or revelation of the divine," can be lost. Nay, he goes farther. It is "good," he tells us, "to do what you can with old Churches and practical symbols of the noble." You are not to "quit the burned ruins of them while you find there is still gold to be dug there."

If, then, Carlyle is logical and consistent, we are forced back on the conclusion that what, at bottom, he denies is Coleridge's sincerity in adhering to Catholic Christianity, and the sincerity of John Sterling in betaking himself, under Coleridge's influence, to the Christian ministry. "What the light of your mind, which is the direct inspiration of the Almighty, pronounces incredible, that, in God's name, leave uncredited; at

your peril do not try believing that." Such is his criterion of
what must *not* be believed. Coleridge and Sterling would of
course have indignantly denied that they forced themselves to
believe anything which the light of their mind pronounced incredible; and the burden of proving insincerity lies, in each
case, upon him who makes the charge.

Carlyle boldly affirms that Coleridge and Sterling had not
fairly vanquished their doubts. The one, he would say, was
an irresolute dreamer; the other he portrays as a brilliant but
restless creature, who entered the Church of England because
the mood of the moment, the influence of Archdeacon Hare,
the mystification of his ideas by Coleridge, his own failure to
find lodgment in any lay profession, and the bitter consequences of his foolish intermeddling with Spanish politics,
made him fancy that he really accepted Church theology.
"Coleridge's talk and speculation," says Carlyle, "was the
emblem of himself; in it, as in him, a ray of heavenly inspiration struggled, in a tragically ineffectual degree, with the weakness of flesh and blood. He says once, he 'had skirted the
howling deserts of infidelity;' this was evident enough; but
he had not had the courage, in defiance of pain and danger,
to press resolutely across said deserts to the new firm lands of
faith beyond; he preferred to create logical fata morganas for
himself on this hither side, and laboriously solace himself with
these." As for Sterling, he told his own brother, long afterward, that his case, in taking orders, was like that of "a young
lady who has tragically lost her lover, and is willing to be half-
hoodwinked into a convent, or in any noble or quasi-noble
way to escape from a world which has become intolerable."
The ground, therefore, on which, justly or unjustly, Carlyle
refuses permission to Coleridge or Sterling to abide in the old
Churches is not that celestial gold may not yet be "dug
there," but that neither the one nor the other really, rationally, honestly believed that it was the gold of heaven.

All this suggests two remarks—first, that one would like . to hear Coleridge and John Sterling themselves on Carlyle's virtual allegation of their insincerity, and secondly, that, apart from all consideration of the circumstances of Coleridge and Sterling, we may challenge the justice of Carlyle's sweeping charges of insincerity against the Christian ministry and religious community in general. The touchstone which Carlyle applies, consciously or unconsciously, to earnestness and sincerity, is vehemence. He makes an exception, indeed, in favor of Goethe, whose procedure in respect of vehemence, and all kinds of heat verging on fanaticism, is directly the reverse of that of his panegyrist, these being in Goethe's eyes the infallible notes of a more or less distempered action of the human mind. But though Carlyle has extolled, in some of his most eloquent passages, Goethe's condor-like poise above the storm region, in the cloudless, windless blue of all-embracing sympathy and perfect tolerance, he has in practice been as unlike Goethe as possible. I can hardly conceive anything that would have affected Goethe with a keener sense of antipathy than the Latter-day Pamphlets, and certain parts of the Life of Sterling. Had Goethe lived to witness the later developments of his disciple's teaching, he would, I believe, have alleged them to be, in some essential respects, deviations from the fundamental principles of his own. The change of the old into the new is figured by Goethe, not under Carlyle's image of a burned-up edifice in the ruins of which you dig for, here and there, a piece of sterling gold or a gem of price, but under that of a dwelling gradually irradiated, in all its stones and timbers, by transforming light, until the whole becomes pure silver. Accordingly, Goethe delights in sympathetically realizing for himself types of Christian character; and not only refers in terms of profoundest reverence to Jesus Christ, but makes contributions of great value and unexceptionable orthodoxy to the exposition of Christian ethics. Goethe never assails or renounces Christianity, but directs all his efforts to purge the popular creed from superstitious or inhuman characteristics, and to elevate its professors into that largeness of intellectual glance, and that breadth of moral nobleness, which befitted the religion that cannot die.

In all this the practice of Carlyle presents, I repeat, a striking contrast to that of his master. It is no doubt true that Carlyle never speaks, except in reverential terms, of Jesus Christ. He agrees with Goethe that Christianity is the supreme religion, and that the race cannot recede from it. And yet he never, so far as I know, alludes, except contemptuously, to those Christian writers who have made it their aim to show how the Christian religion may embrace within its compass all real truth. Take the instance before us—that of Coleridge. Even if Carlyle succeeds in showing that there is no practical value in Coleridge's distinction between reason and understanding, it has still to be considered whether, in his work, The Confessions of an Inquiring Spirit, Coleridge did not do good service by substituting for the old superstitious theory of inspiration, which embraced the unnatural conception of men reduced to mere automata, writing down the Scriptures like machines, the intelligent idea of a succession of men feeling and exemplifying the inspiration they embodied, and representing, in their life and writings, successive stages of the religious education of mankind.

Do we find, on examination, that Carlyle's view of the Christian ministry as obsolete, and bound to make way for men of letters, is practical and sagacious? I answer, No. In all ages hitherto the body of organized preachers of truth and performers of religious rites—in one word, the priesthood—have been recognized as playing a part which was of value in itself, and which was not superseded by the part played by the prophet. One of the main reasons, acknowledged by writers of all schools, why the old Hebrew system performed its inestimable

service to the cause of spiritual civilization, was that the ordinary ministrations of the priest were in it harmoniously associated with the extraordinary ministrations of the prophet.
The office of the prophet was more peculiar, honorable, and
terrible than that of the priest; and the priesthood—the professional clergy—might prove false to the national faith, as in
the days of Elijah, while the prophet risked his life in main-
taining it.   Since Carlyle insists strongly upon the perpetual
existence of prophetic inspiration, and admits again and again
that there is imperishable truth in Christianity, might not
Coleridge have fairly urged that the clergy of the Christian
Churches, on condition of their listening attentively to every
accent of inspired moral genius, and reverently considering every demonstrated fact of science, could still do good service in
their day and generation?   No doubt Carlyle might reply that
the Churches are fenced round with creeds and articles; but
Coleridge might press him to mention where he has declared
that a Christian clergy, *not* hedged in by creeds and articles,
are justified in prosecuting their ministry—that is to say, in •
making the most of those symbols, which, on his own showing,
are not to be cast aside until the sap and verdure of life have
utterly gone from them.   I am not aware that Carlyle could
silence Coleridge by any definite information on this point.

But Coleridge might take up a still stronger position against
Carlyle by asking why, in deference to inspiration in the present, he virtually declares the inspiration of the past to be so
far beneath the level of contemporary progress, that sincere
faith in it, on the part of the Christian clergy, has become incredible and preposterous.   If John Sterling allowed himself
to be "hoodwinked" into orders as a sentimental girl is de-
coyed into a convent, there is not a word to be said for him,
and we must agree with Carlyle that his taking orders was
"the extreme point of spiritual deflection and depression" in
his career.   But before we admit the validity of this precedent,

as applied to the Christian clergy in general, we are bound to inquire what was the nature of the work which, while he acted as Archdeacon Hare's curate, Sterling performed. Let us read what Carlyle says on the subject. He quotes largely from Hare, but does not cast a shadow of suspicion on Hare's trustworthiness as a witness.

JOHN STERLING AS CURATE.

By Mr. Hare's account, no priest of any Church could more fervently address himself to his functions than Sterling now did. He went about among the poor, the ignorant, and those that had need of help; zealously forwarded schools and beneficences, strove, with his whole might, to instruct and aid whosoever suffered consciously in body, or, still worse, unconsciously in mind. He had charged himself to make the Apostle Paul his model; the perils and voyagings, and ultimate martyrdom of Christian Paul, in those old ages, on the great scale, were to be translated into detail, and become the practical emblem of Christian Sterling on the coast of Sussex in this new age. "It would be no longer from Jerusalem to Damascus," writes Sterling, "to Arabia, to Derbe, Lystra, Ephesus, that he would travel; but each house of his appointed parish would be to him what each of those great cities was—a place where he would bend his whole being, and spend his heart for the conversion, purification, elevation of those under his influence. The whole man would be forever at work for this purpose; head, heart, knowledge, time, body, possessions, all would be directed to this end." A high enough model set before one—how to be realized! Sterling hoped to realize it, to struggle toward realizing it, in some small degree. This is Mr. Hare's report of him:

"He was continually devising some fresh scheme for improving the condition of the parish. His aim was to awaken the minds of the people, to arouse their conscience, to call forth their sense of moral responsibility, to make them feel their own sinfulness, their need of redemption, and thus lead them to a recognition of the Divine Love by which that redemption is offered to us. In visiting them he was diligent in all weathers, to the risk of his own health, which was greatly impaired thereby; and his gentleness and considerate care for the sick won their affection; so that, though his stay was very short, his name is still, after a dozen years, cherished by many."

How beautiful would Sterling be in all this: rushing forward like a host toward victory; playing and pulsing like sunshine or soft lightning;

busy at all hours to perform his part in abundant and superabundant meas-. ure! "Of that which it was to me personally," continues Mr. Hare, "to have such a fellow-laborer, to live constantly in the freest communion with such a friend, I cannot speak. He came to me at a time of heavy afflic- tion, just after I had heard that the Brother, who had been the sharer of all my thoughts and feelings from childhood, had bid farewell to his earthly life at Rome; and thus he seemed given to me to make up in some sort for him whom I had lost. Almost daily did I look out for his usual hour of coming to me, and watch his tall slender form walking rap- idly across the hill in front of my window; with the assurance that he was coming to cheer and brighten, to rouse and stir me, to call me up to some height of feeling, or down to some depth of thought. His lively spirit, responding instantaneously· to every impulse of Nature and Art; his generous ardor in behalf of whatever is noble and true; his scorn of all meanness, of all false pretences and conventional beliefs, softened as it was by compassion for the victims of those besetting sins of a culti- vated age; his never-flagging impetuosity in pushing onward to some un- attained point of duty or of knowledge: all this, along with his gentle, al- most reverential, affectionateness toward his former tutor, rendered my in- tercourse with him an unspeakable blessing; and time after time has it seemed to me that his visit had been like a shower of rain, bringing down freshness and brightness on a dusty roadside hedge. By him, too, the rec- ollection of these our daily meetings was cherished till the last."

There are many poor people still at Hurstmonceux who affectionately remember him; Mr. Hare especially makes mention of one good man there, in his young days "a poor cobbler," and now advanced to a much better position, who gratefully ascribes this outward and the other im- provements in his life to Sterling's generous encouragement and charita- ble care for him. Such was the curate-life at Hurstmonceux. So, in those actual leafy-lanes, on the edge of Pevensey Level, in this new age, did our poor New Paul (on hest of certain oracles) diligently study to com- port himself, and struggle with all his might *not* to be a moonshine shad- ow of the First Paul.

If Sterling was "hoodwinked" into this, he was hoodwinked into no base or trivial vocation, and can we rationally doubt that thousands of men might undertake such duties with en- tire sincerity of reason and of understanding? It would hard- ly be a safe or sober experiment to expel all those ministers,

Conformist and Non-conformist, who are trying to awaken something of a Divine glow in the hearts of laborers, mechanics, farmers, and squires, and to leave their work to be done by . Latter-day prophets and by journalists. Thackeray makes it quite plain, by a remark here and there in his writings, that he regarded with a smile of his own gentle but penetrating disdain the big words in which many foolish men, and Carlyle alone among wise men, have denounced as an incubus the Christian ministry at present existing in England.

Under the influence of Carlyle, Sterling threw up his curacy and became a literary man. His success was fair, but not great. Carlyle informs us that "the want of the living, swift looks and motions, and manifold dramatic accompaniments," tells heavily against his writings. "What," says the biographer, who cannot help feeling that he is to some extent in the position of a Johnson writing the life of a Boswell, "can be done with champagne itself, much more with soda-water, when the gaseous spirit is fled!" I have no doubt that Sterling's brilliant talk afforded pleasure to many a clever listener, and that his essays and tales and letters have made time hang less heavily upon the hands of a few rich and polite people, and may even have had an elevating and ennobling effect upon a smaller number; but I cannot help doubting whether, after leaving Mr. Hare, he did so much real good in the world as when he worked among the "many poor people" who "still at Hurstmonceux affectionately remember him, and when he succeeded in making a man of at least one "poor cobbler."

Carlyle proceeds on the assumption that no faith can be sincere unless it is unfaltering. He would have repelled with scorn the man who said to Christ, "Lord, I believe; help Thou mine unbelief," and who was *not* told by the Saviour that there could be no true religion that was shadowed with doubt. "All weakness is not falseness," Browning has just been reminding us; and candid reflection will, I think, justify the assertion that, in ages when light is pouring in from many quarters upon the human mind—in ages like our own, when science has revolutionized our knowledge of God's universe — hesitation and doubt in matters of faith are presumptions in favor of sin- . cerity, rather than the reverse. There will, of course, in such ages, be on each side a number of persons who are spiritually stone-dead. One section of these will affect to be religious if their so doing procures them respectability or bread; another will leap exultantly to any atheistic conclusion that leaves them unvisited by conscientious qualms in the enjoyment of their champagne and their harlots. These two sections may pair off with each other; and I believe that those who reject religion because it clogs vicious enjoyment are at present rather more than less numerous than those who, from selfish motives, pretend to believe. Some persons are naturally believers; they have never found any difficulty in believing what was taught them in their childhood, and they live a simple, innocent, and sincere life, though the storms of doubt are hurtling in the air around them. Some, on the other hand, are born doubters and sceptics, incapable of standing still, perfectly sincere in each phase of belief or unbelief through which they successively pass, but quite sure to believe nothing long. A fine form of this character was presented by John Sterling. But there are in all transition periods, particularly there are in ours, persons who, in so far as they retain the old, do so because they have tested its truth; and, in so far as they accept the new, do so because, having candidly examined it, they find it more true than the old. Tennyson tells us that there lives more faith in honest doubt than in half the creeds; and I dare say he would extend the application of the remark to more than half the vehemently dogmatic rejections of creed.

All the great operations of nature are gradual. There is a time every morning at which you cannot say whether it is day or night. The trees take half the summer to dress themselves, and scarcely has the rich, deep green of their midsummer robes been attained when the process of disrobing commences, and leaf after leaf continues to change color and to fall, until, in midwinter, the branches again are bare. Such is the spiritual revolution which is at present taking place in Western Europe.

It is hardly too much to say that, in the present time, doubt at one period of life or another is for all persons of superior faculties and extensive information an inevitable fate, if not a positive duty. If honor ought to be rendered to those high-minded iconoclasts who find their whole duty summed up in destruction, honor may be claimed for those also who attempt the still more difficult task of transforming the old into the new, and separating the imperishable truth from the perishable form in which men have previously apprehended it. In this point of view Coleridge, Neander, and a host of others, deserve more honorable mention than Carlyle has ever vouchsafed them.

CHAPTER XIII.

JOHN STERLING, we saw, decided to turn away from the Christian ministry. One of the subjects which principally occupied his mind while in a state of transition was Mr. Carlyle's Sartor Resartus. In February, 1835, he bade adieu to Mr. Hare, and to the sick folks and inquiring cobblers of Hurstmonceux, and in the following May sent Carlyle a long letter on Sartor, in which he says that he has read the book "twice with care." Of this letter Mr. Carlyle prints enough to fill nearly seven pages; and there is nothing in the whole range of his writings that strikes me as more curiously or instructively suggestive than a comparison of what he prints with what he suppresses.

Sterling enters into minute verbal criticism of the book, dwells upon its resemblance to the writings of Rabelais, Montaigne, Sterne, and Swift, points out its mannerisms, and pronounces judgment upon particular words occurring in it, such as " vestural," " stertorous," " talented." All this Carlyle prints in full. But the part of his criticism to which Sterling calls particular attention—the part compared with which he rightly pronounces all discussion of the literary and artistic qualities of the book to be mere triviality—is that in which he attempts to define "the principle which lies at the root of, and gives the true meaning to," the character and opinions of Carlyle's hero, who has always been regarded as Carlyle himself. How does Carlyle deal with this all-important passage? Let us see. He quotes from Sterling as follows:

THE MAIN PRINCIPLE OF SARTOR RESARTUS.

This principle I seem to myself to find in the state of mind which is attributed to Teufelsdröckh; in his state of mind, I say, not in his opinions, though these are, in him as in all men, most important—being one of the best indices to his state of mind. Now what distinguishes him, not merely from the greatest and best men who have been on earth for eighteen hundred years, but from the whole body of those who have been working forward toward the good, and have been the salt and light of the world, is this : That he does not believe in a God. Do not be indignant, I am blaming no one;—but if I write my thoughts, I must write them honestly.

Teufelsdröckh does not belong to the herd of sensual and thoughtless men : because he does perceive in all existence a unity of power ; because he does believe that this is a real power external to him, and dominant to a certain extent over him, and does not think that he is himself a shadow in a world of shadows. He has a deep feeling of the beautiful, the good, and the true; and a faith in their final victory.

At the same time, how evident is the strong inward unrest, the Titanic heaving of mountain on mountain : the storm-like rushing over land and sea in search of peace. He writhes and roars under his consciousness of the difference in himself between the possible and the actual, the hoped-for and the existent. He feels that duty is the highest law of his own being; and knowing how it bids the waves be stilled into an icy fixedness and grandeur, he trusts (but with a boundless inward misgiving) that there is a principle of order which will reduce all confusion to shape and clearness. But, wanting peace himself, his fierce dissatisfaction fixes on all that is weak, corrupt, and imperfect around him ; and, instead of a calm and steady co-operation with all those who are endeavoring to apply the highest ideas as remedies for the worst evils, he holds himself aloof in savage isolation ; and cherishes (though he dare not own) a stern joy at the prospect of that catastrophe which is to turn loose again the elements of man's social life, and give for a time the victory to evil ; in hopes that each new convulsion of the world must bring us nearer to the ultimate restoration of all things ; fancying that each may be the last. Wanting the calm and cheerful reliance, which would be the spring of active exertion, he flatters his own distemper by persuading himself that his own age and generation are peculiarly feeble and decayed ; and would even, perhaps, be willing to exchange the restless immaturity of our self-consciousness, and the promise of its long throe-pangs, for the unawakened undoubting simplicity of the world's childhood; of the times in which there was all the evil and horror of our day, only with the difference that conscience had not arisen to try and condemn it. In these longings, if they are Teufelsdröckh's, he seems to forget that, could we go back five thousand years, we should only have the prospect of travelling them again, and arriving at last at the same point at which we stand now.

Something of this state of mind I may say that I understand; for I have myself experienced it. And the root of the matter appears to me: A want of sympathy with the great body of those who are now endeavoring to guide and help onward their fellow-men. And in what is this alienation grounded? It is, as I believe, simply in the difference on that point: viz., the clear, deep, habitual recognition of a one Living *Personal* God, essentially good, wise, true, and holy, the Author of all that exists; and a reunion with whom is the only end of all rational beings. This belief . . .

What means the break? Has the manuscript been torn, or mouse-bitten, or does the stream of discourse run on into drivel, meriting to be curtailed with scornful abruptness? What is perfectly clear is that Sterling has been working up to his point, and that now he believes himself to have reached it. The grand defect which he signalizes in Sartor Resartus is absence of recognition of a Living Personal God, and the moment he begins to show why a Living Personal God is worthier to be accepted than a vague looming of pantheistic deity through the universe, Carlyle thrusts the gag between his teeth. "There follow now," says the biographer, "several pages on 'Personal God' and other abstruse, or, indeed, properly unspeakable matters; these, and a general postscript of qualifying purport, I will suppress."

Can we doubt that, were it possible to consult Sterling on this procedure of his biographer, he would declare that Mr. Carlyle had omitted precisely those pages which, of all he had ever written, whether in book or in letter, he should least like to be suppressed? The literary criticism on Sartor Resartus which Mr. Carlyle prints is good enough of its kind, but not better than may be looked for in a dozen magazines any month in the year; the criticism on the ethical tone and general moral character of the book, even when judged by this truncated specimen, can be seen to be masterly. Let us examine it a little.

The reference made by Sterling to the want, in Sartor Resartus, of healthy sympathy "with the great body of those who are now endeavoring to guide and help onward their fellow-men," is a glance that penetrates to the profoundest roots, not only of what is faulty in Sartor Resartus, but of what has been questionable, uneasy, and, on the whole, lamentable in Mr. Carlyle's life, and particularly in his relation to the Christian Churches, and to the workers in the many divisions of the great army of social improvement. Sterling boldly lays his hand on what he conceives to be the tap-root of the evil. Carlyle's hero, he says, "does not believe in a God." The statement requires explanation, for there are few books in the English language, if any, in which the name of God is more constantly introduced, and the existence of all things in God, and of God in all things, is more constantly asserted, than in Sartor Resartus. In fairness not only to Sterling, but to the readers of so startling an assertion, every word in which he explained and defended his position should be laid before us. Sterling maintains that the verbal recognition of God in the book—the shimmering, so to speak, of God-light through its leaves—is vague, ineffectual, practically equivalent to unbelief. I would give all I have ever seen from Sterling's pen for a sight of what he said in elucidation and support of this thesis. But his biographer, who permits him to descant at any length on the grammatical peculiarities of Thomas Carlyle, shuts his mouth instantly when he begins to speak of a Personal God.

Not only in Sartor Resartus, but in a vast proportion of the most brilliant, original, and fascinating literature of the last hundred years, including the poetry of Goethe, there is that

6*

"abundant use of the name of God," which is affirmed by
Sterling to be neither satisfactory in itself, nor equivalent to
belief, calm, solemn, and steadfast, in "one Living Personal
God." The pantheistic gleaming and glittering in those
books, like lightning along cloud-edges in a stormy sky, is
splendid in an imaginative point of view, and has an effect
which can hardly be described except as a kind of consecration; but it has not the same power to make spiritual corn
grow and spiritual fruit ripen which is possessed by the light
of the central Sun.

There are matters which, though unspeakable and unknow-
able as mysteries, may, nevertheless, be facts, and may admit
of being spoken of, or imperatively require to be spoken of,
in their character as facts. Such is the Divine Personality.
Sterling's mind was eminently clear. He was exactly the man
to discern between the essentials of faith in God and the non-
essentials, and to avoid the error of supposing that it is possible for us to comprehend or to explain either God's life or His
personality. I do not presume to guess at Sterling's line of
argument in the suppressed passage; but the soundness of his
main position, namely, that life and personality are inseparable
from a God believed in to any practical effect, may, I think, be
established by the simple consideration that, as it is impossible
for us to define the human personality, while nevertheless we
cannot believe in the existence of any one without individu-
alizing him as a person, so it is impossible for us, though unable to comprehend and explain the Divine personality, to believe in God to any practical effect, unless we regard Him as
a person. The finite personality, the finite spirit, whether in
myself or in my neighbor, I cannot understand. I never saw
a spirit, never touched, never heard a spirit, never by any of
my senses perceived one; and yet, when my friend speaks, I
am quite sure that I hear him, and that he who speaks is a
person, distinct from all other persons and things, and that

I who hear am a person distinct from all other persons and things. This is the essential condition of my having any benefit from my friend, or of my friend's having any benefit from me, or of our in any practical sense knowing each other. His unity, his personality, may be totally indefinable by me, but while I am clear as to its being a fact, or while, without asking any questions, I proceed upon it as a fact, all relations between us are placed upon a clear practical basis. But if, in my endeavor to penetrate the mystery of my friend's personality, I lose hold of it as a fact, and begin to think of him as a tincture or essence of friend diffused throughout the universe, am I not likely to forfeit clearness of idea as to my obligations to him and his regard for me?

John Sterling suggests precisely that rectification of Carlyleism which it seems to me to stand supremely in need of. The vagueness of pantheism is peculiary ill-fitted to harmonize with much that is most vehemently inculcated by Carlyle. He asserts the infinite nature of duty, the infinite difference between good and evil. He enjoins and exemplifies unappeasable fury as the sentiment with which good men ought to regard bad men. Always when he is in this mood—and he is in it very often—he has the name of God on his lips, and it is the justice of God he invokes. His tone is that of one who not only believes in the power and government of God, but believes in them with the intensity of an Elijah calling down fire from Jehovah to confound the worshippers of Baal. And yet, in this very Life of Sterling, he uses language which might lead us to infer that he would pronounce all such paroxysms of indignation the mere stamping and raving of fanaticism. He cites from Sterling these words, "I find in all my conversations with Carlyle that his fundamental position is, the good of evil: he is forever quoting Goethe's epigram about the idleness of wishing to jump off one's own shadow." On which Carlyle comments as follows:—"Even so:

"'Was lehr' ich dich vor allen Dingen?—
Könntest mich lehren von meinen Schatten zu springen?'*

—indicating conversations on the origin of evil, or rather resolution on my part to suppress such, as wholly fruitless and worthless." Mr. Carlyle adds that the conversations in question had "all grown dark" to him, and as there is nothing in the words quoted from Sterling to prove that it was a particular theory of the origin of evil, held by Carlyle, which he contested, we cannot but conclude that it was Carlyle's view of the nature of evil, not any theory of the origin of evil, that surprised him. He was startled to find Carlyle insisting on the *good* of evil. And well he might be; for Sterling could have told Carlyle that stronger words were not to be found in the language than those in which he, who now seemed to talk lightly of evil as a shadow inseparable from humanity, or even as a producing cause of good, had depicted good and evil as irreconcilable and eternal opposites. It is Carlyle who exclaims that right and wrong are to each other "as life is to death, as Heaven is to Hell." "The one," he cries, "must in nowise be done, the other in nowise left undone. You shall not measure them; they are incommensurable: the one is death eternal to a man, the other is life eternal." No intelligent student of Carlyle's writings can fail to regret that he suppressed that passage in which John Sterling, by placing, as he must have done, the pantheistic view of God in contrast with that which regards God as a Living Spirit and Person, would have forced Carlyle either to choose definitely between the one view and the other, or to admit that there is, in connection with this subject, a certain haziness, a certain inconsistency and incoherence, affecting his whole system of thought and of language?

---

* What do you want me to teach you, first of all?
Could you tell me how to jump off my shadow?

M. Taine, in his lively sketch of Carlyle, remarks that he has
given offence to some persons by adopting a theory of hero-
worship, with fashion of speech to match, in accordance with
which he seems to consider himself a misapprehended great
man, of the race of heroes, to whose hands the human race, if
well advised, would commit itself and its affairs.   To none of
Carlyle's books does this very clever and shrewd remark apply
so pointedly as to the Life of Sterling; for Carlyle was John
Sterling's hero, and the book is, in the main, an account of the
various stages of hero-worship passed through by the devotee.
With wonderful skill — for the task was difficult — does Mr.
Carlyle set Sterling's light on this point on a hill, without pain-
ing his readers by self-praise.   On one occasion, he introduces
Sterling as arguing, by letter, with his father, on the transcendent greatness of Carlyle; and though the biographer does not
in terms adopt his worshipper's estimate, he prefaces it with
the warmest commendation of Sterling as a "son of light,"
loyal to truth, and superior to vanity and petulance, and says
that the passage containing it is "very pertinent."   Sterling's
father had objected to his son's "over-estimate" of Carlyle,
and referred, in support of his view, to the saying attributed to
Talleyrand, "That *all* the world is a wiser man than any man
in the world."   John Sterling will not hear of such a doctrine.
"It is quite certain," he writes to his father, "there is always
some one man in the world wiser than all the rest; as Socrates
was declared by the oracle to be; and as, I suppose, Bacon was
in his day, and perhaps Burke in his."   Is not the suggestion
plain that Mr. Carlyle is, in Sterling's opinion, the wisest man
in the world?   In one word, the biographer finds room for so
much of Sterling's worship of Carlyle, that we must be struck
by the contrast when he peremptorily silences Sterling's plea
for the worship of God.   One cannot wonder at M. Taine's
piquant reference to those who will have it, "qu'il se considère
comme un grand homme méconnu, de l'espèce des héros; qu'à

son avis le genre humain devrait se remettre entre ses mains,
lui confier ses affaires."

Let us beware, however, of doing injustice to Carlyle, or sur-
rendering aught that is precious in his writings. That his
whole system of thought has been injured by its pantheistic
associations ; that, more and more, in his identification of God
with the forces of nature, he has been driven back upon a pagan consecration of strength, and an obliteration of the lines
which eternally discriminate between material success and
moral triumph ; I must hold to be true. But he has never
called himself a pantheist, and I shall not call him one. An
immense number of expressions might be gathered from his
works which are logically irreconcilable with pantheism. His
final deliverance on the subject of God would, I am convinced,
be that no system can adequately name Him, and that, in referring either to the universe or its Maker, it is legitimate to
use the language of various systems, in order to make partly
intelligible what no man can perfectly understand. Shrinking
from atheism as inhuman and incredible, he has shrunk also,
perhaps with too spasmodic a recoil, from that conception of
the universe as a piece of ingenious mechanism, and of God as
a mechanical contriver of transcendent skill, which was in vogue
in the time of his youth. "Atheism," we may say of him as
he says of Frederick of Prussia, " he never could abide : to him,
as to all of us, it was flatly inconceivable that intellect, moral
emotion, could have been put into *him* by an Entity that had
none of its own." Often his references to the universe and its
Maker are those of devout and simple theism. " We speak,"
he says, " of the volume of Nature : and truly a volume it is—
whose author and writer is God. To read it ! Dost thou, does
man, so much as well know the alphabet thereof ? With its
words, sentences, and grand descriptive pages, poetical and
philosophical, spread out through solar systems and thousands
of years, we shall not try-thee. It is a volume written in celes-

tial hieroglyphs, in the true sacred writing; of which even prophets are happy that they can read here a line and there a line." He once very beautifully compares the universe to a rainbow which we see before us on the cloud, while the Sun that has painted it is invisible. We have no right to tie him down to a pantheistic theory of the universe, any more than to allege that, in those expressions which are strictly accordant with orthodoxy, he states an exclusive opinion. He would probably adopt, with some modification, Goethe's declaration that, to express a sentiment which, in its comprehensiveness, is inexpressible, he uses a variety of forms of speech, but that, as a moral being, he is simply a theist, acknowledging his responsibility to God.

This last is the essential point. Our moral nature, our conscience, is the direct link associating us, as moral beings, with God. "The one end, essence, and use of all religion," says Carlyle, "past, present, and to come, is this only: to keep this same moral conscience or inner light of ours alive and shining." It is because of its proclamation of man's responsibility to God that Carlyle finds in the religion of Mohammed, as compared with the idolatries it displaced, a true message from heaven. "'Allah akbar, God is great.' Understand that his will is the best for you; that howsoever sore to flesh and blood, you will find it the wisest, best; you are bound to take it so; in this world and in the next, you have no other thing that you can do! . . . Man does hereby become the high-priest of this temple of a world. He is in harmony with the decrees of the Author of this world, co-operating with them, not vainly withstanding them. I know, to this day, no better definition of duty than that same." This is pure theism, implying, if any words can imply, belief in the personality of God.

CHAPTER XIV.

THE last work of great importance executed by Carlyle was the Life of Frederick of Prussia. In 1856, when he was about sixty, the first chapters of this voluminous biography "got to paper." The pen-portrait of Frederick with which the book opens shows that Carlyle's hand has lost nothing of its vivid and graphic power.

OLD FREDERICK.

About fourscore years ago there used to be seen sauntering on the terraces of Sans Souci for a short time in the afternoon, or you might have met him at an earlier hour, riding or driving in a rapid business manner on the open roads or through the scraggy woods and avenues of that intricate amphibious Potsdam region, a highly interesting lean little old man, of alert, though slightly-stooping figure; whose name among strangers was King *Friedrich the Second,* or Frederick the Great, of Prussia, and at home, among the common people, who much loved and esteemed him, was *Vater Fritz*—Father Fred—a name of familiarity which had not bred contempt in that instance. He is a king every inch of him, though without the trappings of a king. Presents himself in a Spartan simplicity of vesture: no crown but an old military cocked-hat—generally old, or trampled and kneaded into absolute *softness,* if new; no sceptre but one like Agamemnon's, a walking-stick cut from the woods, which serves also as a riding-stick (with which he hits the horse "between the ears," say authors); and for royal robes, a mere soldier's blue coat with red facings, coat likely to be old, and sure to have a good deal of Spanish snuff on the breast of it; rest of the apparel dim, unobtrusive in color or cut, ending in high over-knee military boots, which may be brushed (and, I hope, kept soft with an underhand suspicion of oil), but are not permitted to be blackened or varnished; Day and Martin with their soot-pots forbidden to approach.

The man is not of godlike physiognomy, any more than of imposing stature or costume: close-shut mouth with thin lips, prominent jaws and nose, receding brow, by no means of Olympian height; head, however, is of long form, and has superlative gray eyes in it. Not what is called a beautiful man; nor yet, by all appearance, what is called a happy. On the contrary, the face bears evidence of many sorrows, as they are termed, of much hard labor done in this world; and seems to anticipate nothing but more still coming. Quiet stoicism, capable enough of what joy there were, but not expecting any worth mention; great unconscious and some conscious pride, well tempered with a cheery mockery of humor, are written on that old face; which carries its chin well forward, in spite of the slight stoop about the neck; snuffy nose, rather flung into the air, like an old snuffy lion on the watch; and such a pair of eyes as no man, or lion, or lynx of that century bore elsewhere, according to all the testimony we have. "Those eyes," says Mirabeau, "which, at the bidding of his great soul, fascinated you with seduction or with terror!" Most excellent, potent, brilliant eyes, swift-darting as the stars, steadfast as the sun; gray, we said, of the azure-gray color: large enough, not of glaring size; the habitual expression of them vigilance, and penetrating sense, rapidity resting on depth. Which is an excellent combination; and gives us the notion of a lambent outer radiance springing from some great inner sea of light and fire in the man. The voice, if he spoke to you, is of similar physiognomy: clear, melodious, and sonorous; all tones are in it, from that of ingenuous inquiry, graceful sociality, light-flowing banter (rather prickly for most part), up to definite word of command, up to desolating word of rebuke and reprobation; a voice "the clearest and most agreeable in conversation I ever heard," says witty Dr. Moore. "He speaks a great deal," continues the Doctor; "yet those who hear him regret that he does not speak a good deal more. His observations are always lively, very often just; and few men possess the talent of repartee in greater perfection."

In the Life of Frederick the first thing that strikes me as calling for remark is the astonishing display it presents of literary skill, dexterity, and adroitness. Carlyle was now a veteran, several years older than Scott, when his frame and brain gave way under a pressure of mental toil that seemed at the time to be rather a pleasure than a labor. Scott, no doubt, had the calamity of his bankruptcy to weigh him down, but his literary work never seemed to cost him an effort. Carlyle, on the other hand, has always avowed that, like Goethe, he got nothing in his sleep; his literary work was never a recreation or relief to him; he stood to his tasks with such intensity of application that—so he told the Edinburgh students in his address as their Lord Rector—every book cost him an illness. But the vivacity of the ten volumes on Frederick is as notable as their thoroughness, their elaborate finish, their idiomatic expressiveness and inventive brilliancy of language, and their attestation of enormous research.

The plan of the book, like that of the battle of Marengo, and of many other feats of genius, could have been justified only by success.   Arresting the attention of the reader by placing before him, on the first pages, so bold, picturesque, and interesting a portrait of Frederick at threescore, that it cannot be forgotten, the biographer turns speedily to the cradle of the infant, shows us his father nearly stifling him with caresses, alludes to the "cannon-volleyings, kettle-drummings, metal crown, heavy cloth-of-silver," and other pompous tomfooleries of the christening, and then, with an occasional glance back at "the little boy now sleeping in his cradle at Berlin," puts in two, or almost three, volumes of information not only about his father and mother, but about the origin of the Prussian Monarchy, and even about the general course of German and European history, in so far as this was connected with the rise, progress, and culmination of the Hohenzollerns.   From the time, more than three hundred years before the birth of Christ, when "Pytheas, the Marseilles travelling commissioner, looking out for new channels of trade," sailed along the Baltic coasts, and looked upon the marshy jungles, shaggy bisons, and large-limbed barbarians of "the now Prussian kingdom," to the day of Frederick's birth, nothing of essential importance in the history of Germany, or even of Europe, escapes Carlyle.   It is hardly too much to say that he brings modern history to a focus in the cradle of Frederick.

Such a biographical scheme cannot, on abstract grounds, be commended. The ordinary biographer who should adopt it would be simply unreadable, nor can it be alleged that the success even of Mr. Carlyle, though wonderful, has been complete. All but the most patient and sympathetic readers are sometimes alarmed, and cannot help grumbling, when they are required to peruse lists of "intercalary kaisers," to trace "Baireuth-Anspach" branches, to understand the coils and complications of Court and diplomatic intrigue respecting this marriage project and that, to distinguish between and remember "the seven European crises," and the seventy times seven personages, male and female, that figured in them. Any other writer would have failed disastrously, but Mr. Carlyle succeeds to at least this extent, that, though readers grumble, yet few, I imagine, except the frivolous and unintelligent, would prefer that these preliminary volumes had been left unwritten. Dry as the subject often looks, you find, if you resolutely enter on it, that, under Carlyle's touch, it becomes interesting. His sense of what is essential in history is so true that, in those chapters, we have an unequalled synopsis of what really was going on, what was vital, and growing, and destined to endure, in Europe in the time treated of; and his eye for what is pictorially vivid is so keen, his power of reproducing the past, by felicitous selection of graphic detail, so great, that a few lines or words from his pen often enable us to realize the state of affairs in extensive territories and for long periods, with a distinctness and practical accuracy which we might have failed to obtain after groping for months in libraries, or reading for weeks in the books of stilted or statistical historians.

However far he may seem to range in European history, Mr. Carlyle does not forget for a moment that his express concern is with the Royal House of Prussia, and there is an almost romantic interest in his account of its rise from small beginnings to a place among sovereignties. "Somewhere about the year

1170," Conrad of Hohenzollern set out from the old castle to
seek his fortunes under the great Kaiser Barbarossa. Hohenzollern lies "on the sunward slope of the Rauhe-Alp country,"
a piece of country in that somewhat indefinite region which
holds partly of Germany, partly of Switzerland, "no great way
north from Constance and its lake." Near it springs the Dan-
ube, at its back is the Black Forest; and its name, "fanciful
Dryasdust will tell you," is equivalent to *Tollery*, or Place-of-
Tolls; which "gives one the notion of antique peddlers climbing painfully out of Italy and the Swiss valleys, thus far; un-
strapping their packages here, and chaffering in unknown dia-
lect about *toll*." In point of fact, the dwellers in Conrad's an-
cestral castle appear to have been tax-gatherers on their own
account, and to have known how to combine prudence with
their exactions, so as not to kill the trades on which they lived.

Conrad was a younger son, and decided that in the wide
world, so visible from those high solitudes, he might do better
than help his elder brother to gather in the coppers. "Probably with no great stock of luggage about him," he descended
the Rauhe-Alp and offered his services to the Kaiser. Barbarossa, knowing a man when he saw him, took Conrad by the
hand. "We may conclude he had found capabilities in Conrad; found that the young fellow did effective service as the
occasion rose, and knew how to work in a swift, resolute, judicious, and exact manner. Promotion was not likely on other
terms; still less high promotion." Conrad was presumably a
handsome youth; anyhow, he found favor with an heiress "of
immense possessions, and opulent in territories." The kin of
this heiress had long been hereditary Burg-grafs of Nürnberg,
and to this dignity Conrad was appointed. Such was the lin-
eal ancestor, twentieth in direct ascent, of Frederick the Great.

The Nürnberg Burg-grafs did not lose in their new capacity
those faculties of thrift and energy which evidently ran in the
blood of the ancient tax-gatherers of Hohenzollern. They

seem to have believed, like Byron, that "ready-money *is* Aladdin's lamp," and kept in hand the cash that might enable them to take advantage of likely investments. The Kaisers, on the other hand, were royally in want of money, and few more so than Kaiser Sigismund, who, though he declared himself to be *super grammaticam*, and probably contrived to spell and punctuate according to the freedom of his own will, found that gold was indispensable. In his time the Nürnberg Burg-graf was Friedrich, seventh in descent from Conrad, and to him Sigismund applied for successive advances. In 1411 we find the canny Burg-graf holding the Kaiser's deed of acknowledgment for 100,000 gulden, lent at various times, with Brandenburg pledged by way of security. Sigismund borrows 50,000 more, and is very conscious that the more he borrows the less he is likely to repay. "Advance me, in a round sum, 250,000 gulden more," said he to Burg-graf Friedrich, 250,000 more for my manifold occasions in this time — that will be 400,000 in whole — and take the Electorate of Brandenburg to yourself, land, titles, sovereign electorship, and all, and make me rid of it." That was the settlement adopted, in Sigismund's apartment at Constance, on the 30th of April, 1415; signed, sealed, and ratified—and the money paid. The sum paid might amount, in modern English currency, to £200,000, and would probably go as far as a million in our times. For this was Brandenburg bought and sold; nor does it appear from Mr. Carlyle's narrative that Sigismund took the smallest care to certify himself or the people of Brandenburg that the purchaser would respect any rights or privileges which the people might lay claim to. The country was simply passed from seller to buyer as a pawn-ticket that could not be redeemed. The Nürnberg Burg-graf became absolute sovereign of Brandenburg, and not the smallest speck of constitutional freedom detracts from the beauty of the transaction in Mr. Carlyle's eyes.

The large territory thus acquired was "dog-cheap, it must be owned, for size and capability; but in the most waste condition, full of mutiny, injustice, anarchy, and highway-robbery; a purchase that might have proved dear enough to another man than Burg-graf Friedrich." To him it proved an excellent bargain. He insisted that his bold nobles should give up stealing pigs or anything else that was their neighbor's, and, if they were refractory, he knocked their castles about their ears· with a big gun he had borrowed for the purpose, which his men called *Faule Grete*—Lazy Peg. So marked was his success, and so high did he rise in the esteem of mankind, that he was asked to stand for the Kaisership itself, but this he judiciously declined to do. Among the dozen or so of Electors who succeeded him, some were excellent governors, some bad, some indifferent, and it was not till the dawn of the eighteenth century that the Brandenburg Elector obtained the regal title and became King of Prussia. The winner of the title was an insignificant man, but his son Frederick William, the father of Frederick the Great, was highly remarkable, and of him Mr. Carlyle has a great deal to say. It seems very certain, however, that Frederick William was, in many important respects, a more stunted, cross-grained, mentally and morally ignoble person, than several of those clear-headed Burg-grafs and wise and brave Electors who, before his day, had sprung from Conrad of Hohenzollern.

CHAPTER XV.

WE looked at Mr. Carlyle's portrait of Frederick; we may as well look at his equally graphic delineation of Frederick's father.

FREDERICK WILLIAM.

He was not tall of stature, this arbitrary King; a florid complexioned, stout-built man; of serious, sincere, authoritative face; his attitudes and equipments very Spartan in type. Man of short, firm stature; stands (in Pesne's best portraits of him) at his ease, and yet like a tower. Most solid; "plumb and rather more;" eyes steadfastly awake; cheeks slightly compressed, too, which fling the mouth rather forward, as if asking silently, "Anything astir, then? All right here?" Face, figure, and bearing, all in him is expressive of robust insight and direct determination; of healthy energy, practicality, unquestioned authority—a certain air of royalty reduced to its simplest form. The face, in pictures by Pesne and others, is not beautiful or agreeable; healthy, genuine, authoritative, is the best you can say of it. Yet it may have been, what it is described as being, originally handsome. High enough arched brow, rather copious cheeks and jaws; nose smallish, inclining to be stumpy; large gray eyes, bright with steady fire and life, often enough gloomy and severe, but capable of jolly laughter too. Eyes "naturally with a kind of laugh in them," says Pöllnitz; which laugh can blaze out into fearful thunderous rage, if you give him provocation—especially if you lie to him; for that he hates above all things. Look him straight in the face; he fancies he can see in *your* eyes if there is an internal mendacity in you; wherefore you must look at him when speaking; such is his standing order. . . .

Nothing could exceed his Majesty's simplicity of habitudes. But one loves especially in him his scrupulous attention to cleanliness of person and of environment. He washed like a very Mussulman, five times a day; loved cleanliness in all things to a superstitious extent; which trait is pleasant in the rugged man, and, indeed, of a piece with the rest of his character. He is gradually changing all his silk and other cloth room-furniture; in his hatred of dust, he will not suffer a floor-carpet, even a stuffed chair; but insists on having all of wood, where the dust may be prosecuted to destruction. Wife and womankind, and those that take after them, let such have stuffing and sofas; he, for his part, sits on mere wooden chairs; sits, and also thinks and acts, after the manner of a Hyperborean Spartan, which he was. He ate heartily, but as a rough farmer and hunter eats; country messes, good roast and boiled; despising the French cook as an entity without meaning for him. His favorite dish at dinner was bacon and greens, rightly dressed; what could the French cook do for such a man? He ate with rapidity, almost with indiscriminate violence; his object not quality but quantity. He drank too, but did not get drunk; at the doctor's order he could abstain; and had in later days abstained. Pöllnitz praises his fineness of complexion, the originally eminent whiteness of his skin, which he had tanned and bronzed by hard riding and hunting, and otherwise worse discolored by his manner of feeding and digesting; alas! at last his waistcoat came to measure, I am afraid to say how many Prussian ells, a very considerable diameter indeed. . . .

He girt his sword about the loins, well out of the mud; walked always with a thick bamboo in his hand. Steady, not slow of step; with his triangular hat, cream-white round wig (in his olden days), and face tending to purple—the eyes looking out mere investigation, sharp, swift authority, and dangerous readiness to rebuke and set the cane in motion:—it was so he walked abroad in this earth; and the common run of men rather fled his approach than courted it. For, in fact, he was dangerous; and would ask in an alarming manner, "Who are you?" Any fantastic, much more any suspicious looking person, might fare the worse. An idle lounger at the street corner he has been known to hit over the crown; and peremptorily despatch: "Home, sirrah, and take to some work!" That the apple-women be encouraged to knit while waiting for custom—encouraged and quietly constrained, and at length packed away, and their stalls taken from them, if unconstrainable—there has, as we observed, an especial rescript been put forth; very curious to read.

Dandiacal figures, nay, people looking like Frenchmen, idle, flaunting women even—better for them to be going. Who are you? and if you lied or prevaricated ("Look me in the face, then!"), or even stumbled, hesitated, and gave suspicion of prevaricating, it might be worse for you. A soft answer is less effectual than a prompt, clear one, to turn away wrath. "A *Candidatus theologiæ*, your Majesty," answered a hand-fast, threadbare youth one day, when questioned in this manner. "Where from?" "Berlin, your Majesty." "H-m, na, the Berliners are a good-for-nothing set." "Yes, truly, too many of them; but there are exceptions; I know two." "Two? Which, then?" "Your Majesty and myself." Majesty bursts into a laugh; the Candidatus was got examined by the Consistoriums and Authorities proper in that matter, and put into a chaplaincy.

This is the unprepossessing hero who is declared by Carlyle to have been the most veracious man of his epoch. "Except Samuel Johnson," there was no man of his time gifted with comparable veracity, and even Johnson was not so veracious as the "rugged Orson" of the Spree. In order to comprehend this singular judgment, we must understand what Mr. Carlyle means by veracity. Johnson was personally a truthful man, but his mind was cobwebbed with prepossessions, fallacies, ignorances, respecting which he continued wilfully blind. He was disgracefully ignorant, and was content to remain disgracefully ignorant, of the history of his own country in the preceding age, his ignorance rendering him grossly unjust to the greatest Englishmen of the Puritan time. He was the willing slave of intellectual reaction, standing aside in churlish antipathy from the main current of speculation and progress in his day. But he was abrupt in speech; harsh and overbearing, when any one ventured to disagree with him; arbitrary, irritable, and an admirer of despotically-strong government. I am not called upon to eulogize Johnson's good qualities, which were of a high order; but I cannot help thinking that it is to these drawbacks he owes the honor of being classed by Carlyle as the most truthful man of the eighteenth century except old Frederick William. The truthful man, Mr. Carlyle informs us, "loves truth as truth should be loved, with all his heart and all his soul." Frederick William deliberately told lies. Mr. Carlyle makes no secret of the fact. Let us take an illustration of Frederick William's veracity from his pages.

Czar Peter, who was frequently in Prussia, used to have his

expenses paid by the Prussian authorities. Frederick William, on one occasion, orders what we should call his Financial Board to lay out six thousand thalers (about £900) on behalf of the Czar in his progress from Memel to Wesel; that is to say, through the whole length of the Prussian dominions. The officials think the sum too small, and venture to remonstrate. The King replies, in writing, that he will allow not one farthing more, "but," he adds, "you are to give out to the world that it costs me from thirty to forty thousand." There could hardly be a more barefaced lie than this. Mr. Carlyle himself cannot help dropping a tear over the disgrace of the most veracious man of his epoch. "So that here," says Mr. Carlyle, "is the Majesty of Prussia, who beyond all men abhors lies, giving orders to tell one! Alas! yes; a kind of lie, or fib (white fib or even *gray*), the pinch of thrift compelling!" This is all we have in the way of blame; the next sentence has a tone of extenuation, almost of pity. "But what a window into the artless inner-man of his Majesty, even that *gray* fib; not done by one's self, but ordered to be done by the servant, as if that were cheaper!" The valuation of lies is a slippery business, but it seems plain that a lie which, with all its consequences, you take upon your own head, is less despicable than a lie which you force other people to tell for you. Frederick William's lie strikes me as one of the meanest on record.

By veracity, Mr. Carlyle does not mean what is usually signified by the term. It is far from easy to say what he does mean, nor shall I affirm that he has been consistent in his use of the word; but I take it that we shall not be far wrong if we say that, for him, a truthful man is neither more nor less than an effective man, a man who knows how to fit means to ends, a man who succeeds. He does not, indeed, say that success in the vulgar acceptation of the term is the measure of a man's worth. On no theme does he more congenially expatiate than on the hollowness of that success which has no standard but lucre. "Though you had California in fee-simple, and could buy all the upholsteries, groceries, funded-properties, temporary (very temporary) landed properties of the world, at one swoop, it would avail you nothing." But the picturesque pith or poetical splendor of such denunciations of false success do not compensate for the absence from his works of any definition, even approximately precise, of true success; and when we make such definition for ourselves, however careful we may be to avoid the pedantry of ethical purism, we find that, if moral success is to be distinguished from material success, his Hohenzollern heroes, father and son, can scarcely be called successful.

The pity — the thousand-fold pity — is that, in tracing Mr. Carlyle's literary career, we cannot shut our eyes to the gradual hardening and darkening of his ideal of heroic virtue and of heroic success. In the works which established his reputation, including the History of the French Revolution, he was in sympathy not only with spiritual worth and purity, whether successful or unsuccessful, but with the grand impulse of political progress, in obedience to which all great nations have aspired to be free and self-governing. In his book on Cromwell he reached the zenith of his intellectual and literary power, but for the first time the deep shadow of distrust in the social aggregate—scepticism as to the capacity of nations to choose and loyally obey their governors—may be observed falling across his mind. Since then it has always been his tacitly-assumed axiom that mankind are politically divisible into two parts— the many, whose sole duty is to obey, and the few, the heroic units, whose duty is to compel obedience. England rejected Cromwell, crouching under his sword, but implacably hating him in her heart, and for that shortcoming in hero-worship Carlyle virtually turned away from England as his sphere of historical labor. Individual Englishmen — Chatham, Carteret, Wolfe—he might admire, but in the destiny of England as a whole—in the evolution of political civilization by means of representative institutions—he had ceased to believe. In Germany he found a kingdom, built up from small beginnings, of which the architects were not men of the people addressing Parliaments, but individual rulers who, having bought a territory with money, governed it by arbitrary methods, strangled such representative institutions as had existed from of old, and dealt with patriots as Charles the First dealt with Eliot, and as Strafford would have liked to deal with Pym.

Mr. Carlyle, therefore, in writing of the Hohenzollerns, is satisfied with a much lower kind of success than would have sufficed him in his earlier and better day. Deliberate lying, of a mean and cowardly kind, was not incompatible, in his eyes, with exemplary veracity of the Hohenzollern type. But the lie in question had this redeeming quality, that it was intended to shelter an act of thrift; and we must always, if we are to be just to Mr. Carlyle, and if we are to derive from his writings the amount of instruction which they legitimately afford, take notice that the deviations from a right moral code which he palliates are connected with the public interest, and do not proceed from mere selfish motives. When the despot, however capable, forgets the public interest, thinks only of his own advancement, or that of his family, and has, comparatively speaking, no regard for the life and property of his subjects, he becomes, for Mr. Carlyle, a mere pirate and bandit, deserving of no approbation. It is for this reason that he has finally condemned and abandoned Napoleon. The Hohenzollern kings— and the same may be said of another of his favorites, the Paraguayan dictator, Francia—were no bandits. They were diligent in their business, and their business was to make their subjects happy. Their kingship was no sinecure. Frederick the Great was one of the hardest workers that ever lived. Nor was it in merely extending their dominions that they toiled. Their countries attested the beneficence of their influence by

the smile of prosperity they wore. Their name was stamped
on roads and canals. The traveller, in passing from the Popish
regions of Westphalia into the plains of Brandenburg, passed
from a lower civilization into a higher. Everywhere there was
order, industry, comfort. The churches were commodious and
in good repair. The dwelling-houses and inns were paradisi-
acal, after the slovenly hovels of Westphalia. This was directly due to the Hohenzollerns. In this they took as much
pride as in the extension of their own dominions, or more.
And it is on the condition that their kingship is of this kind
that Mr. Carlyle applauds them. This is a most important
point. Though it may be true, as an acute writer observes,
that the adored Frederick was "not less coarse and material"
than the condemned Napoleon, it can hardly be affirmed that
Napoleon showed the same singleness of eye in his service of
France which the Hohenzollerns showed in their service of
Prussia. That Mr. Carlyle has permitted admiration for military methods to grow upon him with disastrous results, I admit; but he has never consciously honored the sword except
as the pioneer or the ally of the plough.

Where he has erred is in the mildness of his censures of,
or his positive sympathy with, the immoral means which the
Hohenzollerns permitted themselves to use, in the promotion
of their laudable ambition of making Prussia a powerful and
prosperous State. I have given an example of Frederick William's lying. His murderous harshness was shown in putting
to death Lieutenant Katte for aiding and abetting the Crown
Prince in disobedience to his father. He was with difficulty
deterred from killing his own son. The judicial murder of
Katte does not startle Mr. Carlyle into an acknowledgment
that it is not good either for king or for nation that the life
of the subject should depend absolutely upon the will of one
man. The preposterous father, by his narrow and boorish contempt for learning, science, the fine arts, and all that lends re-

finement and adornment to life, as well as by the mixture of
bigotry and ignorant folly which constituted his creed, disgusted the son with religion, and prepared him to become a
scoffer and a cynic.   Hardness breeds hardness, and the prince
grew up a man of polished steel without a heart.   As the murder of Katte does not shake Mr. Carlyle's faith in strenuous
and thrifty despotism, neither is he much scandalized by the
circumstance that a man so thoroughly incapable of forming
an opinion on any philosophical question as was Frederick
William should have had it in his power to order Wolff, one
of the greatest thinkers of his time, without trial, to quit the
Prussian dominions in forty-eight hours, under pain of death.
The crazy eagerness with which he sought for gigantic men,
weak, probably, both physically and intellectually, to be drilled
into grenadiers, might have suggested to Mr. Carlyle the question whether, even in the sense of adjusting himself to fact,
"suppressing platitudes, ripping-off futilities, turning decep-
tions inside out," Frederick William was the model of veracity
which he pronounces him to have been.   If, as Carlyle says,
there is "a mendacity in sham things," there surely was a
streak of mendacity in those knock-kneed hobgoblins whom
this rugged Orson thought the finest soldiers in the universe.

But it is in his description of the "Tobacco Parliament"
that Mr. Carlyle presents Frederick William in the light which
strikes me as reflecting most detrimentally both upon the hero-
despot and upon the worshipper of such royalty.   The theory
of Parliaments propounded by Mr. Carlyle in the Latter-day
Pamphlets was to the effect that their use is exclusively to inform and to advise the monarch, never to declare to him, as authoritative, the nation's will.   It was an ancient custom, he says,
for kings to debate matters with their chief nobles, once before
dinner, when they were probably sober, once after dinner, when
they were pretty sure to be drunk.   The Tobacco Parliament
was shaped on this model rather than on that of the Parlia-

ment which voted the Bill of Rights.   "Friedrich Wilhelm" —I quote from Mr. Carlyle—"has not the least shadow of a Constitutional Parliament, nor even a Privy Council, as we understand it, his Ministers being in general mere clerks, to register and execute what he had otherwise resolved upon: but he had his *Tabaks-Collegium*, Tobacco-College, Smoking Congress, *Tabagie*, which has made so much noise in the world, and which, in a rough, natural way, affords him the uses of a Parliament, on most cheap terms, and without the formidable inconveniences attached to that kind of institution.   A Parliament reduced to its simplest expression, and, instead of Parliamentary eloquence, provided with Dutch clay pipes and tobacco: so we may define this celebrated *Tabagie* of Friedrich Wilhelm's."   In this Parliament "State consultations, in a fitful, informal way, took place; and the weightiest affairs might, by dexterous management, cunning insinuation and manœuvring from those that understood the art and the place, be bent this way or that, and ripened toward such issue as was desirable."   One of the "uses" which Frederick William had of this "Parliament" was, that Seckendorf and Grumkow, two diplomatic gentlemen selected for the task by Austria, availed themselves of its opportunities to make an egregious fool of him, to the destruction of his domestic peace, and almost to the breaking of his own heart and those of his wife and son. Mr. Carlyle looks with great contempt upon constitutional kings and their Parliaments; but it would have been difficult for Seckendorf and Grumkow to practise so villanously against Frederick William under the eyes of a representative Chamber.

It is, however, to the diversions of the Tobacco Parliament, as illustrative of the heroism of Frederick William, that I chiefly call attention.   In the early part of his career Mr. Carlyle spoke with respect of men of letters, honoring the profession of which he has been himself so illustrious an ornament. He seems now to share the opinion of Frederick William, that

bookmen are "generally pedants and mere men of wind," and
lets fall no word of censure upon the treatment to which such
literary men as appeared in the Tobacco Parliament were subjected.   I shall quote Mr. Carlyle's account of the way in
which Frederick William honored literature in the persons of
Gundling and Fassmann, abbreviating to some extent, but not
altering a word.

Gundling and Fassmann.

Gundling was a country-clergyman's son, of the Nürnberg quarter; had
studied, carrying off the honors, in various Universities; had read, or turned over, whole cart-loads of wise and foolish books.   The sublime, long-
eared erudition of the man was not to be contested.   A very dictionary
of a man; who knows, in a manner, all things.   Would not this man suit
Majesty? thought Grumkow; and brought him to his Majesty to read the
newspapers and explain everything.   Gundling came to his Majesty; read
the newspapers and explained everything; such a dictionary-in-breeches
(much given to liquor) as his Majesty had got was never seen before.
Omniscient Gundling was a prime resource in the Tabagie, for many years
to come.   Man with sublimer stores of long-eared learning and omniscience; man more destitute of mother-wit was nowhere to be met with.
None oftener shook the Tabagie with inextinguishable Hahas; daily, by
stirring into him, you could wrinkle the Tabagie into grim radiance of banter and silent grins.   He wore sublime clothes: superfine scarlet coat,
gold button-holes, black velvet facings, and embroideries without end;
straw-colored breeches; red silk stockings, and shoes with red heels; on
his learned head sat an immense cloud-periwig of white goat's-hair (the
man now growing toward fifty); in the hat a red feather:—in this guise
he walked the streets, the gold-key of chamberlain conspicuously hanging
at his coat-breast, and looked proudly down upon the world when sober.
   One day two wicked captains, finding him prostrate in some place, cut
off his Kammer-herr (chamberlain) Key, and privately gave it to his
Majesty.   Majesty, in Tabagie, notices Gundling's coat-breast.   "Where
is your Key, then, Herr Kammer-herr?"   "H'm, hah—unfortunately lost
it, Ihro Majestat!"   "Lost it, say you?" and his Majesty looks dreadfully
grave.   "As if a soldier were to drink his musket!" thinks his Majesty.
After much deliberating, it is found that the royal clemency can be extended.   Next Tabagie, a servant enters with one of the biggest trays in
the world, and on it a wooden key gilt, about an ell long; this gigantic

implement is solemnly hung round the repentant Kammer-herr; this he shall wear publicly as penance, and be upon his behavior till the royal mind can relent. No end to the wild pranks, the Houyhnhnm horse-play they had with drunken Gundling. He has staggered out in a drunk state, and found, or not clearly *found* till the morrow, young bears lying in his bed;—has found his room-door walled-up; been obliged to grope about, staggering from door to door and from port to port, and land ultimately in the big bears' den, who hugged and squeezed him inhumanly there. Once at Wusterhausen, staggering blind-drunk out of the schloss (castle) toward his lair, the sentries at the bridge (instigated to it by the Houyhnhnms, who look on) pretend to fasten some military blame on him: Why has he omitted or committed so and so? Gundling's drunk answer is unsatisfactory. "Arrest, Herr Kammerath, is it to be that, then?" They hustle him about among the bears which lodge there;—at length they lay him horizontally across two ropes; take to swinging him hither and thither, up and down, across the black Acherontic Ditch, which is frozen over, it being the dead of winter; one of the ropes, *lower* rope, breaks; Gundling comes souse upon the ice with his sitting-part; breaks a big hole in the ice, and scarcely, with legs, arms, and the remaining rope, can be got out undrowned.

But the grandest explosions, in Tobacco Parliament, were producible, when you got two literary fools; and, as if with Leyden-jars, positive and negative, brought their vanities to bear on one another. Here is the celebrated Gundling, there is the celebrated Fassmann. Fassmann has one evening provoked Gundling to the transcendent pitch—till words are weak, and only action will answer. Gundling, driven to the exploding point, suddenly seizes his Dutch smoking-pan, of peat-charcoal ashes and red-hot sand, and dashes it in the face of Fassmann; who is, of course, dreadfully astonished thereby, and has got his very eyebrows burned, not to speak of other injuries. Stand to him, Fassmann! Fassmann stands to him tightly, being the better man as well as the more satirical; grasps Gundling by the collar, wrenches him about, lays him at last over his knee, sitting-part uppermost; slaps said sitting-part with the hot pan. Amidst the inextinguishable horse-laughter (sincere but vacant) of the Houyhnhnm Olympus. After which, his Majesty, as epilogue to such play, suggests, That feats of that nature are unseemly among gentlemen; that when gentlemen have a quarrel there is another way of settling it. Fassmann thereupon challenges Gundling; Gundling accepts; time and place are settled, pistols the weapon. At the appointed time and place Gundling stands, accordingly, pistol in hand; but, at sight of Fassmann, throws his pistol away; will not shoot any man, nor have any man shoot him. Fassmann sternly advances; shoots his pistol (powder merely) into Gundling's sublime goat's-hair wig: wig blazes into flame: Gundling falls shrieking, a dead man, to the earth; and they quench and revive him with a bucket of water. Was there ever seen such horse-play? Roaring laughter, huge, rude, and somewhat vacant, as that of the Norse gods over their ale at Yule time;—as if the face of the sphinx were to wrinkle itself in laughter; or the fabulous Houyhnhnms themselves were there to mock in their peculiar fashion.

Frederick William made Gundling President of the Berlin Academy, an institution corresponding to our Royal Society, thus proving that his contempt for science was as great as his contempt for literature. Such a king, brutish in his diversions —for what man that had a soul above a brute's would not have shrunk with pain from the spectacle of such degradation as that of Gundling and Fassmann?—and incapable of any intellectual interest, was a hideous anachronism in the eighteenth century. With wonder, with shame—nay, with unaffected anguish—may we contemplate the spectacle of Mr. Carlyle, standing by with a half-sympathetic smile while this crowned savage insults the intelligence of his time and rolls humanity in the mire. All the spiritual enthusiasm with which Carlyle's earlier essays and nobler books inspire us, rises in protest against this immolation of his better self at the shrine of such a hero.

CHAPTER XVI.

FREDERICK THE GREAT was a preferable man to his
father. Whether he was in the deep sense a better may
be questioned: his father was not steeped in sensual vice as
he was, nor was his father capable of such a crime as the seizure of Silesia: yet it is impossible not to prefer him; for he
could have had no sentiment but loathing in connection with
such scenes in the Tobacco Parliament as his father delighted
to witness; he did not regard art, science, letters with the
spite of a stunted brain; he did not tell lies to cloak miserly
shabbiness; and he did not offend common-sense by kidnap-
ping overgrown blockheads to turn into soldiers. It is to be
remembered also, in extenuation of his faults, that he was
brought up in the household of Frederick William, a household in which Christian faith seemed the characteristic of a
fool, in which he was subjected to ill-treatment, to injustice, to
cruelty, fitted almost to force on him what was his settled conviction in after-life, that God, though certainly existing, did
not concern himself with the affairs of this pitiful world.

Frederick, on ascending the throne in 1740, professed, I
doubt not with sincerity, that the well-being of the State was
his grand concern, which he expressly desired to be regarded
as having a claim prior to his personal interest; acted with
discriminating but real generosity to those who had been kind
to him in his adversity; declared himself the friend of religious toleration and of freedom of the Press; and undertook
the energetic patronage of science, art, and all kinds of noble

culture.   He had composed a book called Anti-Machiavel, the
nature of which may be guessed from its title.   Voltaire spoke
in raptures of its ability, and I think we may believe that Frederick was not consciously insincere in writing it.   This was a
bright beginning; and if any one had told the young King
that within a few months he would be chargeable with one of
the blackest crimes mentioned in history, he would have replied, "Is thy servant a dog, that he should do this thing?"

In October, 1740, Charles VI., Emperor of Austria, died, and
his daughter Theresa, twenty-three years old, in delicate health,
who had given no shadow of offence to Frederick, succeeded
to the throne.   The first impulse of Frederick, on hearing the
news, was to avail himself of the weakness of her situation
and the confusion in which he knew that the outbreak of war
would involve Europe, to lay hold, by military force, of her
large and important province, Silesia.   So soon as he knew
that her father was dead, he sent for his chief general and
chief minister; matured with them his scheme of spoliation;
and within a few weeks entered Silesia at the head of an army
strong enough to overpower all resistance.   Here is Mr. Carlyle's comment on the transaction:

THE SEIZURE OF SILESIA.

Not the peaceable magnanimities, but the warlike, are the thing appointed Friedrich this winter, and mainly henceforth. Those "*golden* or
soft radiances" which we saw in him, admirable to Voltaire or to Friedrich, and to an esurient philanthropic world, it is not these, it is "the *steel-
bright* or stellar kind," that are to become predominant in Friedrich's existence; grim hail-storms, thunders, and tornado for an existence to him,
instead of the opulent genialities and halcyon weather anticipated by himself and others! Indisputably enough to us, if not to Friedrich, "Reins-
berg and Life to the Muses" are done. On a sudden, from the opposite
side of the horizon, see, miraculous Opportunity, rushing hitherward—
swift, terrible, clothed with lightning like a courser of the gods; dare you
clutch *him* by the thunder-mane, and fling yourself upon him, and make
for the Empyrean by that course rather? Be immediate about it, then;

the time is now or never! No fair judge can blame the young man that he laid hold of the flaming Opportunity in this manner, and obeyed the new omen. To seize such an opportunity, and perilously mount upon it, was the part of a young magnanimous king, less sensible to the perils, and more to the other considerations, than one older would have been.

This is one of the passages on account of which Carlyle, since the publication of his Life of Cromwell, has ceased, as a historian, to lead the intelligence, and guide the conscience of Europe. On the French Revolution, and on the character of Cromwell, he was accepted as speaking, in the main, the truth; but this verdict on Frederick's seizure of Silesia has *not* been ratified by the assent of civilized mankind, and deserves to be repudiated. We need not go far afield to discover or establish ethical principles by which to try Mr. Carlyle's decision. His own maxims of veracity, reality, fact, are adequate to the occasion. If my neighbor, as I assert and he denies, owes me ten shillings, and if his coach breaks down when I am passing, and if I rush upon him, filch from him his purse containing twenty sovereigns, and refuse to return him one penny, then I have not honorably taken an opportunity to enrich myself, but have acted as a robber and a thief. Now this is *accurately* what Frederick did to Maria Theresa. Claim to *Silesia* had *never* been made on the part of Prussia until Frederick clutched his prey. Several of Frederick's ancestors, in the last and the preceding century, had claimed *certain parts* of Silesia. Frederick had absolutely no other pretence for seizing *the whole*. Who is our authority for this statement? Mr. Carlyle. From him we learn that, in virtue of a kind of family compact into which the Elector of Brandenburgh entered with the Duke of Liegnitz, a family compact which the Austrian Emperor of the period disallowed and annulled, the Hohenzollerns claimed to inherit certain districts, Liegnitz, Brieg, Jägerndorf, lying either in Silesia or on its borders. The claim was one on which jurists might have disputed in an international court of law; but, sustainable or not sustainable, it bore such a relation to a claim to Silesia as a claim to ten shillings would bear to a claim to twenty sovereigns. Suppose, for example, that Napoleon had claimed two or three Welsh dukedoms, and, to enforce that claim, had seized and retained the whole of Wales, his procedure would have been precisely that of Frederick.

What rendered the seizure of Silesia by Frederick peculiarly atrocious was the fact, of which we cannot rationally suppose him ignorant, that it was sure to bring on a general war in Europe. For many years before the death of the Emperor Charles VI., it had been the object—the reasonable and laudable object—of Austrian policy to secure the succession in favor of his daughter, Maria Theresa. What stood in the way was one of those old laws by which, as in several European kingdoms, women were excluded from the Austrian throne. With the assent of all the provinces of the Austrian Empire, this arrangement had been set aside; and England, France, Russia, Prussia—in short, the Powers of the civilized world, "from Naples and Madrid, to Russia and Sweden"—had accepted the instrument known to historians as the Pragmatic Sanction, binding themselves to maintain Theresa in her heritage. Her accession did injustice to no one, promoted peace in Europe, was welcomed by the population of Austria and Hungary, and had been guaranteed by Frederick's father. Had things been left to take their course, a most important contribution would have been made to the recognition of a public law in Europe; a law of reason and justice superior to that of the sword; a law by which the dictates of common-sense, of honor, and of humanity might pacifically prevail. Frederick interdicted all that. He sprang like a wolf upon the prey, and when the young Empress was seen reeling under his attack, the instincts of blood and burglary, the barbaric lust of conquest masking itself in fine words, awoke throughout Europe. Blood flowed in torrents, and the fountains, stopped for a time, burst out again and again.

It would not be fair to accuse Frederick of having foreseen *all* the consequences of his crime, but he was a most intelligent, well-informed man, twenty-eight years of age, perfectly able to estimate the principal results—in bloodshed and devastation—of a rupture of European peace at that moment. "On the head of Frederick," wrote an author, not so gifted with genius as Mr. Carlyle, but cool and shrewd in his judgments, "is all the blood which was shed in a war which raged during many years, and in every quarter of the globe, the blood of the column of Fontenoy, the blood of the mountaineers who were slaughtered at Culloden. The evils produced by his wickedness were felt in lands where the name of Prussia was unknown; and, in order that he might rob a neighbor whom he had promised to defend, black men fought on the coast of Coromandel, and red men scalped each other by the Great Lakes of North America." There is, doubtless, a touch of rhetoric in the form in which Macaulay's indictment is expressed, but it is substantially just; and if it is substantially just, and if there is one moral law for kings and for common men, then the guilt incurred by Frederick was stupendous.

Frederick—this must be owned—never troubled himself much to defend his act. He began the war, he said, to make a name for himself, to strengthen Prussia, to turn a rare opportunity to good account. Kingly reasons enough! If successful kings are to be worshipped as heroes, they are good reasons; otherwise they are infamously bad reasons. Frederick, we may suppose, was not clearly conscious of the depth and blackness of his villany. But this fact shows only to what an amazing extent, even in the luminous eighteenth century, a naturally vigorous brain had been intoxicated by the fumes of king-worship. Mr. Carlyle, though not pronouncing unre-

servedly in favor of his hero, defends him more expressly than
Frederick ever attempted to defend himself; but Mr. Carlyle's
arguments, though presented with rare skill, not only of a
literary sort, but of that kind which we admire in great plead-
ers at the Bar, prove, when fairly examined, almost incredibly
weak.

In the first place, as much is made as possible of Frederick's
claims upon the Empress - Queen; but these, stated at their
broadest, could extend to no more than *certain bits* of Silesia,
and it was obviously burglarious to snatch the whole. In the
second place, it is studiously represented that the French were
principally to blame for the infraction of the Pragmatic Sanction, and for the sanguinary wars that followed. But the logical nullity of this plea can be demonstrated by reference to
the dates of events, nay, by words which, as if forgetful of the
drift of his own argument, Mr. Carlyle himself allows to fall
from his pen. He tells us that, when Maria Theresa called
upon the European Courts to maintain the Pragmatic Sanction,
they all, except England and Holland, "hung back," and "waited till they saw." What was it they waited to see? What
was the occasion which made Maria Theresa apply to them to
defend her? They waited to see how Frederick's attack would
prosper. The occasion on which she applied to her pledged
protectors was the breaking of Frederick into her dominions,
like, as she said, a thief in the night. "On the first invasion
of Silesia," says Mr. Carlyle, "Maria Theresa had indignantly
complained in every Court; and pointing to the Pragmatic
Sanction, had demanded that such law of nature be complied
with, according to covenant." *She* evidently had no doubt,
therefore, as to who was the first breaker of the Pragmatic
Sanction; and who should know if she did not? Had Frederick been defeated at Mollwitz, the first battle of the war, the
Powers that had guaranteed the Pragmatic Sanction would
likely enough have affected virtuous indignation, and lent her

their aid to crush the robber. He won the battle; and then the Powers, with the exceptions formerly named, flocked like vultures to tear the victim. France may have acted badly and meanly, but there is nothing like evidence that France would have drawn the sword if Frederick's had remained in the scabbard.

The grand argument, however, by which Mr. Carlyle defends Frederick, is independent of all such consideration of facts and dates. It is of a transcendental character. It rests upon that optimism of which we formerly found traces in the works of Mr. Carlyle. "Friedrich," he says, "after such trial and proof as has seldom been, got his claims on Schlesien allowed by the Destinies. . . . For . . . there *are* laws valid in Earth and in Heaven; and the great soul of the world is just." The simple answer to this is that it is a begging of the question, or, rather, a twofold begging of the question—once in respect of the principle implied, a second time in its application to the case in hand. The destinies, even if written with a big D, cannot make right wrong, though they crown it with success, and though the success endures for a thousand years. Success has nothing whatever to do in the spiritual sphere. The destinies bade the wind whistle through Cromwell's bones at Tyburn, and flung his system into the kennel. Was his spiritual triumph any the less on that account? So much for Mr. Carlyle's principle; but is he secure on the ground of fact? Has the seizure of Silesia indeed been sealed with the approval of the destinies? In other words, has this great crime borne such fruits that we can refer to it as part of the providential scheme of human history? It has added to the power of Prussia, but I am not sure that it will be found, in the long run, to have conduced to the well-being of Prussia. It typifies that reliance upon "blood and iron" which has become an integral part of Prussian policy. That member of the German Reichstag who represents the district of Holstein, which Prussia retains in her grasp in direct contravention of the Treaty of Prague, protests, in the name of justice and of European law, against that spirit in the Government of Prussia which was evinced in the seizure of Silesia. The too-manifest fact that the statesmen and people of Prussia are incapable of hearing the voice of justice incarnated in the Holstein member, and of obeying it in spite of all considerations of material advantage, is a proof that the Silesian policy has, in so far, stunted the intelligence and paralyzed the conscience of Prussia. The misery and unrest which, without question, prevail widely in that country—the burden of life rendered intolerable by military constraint and bureaucratic meddling — the spectre of Socialism menacing in the background — suggest a doubt whether it is not too soon to mark the seizure of Silesia as one of those lessons which God has written in the Bible of History.

CHAPTER XVII.

IF the pirate in Shakspeare, who razed the eighth commandment from the Decalogue when he started on a cruise, attended well to his piratical business, and was bold, able, energetic, prompt, adroit, he would have had more success than pi-
rates who played their game less cleverly, and might have been
in many points an instructor. Even his history, therefore,
might be worth reading. But Frederick was no mere pirate,
and in describing his campaigns Carlyle brings into view far
higher than mere piratical virtues. Frederick, in point of fact,
was a hero of the Homeric type, armed with the science of the
eighteenth century. The sacking of any town that came in
his way did not expose Ulysses to the slightest disapprobation
from Homer, and the seizure of Silesia would have excited enthusiastic admiration in the camp of Agamemnon. Not till
we rise to the law of chivalry binding every true knight to defend a woman, or to the law of Christ enjoining every man to
do to others as he would have others do to him, do we meet
with a clear repudiation of such actions as Frederick's seizure.
Frederick fell back upon the heroism of physical force. His
views on chivalry were pretty much those of his friend the author of La Pucelle, and he made no pretence to being a Christian. Voltaire represented a reaction against Christianity in
belief and theory, Frederick a reaction against Christianity in
the practice of life and the management of affairs; and the re-

nown of the one and the success of the other furnish a comment—on the whole a discouraging and melancholy comment
—on Goethe's opinion that the race, having once attained to
the height of Christianity, cannot recede from it.   To follow
the steps of a Homeric hero after seventeen hundred years of
Christianity is not edifying; but when our guide is such a describer as Carlyle, it is interesting; and the adventures of few
heroes are so diversified, picturesque, and startling as those of
Frederick.   The many-counselled, much-enduring Ulysses never
came through one-half so much as the hero of the Seven Years'
War; and whatever were Frederick's faults, he was not only as
sagacious as Ulysses and as brave as Achilles, but had qualities
and characteristics of his own that make his history more piquant than that of either.   If it is the note of a poet to seek
and find relief for his deepest feelings by pouring them forth
in verse, whether the verse is particularly good or not, he was
a born poet.   His wit, also, if not refined, was as biting as his
sword; and the crowned heads of Europe, ally and enemy
pretty much alike, winced under the shafts of his wild mockery
and bitter scorn.   Here was a subject for the most racy historical describer of the century!

It is in the delineation of Frederick's campaigns that Mr.
Carlyle's descriptive power is most signally displayed.   Not
only are the battles placed before the mind's eye with vivid
distinctness, but we are made to understand the precise objects
aimed at by the antagonist commanders, and the means they
took to attain them.   In pictorial descriptions of battles, there
are none but Homer and Scott who can be named in comparison with Carlyle; and Homer almost confined himself to the
single combats of heroes; while Scott, though his Bannock-
burn and Flodden are admirable pictures of feudal fray, did
not, in his Life of Napoleon, describe modern battles with corresponding skill.   Carlyle describes the modern battle with the
science of a military critic, and with the pictorial genius of a

poet. It is totally impossible to do justice to these master-pieces of literary art by brief extracts. They are wholes, and deserve study as such. But I shall give the reader two suc-cessive glimpses of Frederick in the field, first winning, then losing, a battle.

It had been the object of Frederick, in the earlier part of 1745, to entice Prince Karl, who was at the head of an Aus-trian and Saxon army, numbering about 70,000 men, to enter Silesia through the passes from Bohemia. The impression which he had conveyed to the Prince was that he was too weak to face the Austrians in the field, and hoped for nothing better than to secure his retreat upon Breslau. When the French envoy, Valori, a man who knew something of war, ex-pressed surprise to Frederick that he had left the passes unde-fended, "Mon ami," replied the King, "if you want to get the mouse, don't shut the trap!"

Carlyle paints for us a view of the Austrian generals, as they appeared on the top of the mountains overlooking Silesia, while their men were marching past, to descend, as they imagined, in the rear of a retreating foe. I shall quote the account of the battle of Hohenfriedberg from this point, omitting much but altering nothing. The details of the actual fighting are too complicated, and would occupy too much space, to be cited.

THE BATTLE OF HOHENFRIEDBERG, JUNE, 1745.

Prince Karl, with Weissenfels, General Berlichingen, and many plumed dignitaries are dining on the hill-top near Hohenfriedberg: after having given order about everything, they witness there, over their wine, the issue of their columns from the mountains; which goes on all the afternoon with field-music, spread banners; and the oldest general admits he never saw a finer review-manœuvre, or one better done, if so well. Thus sit they on the hill-top in the beautiful June afternoon, Silesia lying beauti-fully azure at their feet; the Zobtenberg, enchanted mountain, blue and high on one's eastern horizon. The Austrian and Saxon gentlemen notice, four or five miles in the distance, a body of Prussian horse and foot, visi-bly wending northward; like a long glittering serpent, the glitter of their muskets flashing back yonder on the afternoon sun and us, as they mount from hollow to height. Ten or twelve thousand of them; making for Strigau, to appearance. Intending to bivouac or billet there, and keep some kind of watch over us; belike with an eye to being rear-guard, on the retreat toward Breslau to-morrow? Or will they retreat without attempting mischief? Serenity of Weissenfels engages to seize the heights and proper posts, over yonder this night yet; and will take Strigau itself, the first thing, to-morrow morning.

Yes, your serenities, those are Prussians in movement; and it is not their notion to retreat without mischief. For there stands, not so far off, on the Stanowitz Fuchsberg, a brisk little gentleman, if you could notice him; with his eyes fixed on you, and plans in the head of him now getting nearly mature. For certain, he is pushing out that column of men; and all manner of other columns are getting order to push out, and take their ground; and to-morrow morning—you will not find him in retreat! Friedrich, I presume, at this late hour of four, may be snatching a morsel of dinner; his orderlies are silently speeding, plans taken, orders given: To start all, at eight in the evening, for the bridge of Strigau; there to cross, and spread to the right and to the left. Never will Valori forget the discipline of those Prussians, and how they marched. Difficult ways; the hard road is for their artillery; the men march on each side, sometimes to mid-leg in water—never mind. Wholly in order, wholly silent; Valori followed them three leagues close, and there was not one straggler. Every private man, much more every officer, knows well what grim errand they are on; and they make no remarks. Steady as Time; and, except that their shoes are not of felt, silent as he. The Austrian watch-fires glow silent manifold to leftward yonder; silent overhead are the stars: the path of all duty, too, is silent (not about Strigau alone) for every well-drilled man. Friedrich's general order is, "No prisoners, you cavalry, in the heat of fight; cavalry, strike at the faces of them. You infantry, keep your fire till within fifty steps; bayonet withal is to be relied on." These were Friedrich's last general orders, given in the hollow of the night, near the foot of that Fuchsberg (Fox-hill) where he had been so busy all day.

To describe the battle which ensued, battle named of Strigau or Hohenfriedberg, excels the power of human talent, if human talent had leisure for such employment. It is the huge shock and clash of 70,000 against 70,000. An enormous furious *simultas* (or "both at once," as the Latins phrase it), spreading over ten square miles. Rather say, a wide congeries of electric simultaneities; all *electric*, playing madly into one another; most loud, most mad: the aspect of which is smoky, thunderous, abstruse; the true *sequences* of which who shall unravel? Prince Karl beats retreat, about eight in the morning; is through Hohenfriedberg about ten: back into the mountains; a thoroughly well-beaten man. Toward Bolkenhayn, the Saxons and he; their heavy artillery and baggage had been left safe there. Not much pursued, and gradually rearranging himself; with thoughts—no want of thoughts! Came pouring down, triumphantly invasive, yesterday; returns on these terms, in about fifteen hours. Not marching with displayed banners and field-music this time; this is a far other march. The mouse-trap had been left open, and we rashly went in!—Prince Karl's loss, including that of the Saxons, is 9000 dead and wounded, 7000 prisoners, 66 cannon, 73 flags and standards; the Prussian is about 5000 dead and wounded.

Having seen Frederick victorious, let us now have a look at him in defeat. The battle of Kunersdorf, one of the most fiercely-contested in the history of war, was fought between the Prussians and the Russians, in August, 1759, on a series of hills, or big sandy knolls, on the right bank of the Oder. The battle, up to the time at which we strike into Carlyle's description, had been magnificently successful on the side of Frederick.

THE ROUT OF KUNERSDORF.

I should judge it must be three of the afternoon. The day is windless, blazing; one of the hottest August days; and "nobody, for twelve hours past, could command a drink of water:" very fresh the poor Prussians cannot be! They have done two bouts of excellent fighting; tumbled the Russians well back, stormed many batteries, and taken in all 180 cannon. At this stage, it appears, Finck and many generals were of opinion that, in the present circumstances, with troops so tired, and the enemy nearly certain to draw off, if permitted, here had been enough for one day, and that there ought to be pause till to-morrow. Friedrich knew well the need of rest; but Friedrich, impatient of things half-done, especially of Russians half-beaten, would not listen to this proposal, which was reckoned upon him as a grave and tragic fault, all the rest of his life; though favorable judges, who were on the ground, are willing to prove that pausing here was not feasible or reasonable. Friedrich considers with himself, "Our left wing has hardly yet been in fire!"—calls out the entire left wing, foot and horse: these are to emerge from their meshwork of Lakes about Kunersdorf, and bear a hand along with us on the Russian front here—especially to sweep

away that raging battery they have on the Big Spitzberg, and make us
clear of it.   The Big Spitzberg lies to south and ahead of the Russian
right as now ranked ; fatally covers their right flank, and half ruins the
attack in front.

The left-wing infantry thread their lake-labyrinth, the soonest possible ;
have to rank again on the hither side, under a tearing fire from that Spitzberg ; can then, at last, and do, storm onward, upward ; but cannot, with
their best efforts, take the Spitzberg ; and have to fall back under its
floods of tearing case-shot, and retire out of range.   To Friedrich's blank
disappointment: " Try it you, then, Seidlitz; you saved us at Zorndorf !"
Seidlitz, though it is an impossible problem to storm batteries with horse,
does charge in for the Russian flank, in spite of its covering battery ; but
the torrents of grape-shot are insufferable ; the Seidlitz people, torn in
gaps, recoil, whirl round, and do not rank again till beyond the Lakes of
Kunersdorf.   Seidlitz himself has got wounded, and has had to be carried
away.

And, in brief, from this point onward, all goes aback with the Prussians
more and more.   Repeated attempts on that Spitzberg battery prove vain ;
to advance without it is impossible.   Friedrich's exertions are passionate,
almost desperate ; rallying, animating, new-ordering ; everywhere in the
hottest of the fire.   " Thrice he personally led on the main attack."   He
has had two horses shot down under him ; mounting a third, this, too, gets
a bullet in an artery of the neck, and is about falling, when two adjutants
save the King.   In his waistcoat pocket some small gold case (*étui*) has
got smitten flat by a bullet, which would otherwise have ended matters.
The people about him remonstrate on such exposure of a life beyond value ;
he answers, curtly, " We must all of us try every method here, to win the
battle ; I, like every other, must stand to my duty here."

Friedrich's wearied battalions fight desperately, but cannot prevail further ; and in spite of Friedrich's vehement rallyings and urgings, gradually lose ground.   The Loudon grenadiers, and masses of fresh Russians,
are not to be broken, but advance and advance.   Fancy the panting death-
labors, and spasmodic toilings and bafflings, of these poor Prussians and
their king !   Nothing now succeeding ; the death-agony now come ; all
hearts growing hopeless ; only one heart still seeing hope.   Back, slowly
back, go the Prussians generally, nothing now succeeds with them.   Back
to the Kuhgrund again; fairly over the steep brow there; the Russians
serrying their ranks atop, rearranging their many guns.   There, once more,
rose frightful struggle ; desperate attempt by the foredone Prussians to
retake that height.   " Lasted fifteen minutes, line to line, not fifty yards

asunder;" such musketry—our last cartridges withal. Ardent Prussian parties trying to storm up; few ever getting to the top, none ever standing there alive one minute. This was the death-agony of the battle. Loudon, waiting behind the Spitzberg, dashes forward now, toward the Kuhgrund and our left flank. At sight of which a universal feeling shivers through the Prussian heart. "Hope ended, then!"—and their solid ranks rustle everywhere; and melt into one wild deluge, ebbing from the place as fast as it can.

It is toward six o'clock: the sweltering sun is now fallen low and veiled; gray evening sinking over these wastes. "*N'y a-t-il donc pas un bougre de boulet qui puisse m'atteindre* (is there then not one b—— of a ball that can reach me, then)?" exclaimed Friedrich, in his despair. Such a day he had never thought to see. The pillar of the State, the Prussian army itself, gone to chaos in this manner. Friedrich still passionately struggles, exhorts, commands, entreats, even with tears, "Children, don't forsake me in this pinch!" but all ears are deaf. Friedrich was among the last to leave the ground.

It is not in the heart of man to deny some sympathy to a king so brave and resolute as Frederick showed himself at Kunersdorf. He might not have left the field at all, had not his adjutants seized his bridle and galloped off with him. He felt that all was lost. His determination seems to have been to commit suicide, and he actually wrote and sent away, the same night, an order respecting the command of the army and the succession to the throne. But, before writing this letter, he found opportunity to display a tenderness for which my readers may hardly have given him credit.

FREDERICK AFTER THE BATTLE.

Friedrich found at Œtscher nothing but huts full of poor, wounded men, and their miseries and surgeries; he took shelter himself in a hut "which had been plundered by Cossacks," but which had fewer wounded than others, and could be furnished with some bundles of dry straw. Kriele has a pretty anecdote, with names and particulars, of two poor lieutenants who were lying on the floor as he entered this hut. They had lain there for many hours; the surgeons thinking them desperate, which Friedrich did not. "Alas, children, you are badly wounded, then?" "*Ja*, your Majesty: but how goes the battle?" (Answer evasive on this point.) "Are

8

you bandaged, though?   Have you been let blood?"   "*Nein, Euer Ma-jestät, kein Teufel will uns verbinden* (not a devil of them would bandage us)!"   Upon which there is a surgeon instantly brought; reprimanded for neglect: "Desperate, say you?   These are young fellows; feel that hand, and that; no fever there: nature in such cases does wonders!"   Upon which the leech had to perform his function; and the poor young fellows were saved—and did new fighting, and got new wounds, and had pensions when the war ended.   This appears to have been Friedrich's first work in that hut at Œtscher.

As he did not swallow poison or blow his brains out before the morning after the battle, and as the nucleus of an army soon gathered round him, the likelihood that he would take his own life passed speedily away.   Had his enemies been as active as himself, he would certainly have been overpowered. He struggled on, however, amidst unparalleled difficulties, two years longer.   The expedients to which he had recourse in or-der to find men and horses, and food to keep them alive, read like fables.   The coin of the realm was debased wholesale. Prisoners were forced to take rank as soldiers of their captor. Agents were employed in the various German States to cajole or crimp recruits, and the wild adventurers who engaged in this business shrank from no extravagance of deception that could induce hair-brained lads to enter the service of the King of Prussia.   Idle students, apprentices who had made free with their masters' tills, sons who had quarrelled with their fathers, were told that they might be lieutenants or captains in the Prussian army.   Their commissions were actually made out by the crimpers.   When they presented themselves with these precious documents at some Prussian centre of recruiting ope-rations, they were handed over to the drill-sergeant, cuffed and caned into soldiers, and in a short time sent to meet the ene-my.   It is said that sixty thousand men were thus brought into the Prussian ranks in the closing years of the war.   Strange to say, the quality of Frederick's troops continued excellent. Stern discipline did not quench the enthusiasm of the soldiers for their unconquerable king, and the contagion of courage and endurance was caught even by the losels and scapegraces who entered the nets of the crimpers.

We may, I think, regard, on the whole, with satisfaction the attitude assumed by our Government and countrymen in relation to Frederick. The seizure of Silesia was seen to be criminal, and George II., with the Parliament and people of England at his back, lent a helping hand to the Empress-Queen. In drawing the sword to maintain the Pragmatic Sanction, England was right. At the outbreak of the Seven Years' War, the situation had changed. Frederick was no longer the aggressor. Austria and France, with other formidable allies, had united to snub and put down the upstart of Brandenburg. That Frederick had given both France and Austria good cause to detest and assail him will hardly be questioned by the candid reader of Frederick's life; but the instinct of the British nation decided that, whatever might be Frederick's faults, it was not fair to stamp him out; and the spectacle of a king with less than five millions of population, pitted against Powers commanding fourscore millions, appealed irresistibly to an Englishman's admiration for courage and fortitude. Accordingly, England, led by Pitt, took Frederick's side at the beginning of the Seven Years' War, and gave him most important assistance, both in money and by drawing upon English troops the attack of France.

Frederick made no concession to his enemies at the end of the struggle, but he was surfeited with fighting, and engaged in no serious war during the twenty years that still remained of his life.

CHAPTER XVIII.

CARLYLE expresses the opinion that Frederick was as great in peace as in war, "a first-rate Husbandman," who not only defended Prussia, but instructed the nation in industry and in thrift. Nothing that is recorded of Frederick does him more credit than the pride he took in his victories of peace as compared with those purchased by human blood. At the end of the Seven Years' War, he set himself, with the promptitude, energy, and insight that had shone so conspicuously in his campaigns, to repress the anarchy into which the country had fallen during the struggle, and to repair the frightful waste in its resources. "There is something," says Carlyle, "of flowingly eloquent in Friedrich's account of this battle waged against the inanimate Chaos; something of exultant and triumphant, not noticeable of him in regard to his other victories. On the Leuthens, Rossbachs, he is always cold as water, and nobody could gather that he had the least pleasure in recording them. Not so here."

When, at last, those seven years of calamity, in which a Hebrew prophet might have discerned the vengeance of Heaven for the crime of seizing Silesia, were at an end, the spectacle presented by Frederick's dominions was appalling. So thoroughly had some districts been laid waste that the very traces of the houses could hardly be found. Some towns were destroyed wholly, some half-burned. The very vestiges of thirteen thousand dwellings had disappeared. The fields lay unsown, no seed to cast upon them; the inhabitants lacked grain for food; and a kind of bewildered and amazed dispiritment had sunk down upon the heart of the population. The ground could not be ploughed for want of horses; sixty thousand, it was calculated, were required to start once more the regular cultivation of the soil. "In the provinces generally, half a million less population," according to Frederick's estimate, were on the land than when the war broke out; "upon only four millions and a half, the ninth man was wanting." It is strange that the question never seems to have pressed itself on Frederick's conscience, *who* was expressly responsible for that haggard spectacle of death and misery. If he had never attacked Silesia, and if he had not infuriated other European Courts, besides the Austrian, by his diplomatic falsity and political selfishness, not to mention his arrogance and blistering scorn, there is no reason to believe that one drop of that blood would have been shed. Frederick is Mr. Carlyle's last model king — the type of a kind of man without whom there can be no right governing authority, nothing but anarchy and chaos—and, on Frederick's own estimate, five hundred thousand of his subjects pay for his kingship with their lives in one grim week of years! Might we not reply to Mr. Carlyle that this one fact affords demonstration that the dependence of millions of lives upon the will of a single man—the very existence of kingship, except in the constitutional and representative sense — is a ghastly anachronism in modern civilization?

Frederick had been a close student of history, and one of the soundest of his father's educational notions was that the boy ought to be made thoroughly acquainted with the history of recent times and of his own country. He knew, therefore, that after the Thirty Years' War the wasted districts, left to the mere natural action of time, had required for their recovery about a hundred years. Warned by this deterrent example, he resolved not to trust to time, but to step in at once with active remedies. Mr. Carlyle thinks that political economists are pledged by their science to disapprove of this decision, but

I see no cause why this should be so. The doctrine that it is
unwise to do by artificial means what will be consummately
well effected by natural means does not conflict with the common-sense rule of applying exceptional means to exceptional
emergencies. A system of bounties to secure the growing of
corn is likely, under ordinary circumstances, to be superfluous
or pernicious; but if the farmers of a particular district are so
impoverished that it is hardly possible for them to plough and
sow their fields, they may be relieved, without injury to any
one, by help in money, or by a temporary remission of taxes.
The charge which "professors of the dismal science" have
made against Frederick is sufficiently illustrated in a single
well-packed sentence of Macaulay's, and there is no allusion in
it to the extraordinary assistance which he lent his subjects
when such had been rendered indispensable by war. "The
public money," says Macaulay, "of which the King was generally so sparing, was lavishly spent in ploughing bogs, in
planting mulberry-trees amidst the sand, in bringing sheep
from Spain to improve the Saxon wool, in bestowing prizes for
fine yarn, in building manufactories of porcelain, manufactories
of carpets, manufactories of hardware, manufactories of lace."
Whether Frederick was far wrong in stimulating his people to
improve their wool and their yarn may be doubted, but it is
clear that the case of a country desolated and demoralized by
war does not fall within any of the categories specified by
Macaulay, nor does he, in his other remarks upon Frederick's
administration, pronounce one syllable of censure upon the
policy of exceptional outlay in that instance.

During the war, Frederick had not burdened himself with
any considerable debt, and at its close he had upward of
three millions sterling ready for another campaign. With
this money he set about rebuilding the towns, repaying the
impositions wrung from the provinces by the enemy, and giving aid to the necessitous. The artillery, baggage, and com-

missariat horses were distributed among those who had none, to be employed in tillage of the land. The Government grain stores were taken for the food of the people, and to sow the ground. All taxes were remitted to Silesia for six months; to Pomerania and the Newmark for two years. "Repeated gifts restored courage to the poor husbandmen, who began to despair of their lot; by the helps given, hope in all classes sprang up anew; encouragement of labor produced activity; love of country arose again with fresh life; in a word, the fields were cultivated again, manufacturers resumed their work, and the police, once more in vigor, corrected by degrees the vices that had taken root during the time of anarchy." Within the second year improvement was manifest, and within seven years the country had regained its wonted look of prosperity. "In Lower Silesia," says Frederick, with glowing satisfaction, "we managed to increase the number of husbandmen by four thousand families." With like alacrity and energy, he set about restoring the currency, and getting rid of the debased coinage which war had forced upon him. Within some fourteen months of the cessation of hostilities, the money was pure. One can understand enthusiasm for a King who could work for his people in this fashion!

CHAPTER XIX.

FREDERICK has been much blamed for his share in the partition of Poland; but if we are to do him anything like justice in that matter, we must view him, in Poland also, in capacity of regal husbandman. Mr. Carlyle goes much farther than merely to commend his administration of the part of Poland which fell to his share, averring that much is to be said in defence of the partition itself; and I own that, after considering the question as carefully as I can, I regard Mr. Carlyle, in this instance, as on the whole, right. He by no means pronounces an unqualified approval on Frederick. Poland, he says, was looked upon by Frederick as "a moribund anarchy, fallen down as carrion on the common highways of the world; belonging to nobody in particular; liable to be cut into on a great and critically stringent occasion." He does not say that Frederick's conception of the way in which the Polish problem ought to be solved was morally right, or that "a higher rectitude" might not have dictated a different course from that pursued by the Prussian king. The case was exceptional, and no precedent is to be founded on it. "Were it never so just, proper, and needful, this is by nature a case of *Lynch Law;* upon which, in the way of approval or apology, no spoken word is permissible. Lynch being so dangerous a law-giver, even when an indispensable one!"

It is difficult to conceive a case in which the intervention of Lynch law could have been more called for than in that of Poland. Not only was the anarchy of the country inveterate, chronic, incurable; not only did it involve risk to the neighboring countries; it was in itself peculiarly execrable. The Poles had fallen in great part under the influences of the Jesuits, and were fanatically intolerant of every form of faith except their own intensely superstitious Catholicism. The country, with its furious priests and weeping images of the Virgin, was fast retrograding to barbarism, and was, in fact, a scandal to Europe. In their frantic wilfulness and hatred of all restraint, the Poles had made government an impossibility among them, unless it came from without. Had Frederick exerted his influence with the Austrian and Russian Courts to have his brother Henry, a man of great ability and an admirable commander, appointed King of Poland, as some intelligent Poles desired, the issue might have been better for all parties; but I am not prepared to prove that such a course was practicable. Mr. Carlyle translates for us, from Herr Freytag, the following account of what Poland was when Frederick got his share of it, and what that share (West Preussen) became under Frederick's management.

POLAND BEFORE PARTITION AND AFTER.

During several centuries, the much-divided Germans had habitually been pressed upon, and straitened and injured, by greedy, conquering neighbors; Friedrich was the first conqueror who once more pushed forward the German frontier toward the East; reminding the Germans again that it was their task to carry law, culture, liberty, and industry into the East of Europe. All Friedrich's lands, with the exception only of some old-Saxon territory, had, by force and colonization, been painfully gained from the Sclave. At no time since the migrations of the Middle Ages had this struggle for possession of the wide plains to the East of Oder ceased. When arms were at rest, politicians carried on the struggle.

In the very "century of enlightenment" the persecution of the Germans became fanatical in those countries; one Protestant church after the other got confiscated; pulled down; if built of wood, set on fire: its church once burned, the village had lost the privilege of having one. Ministers and school-masters were driven away, cruelly maltreated. "Wring the Lutheran, you will find money in him," became the current proverb of the Poles in regard to Germans. A Protestant Starost of Gnesen, a Herr Von Unruh, of the House of Birnbaum, one of the largest proprietors of the country, was condemned to die, and first to have his tongue pulled out, and his hands cut off, for the crime of having copied into his note-book some strong passages against the Jesuits, extracted from German books. Patriotic Confederates of Bar, joined by all the plunderous vagabonds around, went roaming and ravaging through the country, falling upon small towns and German villages. The Polish nobleman, Roskowski, put on one red boot and one black, symbolizing *fire* and *death;* and in this guise rode about, murdering and burning, from place to place; finally, at Jastrow, he cut off the hands, feet, and, lastly, the head of the Protestant pastor, Willich by name, and threw the limbs into a swamp. This happened in 1768.

When Prussian Poland came into possession of Friedrich, the towns, with some few exceptions, lay in ruins; so also most of the hamlets of the open country. Bromberg, the city of German colonists, the Prussians found in heaps and ruins: to this hour it has not been possible to ascertain clearly how the town came into this condition. No historian, no document tells of the destruction and slaughter that had been going on, in the whole district of the *Netze* there, during the last ten years before the arrival of the Prussians. The town of Culm had preserved its strong old walls and stately churches; but in the streets, the necks of the cellars stood out above the rotten timber and brick heaps of the tumbled houses; whole streets consisted merely of such cellars, in which wretched people were still trying to live. Of the forty houses in the large market-place of Culm, twenty-eight had no doors, no roofs, no windows, and no owners. Other towns were in similar condition.

The country people hardly knew such a thing as bread; many had never in their life tasted such a delicacy; few villages possessed an oven. A weaving-loom was rare, the spinning-wheel unknown. The main article of furniture, in this scene of squalor, was the crucifix and vessel of holy-water under it. The peasant-noble was hardly different from the common peasant; he himself guided his hook-plough and clattered with his wooden slippers upon the plankless floor of his hut. It was a desolate land, without discipline, without law, without a master.

The very rottenness of the country became an attraction for Friedrich; and henceforth West Preussen was, what hitherto Silesia had been, his favorite child; which, with infinite care, like an anxious, loving mother, he washed, brushed, new-dressed, and forced to go to school and into orderly habits, and kept ever in his eye. The diplomatic squabbles about this "acquisition" were still going on, when he had already sent a body of his best official people into this waste howling scene, to set about organizing it. The Counties were divided into small Circles; in a minimum of time, the land was valued, and an equal tax put upon it; every Circle received its *Landrath*, Law-court, Post-office, and Sanitary Police. New parishes, each with its church and parson, were called into existence as by miracle; a company of 187 school-masters were sent into the country; multitudes of German mechanics, too, from brick-makers up to machine-builders. Everywhere there began a digging, a hammering, a building; cities were peopled anew; street after street rose out of the heaps of ruins; new villages of colonists were laid out, new modes of agriculture ordered. In the first year after taking possession, the great canal was dug, which, in a length of fifteen miles, connects, by the Netze river, the Weichsel with the Oder and the Elbe: within one year after giving the order, the King saw loaded vessels from the Oder, 120 feet in length of keel, enter the Weichsel. The vast breadths of land, gained from the state of swamp by drainage into this canal, were immediately peopled by German colonists.

We saw that, immediately on his accession, Frederick proclaimed toleration to all religions, and freedom of the Press. He at once put a stop also to the use of torture in the legal system of Prussia. But his enthusiasm for Law Reform was by no means content with these memorable improvements. The sword once in the sheath, after the second Silesian war, he summoned to his help, as his manner was, the most effective men whom he could find to undertake the reform of the law. It is notable of Frederick—and one of the proofs of his consummate practical talent—that he never undertook work for which he was unfitted, seldom forced his own views upon men whose mastery in their department was clear. As his Chief Law Minister he named Samuel Von Cocceji, whom Mr. Carlyle describes as "one of the most learned of lawyers, and a very Hercules in cleansing law stables;" and, a fortnight after the peace was signed, an express order was written by Frederick directing Cocceji to begin. The Law Minister had a Commission of Six appointed to assist him, "riddled together" out of

Prussia, the best men producible for the work. "To sweep out pettifogging attorneys, cancel improper advocates, to regulate fees; to war, in a calm but deadly manner, against pedantries, circumlocutions, and the multiplied forms of stupidity, cupidity, and human owlery in this department;" such, in Mr. Carlyle's picturesque language, was their duty. They took up the provinces successively, beginning with Pomerania and ending with Prussia proper.

Their method was bold, and involved one change which, to our friends of Westminster Hall and Lincoln's Inn, may seem appalling and incredible. They actually swept away the attorney species. The advocate was himself to take charge of the suit, no middle-man permitted. In the next place they sifted out and dismissed incompetent advocates, retaining in each Court a fixed number of qualified men. Inefficient judges were shelved, and those who remained were better paid. The standard of fees was accurately fixed—another of those things which, with freedom granted to solicitors and clients to make personal bargains, and with taxation of costs left very much a sham from not being enforced in all cases, has been found a practical impossibility in England. They made it imperative—this seems to have been Frederick's own suggestion—that every suit, even if twice carried by appeal to higher Courts, should terminate within a year of its inception. Cocceji crowned his general Law Reform with the project of a code, which, in due time, was realized. "Friedrich's fame," says Mr. Carlyle, "as a beneficent Justinian, rose high in all countries."

CHAPTER XX.

IN every case occurring within the Prussian dominions there was an appeal to the King direct. Frederick proclaimed himself the advocate of the poor man and of the common soldier. The opinion of educated Prussia, both during Frederick's life and in our own time, has been that, in one instance, at least, his desire to do justice to a poor man, and his suspicion of legal pedantry, led him to a wrong decision. Miller Arnold, who claimed compensation for the water which, as he alleged, had been drawn from his mill-stream by a landed proprietor, and whose cause was so vehemently espoused by Frederick that he actually imprisoned his Berlin judges for refusing to decide in Arnold's favor, is commonly believed to have befooled His Majesty. Mr. Carlyle, indeed, thinks differently, but the evidence on the other side appears to be overwhelming. In the well-known case of the *Sans Souci* miller, a Prussian Naboth who would on no account give up to the King his bit of ground and mill, Frederick showed himself a wiser as well as a more magnanimous ruler than Ahab, and left the mill to be a picturesque ornament in his garden. Generally speaking, the right of appeal to Frederick worked well, checking the blunders of mechanical routine, and tending greatly to endear him to his subjects. One instance in which the crowned advocate of the poor man served his client well, deserves to be more fully detailed.

Linzenbarth was a "rugged poverty-stricken old licentiate of theology," tall, awkward, rawboned, a kind of German Dominie Sampson, who had failed in the pulpit, and managed to keep body and soul together by school-mastering among the hill-villages of Thuringia. When he was about sixty years of age, Cannabich, pastor of the "thrice-obscure village of Hemmleben," died, and the landed proprietor, who had the living in his gift, sent a messenger announcing to Linzenbarth that he might have the place. The offer which, at the first moment, filled the poor old hungry soul with gladness, was, at the second, on his learning that the condition annexed was marriage to a cast-off dependent of the great house, peremptorily rejected. The mean wretch who took the living and the wife, was worried to death by the latter in three years' time; but Linzenbarth found that his poor prospects in his native district were ruined, and set out for Berlin, where he arrived on the 20th of June, 1750.

Hard as his life had been, he had contrived, by more than Spartan frugality, to save some £60, which he carried with him in Nürnberg silver money of very bad quality. By a decree made some six years before, this Nürnberg money had been excluded from Prussia, and the Custom-house officials no sooner caught sight of Linzenbarth's "batzen," than they seized and sealed up the whole. He exclaimed and gesticulated, vowed that he was ignorant of the decree, asked how he was to live in a strange place upon nothing. With calm professional cruelty the officials told him it was his duty to have informed himself, theirs to put the law in force. Not a stiver of his hoard could circulate in Prussia. One advocate, who took up his case on the chance of being paid in the event of success, was sharply rebuked by the magistrate for countenancing a breach of the King's laws, and told that, if he went on so, he would land in the common jail. At last some simple persons advised Linzenbarth to appeal direct to the King. "Write out your case," said Linzenbarth's advisers, "with extreme brevity; nothing but the essential points, and those clear." Linzenbarth did so, and one August morning, at the opening of the gates of Berlin, went off "without one farthing in my pocket, in God's name, to Potsdam." We shall now take his own narrative, with Carlyle's intercalated remarks, abridging but not altering.

LINZENBARTH AND FREDERICK.

At Potsdam I was lucky enough to see the King; my first sight of him. He was in the palace esplanade there, drilling his troops. When the drill was over, his Majesty went into the garden, and the soldiers dispersed; only four officers remained lounging upon the esplanade, and walked up and down. For fright I knew not what to do; I pulled the papers out of my pocket. These were my memorial, two certificates of character, and a Thüringen pass. The officers noticed this; came straight to me and said, "What letters has he there, then?" I thankfully and gladly imparted the whole; and when the officers had read them, they said, "We will give you a good advice. The King is extra-gracious to-day, and is gone alone into the garden. Follow him straight. Thou wilt have luck." This I would not do; my awe was too great. They thereupon laid hands on me (the mischievous dogs, not ill-humored, either): one took me by the right arm, another by the left, "Off, off; to the garden!" Having got me thither, they looked out for the King. He was among the gardeners, examining some rare plant; stooping over it, and had his back to us. Here I had to halt; and the officers began, in underhand tone (the dogs!), to put me through my drill: "Hat under left arm! Right foot foremost!—Breast well forward!—Head up!—Papers from pouch! Papers aloft in right hand!—Steady! steady!" And went their ways, looking always round, to see if I kept my posture. I perceived well enough they were pleased to make game of me; but I stood, all the same, like a wall, being full of fear. The officers were hardly out of the garden, when the King turned round, and saw this extraordinary machine — telegraph figure, or whatever we may call it, with papers pointing to the sky. He gave such a look at me, like a flash of sunbeams glancing through you; and sent one of the gardeners to bring my papers. Which having got, he struck into another walk with them, and was out of sight. In a few minutes he appeared again at the place where the rare plant was, with my papers open in his left hand; and gave me a wave with them to come nearer. I plucked up a heart, and went straight toward him. Oh, how thrice and four-times graciously this great monarch deigned to speak to me!

KING: "My good Thüringian, you came to Berlin, seeking to earn your bread by industrious teaching of children, and here, at the Packhof, in searching your things, they have taken your Thüringen hoard from you.

True, the batzen are not legal here; but the people should have said to you: You are a stranger, and didn't know the prohibition;—well, then, we will seal up the bag of batzen; you send it back to Thüringen, get it changed for other sorts; we will not take it from you!—Be of heart, however; you shall have your money again, and interest too.—But, my poor man, Berlin pavement is bare, they don't give anything gratis; you are a stranger; before you are known and get teaching, your bit of money is done; what then?" I understood the speech right well; but my awe was too great to say, "Your Majesty will have the all-highest grace to allow me something!" But as I was so simple, and asked for nothing, he did not offer anything.

When we got out of the garden, the four officers were still there on the esplanade. For twenty-seven hours I had not tasted food; not a farthing *in bonis* to get bread with; I had waded twenty miles hither, in a sultry morning, through the sand. In this tremor of my heart, there came a *Kammer-hussar* (soldier-valet, valet reduced to his simplest expression) out of the palace, and asked, "Where is the man who was with my King in the garden?" I answered, "Here!" And he led me into the Schloss, to a large room, where pages, lackeys, and Kammer-hussars were about. My Kammer-hussar took me to a little table, excellently furnished; with soup, beef; likewise carp dressed with garden-salad, likewise game with cucumber-salad; bread, knife, fork, spoon, and salt were all there (and I with an appetite of twenty-seven hours; I, too, was there). My hussar set me a chair, said, "This that is on the table, the King has ordered to be served for you; you are to eat your fill, and mind nobody; and I am to serve. Sharp, then, fall to!" I was greatly astonished, and knew not what to do; least of all could it come into my head that the King's Kammer-hussar, who waited on his Majesty, should wait on me. I pressed him to sit by me; but, as he refused, I did as bidden—sat down, took my spoon, and went at it with a will (*frisch*)! The hussar took the beef from the table, set it on the charcoal-dish (to keep it hot till wanted); he did the like with the fish and roast game, and poured me out wine and beer. I ate and drank till I had abundantly enough. Dessert, confectionery, what I could. A plateful of big black cherries and a plateful of pears my waiting man wrapped in paper and stuffed them into my pockets, to be a refreshment on the way home. And so I rose from the royal table, and thanked God and the King in my heart that I had so gloriously dined.

At that moment a secretary came, brought me a sealed order to the Packhof at Berlin, with my certificates and the pass; told down on the table five tail ducats and a gold Friedrich under them (better than £10 of our day), saying the King sent me this to take me home to Berlin again. The secretary took me out, and there, yoked with six horses, stood a royal Proviant-wagon, which having led me to, the secretary said : " You people, the King has given order you are to take this stranger to Berlin, and also to accept no drink-money from him." I again, through the Herrn Secretarium, testified my most submissive thankfulness for all royal graciousness ; took my place, and rolled away. On reaching Berlin, I went at once to the Packhof and handed them my royal rescript. The head man opened the seal; in reading he changed color, went from pale to red, said nothing, and gave it to the second man to read. The second put on his spectacles, read, and gave it to the third. However, I was to come forward, and be so good as write a quittance, " That I had received for my batzen the same sum in Brandenburg coin, ready down, without the least deduction !" My cash was at once accurately paid. And thereupon the steward was ordered, To go with me to the White Swan in the Judenstrasse, and pay what I owed there, whatever my score was. This was what the King meant when he said, " You shall have your money back, and interest too." Our gray - whiskered, rawboned, great - hearted Candidatus lay down to sleep, at the White Swan ; probably the happiest man in all Berlin. Meat, clothes, and fire he did not again lack for the time he needed them, some twenty-seven years still. He died of apoplexy at the age of eighty-eight.

Of the general success of Frederick's administrative system, and the security and prosperity of his subjects, no better proof could be afforded than the fact that only fourteen or fifteen criminals were executed annually in Prussia.

CHAPTER XXI.

WITHIN his book on Frederick Mr. Carlyle has given us what is, in effect, the best biography of Voltaire in existence, and I must not conclude my talk about Carlyle without saying something of it.

Carlyle pronounces Voltaire "the spiritual complement" of Frederick. Between these two lies mainly "what little of lasting their poor century produced." Frederick stands for what it "*did*," Voltaire for what it "*thought*." One can hardly help fancying that this generalization is too broad to be of much practical value. A century which produced the sceptical philosophy of Hume, the constructive philosophies of Reid and of Kant, Butler's Doctrine of Conscience, Adam Smith's Political Economy, and the most important poems of Goethe, has surely left us fruits of thought more permanent and more precious than the works of Voltaire. Frederick and he were, however, the most conspicuous men of their century, the orbit of Napoleon touching only on its close; and the interest now felt in Voltaire is at least as great as that felt in Frederick. Probably, also, Voltaire's writings have directly influenced a greater number of minds than those of any of the thinkers named, his popularity being quite unrivalled until the end of his own century, and remaining to this day unsurpassed. "This poor Voltaire," says Carlyle, "without implement, except the tongue and brain of him—he is still a shining object to all the populations; and they say and symbol to me, Tell us of him! He is the man!" In fundamentals Carlyle does not abandon the estimate of Voltaire published in his famous essay of 1828; it was indeed impossible that the grand preacher of earnestness should reconcile himself with the least earnest of all great writers, the man who, more, perhaps, than any one that ever lived, treated life as a jest; but it is unmistakable that his feeling toward Voltaire had relented between 1828 and 1858; and the high lights in the portrait executed in the second period are warmer and brighter than those of the earlier likeness. He now, grudgingly indeed, and with many qualifications, yet decisively, classes Voltaire among the prophets. There was in him "a spark of heaven's own lucency, a gleam from the Eternities (in small measure)." The facts of Voltaire's life are, therefore, carefully sifted for us from the rubbish heaps of former biographies; his intercourse, personal, and by letter, with Frederick, is described; and, on the whole, we are enabled to form an idea of Voltaire no less distinct than of Frederick himself.

Voltaire's father was a Paris lawyer, flourishing and influential, and it was his wish that his clever second son, born in 1694, should advance to fortune on the legal road which he was able to open for him. The mere boy seems to have been docile enough, and took his place among his father's clerks, with whom he was an immense favorite, being already "the most amusing fellow in the world;" but the youth, though he went through the regular stages of a legal education, and "even became an advocate," showed invincible impatience of the professional harness, "took to poetry, and other airy dangerous courses," and was a sorrow to the parental mind. Meanwhile his social talents made him friends, and he became known in exalted circles as one of the most brilliant young fellows in France. He was hardly of age when, under the false suspicion of having written a popular political squib, he was flung into the Bastile for eighteen months. Such a mishap might have sobered another man into dulness or soured him into misanthropy; but young Voltaire was nowise discomposed or dis-

heartened; and retained, as always afterward under similar circumstances, the perfect and joyous use of his faculties. He
employed himself in composing an epic poem which he called
La Ligue, and which, recast and published a few years subsequently, has become known to all the world as the Henriade.
He was but twenty-four when his first drama, " Œdipe the renowned name of it," was successful on the Parisian stage. " All
of us princes, then, or poets!" he could exclaim, as he glanced
round the company with which he sat at supper.

Dining one day with the Duc de Sulli, and, as usual, leading
the conversation, and illuminating the circle by the coruscations of his wit, he attracted the unfavorable notice of " a certain splenetic, ill-given Duc de Rohan, grandee of high rank,
great haughtiness, and very ill-behavior in the world." " Who,"
asks Rohan, " is this young man that talks so loud, then?"
" Monseigneur," says Voltaire, " it is one who does not drag a
big name about with him, but who secures respect for the name
he has." Rohan stalked from the room " in a sulphurous frame
of mind," and took the mean revenge of having Voltaire horse-
whipped by hired bullies. Voltaire challenged him, and Rohan
pretended to accept, but told the secret to his wife. Voltaire
was a second time flung into the Bastile. On regaining his
freedom, he at once quitted France for England.

His new residence had a great effect on him. " England
was full of constitutionality and free-thinking; Tolands, Col-
linses, Wollastons, Bolingbrokes, still living; very free, indeed.
England, one is astonished to see, has its royal-republican ways
of doing; something Roman in it, from peerage down to plebs;
strange and curious to the eye of M. de Voltaire. Sciences
flourishing; Newton still alive, white with fourscore years, the
venerable hoary man; Locke's Gospel of Common Sense in
full vogue, or even done into verse, by incomparable Mr. Pope,
for the cultivated upper classes. In science, in religion, in politics, what a surprising liberty allowed or taken!" On the

whole, he liked England, and though the figure of the Englishman in his works is "pretty much the *reverse* of Voltaire's own
self," he delineates it, though not without mockery, yet "with
evident love." Here was no Bastile; toleration was in full
play; no Jesuits, "strong in their mendacious, malodorous stupidity, despicablest yet most dangerous of creatures," checked
freedom of thought. He studied Newton's astronomy with enthusiasm, went full sail into English freethinking, and displayed
henceforward a contempt for Popish superstition and a detestation of the Jesuits as cordial as could have been displayed
by any Englishman. When he returned to France in 1728,
his character was fully formed, and the education had been received which fitted him to play the extraordinary part which,
for the next half century, he enacted on the stage of Europe.

We have had no Englishmen at all like Voltaire, and I cannot pretend to have got any tangible grasp of his personality.
More than any man I have ever heard of, he strikes me as not
so much a living unity as a selection of several well-marked
types of man, working in partnership and passing under one
name.

First of all, and most easily intelligible, we have the Voltaire
of society, the "brilliant, swift, far-glancing" wit and talker,
who dazzled and delighted every circle in which he appeared.
Then there is the poetical Voltaire, in which capacity he shows
by no means to advantage, his nature being essentially defective in those elements of earnestness, reverence, enthusiasm,
passion, conviction, without which there can be no rhythmic
melody of speech. Artificiality, tunelessness, surface-glitter,
seem to me the salient characteristics of Voltaire's poetry.
Versification was with him an acquirement, an accomplishment
—a particular knack, used for purely literary purposes, rather
than a flood of expression, modulated and colored by the emotional fervor which compelled it to rush forth. Frederick
could not round a stanza or burnish a similitude so well as

Voltaire; but when, in the Seven Years' War, he poured his anguish, in what Carlyle well calls Psalms of Lamentation, into the ear of a beloved sister, he was a poet in a sense in which Voltaire never deserved the name. No one can even cursorily examine Voltaire's twenty-one cantos on Joan of Arc without feeling that mockery was the dominant mood of his mind. He must, to a considerable extent, be judged by that poem. La Pucelle was written two years after he left England, when he was nearly forty years of age. The most pathetic episode in the history of France, one of the most solemn and heart-rending episodes in the history of the world, affects him solely as furnishing the suggestion for a wildly profane, licentious, heartless poem, in which every virtue that beautifies and ennobles the life of man, and every aspiration that lifts him heavenward, are laughed to scorn. It is to this, beyond any book known to me in literature, that Victor Hugo's judgment on Voltaire's writings generally will apply, namely, that they kill the sentiment of God in the soul. A fathomless scepticism is the doctrine of the book, pervading, underlying, overarching it like an atmosphere — scepticism in man as well as in God, scepticism in everything except the pleasantness—the fleeting and ignoble pleasantness—of pleasure. Life is a detected illusion; it might be extremely agreeable to believe in it, but that would be enthusiasm, and all enthusiasm is folly. Byron was accused by the highest literary authorities of his day of preter-human wickedness for writing Don Juan; but, bad as Don Juan is, you always feel in reading it that the author has capacities of goodness, and that his heart of hearts is in the right place. La Pucelle conveys to me the idea of sheer incapacity of goodness, absence of heart altogether.

That Voltaire was capable of acts of generosity, and that he could be stirred to unfeigned indignation by injustice and cruelty, cannot be called in question; but his life, on the whole, bears much the same testimony to his character as the

Pucelle. Carlyle is scrupulously just to Voltaire, dwelling with evident enjoyment and not a little sympathy on the mellow evening of his life at Ferney; but Carlyle makes it abundantly plain that he could not be relied on, that he was incurably selfish, incurably false, and that, with all his easy amiability to dependents, he was bitterly revengeful. It is with a feeling of positive shame for human nature that we hear of his greedy scheming to get money out of Frederick. It may be incredible that he actually cheated the palace valets of their perquisite of candle-ends, but would it have been possible for such a story to be current at the Prussian Court, and to be printed for the instruction of posterity, if Voltaire had not been execrably mean as well as rapacious? He suffered a good deal from Frederick, though the mendacity of his own account of what he suffered has been amply exposed; and one could make allowance for a strong feeling of anger retained by him against his former benefactor, or pardon a vigorous blow dealt in a manly way; but we should deserve our own contempt if we did not spurn him when he tries, in spite of rebuffs, to sneak back into Frederick's favor, and when, with one and the same pen, he writes maudlin sycophancies for Frederick's eye, and venomous disparagements for the eyes of others. No one who was not habitually false could have been the author of what Carlyle quotes as written by Voltaire *to* Frederick, and also of what he quotes as written by Voltaire *of* Frederick. The King's settled opinion was that Voltaire was utterly bad, thoroughly heartless, and there are few things recorded of Frederick more creditable either to his manliness or his penetration than his steadfast resistance of Voltaire's blandishments, and his determination to avoid a renewal of their intercourse, after he had fairly satisfied himself as to the kind of man he had to deal with.

A third Voltaire whom I discern in this complex and marvellous personality, distinct both from the wit and the poet, is

Voltaire the money-maker. His father thought him an intellectual scapegrace, brilliant it might be, but as incapable of practical success as a pyrotechnic firewheel is of turning a mill; but there never was a man more shrewdly practical. It was in England that his character took final form in relation to economics as well as to other things. Furbishing up the poem he had written in the Bastile when he had but emerged from boyhood, he brought it out in London by subscription. Having come to England well furnished with introductions, and having taken care, by learning English in France, to prepare himself to take a place in London society, he had many friends in this country. Princess Caroline headed the list of subscribers. The venture yielded him " an unknown but very considerable sum of thousands sterling, and grounded not only the world-renown but the domestic finance of M. de Voltaire." The Henriade carried his name into all civilized countries. "And such fame, and other agencies on his behalf, having opened the way home for Voltaire, he took this sum of thousands sterling along with him; laid it out judiciously in some city lottery, or profitable scrip then going at Paris, which at once doubled the amount; after which he invested it in corn-trade, army clothing, Barbary-trade, commissariat-bacon trade, all manner of well-chosen trades—being one of the shrewdest financiers on record;—and never from that day wanted abundance of money, for one thing: which he judged to be extremely expedient for a literary man, especially in times of Jesuit and other tribulation." By his books he made "almost nothing." Generally he had "to disavow them, when some sharp-set bookseller, in whose way he had laid the savory article as bait, chose to risk his ears for the profit of snatching and publishing it." Yet he had money enough always, and had so disposed it that, wherever he went, he had resources, "and no conceivable combination of confiscating Jesuits and dark fanatic official persons could throw him out of a livelihood, whithersoever he might be forced to run." His yearly income at his death was equal, Mr. Carlyle estimates, to £20,000 of our money. "The richest literary man ever heard of hitherto."

Voltaire had a light way of accounting for his pecuniary success. "You have only to watch," he would say, "what scrips, public loans, investments in the field of agio are offered; if you exert any judgment, it is easy to gain there: do not the stupidest of mortals gain there, by intensely attending to it?" This is a highly self-flattering account of the matter; for we are expected to believe that his transcendent cleverness, honestly applied and with no particular furtherance, brought him his wealth. But there is something more to be considered in the solution of the problem. From the first he was the companion of influential people, and had extraordinary opportunities of becoming acquainted with good public investments. "Army clothing and commissariat-bacon trades" are exactly the kind into which entrance might be got by interest in high quarters, and one has a suspicion that the feeding and clothing of the poor soldiers thus provided for might be perfunctory. Voltaire, besides, never lost anything that could be got for begging, and he had no scruple about engaging in speculations forbidden by law. When driven to extremity, he told lies. On one occasion he was guilty of forgery, and offered to swear to a falsehood. Frederick found that he was not only excessively greedy in relation to salary and allowances, but that he was prepared to do illegal business at the expense of his royal patron. By the treaty of peace with Saxony, Frederick had stipulated that certain Exchequer Bills should be paid by the Saxon Treasury in gold to *bona fide* Prussian subjects. The judicious Voltaire, on the watch for investments, bethought him that if he could buy the Bills from persons who, not being Prussian subjects, had no legal claim to gold for them, and then demand gold in character of a Prussian subject, he might clear 35 per cent. Accordingly, he hired a Jew money-lender, or jeweller, to proceed to Dresden and buy the Bills, it being arranged between them that, in talking or corresponding on the subject, Voltaire and the Jew were to call the goods bought *furs* or *diamonds*. This was a direct attempt to cheat the Saxon Treasury, and the Saxon Court, getting wind of it, " made grievous complaints " to Frederick. No one could better understand the nature of the whole transaction than Frederick, and he looked upon Voltaire as playing in it the part of an unprincipled trickster. The business did not prosper. The Jew either could not or would not buy the Bills, and he and Voltaire got into a furious quarrel, ending in a lawsuit. " You have had the most villanous affair in the world with a Jew," wrote the King to Voltaire. Mr. Carlyle distinctly states that, before he was done with the affair, Voltaire lied, forged, and offered to commit perjury. Voltaire had calculated that he might gain £800 by the transaction. Frederick wrote him in terms of sharp reproof, almost with a spice of contempt in them, and it makes one blush to hear that the King received " four lamenting and repenting, wheedling, and ultimately whining " letters from the first literary man in Europe. Frederick was at this time forty years old, Voltaire fifty-eight.

These facts respecting Voltaire's financial operations qualify to a considerable degree that apparently light and off-hand, but no doubt carefully-studied, attempt of his to make it appear that his wealth was obtained by the semi-sportive choice, at leisure moments, of profitable investments. Money - making was a very serious business with him, and he evidently estimated with penetrating vigilance the advantages offered by every situation for gainful bargaining. His education as a lawyer could not fail to be of immense use to him in stock-jobbing, and in his trading speculations generally. The Berlin Jew probably thought that a man of letters at Court, with appearances to keep up, would be an easy prey ; but the sharpest man in Europe would have found it dangerous to engage in a game of diamond cut diamond with Voltaire.

As biographer, as historian, as man of science, as philosopher even, this most versatile and comprehensive of authors might be separately delineated. The only point on which Carlyle seems to me to do him something less than justice is in respect of his humor. Carlyle denies Voltaire any humor except in the sense of wit and persiflage. The wittiest man he certainly was that ever existed, the man with the keenest sense of the ridiculous, and the nimblest adroitness in expressing his sense of it, and making the thing he wished to mock ridiculous in all eyes. But in such works as Zadig and Candide, particularly the second, there is much more than wit, much more than that thin laughter, from the teeth outward, of which Carlyle so often speaks. No books suggest to me more forcibly than those, not even Dickens's Christmas Carol or Scott's Antiquary, that the author thoroughly enjoys the fun that is going, and has in him a great power of laughter. In Candide there is a humor which, in breadth, equals that of Swift, in heartiness that of Cervantes; and a rollicking mirthfulness, and wild, bright, dancing gayety, wholly Voltaire's own. I wish Carlyle had given us a careful critique of Candide. It is surely, beyond all comparison, the finest philosophical satire in the world. And it has a great truth in it—this, in fact, was essential to its consummate excellence as a satire. The truth on which it rests is that optimism is a lie—a dangerous, hypocritic lie— poison of lead disguised in sweetness of sugar. Leibnitz's famed hypothesis of this being the best of all possible worlds was immensely in vogue in those days; and always it is a popular thing, pleasing to sentimentalists and simpletons, to paint up the world and to veneer pain with platitude. On this optimistic habit Voltaire has his say—not in cruel, Swiftian mood, but in that of resolutely honest, though wildly jocular, respect for facts; and so long as Dr. Pangloss and his observations

and adventures, his sketches of Europe tormented by armies
and rent by Lisbon earthquakes, his record of facts and optimistic decoration of the same, survive, the rose-water version
of things will be tempered, and most profitably tempered, by
derisive laughter.

Frederick and Voltaire met in transports of mutual admiration, lived for years in close intimacy, and parted with the unal-
terable persuasion, on each side, that the other was bad.   That
this was Frederick's estimate of Voltaire is open to no dispute; he attested it in word and in deed, unmistakable both.
Whether Voltaire was really convinced of Frederick's badness
is not so certain.   It is indeed a most difficult thing to know
what Voltaire in his heart believed on any subject whatever.
He professes faith in Christianity, abjuring only the supersti-
tions which have disguised or defaced Christianity, with an air
of engaging and frank sincerity — if his correspondent is a
bishop or cardinal.   He writes to Frederick in tones of im-
ploring tenderness, plaintively dwelling on his inextinguishable
friendship, until he convinces even Mr. Carlyle that he had a
genuine esteem for the King; and yet no expressions could
appear to come more authentically from the heart, no expressions could seem more deeply steeped in passionate conviction,
than those in which he reviles Frederick behind his back, and
compares him to a spiteful, untamable, dangerous ape.   Voltaire and the other French literary men with whom he tried to
surround himself did Frederick a great deal of harm.   One of
his remarks in a letter to Voltaire is that, if Voltaire's works
deserve statues, himself deserved chains; and the plain truth is
that, having summoned around him a number of men whose
books might suggest that they were incarnations of the cardinal
virtues, Frederick found them to be the most paltry, vain, envi-
ous, quarrelsome, unprincipled, and vindictive of human beings.
The most brilliant genius in Europe he believed to be the greatest scoundrel breathing.   And so, in a mind which, at the first,

seems to have been clear and radiant, open to all celestial influences, faith, hope, reverence, gradually died away; "star after
star went out, and all was night:" his settled conviction being
that there is more evil than good in the world, and that, if God
indeed made it, he has entirely forgotten it.

Among the many portraits of celebrated men, German and
not German, executed for us in the Life of Frederick, there occurs, near the end of the work, one of Pitt, Earl of Chatham,
which has a peculiar interest, as affording Mr. Carlyle an opportunity of expressing his final views upon English history since
the time of Cromwell, and upon the British system of constitutional government. Pitt was at the head of affairs for four
years before his brain gave way, and Mr. Carlyle avers that this
four years' kingship was the only one England has had "since
the constitutional system set in." Oliver Cromwell was indeed
a king after Mr. Carlyle's own heart, but "he died, and there
was nothing for it but to hang his body on the gallows."
Dutch William "to us proved to be nothing." While Sarah
Jennings ruled Queen Anne, and Marlborough commanded the
English army, there were "some gleams of kinghood for us."
Then came "noodleism and somnambulism," till Pitt arose.
His reign was brief, and since its close there has been "never
again one resembling him — nor, indeed, can ever be." That
Pitt should have believed in British constitutionalism is an
amazement to Mr. Carlyle. "Stranger theory of society, completely believed in by a clear, sharp, and altogether human head,
incapable of falsity, was seldom heard of in this world." The
point of its strangeness lies in its recognition of a king, who,
nevertheless, is tied up "with constitutional straps, so that he
cannot stir hand or foot for fear of accidents." No man like
Pitt will "ever again apply in Parliament for a career. 'Your
voices, *your* most sweet voices; ye melodious torrents of Gadarene swine, galloping rapidly down steep places — I for one
know whither!'"

These melancholy words are a condensation of that political philosophy of despair which Mr. Carlyle definitively adopted in the Latter-day Pamphlets. In kings, curbed by no representative Parliament, lies, he stubbornly insists, the only hope of peoples; these, being but Gadarene swine, cannot even know and choose them. How the kings are to be got at he does not say, giving us no glimpse of hope that somewhere, among high Alpine crags, there is an eyrie of royal birds, from which, as from the old castle of the Hohenzollerns, may one day descend a ruler fit to govern England. The era of order and authority has gone; the era of anarchy and dissolution has come. I am unable to extract any articulate theory of the prospects of modern society from Mr. Carlyle's later writings, except that which John Sterling saw dimly looming in Sartor Resartus, namely, that a series of recurrent catastrophes, deluging the world with blood, will at last destroy in all men the faith that nations can be representatively and freely governed, and will compel them to fall back upon some form of feudal despotism. It is strange and lamentable that Mr. Carlyle should find nothing worth mention in modern English history, except a few brief periods when England spent blood and money in Continental wars; nor can I imagine why, even if we accept this view, it should be less kingly for modern Englishmen to check the encroaching despotism of Napoleon under Wellington, than it was for their fathers to check that of Louis XIV. under Marlborough. Still more difficult is it for me to conceive why it should be in the nature of things impossible, even if war is granted to be a nation's only noble work, for a self-governing nation to understand the necessity of having, especially in time of war, a strong executive. Swine do not wish to be well governed, but rational men do. After what has been effected by consuls of Rome, by marshals of Republican France, by generals of Republican America, and by commanders of constitutional England, it is really too late to maintain that work as vigorous as the work of despots cannot be done by the servants of a free nation. Another question is, why the England which listened to, accepted, obeyed, exulted in Pitt, should have subsequently become incapable of recognizing heroic men, and even unworthy of being "asked kindly" by them for the authority to do great things in her name. But it is unnecessary to go further into these questions.

The Life of Frederick was Mr. Carlyle's last great book. His volume upon the Early Kings of Norway, though interesting from its Carlylian mannerism, and though wonderful as the work of a man nearly fourscore years of age, is not equal in power to his earlier writings; and his Niagara brochure, a protest against the latest extension of the franchise in England, is but the last and most extravagant of the Latter-day Pamphlets.

From the books of his afternoon and evening I turn, for manlier and stabler truth, to the books of his prime. His magnificent exposition of the uses of great men, his spirit-stirring exhortation to us to recognize and respect them, to select them for our governors and loyally to obey them, cannot, if we are wise, be neutralized for us even by his own astounding doctrine of despair that we, the many, are forever incapable of discerning those gifted few who are our natural governors. And if we exhaust the lessons of his books we have still the lesson of his life to fall back upon; a life instinct with true epical grandeur; a life upon which even calumny and slander have never cast a tarnishing breath; a life based upon realities.

ALFRED TENNYSON.

9*

CHAPTER I.

HOW vividly I remember the place and hour when I first became acquainted with Tennyson's poetry! Two volumes, one of them very tiny, then contained all that he had given to the world, and, as I carried these home from the library of King's College, Old Aberdeen, I stole one or two glances at my treasure. I was perfectly familiar with the poetry of Scott and Byron, had dipped into Keats and Shelley, and had read with passionate and boundless admiration the principal dramas of Shakspeare. The first thing in Tennyson on which my eye fell was the word-portrait of Lilian.

> Airy, fairy Lilian,
> Flitting, fairy Lilian,
> When I ask her if she love me,
> Claps her tiny hands above me,
> Laughing all she can;
> She'll not tell me if she love me,
> Cruel little Lilian.

This, at least, was new, and I thought it exquisitely nice. It reminded me of nothing I had ever read in poetry or in prose. No strong feeling was produced, but I experienced a distinct sensation of pleasantness like that of seeing a delicately tinted, quaintly shaped china cup, or finding a curiously veined, richly flushed shell on the sea-shore not far from which I was walking. The picture of Lilian was in the tinier of the two volumes. I closed it and opened the other. The lines that met my glance were these:

I see the wealthy miller yet,
    His double chin, his portly size,
And who that knew him could forget
    The busy wrinkles round his eyes?
The slow wise smile that, round about
    His dusty forehead dryly curl'd,
Seemed half-within and half-without,
    And full of dealings with the world?

In yonder chair I see him sit,
    Three fingers round the old silver cup—
I see his gray eyes twinkle yet
    At his own jest—

I liked this still better than Lilian—a good deal better; the old miller planted his chair in my memory forthwith, and has sat there ever since. Thirty years have gone by, and the fountain of genuine, refined, serenely intense enjoyment then opened to me is not yet exhausted. My life has been happier, greatly happier, than if I had not known Tennyson's poetry. There are many poets who have moved me more, and some whose works appear to me more wonderful, but I am not sure that there is any poet whatever who has produced in me so keen and deep a feeling of pleasure.

Of course I cannot be quite sure that my experience on this point has been general; but if I may take my own experience as an indication of the nature of Tennyson's influence generally, I should say that he is pre-eminently distinguished by the quality of *charm*. The element of sweetness pervades his poetry; sweetness too subtle to define, sweetness never permitted to cloy the reader, sweetness cunningly allied with, or relieved by, what the poet himself calls "the bitter of the sweet," but which, nevertheless, some critics have declared to be akin to weakness, and to have fitted him to be the poet of women rather than of men. For my own part, I accept the ancient canon of criticism—that poetry ought to be not only beautiful, but sweet (*Non satis est pulchra esse poemata; dulcia sunto*); and I think that it is in the exceeding beauty of Tennyson's that one chief secret of its sweetness lies.

It was in 1830 that his first thin volume appeared. Scott still lived, but his genius was in the sere and yellow leaf, and the works on which his poetical reputation rests had been long since produced. It is worth noting that Tennyson, in his boyhood, was insatiably fond of the poetry of Scott. No two poets could be more strongly contrasted in their habits of work, Scott being one of the most rapid and spontaneous, Tennyson one of the most elaborate of writers; and yet I fancy that Tennyson caught from Scott more than from any other of his poetical teachers the magical art—for magical it is in the sense of being entirely incommunicable by formal instruction—of fascinating his readers. Regarded as a poetical creator in connection not only with his poems, but his novels, Scott must be pronounced one of the greatest masters of charm that ever lived. He modestly claimed only one power, that of knowing how to "interest" readers; and while his faculties continued unimpaired he certainly did possess this power in a degree unexampled in recent times. It would be nearer the truth than such generalizations often are, to say that Tennyson has combined a studious elaboration, reminding us of Keats, with a warmth and depth of human feeling and a power of interesting readers comparable to Scott's.

The moment was not inauspicious for the appearance of a new poet. The fashions of thought and feeling which had prevailed during the last years of the war and the first years of the peace had begun to change. Byronism, still powerful with the multitude, was ironically smiled at in cultivated circles. Political excitement had succeeded to the fierce passions of martial conflict; industry was in the enthusiasm of youth renewed after long decrepitude; the genius of mechanism, already laying down here and there an iron line between town

and town, made infinite promises and awakened infinite hopes.
Carlyle and Macaulay had announced themselves in prose
essays more fervid and more richly ornamented than most of
the poetry of the waning generation, and almost as melodious.
"Many influences," as I have said elsewhere, "were working
toward undefined issues:" more aspiring and earnest thought,
more searching culture, bolder speculation, more exacting taste,
and deeper reflectiveness were replacing the somewhat shallow
and showy modes of the Regency.

Such was the time when Alfred Tennyson, a Cambridge
man of twenty-one, offered to the world, through the medium
of Mr. Moxon, his slender volume of poems.   In 1832 a
second appeared.   The great public paid slight attention to
either, but their share of critical notice was much above the
average obtained in similar cases.   One critic, writing in the
powerful *Westminster Review*, hailed the young author as a
man of original and mighty genius, who had the mallet hand
of the great Elizabethans, and promised higher things in English literature than recent years had seen.   The *Westminster
Review* was the organ of philosophical Radicalism, and Tennyson came from the Liberal University, Cambridge; both the
poet and the reviewer, therefore, were likely to be viewed
askance by Professor Wilson, who, under the name òf Christopher North, did the critical bludgeoning in that giant's castle of old Toryism, *Blackwood's Magazine.*   There were one or
two feeble poems in the first little volume, and some lines in
other pieces which showed a trace of that namby-pambyism,
that childishness, that tinkle-tinkle of pretty, meaningless
words, into which, at those rare moments when, like Homer,
he nods, Tennyson lapses.   Wilson quoted with scorn the
weakest lines he could find, pronounced Tennyson an "ingenious lad," declared that one sample was "drivel," another
"more dismal drivel," a third "more dismal drivel even than
that," and savagely belabored the Westminster panegyrist.   ·It

is interesting, however, to observe that, toward the end of his article, Wilson betrays strong misgivings as to the justice of his censure. He confesses that "he may have exaggerated Mr. Tennyson's not unfrequent silliness," but is sure that he has "not exaggerated his strength," and says that the extracts are better than anything else in his article. He gives the young poet very sound advice, telling him to get rid of affectation, to distrust verbal conceits and mere polish or brilliancy of diction, to court simplicity in thought and expression, to have more faith in great common truths, in home-bred feeling and pathos welling from the heart, than in superfine æsthetic sensibilities.

When we turn to the poems which Wilson had before him —those exclusively of the first volume—we are constrained to say that, though few, they were so original and excellent, that an experienced critic like Wilson might have spoken more enthusiastically about them. They bear curiously vivid marks of the Lincolnshire birth-land of the poet. In fact, knowing that Lincolnshire is one of the most flat and prosaic counties in England, a region of vast plains, interminable water-courses, with only a few trees of the willow and poplar kind, we seem, as we read these early verses of Tennyson's, to be actually transported to the scene. Already he has become Dantesque, if not in sternness of mood, at least in minuteness of delineation; he trusts nothing to random strokes, to sounding epithets; he sees the landscape and details its features. Not content with telling us that the lonely moated grange stood among gloomy meadows, with bats flitting about its weathered gables, he localizes it for us by minute specific touches.

> About a stone-cast from the wall
>   A sluice with blackened waters slept,
> And o'er it many, round and small,
>   The clustered marish-mosses crept.

Hard by a poplar shook alway,
　　All silver-green with gnarled bark :
　　For leagues no other tree did mark
　　The level waste, the rounding gray.

Scenery like this has not much on which the eye of the boy-poet can rest enraptured ; but what there is of beauty in it, or in the sky above it, will be dearly prized, exactly observed, accurately remembered.　Accordingly we find that, as a landscape word-painter, Tennyson is intensely true.　A painter might perfectly rely upon his statement of facts, and lay fearlessly on the canvas the "little clouds *sun-fringed*" which float in his skies.　This last epithet is quite exquisite in its accuracy, as you may satisfy yourself by noting, any summer day, how the little clouds, delicate pearl-blue in the middle, are lit with white fringes all round the edge, where the sun changes their vapor into snow.　This rightness of local color has distinguished Tennyson from first to last, and in respect of it a place has been claimed for him beside the very greatest poets.

Perhaps, compared with the great old masters,
　　His range of landscape may not be much ;
　　But who, out of all their starry number,
　　Can beat our Alfred in *truth of touch ?*

We have the sounds even, of the Lincolnshire landscape, as they reach the desolate Mariana in the night.

From the dark fen the oxen's low
　　Came to her.

He tells us in his Ode to Memory—for that poem is unmistakably autobiographic — that it was not upon "flaunting vines" that the eye of his memory opened, nor upon a waterfall sounding and shining forever, a pillar of white light seen against purple cliffs, but on a more prosaic scene.　Yet it is very dear to him, and he invokes memory to bring its quaint pictures back.

Come from the woods that belt the gray hill-side,
The seven elms, the poplars four
That stand beside my father's door,
And chiefly from the brook that loves
To purl o'er matted cress and ribbed sand,
Or dimple in the dark of rushy coves,
Drawing into his narrow earthern urn,
In every elbow and turn,
The filter'd tribute of the rough woodland.

Who will say that it is the landscape that makes the poet, and not the poet that sees tints of loveliness in, draws tones of melody from, the dreariest landscape, after Tennyson has found so much beauty in one of those drowsy brooks, that "purl" through cresses and over sand, a few feet below the level of the meadow? It is the love that lends the charm—the affection of a good heart for all that was associated with the peace and kindness of a happy home. There is, besides, as the poet himself informs us, a charm for the young describer in those subjects on which his capacities as a word-artist were *first* exercised. Ruskin says that Turner's drawing of hills, even when he had to represent the stupendous masses of the Alps, was to the last influenced by the forms of hill which he learned to draw in Yorkshire in his youth; and Tennyson, addressing the "great artist Memory," says:

Needs must thou dearly love thy first essay,
And foremost in thy various gallery
    Place it, where sweetest sunlight falls
    Upon the storied walls;
        For the discovery
And newness of thine art so pleased thee,
That all which thou hast drawn of fairest
    Or boldest since, but lightly weighs
With thee unto the love thou bearest
The first-born of thy genius.

And then he adds, in narrow compass, but with marvellous opulence, vividness, and precision of detail, a variety of aspects of Lincolnshire country, from the windy dunes that barricade the sea, to the garden which has been coaxed into beauty by tender culture, where the wind of the wold swoons and dies amidst scents of rose and lavender.

> Artist-like,
> Ever retiring thou dost gaze
> On the prime labor of thine early days:
> No matter what the sketch might be;
> Whether the high field on the bushless Pike,
> Or even a sand-built ridge
> Of heaped hills that mound the sea,
> Overblown with murmurs harsh,
> Or even a lowly cottage whence we see
> Stretch'd wide and wild the waste enormous marsh,
> Where from the frequent bridge,
> Like emblems of infinity,
> The trenched waters run from sky to sky;
> Or a garden bower'd close
> With plaited alleys of the trailing rose,
> Long alleys falling down to twilight grots,
> Or opening upon level plots
> Of crowned lilies, standing near
> Purple-spiked lavender.

Sometimes, on strong wings of imagination, he rises out of this region of pencilling fancy, becomes broad and bold in his stroke, and crowns his Lincolnshire landscape with splendors brought from other climes. So it is in that superb poem, The Dying Swan. The scene is sketched in the first four lines with a breadth worthy of the most mature artist.

> The plain was grassy, wild, and bare,
> Wide, wild, and open to the air,
> Which had built up everywhere
> An under-roof of doleful gray.

A few lines after this there is a marvellous bit of minute realization.

> Ever the weary wind went on
> And took the reed tops as it went.

Do we not seem to stand by the marsh and shiver with the shivering reeds? But the dying swan, singing in death, is too imaginative an affair to suit a strictly realistic scene in Lincolnshire. Accordingly there are features added which even England could not supply, and it is only in the foreground that the landscape continues to be exact and most expressive in its local truth.

> Some blue peaks in the distance rose,
> And white against the cold-white sky
> Shone out their crowning snows.
>   One willow over the river wept,
> And shook the wave as the wind did sigh;
> Above in the wind was the swallow,
> Chasing itself at its own wild will,
> And far through the marish green and still
> The tangled water-courses slept,
> Shot over with purple, and green, and yellow.

The comparison of the song of the dying swan to the acclamations of a mighty people is worked out with great imaginative power, and the poem ends with an enumeration of details of fen landscape in striking contrast with the few broad strokes that realize for us, in the outset, the gray sky and the grassy plain.

> Anon her awful jubilant voice,
>   With a music strange and manifold,
> Flowed forth on a carol free and bold;
>   As when a mighty people rejoice
> With shawms, and with cymbals, and harps of gold,
> And the tumult of their acclaim is roll'd
> Thro' the open gates of the city afar,
> To the shepherd who watcheth the evening star.
> And the creeping mosses and clambering weeds,
> And the willow-branches hoar and dank,
> And the wavy swell of the soughing reeds,
> And the wave-worn horns of the echoing bank,

> And the silvery marish-flowers that throng
> The desolate creeks and pools among,
> Were flooded over with eddying song.

One sublime component of landscape Tennyson had before him in perfection in his native Lincolnshire, namely, the sea; and, not forgetting Heine's remarkable series of pieces on the ocean, I know of no poems in which so grand, and, at the same time, so natural and heart-felt a use is made of the imagery of the world of waters as in those of Tennyson. He knows it in all its aspects: whether the " Norland winds pipe down the sea," or " the spangle dances in bight and bay," and " the rainbow hangs on the poising wave ;" whether the moonlight falls into the silent pools left by the tide, or the mid-day sun flames down on " glaring sand and inlets bright ;" whether the hollow ocean ridges roar into cataracts, or the low wave breaks monotonously on cold gray stones.

Among the products of his fanciful dallying in boyhood and youth with things relating to the sea, none are more delightful than the three pieces, unique in their quaint sprightliness and delicate bloom, in which he presents us with his notion of mermaids, mermen, and those Sirens who tried to entice the mariners of Ulysses from their ship. The Sirens, who to the Greek imagination were alarming creatures, beautiful exceedingly, but of deadly influence, he turns into " sea-fairies," with whose girlish beauty we cannot associate anything very wicked or dreadful.

> Slow sailed the weary mariners and saw,
> Betwixt the green brink and the running foam,
> Sweet faces, rounded arms, and bosoms prest
> To little harps of gold.

There is something nice and naïve in this transmutation of the serenely beautiful, but false and cruel, sea-women of the Greek legend into sweet, harmless fairies, by the tuneful boy of Lincolnshire. The most powerfully imagined, however, of the three poems is that on the mermaid. It is the office of imagination, in its most original mood, to summon up creatures of the mind, to bestow upon them local habitation and name, and, by sheer force of sympathetic realization, to give them poetic life. There is no test of imagination so sure and searching as capacity to endue its figures with life ; and nothing impresses me more deeply with the power of young Tennyson's imagination than the fact that, in this poem on the mermaid, he not only makes me think of the mermaid herself as alive, but of the sea-snake, which she fascinates, as also a living thing. In the following lines it is the mermaid that speaks.

> I would comb my hair till my ringlets would fall
>   Low adown, low adown,
>   From under my starry sea-bud crown
>   Low adown and around,
>   And I should look like a fountain of gold
>   Springing alone
>   With a shrill inner sound,
>   Over the throne
>   In the midst of the hall ;
>   Till that great sea-snake under the sea
>   From his coiled sleep in the central deeps
>   Would slowly trail himself seven-fold
>   Round the hall where I sate, and look in at the gate
>   With his large calm eyes for the love of me.

One of these earliest contributions which decisively announced the rise of a great poet is the Recollections of the Arabian Nights. The linguistic opulence of the poem is a small matter compared with the imagination required to plan and the fancy to execute such a work. The whole is a thing of the mind, a vision founded upon no fact, and yet we accompany the poet in his voyage down the Tigris with as distinct a realization of his whereabouts as if he were detailing the stages of a journey by boat between Oxford and Twickenham. We see the blaze of light falling in golden green upon the leaves, when suddenly the million tapers of the Caliphate illuminate the scene ; and we, as well as the poet, are drawn on in wondering curiosity until we are in presence of the monarch.

> Six columns, three on either side,
> Pure silver, underpropt a rich
> Throne of the massive ore, from which
> Down-droop'd, in many a floating-fold,
> Engarlanded and diaper'd
> With inwrought flowers, a cloth of gold.
> Thereon his deep eye laughter-stirr'd
> With merriment of kingly pride,
> Sole star of all that place and time,
> I saw him—in his golden prime—
> THE GOOD HAROUN ALRASCHID!

It is to be remarked of these first-fruits of Tennyson's poetical garden that there is nothing lawless, irregular, or extravagant about them, no trace of license, of moody bitterness, of discontent with the society into which the poet finds himself born, no conventional satire or flippancy. For him, as for Schiller, life is earnest, but not cruel, horrible, or contemptible. The conception he has formed of his mission as a poet is not more sublime than sincere.

> The poet in a golden clime was born,
> With golden stars above :
> Dower'd with the hate of hate, the scorn of scorn,
> The love of love.

It is his to sow the world broad-cast with seeds of truth, winging them and heading them with the flame of his burning words.

> Thus truth was multiplied on truth, the world
> Like one great garden show'd,
> And thro' the wreaths of floating dark upcurl'd,
> Rare sunrise flow'd.

> And Freedom rear'd in that august sunrise
>   Her beautiful bold brow,
> When rites and forms before his burning eyes
>   Melted like snow.

It can be said of Tennyson that he has never been false to the noble ideal which he set before himself in this poem.

The ballad of Oriana, and the lines entitled The Deserted House, occupy an important place in the tiny volume of 1830. They attest a massiveness of power, a breadth of imaginative handling, which the verbal richness, the almost too florid ornamentation, of several of the poems, would not lead us to expect. There is no fanciful word-painting, no elaborate laying on of tint after tint, in these pieces. Their supreme human interest swallows up all other interests. Imagination, merely painting, by a few broad sweeps of the brush, a stage suited to the occurrences described, dwells on the human action and passion alone. "The long dun wolds are ribbed with snow, and loud the Norland whirlwinds blow;" yes; but we think only of the lover who has slain his Oriana, and of the woe in his heart that seeks relief in the companionship of winter and of tempest. The five stanzas in which a dead body is compared to a deserted house are stern and true as the most severe of the sonnets of Milton.

> All within is dark as night:
> In the windows is no light:
> And no murmur at the door,
> So frequent on its hinge before.
> Close the door, the shutters close,
>   Or through the windows we shall see
>   The nakedness and vacancy
> Of the dark deserted house.

I may mention that Wilson, in his review, does full justice to Oriana and The Deserted House. The former he pronounces "perhaps the most beautiful" in the volume; and of the lat-

ter he says: "Every word tells, and the short whole is most
pathetic in its completeness—let us say perfection—like some
old Scottish air sung by maiden at her wheel—or shepherd in
the wilderness." The reader would do well to compare Tennyson's wonderful lines with Shakspeare's description of the
death of Cardinal Beaufort in the Second Part of Henry VI.
"Close up his eyes, and draw the curtain close," are Shakspeare's final words.

CHAPTER II.

M. TAINE ON TENNYSON AND ALFRED DE MUSSET.

I SAID that the first poetical efforts of Tennyson were characterized by an absence of extravagance, moody bitterness, discontent with existing social arrangements, and all kinds of lawlessness or irregularity. Neither of licentiousness nor of satiric fury do we find a trace. We have exquisite perception of beauty, impassioned love of beauty, resolute trust or at least sustaining hope that beauty, unaided by ruder spells, will prove strong enough to attract an audience fit though few. Meaner allurements are proudly rejected. "There is a strange earnestness," says Arthur Hallam, in his valuable review of his friend's poems, "in his worship of beauty." Not only do these poems display no vulgar smartness, but no fun, no humor, no caricature. A Greek severity of style is everywhere apparent; a reverence as of one for whom song has in very truth the sacredness of worship. And even if we decide that, in the work of Tennyson as a whole, there is too much of rule and measure, too marked an absence of humor, too little of the wild witching graces of freedom, we are, I think, safe in regarding the classic purity, the chastened enthusiasm—in one word, the moderation, of his first poems, as a good omen. The earnestness noted by Hallam was the best proof of capacity to take pains, the best guarantee of staying power. A similar spirit was strong in young Milton, strong also in Keats. Not only colossal genius, but concentrated and intense effort, are attested by *Endymion, Lamia, Hyperion.* I have been deeply impressed, in studying the early drawings of Turner, with the witness they bear that, for him also, the ministry of beauty

10

had in it something of the earnestness of worship. It is not
only that they show invincible patience, untiring pains, but
that there is in them an instinctive shrinking from all exaggeration, from all sensational emphasis, from all tendency to
jest. An imperious consciousness seems to warn him, as it
warned the great Greek sculptors, that the slightest indulgence
in caricature unfits the eye and the hand for their highest
achievement—namely, to strike, in obedience to the sovereign
imagination, the line of art. There is a gravity, a pure and
solemn graciousness, in all Turner's early work, which only his
superlative sense of beauty and love for light prevent from becoming formal. These are not the only instances that might
be adduced to prove that a religious earnestness of application,
and a reverent regard for purity and truth, have generally characterized the early period of those who have done great things
either in painting or in poetry.

"The early period;" yes, but has not Tennyson carried too
much into manhood the moral fastidiousness, as well as the patient elaboration, of his first manner? M. Taine answers the
question, not formally, indeed, yet explicitly enough, in the affirmative; and devotes fourteen or fifteen pages of his clever,
but, I must be permitted to say, rather shallow essay on Tennyson, to a demonstration that he is the *magnus Apollo* of
respectable mediocrity. M. Taine is too skilful a literary artist
to give us a regular argument upon the subject. He adopts
the more entertaining but equally effective method of setting
before us a picture of that particular aspect of English society
of which Tennyson's poetry is, he holds, at once the outcome
and the mirror, contrasting it with a corresponding picture of
French society, of which Alfred de Musset's poetry is the reflection, and leaving us to decide for ourselves, or rather sug-
gesting very clearly that we ought to agree with him in decid-
ing, that Alfred de Musset's is the greater and the manlier.
M. Taine is one of the liveliest of companions; and though it is

wholly impossible for me to quote so long a passage, I shall
need no apology for placing, in a brief summary, the main
features of his description of the country and people whose
favorite poet is Tennyson, and of the country and people
whose favorite poet is Alfred de Musset, before my readers.
He begins with England.

Landing at Dover or Newhaven, you take rail and survey
the country through which you are rapidly whirled. On all
hands there are gentlemen's mansions, on the sides of lakes, on
the shores of bays, on the banks of rivers, on every point where
the hill-side offers a picturesque view. In these houses live
the men who constitute the great world of England; London
is for them but a place of business (*rendezvous d'affaires*); in
the country they live, amuse themselves, receive their friends.
The mansion is pretty and well-arranged; the lawn, soft as
velvet, is rolled every morning. Here a huge rhododendron
blooms like a bouquet, murmuring with bees; there honeysuckles and roses hang in clusters and festoons; elms, yew-
trees, oaks show in the background their masses of foliage and
their strength of stem. If we walk into the meadows, we see
great oxen couched upon the rich grass, and sheep whose
snowy wool suggests that they have just come from the wash-
ing. Entering the house, we note the careful commodiousness,
we experience a studious anticipation of our least wants. All is
correct, trim, highly finished; you fancy that the objects have
had prizes at an Industrial Exhibition, or at least honorable
mention. A fastidious cleanliness, as of Holland, reigns around,
and the look of spick-and-span faultlessness is kept up by an
array of domestic servants three times as numerous as in France.
The whole domestic machine moves without a jar. You enter
into conversation with your host. You find that his soul is
serene and balanced. On leaving the university, he found his
path in life marked out for him; he had no call to revolt
against his Church, which is half reconciled to reason (*à demi*

raisonnable), or against the constitution of his country, which is nobly liberal.   He is tormented with no doubts, carried away by no theories, puzzled by no contradictions.   He marries, looks after his tenantry, performs magisterial duties, cultivates politics, gets up associations, speaks at meetings, inspects schools, introduces improvements.   He is potent and respected. He has the pleasures of self-complacency and of a quiet conscience.   "Without doubt he is cultivated and occupied ; he is instructed, knows several languages, is desirous of precise information, and is kept by his newspapers *au courant* of all new ideas and discoveries."   He rides, walks, hunts, lives much in the open air, and resists the ensnarements of that sedentary life which elsewhere conducts the man of our time to agitation of brain, enfeeblement of muscle, and excitement of nerves.   "Such is the world, elegant and sensible, refined in point of well-being, regulated in point of conduct, which the tastes of a dilettante and the principles of a moralist shut into a kind of flowery enclosure, and prevent from looking beyond it."

Could any poet, asks M. Taine, be better adapted for such a world than Tennyson ?   Without being a pedant, he is moral. You can read him in the bosom of the family.   He is not at war with society and life ; he speaks nobly, tenderly, of God and the soul, without ecclesiastical partisanship ; he has no violent expressions, no scandalous sentiments ; there is no fear of his perverting any one.   You could close his book, and straightway, without sense of contrast, hear " the grave voice of the master of the mansion, who, before his kneeling domestics, reads family prayers."   Nevertheless, in turning from his volume, you have on your lips a smile of pleasure.   Its landscape painting delights the lover of the country.   The ladies have been charmed with the poet's portraits of women.   "They love him because they feel that he loves them."   The exquisite finish of his style, his carefully-selected ideas, his chiselled sentences, suit the elegance of the scene.   His poetry seems made expressly for those citizens, rich, cultivated, and free, who are the chiefs of modern England. "It forms part of their luxury as of their morality, is an eloquent confirmation of their principles, and a costly piece of furniture in their saloons."

Crossing now to France, and taking train for Paris, we find ourselves in a different world. There are on the route chateaux of nobles and houses of rich citizens; but it is not among these that you can look, as in England, for the world of thought, of elegance, of taste, that leads the nation. There are two peoples in France—the dining, sleeping, yawning Provincials; the thinking, daring, wide-awake and voluble Parisians. It is at the men of Paris we must look if we would know France. Behold them in the evening when the streets are lit up, and a luminous dust-haze envelops the busy, noisy, elbowing crowd, that swarms before the theatres, and sits behind the panes of the *cafés*. Their faces are haggard, their glance unquiet, their gestures nervous. Most of them are bald before thirty. If they are to have pleasure, they must have it in the form of excitement. "The dust of the boulevard impregnates the very ice that they eat." Their joys are artificial, and, as it were, snatched hastily while hurrying past; there is in those joys, therefore, something distempered and irritating, something akin to the glare of the *cafés* and the hollow gayety of the theatres. Patience, moderation, are unknown. Haste and exaggeration are the rule. Their minds are athirst for excitement, and they require every day "a provision of colored words, of piquant anecdotes, of new truths, of diversified ideas." They soon fall victims to *ennui*, and yet *ennui* is to them insufferable. They devote all their powers to self-amusement, and yet find that they are hardly amused at all. The succession of excitement and fatigue keeps their nerves on the strain, and their varnish of heartless gayety cracks twenty times a day, to reveal, beneath, a gulf of pain and of burning. But how keen-edged is their intellect, how free is their spirit! How

that incessant friction has sharpened their wits! The great
town is cosmopolitan; all ideas start into life; there is no bar-
rier, no prescribed course, to restrain the flights of the mind.
Neither in Church nor in State have they any faith; the one
and the other is for them but a show (*on ne les regarde qu'à la
façon d'un spectacle*). All great questions are subject to doubt
and discussion. In the conflict of opinion every one must make
his faith for himself; and as this is practically an endless business, every mind lies open to all incertitudes. In the hollow
void thus formed, dreams, theories, fantasies, chase each other
like clouds.

Such is the world of which Alfred de Musset was the poet.
He must be read in Paris. The localities of his poems are
familiar to every Parisian, and the spirit and sentiments of the
Parisian crowd vibrate in every line. Its impetuous passions,
its feverish joys, its wild agonies, its aspirations, its dreams,
are reflected in his verse. "What! so young and already so
weary! So many precious gifts, a wit so fine, a tact so delicate, a fancy so mobile and so rich, a renown so early, a blooming out so suddenly of beauty and of genius, and at the same
instant anguish, disgust, tears, and cries! What a mixture!
With the same gesture he adores and curses. The eternal
illusion, the invincible experience, are in him side by side, to
combat and rend each other. He is old, and, at the same
time, young; a poet and yet a sceptic. The Muse and her
pacific beauty, Nature and her immortal freshness, Love and
its happy smile, all the procession of Divine visions, had hardly
passed before his eyes, when they were followed by the spectres of debauchery and of death, pouring out maledictions and
sarcasms." All this is terrible and sad, and from this poet of
the ghastly tumult of Paris, we turn to that other singer who,
"down there in the Isle of Wight," amidst his roses and his
honeysuckles, amuses himself with singing of Adelines and
sleeping beauties, of Arthur and the Round-table. It is very

pretty, and the audience of the English laureate is more distinguished than the *aristocratie de bourgeois et de bohèmes* that
rejoices in the poet of Paris; "but," says M. Taine, "I like
Alfred de Musset better than Tennyson."

M. Taine may claim to speak with authority of France, and
I have no doubt that his picture of Paris and his description
of the Parisian school of poetry may be relied upon as accurate; but it was not to be expected that he should see so
deeply into England, and while admitting that there is a good
deal of truth in his sketch of English life, with its elegance
and comfort, I must insist that it falls far short of the whole
truth. Even what truth there is in the presentation of Tennyson, as the poet of the cultivated and comfortable classes of
England at the present day, falls away from it if applied to
the England of fifty years ago. Tennyson has educated his
public. When he appeared, a few were attracted, a much
larger number were repelled, but all admitted that the music
was new. It may be doubted whether many country gentlemen read him even now. He began his poetical career in
England at almost exactly the same time when Alfred de
Musset began to publish in France. The poetical position of
both men was determined by their relation to that extraordinary genius who had made the whole European world his
audience a few years before. Like Carlyle in prose, Tennyson in poetry represents a triumphant reaction against the
spirit and influence of Byron. Alfred de Musset, on the other
hand, was the poetical child of Byron. I do not presume to
pronounce upon his merits as a whole, but from what I know
of his writings, I should hold it fair to describe him as a less
earnest, less sagacious, less able Byron, superior, probably, in
some poetical qualities, to his model, but greatly his inferior
in strength. It is, indeed, remarkable that the Byronic school,
having died out quickly and utterly in the land of its birth,
should have flourished vigorously in France.

The question of essential importance, however, is whether it was Tennyson or Alfred de Musset that went to the purer fount' of inspiration, whether it was the accepted poet of France or the accepted poet of England, that based his reputation upon the nobler originality, the deeper and stabler truth. Byron was the poet of rebellion; and in their own place and time, rebellion and revolution are indispensable. You must storm the batteries of old error, oppression, falsehood, before you can lay bare a foundation for the new temple of truth. A revolutionary process has been going on in our general European system for upward of a hundred years, a process involving enormous demolition; and if any one reflects for a moment on the number of infamous and cruel laws, class privileges, effete institutions, pernicious dogmas, which in that time have been swept from the face of the earth, and from the heaven of man's spirit, he will find reason to conclude that this revolutionary demolition has been salutary and beneficent. But far more difficult than the work of demolition is the work of construction; and it is to constructive work that the greatest poets, thinkers, and men of science in the last fifty years have been more and more addressing themselves. Granted that all falsehood and superstition must be cast aside, that kings and priests, if they are to exist at all, must, like the Sabbath, exist for man—What then? Is there any truth that will endure? Are there any laws in accordance with which society can be rightly constituted? M. Taine does not allege that Alfred de Musset professed or attempted to answer such questions. There is, indeed, a living French poet who has attempted to answer them, and I confess to being somewhat surprised that M. Taine, in selecting from the French poets of the century a rival to Tennyson, did not mention one who seems to me incomparably greater than De Musset—Victor Hugo. To rear the edifice of a reconstituted society is a task which Hugo expressly undertakes, proudly claiming for himself to have con-

tributed something toward setting up two of its chief pillars—
"respect for the old, and love for children." But it is not to
the streets of Paris, glaring with the lights of *café* and theatre,
that Victor Hugo would send the poet for a true inspiration;
nor would he accept it as the task of the poetic seer to minister
new excitement to forlorn profligates, whose faces are wrinkled
and heads bald at thirty. His counsel to the poet is to go to
the woods and the shores, and to beat out the music of his
verse in tune with the song of the leaves, and the hymn of the
waves; or, to take it in his own bright, melodious French:

> Va dans les bois, va sur les plages;
> Compose tes chants inspirés
> Avec la chanson des feuillages
> Et l'hymne des flots azurés!

Adopting Hugo's imagery, I should say that, among the pillars of a reconstituted society which Tennyson has labored to
set up, the most conspicuous have been responsibility to God
and reverent trust in the Supreme; faithfulness and constancy
in the marriage relationship; mutual affection and mutual fitness, in contradistinction to worldly advantage, as the terms and
motives of the marriage tie; love of mankind, love of country,
enthusiasm for knowledge, faith in freedom, hope of immortality. A stable and happy society in which these, or at least
most of them, should not be found, is the dream of sheer delirium, and any "liberty" which should permit them to be
trodden down would but unchain the brute elements in human
nature, to tear and rend each other in the slime of a devastated
civilization. I do not, of course, affirm that society must be
constituted as our present society is constituted. Plato, in his
Republic, sketches a very different order of society from ours,
but in his scheme also license and disorder are absolutely put
down. The day has gone by when civilized nations can un-
dergo the discipline of political or ecclesiastical slavery; but it

is essential to their well-being that the discipline of freedom, the discipline of virtue, the discipline of justice, truth, and law, should succeed the discipline of slavery. Tennyson has been the foe of conventionality, and has cut sharp and deep into " the social lies that warp us from the living truth;" as M. Taine admits, he has been the partisan of no ecclesiastical system; but Carlyle himself has not looked with loftier disdain upon those ravings of the Satanic school, according to which the coming race is to obliterate all moral codes, and to pig in sensual brutishness amidst the crumbling *débris* of the sanctuary and the home.

M. Taine has all the right in the world to prefer Alfred de Musset to Tennyson, but I cannot recognize the justice of his application to Tennyson of the term " dilettante." To be scrupulously fair, indeed, I must say that he does not give Tennyson this name directly. Alfred de Musset, he tells us, " was not a mere dilettante, content with tasting and enjoying;" and as he is expressly contrasting the French with the English poet, we cannot help feeling that he intends to imply that Tennyson is what De Musset was not. A dilettante poet I take to be one who puts together his poems and polishes them up verse by verse, in the spirit in which a virtuoso collects cups or vases, for the pleasure of looking at them, and the vanity of being known to possess them, without any view to expressing truth or benefiting mankind. Once or twice Tennyson may have written in this mood. The Day-dream, perfect as is its workmanship, is little more than a play of fancy, light and brilliant as the tints of sunlight in foam. If its delightfulness is not enough to warrant its production, as I believe it to be, the poet has no better apology for producing it. But in general Tennyson writes with deep and solemn purpose, and it ought to have occurred to M. Taine that an English poet might be as sincere and earnest in celebrating a pure morality as a Parisian poet in revelling in paradox, extravagance, and vice. . Tennyson grew up amidst a society which, in the vital organs, was substantially sound. In France the succession, since the seventeenth century, had been triumphant Popery, consolidated despotism, Voltaircism, rebellion, despair; in England it had been Protestantism, constitutional government, scientific and industrial progress. If Alfred de Musset proved his sincerity by being true to the prevailing sentiment of France, Tennyson proved his sincerity by being true to the practical ideal which he saw around him in England. Society in France I believe to be now much more sound; but it is of the France and the England of 1830 that I have been speaking.

CHAPTER III.

THE earliest poem in which Tennyson takes for his subject
the marriage relationship is The Miller's Daughter, the
earliest, and in some respects the most delightful, though not,
by a great deal, the most powerful. What is, perhaps, most
surprising about it is that it should be the work of a young
man ; for though it breathes the sweetest freshness of youth,
it contains the quintessence of what I cannot define except by
coining the queer-looking word, "elderly-gentleman-liness."
It is pervaded with the pensive quietude, the subdued but mellow radiance, of life's afternoon. With consummate dramatic
power the unmarried poet relates the experience, and depicts
the feelings, of one who has been long married. Other young
poets have bestirred themselves to give burning expression to
the ardor of the lover—to show the flaming eyes and heaving
breast of Apollo as he *pursued* his Daphne ; young Tennyson
throws his strength into verses in which are described the proud
constancy, the satisfied devotion, of the husband.

> Look thro' mine eyes with thine. True wife,
> Round my true heart thine arms entwine ;
> My other dearer life in life,
> Look thro' my very soul with thine !

Goethe's, Schiller's, Burns's lovers speak of moments of
rapture ; this lover speaks of the peace that has been the atmosphere of his life for many years.

> The kiss,
> The woven arms, seem but to be
> Weak symbols of the settled bliss,
> The comfort, I have found in thee.

The scenery of the poem is no longer that of Lincolnshire; it is that which surrounds Cambridge. A mill is pointed out in the vicinity of that town, which can stand as well for the mill of the poem as the cottage under Salisbury Crags at Edinburgh, shown as that of David Deans, stands for the cottage in which Scott placed the heroine of the Heart of Midlothian. Here, as always, Tennyson paints by particular touches, not by vague generalities. In the crystal eddies of the mill-dam, the minnows "glance and poise." If you looked at minnows every day for a week, you would not learn much more about them than lies in these two words. The whole biography of a minnow is there. To poise in perfect stillness and almost perfect invisibility, and then to become visible for the tenth part of a second in that strange glancing gleam, or glint, of the silvery side, as the tiny creature darts away—this is the complete circle of a minnow's observable activities. There is a subtle imaginative keeping, though the poet probably had no thought of it, between the quietness of emotional tone throughout the poem and the circumstance that the lover first sees Alice reflected in water. "The reflex of a beauteous form, a glowing arm, a gleaming neck," caught his eye in the mill-dam as he was listlessly angling; he looked up, he saw her leaning from the window-ledge, their eyes met, and they loved. There is a curious maturity of observation in the following verse:

> My mother thought, What ails the boy?
> For I was alter'd, and began
> To move about the house with joy,
> And with the certain step of man.

A piece of knowledge this which one would expect to be more clearly apprehended by an old man than by a stripling. Often, indeed, as life goes on, and as we live over again in meditation the scenes of by-gone years, our own actions and the feelings and motives of other people, which were dim to us at the time, become distinct. Experience has taught us to interpret. In exquisite dramatic accordance, also, with the retrospective interest of an elderly man, is the specification of objects which happy love clothed, for him, with a new charm. Had you asked the youth, he would have spoken only of his Alice; the old man dwells garrulously, and with Morland-like picturesqueness of detail, on the objects which had been gilded with the light of love.

> I loved the brimming wave that swam
>   Thro' quiet meadows round the mill,
> The sleepy pool above the dam,
>   The pool beneath it never still,
> The meal-sacks on the whiten'd floor,
>   The dark round of the dripping wheel,
> The very air about the door
>   Made dusty with the floating meal.

But quiet as is its tone and tenderly domestic as is its spirit, there is nothing conventional in The Miller's Daughter. Here, as decisively as in any work of Byron's or Alfred de Musset's, the rights of the heart are asserted, the essentials of a just, wise, and seemly marriage are postulated, the fundamental ordinance on which a healthful and happy social system can be reared is laid down. When I refer to Byron and Alfred de Musset I do not mean to imply that they give the good side of domestic life, but only that Tennyson casts out, as vigorously as they cast out, the demon of worldliness that turns the hearth into a pandemonium. Writers of the atheistic-revolutionary or Satanic school jeer at the family, laugh domestic sentiment to scorn, and thus in effect advocate a dissolution of society. Tennyson addresses himself to the more difficult task of denouncing the conventionality and Mammon-worship, by which marriage may be rendered the vilest slavery and the bitterest torment, while, at the same time, he celebrates that true marriage, that healthful and holy family life, which has its roots in mutual affection, in mutual fitness, and which is guarded by a constancy as strong as heaven's blue arch, and yet as spontaneous as the heart-beats of a happy child.

In this poem we have these things only in germ, but the germ is beautiful. The young squire marries the miller's daughter. All the traditions of worldliness, all the rules of Mammon-worship, all those buckram proprieties which are woven into shrouds and cerements to crush the soul out of living men and women, are defied in such an arrangement. Had the boy-squire's father been alive, it might not have been practicable. In no instance does Tennyson make the father bend his pride to consent to the unequal marriage of a son or of a daughter. But, like Chaucer, Shakspeare, and Ruskin, he seems to have lurking somewhere in his heart a faith that women, when they *are* good, are infinitely good, infallibly wise, capable of getting nearer to the mother-heart of nature than men. The squire, had he been alive, might have made insuperable difficulties, but the mother did what was right.

> And slowly was my mother brought
> To yield consent to my desire:
> She wish'd me happy, but she thought
> I might have look'd a little higher;
>
> And I was young—too young to wed:
> "Yet must I love her for your sake;
> Go fetch your Alice here," she said:
> Her eyelid quiver'd as she spake.

What I have said, however, in praise of Tennyson's treatment of the marriage relationship would require grave qualification if The Miller's Daughter were his sole poem upon the subject. Perfect as the piece is in its way, its character is too negative. The Satanic people might plausibly urge that, if this is a delineation of ideal marriage, it is indeed a state of ignoble though pleasurable repose. The bracing and inspiring influences of rightly constituted marriage are not even hinted at.

The good old fellow who runs on with garrulous *näivete* over the walnuts and the wine seems to have done little or nothing all his life but look into his wife's eyes. The limitation of Tennyson's sympathy with action in the period of the first efflorescence of his genius is very remarkable. But when we glance along his works as a whole we perceive that he, least of all men, can be accused of having eulogized marriage as a state of sweetly sordid rest. The main theme of his most extensive poem is the marriage relationship, exhibited in the persons of a king and queen, and viewed as the centre and crown of the beneficent influences that act upon society. Had the marriage of Arthur been all that the king and his poet deemed it capable of being, Arthur would have found the influence of Guinevere not only a stay, but an impulse and inspiration in his kingliest enterprises. The scheme was baffled; but its being baffled is the tragic burden and issue of the poem; nor is it easy to imagine Tennyson or any other poet conveying an impression of the positive and aggressive energy for good of such marriage as Arthur's and Guinevere's *might* have been, so strong as the reader now derives from the collapse of the king's hopes and the defeat of his life-purpose, and from Guinevere's cry of passionate despair—

> Ah, my God,
> What might I not have made of Thy fair world,
> Had I but loved Thy highest creature here!

It is, in fact, to be noted that The Miller's Daughter is almost the only poem in which Tennyson sets married life in a wholly prosperous and happy light. The Lord of Burleigh disguises himself as a landscape-painter, marries a village maiden, and is a gentle and joyous husband; but the lady sinks into her grave under the burden of an honor unto which she was not born. In Lady Clare it is a single incident in the course of Lord Ronald's and his bride's true love that furnishes the subject of the poem. The perfect trust and perfect constancy

of a woman's heart are its theme; but, though the reader sees
in long perspective the happy wedded life of Lord Ronald and
his low-born wife, he actually hears only of their espousals. In
Locksley Hall, in Maud, in Aylmer's Field, and in that Arthurian Epic which gathers itself together out of many idyls, love
becomes, through worldliness, pride, or faithlessness, the source
of sorrow.

It is, I fancy, to Locksley Hall, more than to any other of his
poems, that Tennyson owes his hold upon the heart of the
world. Partly this may be due to its being a peculiarly fascinating and piquant variation from his usual manner. It is trochaic in melody, the beat coming upon the first syllable in the
metrical foot, instead of, as in the iambus, on the second.

> Comrades, leave me here a little while, as yet 'tis early morn;
> Leave me here, and when you want me, sound upon the bugle horn.

The corresponding iambic measure, in which the beat falls
upon the second syllable, is exhibited in Macaulay's Lays of
Ancient Rome.

> Then Ocnus of Falerii, rushed on the Roman three,
> And Lausulus of Urgo, the rover of the sea.

Tennyson generally uses the iambus. This is, indeed, the organic unit of measurement in English verse, forming the basis
of the heroic stanza, rhymed and unrhymed, as employed in all
the monumental works of English poetry, the Canterbury Tales,
Paradise Lost, Pope's Essays and Satires, Dryden's Fables, the
Shaksperian drama, the Faëry Queen, the Revolt of Islam,
the Excursion, Don Juan, and Childe Harold. So long ago as
the days of Aristotle the iambic measure was considered "the
natural march-music of action and business." It is most consistent with the genius of the English tongue, and Tennyson
has evidently found it harmonize best with that patient elaboration, that minute and symmetrical working-up of the pictures

of his mind, in which he delights. In Locksley Hall, however, he gives voice to one of those high tides of emotion in which the full heart sometimes relieves itself, and on such an occasion it was more important to render the force and billowy splendor of the waves, to express sympathy with their glorious freedom, their magnificent boldness, and wildness, and tumult, their clapping of hands and revelry of infinite laughter, or passionate sobbing of grief, than to mould their particular forms or to time their march upon the beach. In Locksley Hall, therefore, as under somewhat different conditions in Maud, Tennyson escapes from that iambic regularity, that dignified perfection and repose, so characteristic of his general manner, into the fitful and ringing, or wildly wailing and throbbing, melody of a trochaic measure. Rich as is the color of the poem, there is a racy picturesqueness in it from first to last—a picturesqueness of soldier-life and vagrant comradeship, of windy hillocks by the sea, and morning copses and bugle-horns.

The soldier tells, or rather chants, his own history, of which the key-note is his unhappy love, moving at once with superb energy of soldier-like purpose into the heart of the tale, bringing the past before us with all the vividness of the present. In two lines he dismisses his comrades, and makes for himself a solitude; in four more, of as masterly breadth and precision of landscape painting as could be paralleled in the language, he sets before us the scene of the occurrences that are to form the main subject of the poem.

> 'Tis the place, and all around it, as of old, the curlews call,
> Dreary gleams about the moorland, flying over Locksley Hall;
> Locksley Hall, that in the distance overlooks the sandy tracts,
> And the hollow ocean-ridges roaring into cataracts.

Then follows that description of the youth of an aspiring, gifted, ardent boy of the nineteenth century, which has been familiar as household words upon the lips of all readers of

English poetry for something like forty years. We of the last quarter of the nineteenth century cannot, as I hinted before, without a strong imaginative effort, recall the enthusiasm of eager hope with which, in its second quarter, people still looked into the future and saw the commercial, scientific, and political "vision of the world." The "fairy tales of science" have now rather lost their charm for those who, causelessly or with good cause, charge our prominent scientific authorities with wishing to chain up or to petrify the soul of man in universal materialism. "The promise" that the future "closed" for the youthful singer of Locksley Hall has turned out to be a dreadfully prosaic future of iron roads, towns choked with soot, rivers poisoned with chemicals, nations taxed to the bone for iron-clads, groaning, as in the hopeless anguish of a torturing dream, under nightmare armies. The "argosies of magic sails" have, with lamentable frequency, carried cargoes of shoddy. "The parliament of man, the federation of the world," has not yet come; but the Parliament of the United Kingdom has been repeatedly reformed; and yet it is not found that "the common-sense of most" holds the gallant Major O'Gorman in awe, or prevents Mr. Roebuck from announcing with exultation that "Benjamin Disraeli rules the world."

From visions of the future, however, as well as from vague glancings at Orion and the Pleiades, our soldier-bard is suddenly recalled to a personal, present, and transcendent interest. A few brief, living touches place his Amy before us, and, though we are furnished with almost no details of his love-making, yet so vivid and so suggestive are those few that are given—so effectually do they awake our own imagination and set it to work—that we seem to have been present at ever so many delightful wanderings amidst the copses dewy with dawn, and to have again and again, with the lovers, watched the sun reddening the evening wave. He told his love; then

On her pallid cheek and forehead came a color and a light,
As I have seen the rosy red flushing in the northern night.
And she turn'd—her bosom heaving with a sudden storm of sighs—
All the spirit deeply dawning in the dark of hazel eyes—
Saying, " I have hid my feelings, fearing they should do me wrong;"
Saying, " Dost thou love me, cousin ?" weeping, " I have loved thee long."
Love took up the glass of Time, and turn'd it in his glowing hands ;
Every moment, lightly shaken, ran itself in golden sands.
Love took up the harp of Life, and smote on all the chords with might;
Smote the chord of Self, that, trembling, pass'd in music out of sight.

This last line concentrates into itself a large part of Tennyson's noble conception of love, or conception of the nobleness
of love.   Love annihilates Self, even while exalting it, and
crowns life in a twofold ecstasy of renunciation and attainment.   A life of unselfish, beneficent occupation—of sympathy
in mental culture—of co-operation in benevolent effort—would
have been the natural sequel.   But Mammon and conventional
respectability tore the strings from the harp of Life, and shattered the glass of Time with its golden sands.   " Puppet to a
father's threat, and servile to a shrewish tongue," Amy jilts
her soldier laddie ; and the latter has no better consolation than
to pour out anathemas upon paternal worldliness, to describe
the misery of a forced and loveless marriage, to inveigh, not
without bitterness, against the girl, and to rush out into the
melancholy yet stimulating activities of life.   Exception has
been taken to the tone which the discarded lover assumes toward her who has forsaken him, as if its harshness were impossible for a generous and magnanimous nature, which Tennyson, without question, intends his lover to be.   But I think
this is to bring the air of Rosa Matilda romance over the world
of reality.   It would have been very pretty for the poet to
represent his lover as breathing nothing but admiration and
broken-hearted forgiveness.   Schiller might perhaps have told
the story so ; but Goethe or Shakspeare would not.   Heroes
that are too angelic cease to be men.   Too high-flown mag-

nanimity is the sign-manual of the false sublime. Tennyson
makes it plain, also, that it is only what is degrading in Amy's
life that the lover blames and hates.   Beneath all his angry
words, his love for her remains ineradicable, and he would wish
her happy, if he could do so and at the same time save her
from his contempt.

After ranging through many moods, sometimes rising almost
into rapture, sometimes settling almost into despair, the hero
decides for progress and for hope.

> Not in vain the distance beacons.   Forward, forward, let us range.
> Let the great world spin forever down the ringing grooves of change.
> Thro' the shadow of the globe we sweep into the younger day:
> Better fifty years of Europe than a cycle of Cathay.

The "palsied heart" and the "jaundiced eye" are but signs
of disease; the idol-gods of fashion and conventionality may
be hurled from their thrones; "one increasing purpose" runs
through the ages, "and the thoughts of men are widened with
the process of the suns."

Aylmer's Field seems to me the companion picture to Locksley Hall.   It is one of the most tragic of Tennyson's pieces—
one of the saddest, sternest, and I would almost add mightiest,
poems in the world.   In Locksley Hall we see desecrated affection making two persons unhappy; in Aylmer's Field the
blight is more deadly and more comprehensive.   I know nothing of Tennyson's in which the moral earnestness is so prophet-
like as in this great poem.   With all the might of his genius
in its maturity, he pours a molten torrent of indignation and
of scorn upon that pride which is, perhaps, the central vice of
England, that pride which displays itself in many ways—in
pride of birth, in pride of gold, in pride of insular superiority,
and which is always desolating and deadly.   Pride, in this instance, trampling love under its feet, provides exquisite pain
for all the chief personages in the poem, and obliterates two
ancient families from the face of the earth.

Briefly, in stern, compact enunciation, the moral thesis or text of the poem is stated in the opening lines.

> Dust are our frames; and, gilded dust, our pride
> Looks only for a moment whole and sound;
> Like that long-buried body of the King,
> Found lying with his urns and ornaments,   .
> Which at a touch of light, an air of heaven,
> Slipt into ashes and was found no more.

Edith, the daughter of the proud squire, is one of the love-liest of Tennyson's creations; lovely specially in this, that her beauty, far more than commonly with Tennyson, is a thing of the heart and the mind, rather than of form or feature. We love her for her home-bred truth and tenderness, for the deli-cate tact and gentleness that make her a ministering angel in the dwellings of the poor. Tennyson opens his sketch-book, and gives us a series of pen-pictures—each a line or two in length—of the laborers' homes which she loved to haunt.

> Here was one that, summer-blanch'd,
> Was parcel-bearded with the traveller's-joy;
> In autumn, parcel ivy-clad; and here
> The warm-blue breathings of a hidden hearth
> Broke from a bower of vine and honeysuckle:
> One look'd all rose-tree, and another wore
> A close-set robe of jasmine sown with stars:
> This had a rosy sea of gillyflowers
> About it; this, a milky way on earth,
> Like visions in the Northern dreamer's heavens,
> A lily-avenue climbing to the doors;
> One, almost to the martin-haunted eaves
> A summer burial deep in hollyhocks;
> Each, its own charm: and Edith's everywhere.

What a constellation of English cottages!

Edith, the squire's daughter, loved Leolin, the rector's son, who in all fine and strong qualities was worthy of her; who,

even in ancientness of blood, was not much her unequal, and
lacked only gold.

> A grasp
> Having the warmth and muscle of the heart,
> A childly way with children, and a laugh
> Ringing like proven golden coinage true,

attested his sterling goodness. The boy and girl, neighbors
in the village, grew up together. The pride of the squire and
his lady blinded them to the possibility that love could arise
between the two. When at last the truth flashes on them,
Leolin is spurned from their door like a dog. He and Edith
remain true to each other; but, by her imprisonment in the
Hall and its grounds, and by interception of letters, in a way
analogous to that practised against Lucy, in the Bride of Lam-
mermoor, they are debarred from all intercourse. After twenty
months of silence Edith droops, and then

> Some low fever ranging round to spy
> The weakness of a people or a house,
> Like flies that haunt a wound, or deer, or men,
> Or almost all that is, hurting the hurt—
> Save Christ as we believe him—found the girl
> And flung her down upon a couch of fire,
> When careless of the household faces near,
> And crying upon the name of Leolin,
> She, and with her the race of Aylmer, past.

Maddened with the news of her death, Leolin strikes to his
heart a dagger, which she had once playfully presented to him.
The rector, Leolin's brother (their father had been dead long
before), is asked by the mother of Edith to preach a funeral
sermon on her daughter, and he preaches on the desolation
wrought by pride. It is one of the grandest and most terrible
sermons ever penned. We know nothing in modern verse, except Jean Ingelow's wonderful sermon, preached by the old pastor to fisher-folk in the little chapel by the sea, that will at all

compare with it.   It was the death-knell of the guilty parents.
The lady died soon; the squire lingered for awhile, but spoke
only one word, " desolate."

> Then the great Hall was wholly broken down,
> And the broad woodland parcell'd into farms ;
> And where the two contrived their daughter's good,
> Lies the hawk's cast, the mole has made his run,
> The hedgehog underneath his plantain bores,
> The rabbit fondles his own harmless face,
> The slow-worm creeps, and the thin weasel there
> Follows the mouse, and all is open field.

" The two contrived their daughter's good !"—the irony of
that is tremendous in its calmness.   In this poem Tennyson
has reaped the highest honor man can attain, namely, that of
adding to the Scripture of his country ; nor should I think it a
much less dark or pernicious error than the pride which caused
all this woe, to hold that the Almighty could speak only through
or to Jewish seers, and that there is no true inspiration in such
writing as this.

CHAPTER IV.

THE TWO VERSIONS OF MAUD.

MAUD has a particular interest for me; I reviewed it long since; and with that postprandial freedom which I craved liberty to take, I have to inform my readers that my old criticism now seems to me unsatisfactory. The poem appeared in 1855, the year when I first got into journalistic harness, and I was one among many ardent admirers of Tennyson who expressed disappointment with the production. [In my essay on Tennyson and his Teachers, published (along with others) in America in 1858, and in this country in the following year, I devoted several pages to a notice of Maud, reiterating my unfavorable judgment, declaring the work deficient in beauty, and pronouncing it, on the whole, a failure. That estimate I still look upon as not altogether wrong or unreasonable; and I have the comfort of believing that it was much less wrong in 1855 than it would be if first put forward in 1879.] When Maud appeared, Tennyson's reputation rested upon the early poems and In Memoriam, and the difference between these and the new work was hardly more startling than the inferiority of the new to the old seemed to be conspicuous. But now that Tennyson has written as much again as he had then given to the world, and when it has been proved that the somewhat crude realism of Maud was but a passing variation in his manner of composition, the right of such a poem to take its place in the totality of his works—to play its part in the general Tennysonian orchestra—is much more easily recognizable. What is still more important, the Maud of 1879 is a much more excellent poem than the Maud of 1855. With a massive sense and a profound geniality of temper, that do him infinite credit, setting him on a pedestal of marked superiority to those authors who, when sharply criticised, have hugged their defects and shrieked out asseverations of their infallibility, Tennyson listened to reasonable criticism, and mended his work. The man who can do that must be rarely free of egotism, and have a command of his own spirit entitling him to Solomon's signalization as greater than one that taketh a city. To retouch a poem without destroying it is, besides, one of the most difficult operations that a poet can undertake, and I do not know that I have ever been more struck by any display of literary skill than I am by the consummate power and the supreme felicity of Tennyson's improvement of Maud.

First of all, it is now announced as a Monodrama. We are thus taught to expect that the hero will speak throughout for himself. If it is improbable that he should do so in real life, still we are bound to recognize the right of an artist, within certain limits, to adopt what artistic machinery he pleases, every possible arrangement involving more or less of improbability. In the next place, the work is now divided into three Parts. This is an important circumstance. It leaves us at liberty to suppose, if it does not actually suggest, that some change in the position or state of the hero has taken place in the interval between Part and Part. That bewilderment which we naturally felt in listening to a speaker who at one moment was sane, and at another mad, at one moment at large, and at another in confinement, is thus obviated. The changes in melody, also, are thus rendered more appropriate. "If," I remarked in my earlier criticism, "we suppose the poem written by its hero at four or five different periods of his life—a period of silly juvenile raving, a period of joyous love, a period of melancholy but tranquil madness, a period of raging insanity, and a period of new life and reviving strength—its rugged and varying rhythm will appear more defensible." Tennyson has now marked off the great divisions of the poem. Part I. contains the period of restless, unhappy, cynical youth, and also that of accepted and exultant love; Part II. is occupied with successive phases of anguish and madness; in Part III. the rage has passed away, the fires of madness have ceased to burn into the heart and brain, and the meaning and result of the whole are summed up in words of mature and lofty wisdom. By this arrangement, and by the stanzas—extending in one instance to so many as a hundred lines—deftly added here and there, that atmosphere of stormy tumult and distraction, which flickered over the poem, is penetrated with shafts of light; the brooding cloud lifts; and though the air continues electric, we can perceive with entire distinctness the direction of the road and the articulation of the landscape.

The opening lines contain a description, by the sole speaker, of the scene of a catastrophe which has a determining influence on the whole course of the poem.

I hate the dreadful hollow behind the little wood,
Its lips in the field above are dabbled with blood-red heath,
The red-ribb'd ledges drip with a silent horror of blood,
And Echo there, whatever is ask'd her, answers "Death."

For there in the ghastly pit long since a body was found,
He who had given me life—O father! O God! was it well?—
Mangled, and flatten'd, and crush'd, and dinted into the ground:
There yet lies the rock that fell with him when he fell.

Did he fling himself down? who knows? for a vast speculation had fail'd,
And ever he mutter'd and madden'd, and ever wann'd with despair,
And out he walk'd when the wind like a broken worldling wail'd,
And the flying gold of the ruin'd woodlands drove thro' the air.

I will here digress for a few moments. The last of these lines is quoted by Mr. Ruskin as an exquisite example of the " pathetic fallacy." The true imagination, he holds, works with nature as nature is; the fancy imputes to nature some-

thing which is not there, as prodigality to the crocus, cruelty
to sea-foam, speech to lilies and roses. The sere leaves of
autumn woodland are not gold, and in calling them gold,
Tennyson (thinks Mr. Ruskin) indulges in the pathetic fallacy.
Though, however, the temperament which admits the pathetic
fallacy is "that of a mind and body in some sort too weak to
deal fully with what is before them or upon them, borne away,
or over-clouded, or over-dazzled by emotion," there is "a point
beyond which it would be inhuman and monstrous" for a
man to push the government of his feelings, "a point at which
all feverish and wild fancy becomes just and true." This
point was reached, for example, by a Hebrew prophet when he
contemplated the destruction of the Kingdom of Assyria.
The thought of so tremendous an occurrence "dashed him
into a confused element of dreams," and filled the world with
strange voices. A similar effect was produced when he realized
the presence of the Deity. "The mountains and the hills shall
break forth before you into singing, and all the trees of the
field shall clap their hands." If Mr. Ruskin intends to maintain that these last words, though a noble instance of pathetic
fallacy, are inferior to truly imaginative work, I can only say
that I have never met with and cannot conceive any purer or
nobler exertion of imaginative power. The "pathetic fallacy"
which the great critic points out in the last of Tennyson's
lines is pronounced by him exquisite, chiefly, I presume, because whether it is to the son, musing distractedly on his virtually murdered father, or whether it is to the father himself,
rushing about the woods in frantic despair, that the leaves take
the semblance of flying gold, the excitement in either case was
great enough to render the transformation "just and true."
But if it is just and true, why call it a fallacy at all?

After considering the matter long and carefully, I find it
impossible to draw a line, with Coleridge, between fancy and
imagination, or, with Ruskin, between the pathetic fallacy and

true imaginative work; but I doubt whether there is any poem of Tennyson's in which we have more instances of what Mr. Ruskin would call pathetic fallacy than in Maud. In the first verse things so tenderly sweet as blooming heather, and so delicately beautiful as lichened rock, are bathed in blood; in the third, the falling leaves become gold, swept from the bankrupt branches by the blast of ruin; farther on, we hear the scream of a maddened beech dragged down by the wave; the gale is a ruffian, catching and cuffing "the budded peaks of the wood:" and then, as circumstances change, the birds cry, and call "Maud, Maud, Maud, Maud;" the stars look down in new brightness of sympathetic splendor; the larches and pines are "perky" about a rival's castle; and roses, lilies, larkspurs, passion-flowers, weeping, listening, crying, all become vivaciously alive in the presence or expectation of the lady. If the reader pleases, he may set down all these modifications of the actual fact of things to pathetic fallacy, and call them signs that Tennyson belongs to the "inferior school of poets;" inferior, that is, to the school of the great creative masters, Homer, Dante, Shakspeare; to my thinking, they illustrate the normal action of imagination, but not uniformly of imagination in her mood of deepest inspiration and most majestic power. Although there is a subtlety inexpressible by words in the closeness of truth to nature which may be, and perhaps generally is, *preserved* by imagination in her noblest action upon things, it is, nevertheless, the splendor of the flash of irradiating, transfiguring, or even distorting and darkening color, poured by imagination over the object, rather than the mere truthfulness of delineation, which is the index of imaginative power. "Thou hast clothed his neck with thunder" —that is a more nobly imaginative description of the neck of the war-horse than if it were literally correspondent with fact. Mr. Ruskin, I presume, would say that, as the hero in Maud is a typical representative of conditions of thought in the morbid

nineteenth century, the prevalence of pathetic fallacy in his
outpourings is peculiarly appropriate; the statement I should
prefer is that the poem furnishes admirable illustrations of a
particular kind of true imagination. The difference may, after
all, be one of words. *Revenons à nos moutons.*

Having shown the dreadful hollow behind the little wood,
the mono-dramatic speaker adds a few touches delineative of
the circumstances attending the discovery of the corpse:

> I remember the time, for the roots of my hair were stirr'd
> By a shuffled step, by a dead weight trail'd, by a whisper'd fright,
> And my pulses closed their gates with a shock on my heart as I heard
> The shrill-edged shriek of a mother divide the shuddering night.

He then launches into fierce denunciation of society. The
blessings of peace have been made a curse; the lust of gain,
the spirit of Cain, are abroad; "who but a fool would have
faith in a tradesman's ware or his word?" Such a state of
things is not peace, but civil war, and war viler than that of
the sword, because underhand. Then follow four verses, which
may take rank with the most picturesque invectives uttered by
Hood in verse or Carlyle in prose, against our poor nineteenth
century:

> Peace sitting under her olive, and slurring the days gone by, ˋ
> When the poor are hovell'd and hustled together, each sex, like swine,
> When only the ledger lives, and when only not all men lie;
> Peace in her vineyard—yes!—but a company forges the wine.

> And the vitriol madness flushes up in the ruffian's head,
> And the filthy by-lane rings to the yell of the trampled wife,
> And chalk and alum and plaster are sold to the poor for bread,
> And the spirit of murder works in the very means of life.

> And Sleep must lie down arm'd, for the villanous centre-bits
> Grind on the wakeful ear in the hush of the moonless nights,
> While another is cheating the sick of a few last gasps, as he sits
> To pestle a poison'd poison behind his crimson lights.

When a Mammonite mother kills her babe for a burial fee,
And Timour-Mammon grins on a pile of children's bones,
Is it peace or war? better, war! loud war by land and by sea,
War with a thousand battles, and shaking a hundred thrones.

That war would purge the moral atmosphere, and convert knaves into heroes, was this philosopher's fixed persuasion. If an enemy's fleet "came round the hill," and a battle-bolt or two "sang" from the foam, "the smooth-faced, snub-nosed rogue would leap from his counter and till, and strike, if he could, were it but with his cheating yard-wand, home."

This climax gave great offence to the unfavorable critics of the first edition of Maud. "The author of Locksley Hall and the Palace of Art," it was said, "demands our assent to profound social and moral truths, by letting us hear a jargoning, ill-conditioned misanthrope declare that a tailor, dishonest in peace, would be brave in war." The censure, I still think, was reasonable. But exactly at this point Tennyson now adds three very noble stanzas, attuned so perfectly to the context that, unless the reader were minutely familiar with the earlier version, it could not possibly occur to him that they had been inserted, and yet admirably adapted to set the poet right with his audience. After depicting the snub-nosed man of thrums lunging with his yard-wand, the speaker pauses, rebukes himself, tacitly admits the weakness of his reasoning:

What! am I raging alone as my father raged in his mood?
Must *I*, too, creep to the hollow and dash myself down and die,
Rather than hold to the law that I made, nevermore to brood
On a horror of shatter'd limbs and a wretched swindler's lie?

Another point is to be noted here. All obscurity as to the nature of the father's death is cleared up. Formerly we might vaguely have fancied that he had been murdered; now we learn that he dashed himself down and died. Tennyson thus complies with what is assuredly a sound canon of criticism—

that, though the artist has a right, with a view to quickening
the attention, and stimulating the curiosity, of his reader, to
impart or to withhold information bearing upon his plot, yet
he is not at liberty to perplex the reader with mere puzzles, or
to refuse definite statement of such facts as are necessary to
the intellectual and imaginative appreciation of his work.   One
other change ought to be observed in this highly-important
opening chant.   The last line in the first edition was as follows:

> I will bury myself in my books, and the devil may pipe to his own.

In the second version the words are, "I will bury myself in
myself," etc.   No change could be more expressive.   Of all
the graves in which a man can bury himself, self is the worst
—haunted with the ghastliest visions, tormented with the
loathliest worms.   Accordingly, the recluse now sinks into a
mood of contented and cynical Epicureanism, more venomously
bad than that in which he had invoked Mars to shame Belial
and Mammon.   He will let the world have its way.   Man
preys on his weaker brother, as the swallow on the May-fly, the
shrike on the sparrow; "nature is one with rapine, a harm
no preacher can heal."   Let Poland fall, let Hungary fail; "I
have not made the world, and He that made it will guide."

> Be mine a philosopher's life in the quiet woodland ways,
> Where if I cannot be gay let a passionless peace be my lot,
> Far off from the clamor of liars belied in the hubbub of lies;
> From the long-necked geese of the world that are ever hissing dispraise,
> Because their natures are little, and, whether he heed it or not,
> Where each man walks with his head in a cloud of poisonous flies.

This is his point of deepest degradation; henceforward he
ascends.   He hears Maud singing "by the cedar-tree in the
meadow under the Hall," and her song is of such regal and
martial strain, so full of hope, joy, patriotism, courage, that it
sounds like an appeal to the higher nature that slumbers within him.   He awakes to the nobleness of self-contempt, and

could weep not only for the meanness of the time, but for himself, "so languid and base." Then they meet; she touches his hand, and smiles upon him; the thought of that blissful moment is as "a delicate spark of glowing and growing light" through the dark hours, but with morning his suspicion and cynicism return. He fancies that Maud may wish to make him the victim of her pride, nay, that she may have an eye to his vote when her brother presents himself at the hustings in the approaching election. Her brother treats him with haughty disdain, and he responds with fiercest scorn. As both her father and her mother are dead, the brother is in a position to exercise great influence over her. The notions of the lover— for now he is clearly in love with Maud—both as to the brother's character and as to the probable nature of his influence over the lady, are indicated in these lines:

> What if tho' her eye seem'd full
> Of a kind intent to me,
> What if that dandy despot, he,
> That jewell'd mass of millinery,
> That oil'd and curl'd Assyrian Bull,
> Smelling of musk and of insolence,
> Her brother, from whom I keep aloof,
> Who wants the finer politic sense
> To mask, tho' but in his own behoof,
> With a glassy smile his brutal scorn—
> What if he had told her yestermorn
> How prettily, for his own sweet sake,
> A face of tenderness might be feign'd,
> And a moist mirage in desert eyes,
> That so, when the rotten hustings shake
> In another month to his brazen lies,
> A wretched vote may be gain'd.

"That oil'd and curl'd Assyrian Bull" I consider one of the crudest lines Tennyson ever penned. It is grotesque, without being expressive, and has neither true facetiousness, nor cutting

11*

satire, nor imaginative appropriateness, nor fanciful aptness.
The last thing the "wingèd beast from Nineveh" suggests is a
dandy. Rossetti has entered into the spirit of the creature
very differently :

> A human face the creature wore,
> And hoofs behind and hoofs before,
> And flanks with dark runes fretted o'er,
> 'Twas bull, 'twas mitred Minotaur.

Under the auspices of the brother, a "new-made lord, whose
splendor plucks the slavish hat from the villager's head," pays
his addresses to Maud, and adds jealousy to the other distract-
ing influences at work upon our hero's mind. But love gradually gains the mastery, and as love becomes strong and hopeful his better self begins to gain the ascendant. In a new
verse, which greatly strengthens the poem at this point, he
wishes that he could hear Maud once more singing "the chiv-
alrous battle-song" that formerly roused him ; and two lines,
set by themselves, are like a jewelled clasp knitting the earlier
to the later portions of the first Part—

> And ah, for a man to arise in me,
> That the man I am may cease to be!

The process, however, of the new man's emergence into light
is gradual, and immense and subtle power is displayed by the
poet in tracing the hero's variations of mood. Some of those
crudenesses, nevertheless, occur, which were characteristic of
the poem from the first, and are now, I suppose, destined to
remain in it to the last. It is crude, I think, to speak of Maud
coming down from a window to meet her lover "like a beam
of the seventh Heaven ;" and I doubt whether, at this stage of
the love-cure, he ought to have been represented as still so
morbidly self-conscious as is implied in his saying, of Maud's
beauty—

I know it the one bright thing to save
My yet young life in the wilds of Time,
Perhaps from madness, perhaps from crime,
Perhaps from a selfish grave.

The words I have put into italics are more curiously expressive of a brooding, inward-looking habit of mind than any I know in literature. But the triumph of love now becomes complete. He is a new man, living in a new world, and as he looks up to the stars, he addresses them thus:

And ye, meanwhile, far over moor and fell
Beat to the noiseless music of the night!
Has our whole earth gone nearer to the glow
Of your soft splendors, that you look so bright?

At this point occurs the most extensive and important of all the additions made to the first draft of the poem. It had been objected, not, I think, without grounds, that, though the hero might love Maud, there was no cause why she should love him. "Why," it was asked, "does Maud love him? He is a sour, sulky, shabby, purposeless soliloquizer. By all physiological and physiognomical symptoms, he is sallow, squalid, with his skin hanging loose on his bones, with matted hair, shuffling, awfully conceited, probably squint-eyed, demonstrably a sloven. Why does she love him? He hates her kith and kin, and all men and women. He is moody, idle, given to night-walking. Worst of all, he writes such verse as this:

I kiss'd her slender hand,
  She took the kiss sedately;
Maud is not seventeen,
  But she is tall and stately.

Why does Maud love him? He goes about with an aggrieved, injured-looking, gingerly expression, which makes you expect he is going to knock you down. Poe's raven is the only hero in literature who is nearly his counterpart; but the raven had some dignity, and was not so intensely egotistical, so profoundly selfish, as this ungainly, gaunt, and ominous Radical."

The verse quoted has always seemed to me very bad, and I am not sure that the unlikelihood of Maud's loving such a man is much exaggerated. But in the passage now added a potent reason is assigned why Maud should be attracted toward the solitary, why she should sympathize with his distress, understand his brooding indignation with things in general, and give him the opportunity of making her acquainted with that better nature which lies indestructible beneath his repellent manners. When Maud's mother was dying, and she and her brother hung over the bed, she, the mother, had said something which left an indelible impression upon Maud's mind :

> She said,
> When only Maud and the brother
> Hung over her dying bed—
> That Maud's dark father and mine
> Had bound us one to the other,
> Betrothed us over their wine,
> On the day when Maud was born ;
> Seal'd her mine from her first sweet breath.
> Mine, mine by a right, from birth till death.
> Mine, mine—our fathers have sworn.

This bond had been dissolved by the suicide of one of the fathers, in a state of madness induced by the ruin brought upon him by the dishonorable conduct of the other ; but Maud had always nursed the idea that it was her duty, for her mother's sake, to be reconciled to the son of the suicide, and while he was gloomily cursing the family of his father's destroyer, Maud was kneeling in foreign churches praying that they might be friends. This accounts for everything ; varies the interest and deepens the pathos of the poem ; is, in one word, masterly. The love of Maud is no longer unintelligible.

I need not linger on what remains of the poem. The brother and the enamored lord surprise Maud and her lover at a secret interview. A duel between the brother and the lover follows, and, as Aytoun said, *procumbit humi bos*, the dandy-despot falls. This brings back over the sky of the hero darkness thicker than had formerly wrapped it. A new verse definitely informs us that Maud dies—the fact could previously be but guessed at. The mind of her lover, never very firm, now gives way completely, and when he next opens his mouth to sing, he is a moaning invalid over whom there seem to have passed long years of grief and pain. He is haunted by a phantom, that reminds him of Maud, but cannot be recognized for her:

> A shadow flits before me,
> Not thou, but like to thee :
> Ah Christ, that it were possible
> For one short hour to see
> The souls we loved, that they might tell us
> What and where they be.

A period of wilder lunacy succeeds. He fancies himself dead and buried, and yet, with the contradictory persuasions of frenzy, that he is with others in an asylum, or, perhaps, with a company of dead men in some unimaginable place:

> See, there is one of us sobbing,
> No limit to his distress ;
> And another, a lord of all things, praying
> To his own great self, as I guess ;
> And another, a statesman there, betraying
> His party secret, fool, to the press ;
> And yonder a vile physician, blabbing
> The case of his patient—all for what ?
> To tickle the maggot born in an empty head,
> And wheedle a world that loves him not,
> For it is but a world of the dead.

He wails and raves, cursing the "wretchedest age since time began," that cannot even "bury a man ;" while now and then the thought of Maud comes in like a gleam of pallid light, a strain of melancholy music.

In Part III. he is sane and calm, capable of sympathizing with the high ambition of a people resolute to do justice, and glad that England, in the Crimean war, has undertaken to wreak God's wrath " on a giant liar," and that there flames along the Baltic deep " the blood-red blossom of war with a heart of fire."

Last of all, six lines are added, in which the meaning and moral of the poem are grandly summed up.

> Let it flame or fade, and the war roll down like a wind,
> We have proved we have hearts in a cause, we are noble still,
> And myself have awaked, as it seems, to the better mind ;
> It is better to fight for the good than to rail at the ill :
> I have felt with my native land, I am one with my kind,
> I embrace the purpose of God, and the doom assign'd.

Instead of calling Maud, as we now have it, a failure, I should pronounce it well worthy of Tennyson's genius.

CHAPTER V.

IT is from the publication, in two volumes, in 1842, of the early poems in the form which they have since, on the whole, until quite recently, retained, and of English Idyls and additional pieces, that the world-wide range and firm establishment of Tennyson's reputation are to be dated. With great judgment and self-control, he put aside comparatively weak and questionable matter, a large portion of which had been pointed out by Christopher North—dressing his line of battle like a skilful general, for the decisive charge. When thirty years more had gone by, he was able to replace in his volumes not a little of what had, in 1842, been excluded—as troops might be admitted to a festive review, or triumphant march into the capital, which had not been trusted in the crisis of the campaign. It would have been well—I cannot help remarking as I pass—for the fame of his reviewer if a similar process had been applied to his own works. Professor Wilson had great genius and rich culture; he impressed Scott as fitted to become the foremost man of his time, and awoke enthusiasm in the more severely critical mind of Carlyle; his writings abound with imaginative exuberance, pathetic tenderness, and picturesque beauty: but he composed with immense haste; had no idea, as is memorably evinced in his critique on Tennyson, when he began an article, of what he might say before he got to the end; and availed himself, for the sake of present effect, of any triviality, jest, political squabble, or social fashion which flitted across the public stage at the moment. The consequence is that the *Noctes Ambrosianæ,* to which Wilson's contemporaries never referred save in terms of positive ecstasy, has, as a whole, become unreadable by the present generation, nor am I sure that even the selection from it by so qualified a hand as Mr. Skelton's will escape oblivion; while the critical and descriptive essays, though redolent of life and brightness, and containing "rural pictures" which, says Ebenezer Elliot, "before God, I believe have lengthened my days on earth," have many passages which weaken the general impression.

And yet Wilson was professionally a critic. So rare is the combination of a consummate critical faculty with great productive genius. Tennyson has proved himself to be possessed of both. I am far from sure, however, that his emendations of his early poems have been uniformly felicitous. He appears to me to have sometimes forgotten what was due to the feelings under which he first wrote—the legitimate jurisdiction and authority, within limits, over the text, of that fervor of inspiration which originally gushed forth in song. In the first version of Clara Vere de Vere, for example, there is this stanza:

> Trust me, Clara Vere de Vere,
>   From yon blue heavens above us bent,
> The grand old gardener and his wife
>   Smile at the claims of long descent.

These words came glowing from Tennyson's heart, and the third line took the ear of the world, and obtained domicile in current literature wherever the English tongue is spoken. In recent editions it runs thus—

> The gardener Adam and his wife,

a line which, formally unexceptionable though it may be, would hardly have struck the general imagination like the other.

In the later version of A Dream of Fair Women, a much more important alteration occurs. In that poem, one of Tennyson's masterpieces, there is a description of the death of Iphigenia. My readers may recollect that, according to the legend, or, rather, according to a particular version of the legend, Iphigenia, the daughter of Agamemnon, was offered up as a sacrifice to appease the wrath of Diana, who detained the Greek fleet, about to sail for Troy, by a dead calm. In the poem, Iphigenia, who speaks for herself, is very effectively placed face to face with Helen, the original cause of the Trojan expedition. The poet calls upon the daughter of Agamemnon to join him in admiring Helen's sovereign beauty, and the manner in which Iphigenia meets the appeal is recorded in the following verses :

> But she, with sick and scornful looks averse,
>   To her full height her stately stature draws;
> "My youth," she said, "was blasted with a curse:
>   This woman was the cause.
>
> "I was cut off from hope in that sad place,
>   Which yet to name my spirit loathes and fears:
> My father held his hand upon his face;
>   I, blinded with my tears,
>
> "Still strove to speak: my voice was thick with sighs,
>   As in a dream. Dimly I could descry
> The stern, black-bearded kings, with wolfish eyes,
>   Waiting to see me die.
>
> "The tall masts flicker'd as they lay afloat,
>   The temples, and the people, and the shore;
> One drew a sharp knife through my tender throat,
>   Slowly—and nothing more."

The last stanza I quote from memory. Its second, third, and fourth lines have not appeared thus in any edition published within the last twenty years, and I am not aware of having seen them in this form since boyhood; but they stamped themselves upon my imagination at once and ineffaceably. The picture, as drawn by the poet, is perfectly in keeping with itself, perfectly complete. With a force of dramatic sympathy which it would be quite reasonable to compare with Shak-

speare's, Tennyson enters into the person of the girl that is
about to die, and enables the imaginative reader to see through
her eyes, to gasp and sigh with her in her swooning anguish.
All is intensely real; no pathetic fallacy modifies the dreadful
fact. The light glimmers on her through blinding tears; she
strives, as one has so often striven in a nightmare dream, to
speak, but cannot; the actual kings are there, not phantoms or
spectres, but stern men with black beards and wolfish eyes.
Dimly, through burning tears, the whole scene quivers before
her, "the temples, and the people, and the shore," and then,
real as everything else is real, the knife is drawn slowly through
her throat. The altered version of the stanza runs thus:

> "The high masts flicker'd as they lay afloat;
>   The crowds, the temples, waver'd, and the shore;
> The bright death quiver'd at the victim's throat;
>   Touch'd: and I knew no more."

This is not merely inferior to the former, but, what by no
means necessarily follows, is capable of being demonstrated to
be inferior, by reference to simple and irrefragable principles
of criticism. Is it permissible that Iphigenia should begin her
narrative in such a fervor of imaginative passion, that she no
longer speaks of the scene or of herself, but *sees* the whole in
vision; and should thus carry it on until it reaches its most
agitating point; and should *then* sink back into the infinitely
colder and less imaginative mood of one who speaks from
memory, who coolly separates her present self from her past,
and talks of herself as "the victim?" She passes from poetic
vision—"*I* strove to speak, *I* could descry"—to prosaic recollection. If criticism has any principles at all, such a declension
ruins the passage. The "bright death" is due to the same unparalleled error. Seeing, as Tennyson originally saw, through
the eyes of the swooning girl, the wolfish kings and flickering
crowd, he had no leisure to think of "bright death," no idle

ingenuity of spirit to hit upon such a conceit. "Bright death" means nothing in particular, and would probably suggest a flash of lightning if the knife had not been mentioned in the earlier version.

I am entirely at a loss to conjecture how Tennyson could have been led to substitute the second form of the stanza for the first, unless he allowed his better judgment to be overruled by some critic,* learned, perhaps, but devoid of imagination. Is it possible that skill in the use of words may occasionally produce in readers a vividness of imaginative perception greater than that of the poet when he wrote them down? If I live for a hundred years, I shall always *see*, with my mind's eye, those wolfish kings, those quivering masts, that shore, that crowd, and most clearly of all that knife, as they flashed on me when Ten-

---

* After the publication of this conjecture in the *Literary World*, I received a letter from Mr. Edward Taylor, of 90 Isledon Road, Finsbury Park, containing this pertinent and interesting passage:

In the *Literary World* for October 25, you very naturally inquire, What could have induced Tennyson to make such an unfortunate alteration as he has introduced into the speech of Iphigenia, in the Dream of Fair Women? Perhaps the following may furnish a clew to the mystery:

Tennyson's second volume was reviewed, shortly after its first appearance, in the *Quarterly*, in an article that, in its way, is a masterpiece of mock respect—full of sardonic praise and spiteful depreciation most dexterously insinuated.

On coming to the Dream of Fair Women, after promising the reader a touch of pathos that will throw into the shade every previous device of ancient or modern poets, the reviewer quotes the lines—

> "The tall masts flicker'd as they lay afloat;
> The temples, and the people, and the shore;
> One drew a sharp knife through my tender throat,
> Slowly—and *nothing more!*"

And then adds, "What touching simplicity! What genuine pathos! *He cut my throat—nothing more!* One might indeed ask, *What more she would have?*"

I suppose this was too much for the youthful poet, and he altered the poem regardless of all consequences.

nyson showed me them in my boyhood; and it amazes me beyond measure that he should not resent, as I have resented, the
attempt to dissolve the vision by intrusion of bright deaths,
and historical talk about victims.

I said that the Dream of Fair Women is one of Tennyson's
masterpieces. There is none of his poems more characteristic,
few, if any, more splendid. It would be one of those poems
to which I should refer if I were asked to name a number of
pieces illustrative of the superiority of the pictorial art that
works with words to the pictorial art that works with color.
What could painter or sculptor do to represent a reader, who
has been hanging over a book of poetic tales, first, as he gradually reproduces their scenes and images while falling asleep,
and then, as he continues to exhibit the same train of influence
under the conditions of profound slumber? Poetry is the art
that paints the soul—that describes thought and feeling in their
mental fountains, and that is confined to no one moment, to no
one mood.

When a man is wide awake he thinks and imagines connect-
edly; when he is deep asleep, his dreams have again a dream-
like coherence and consistency; in the interval between perfect
wakefulness and perfect sleep, image follows image without definable bond of connection. All this Tennyson realizes in the
opening of the Dream of Fair Women. He has been reading
Chaucer's Legend of Good Women, and his head is full of it
when he begins to nod.

> Those far-renowned brides of ancient song
>   Peopled the hollow dark, like burning stars,
> And I heard sounds of insult, shame and wrong,
>   And trumpets blown for wars;
>
> And clattering flints batter'd with clanging hoofs:
>   And I saw crowds in column'd sanctuaries;
> And forms that pass'd at windows and on roofs
>   Of marble palaces;

>   Corpses across the threshold; heroes tall
>   Dislodging pinnacle and parapet
>   Upon the tortoise creeping to the wall;
>   Lances in ambush set.

Hitherto there is something like unity in the varying pageantry; it has all some connection with the pomp, and circumstance, and terror, and anguish of war; but in the next verse, which I need not quote, we are out at sea, the wind scattering the surf over sails and masts; and then the imagery returns to the land.

>   Squadrons and squares of men in brazen plates,
>   Scaffolds, still sheets of water, divers woes,
>   Ranges of glimmering vaults with iron grates,
>   And hush'd seraglios.

The last stage, when sleep is just gaining the mastery, is represented with astonishing felicity:

>   All those sharp fancies, by down-lapsing thought
>   Stream'd onward, lost their edges, and did creep
>   Roll'd on each other, rounded, smooth'd, and brought
>   Into the gulfs of sleep.

Then all is calm. The dreamer has wandered far in an old wood.

>   Fresh-wash'd in coolest dew,
>   The maiden splendors of the morning-star
>   Shook in the steadfast blue.

In this old wood he sees the fair women whose beauty and sorrow are commemorated in the poem. The most elaborate of the portraits is that of Cleopatra. At an exceedingly early age—in mere boyhood—Tennyson's imagination had been impressed by the Egyptian enchantress, and in puerile rhymes from his pen which still exist, and some of which have been brought under my attention by that indefatigable bibliographer, Mr. Shepherd, are to be found touches which reappear in this finished and almost faultless poem.   The exultation of the wild, splendid, witch-like woman when she thinks of her Antony is grand.

> " We drank the Libyan sun to sleep, and lit
>   Lamps which outburn'd Canopus.   O my life
>   In Egypt!   O the dalliance and the wit,
>   The flattery and the strife.

> "And the wild kiss, when fresh from war's alarms,
>   My Hercules, my Roman Antony,
>   My mailed Bacchus leaped into my arms,
>   Contented there to die !"

The Bacchus had figured as a "captain" in the boyish rhymes.

With almost too strong a sense of contrast, we turn from Cleopatra to Jephtha's daughter.   She comes through the wood singing.

> " The torrent brooks of hallow'd Israel
>   From craggy hollows pouring, late and soon,
>   Sound all night long, in falling thro' the dell,
>   Far heard beneath the moon.

> " The balmy moon of blessed Israel
>   Floods all the deep-blue gloom with beams divine:
>   All night the splinter'd crags that wall the dell
>   With spires of silver shine."

The crags turned to frosted silver in the moonlight—how delicately beautiful !   And how solemn, how true to the religious enthusiasm of a Hebrew maiden, are not only these verses, but all that "the daughter of the warrior Gileadite" sings and says !   At last

> She lock'd her lips ; she left me where I stood :
>   " Glory to God," she sang, and past afar,
> Thridding the sombre boscage of the wood,
>   Toward the morning-star.

A sifted and brilliant diction is appropriate in a poem of which the subject is the love and the sorrow of renowned queen-like women; but I think that the exclusion of all common words—the elaborate burnishing of phrase—is carried in this poem almost to the point that suggests artificiality. The very grass is rather the enamelled green of costly porcelain than the mossy sward of an old English wood. Cleopatra lays bare the "polished argent" of her breast. Surely it would have been better to say silver than argent. Christopher North scored one against Tennyson when he hinted that dewdrops might look as well though not always called "orients." The dread of commonplace has lain heavy on Tennyson. In an address to Queen Victoria he does not dare to speak of Waterloo, but must say "Hougoumont." All artists, as well as authors in prose and verse, labor in these days under the disadvantage involved in the fact that people have been singing, carving, painting now for some three thousand years, and that all themes and all words are getting used up. The vast deluges of literature of the hour—newspapers, magazines, novels, books of travel—which flood all highways, take the edge and brilliance, the freshness and power, from word and image. Such is the condition under which literary artists of these times must work. Some men are driven by it to wild extravagance, like Walt Whitman; but the more general effect is that which has been produced in the case of Tennyson, namely, to enforce an intensity of elaboration unknown in former times. The great poetic schools of England have always favored high finish, but no poet since Spenser, with the doubtful exception of Keats, has finished so carefully as Tennyson. Rossetti's poetry also strikes me as an agony of effort and elaboration. Whatever may be the qualities of such verse, it cannot be said to come, as Goethe said that his came, straight from the heart of the poet, like the song from the bird on the bough. How different the manner in which Burns worked!—the immortal

stanzas leaping from his pen, as if at hap-hazard, amidst poor·
stuff, in a rhyming letter to some Blacklock, or Lapraik, or
Simpson, or welling up, in more pure completeness, as he followed the plough, musing upon some slightest incident of the
moment, the sight of a scampering mouse, a trodden daisy, a
wounded hare. Scott composed parts of Marmion in jubilant
gallops along the sea-shore. It was inevitable that a proportion
of the poetry thus composed should be loosely knit or commonplace. Byron, who wrote with headlong speed, laughed to
scorn the idea that a poem could be expected to be poetical
throughout. It may be said that Byron, Burns, and Scott
would have left us better poetry if they had taken more conscious pains, and had pruned their superfluous foliage; and I
do not care to maintain the contrary; but a strong thought or
happy image has an enhanced effect when it occurs among
others of a more ordinary kind; and in the rapid, sketchy manner there is a charm of lightness, grace, and freedom—a charm
as of nature's very self—which goes far to compensate for the
high-wrought beauty of the other.

With the Dream of Fair Women we naturally, from identity
of metre and similarity in the texture and polish of the versification, associate The Palace of Art. It is one of many
poems in which Tennyson becomes the ethical instructor as
well as the poetical entertainer of his age. The truth he ex-
pounds and inculcates is very old, very simple, but of infinite
importance, and specially requiring enforcement in a time of
ripe intellectual civilization, and of the fastidiousness, cynicism,
and cultured pride which are its besetting sins. Avoiding,
with a willingness to make himself intelligible and useful which
I wish he had exhibited in some other instances, the risk of
being treated as having many meanings or none, he states, in
a few lines addressed to an unnamed friend, his purpose in the
poem. It is an allegory of a soul possessed of many gifts,
loving beauty and knowledge, and even good in so far as good-

ness may gratify an æsthetic taste, but forgetting that beauty, knowledge, and goodness ought to be vassals unto charity.

> And he that shuts Love out, in turn shall be
> Shut out from Love, and on her threshold lie
> Howling in outer darkness.

The palace of art is "a lordly pleasure-house," built by the poet for his soul, in which all the delights of intellect and imagination—all the charm of fancied superiority to the mass of men—combine to make her happy. The problem to be solved is whether man *can* thus be made nobly and permanently happy, and the solution is experimental; that is to say, the poet places imaginatively before us a soul in the enjoyment of all delights, save spiritual and moral, realizes her experience step by step, and finds, in the concluding stage of that experience, the solution of which he is in quest.

First of all, we are present at the building of the palace; and this is not managed in the way in which Byron would very likely have managed it, by a stanza or two of vague allusion to curtains of cloud and the azure and vermilion that are mixed at eventide for the pavilion of the sun, but with an explicitness and fulness of detail that leave nothing to the imagination of the reader, and might have excited the wonder of Keats or of Spenser. On a huge crag-platform, high above the common world, it stands; we see its courts, its cloisters, its squared lawns, its four fountains spouted from the golden gorge of dragons, which unite in one swell, and stream from the mountain-like platform "in misty folds, that floating as they fell lit up a torrent bow." Within, long-sounding corridors "over-vaulted grateful gloom," and along these the soul passed from chamber to chamber. Each room was a perfect whole, but no two rooms were alike. In a succession of incomparable stanzas, Tennyson describes first the landscape adornment of some of the rooms, then the figure-subjects treated pictorially in others. Here are two of the landscapes:

12

> One show'd an iron coast and angry waves.
>   You seem'd to hear them climb and fall,
> And roar rock-thwarted under bellowing caves,
>   Beneath the windy wall.
>
> And one, a full-fed river winding slow
>   By herds upon an endless plain,
> The ragged rims of thunder brooding low,
>   With shadow-streaks of rain.

Any artist who is master of his business could put these pictures upon canvas; and I feel sure that Turner, austere critic as he was, would have confessed that he could not paint them in color more truthfully than Tennyson has painted them in words. Even Turner's pictures must have been dumb; but we *hear* the waves roaring rock-thwarted under the bellowing caves. It is not impossible that Turner's knowledge that words could convey more in the way of natural description than can be done by the brush may have been one of those motives which impelled him, during something like thirty years of his life, to make attempts in poetry, and, latterly, to sign himself "author" rather than artist. The following has been very often painted, and is probably familiar to all my readers :

> And one, an English home—gray twilight pour'd
>   On dewy pastures, dewy trees,
> Softer than sleep—all things in order stored,
>   A haunt of ancient Peace.

The figure subjects are Christian, Mohammedan, or classical.

> Or in a clear-wall'd city on the sea,
>   Near gilded organ-pipes, her hair
> Wound with white roses, slept St. Cecily;
>   An angel look'd at her.
>
> Or thronging all one porch of Paradise,
>   A group of Houris bow'd to see
> The dying Islamite, with hands and eyes
>   That said, We wait for thee.

In one, King Arthur, in sleep that may be death, is watch-ed by weeping queens; in another, Numa meets the nymph Egeria; in a third, Ganymede shoots through the sky, borne upward by the eagle. I have often wondered whether this last was suggested by Titian's picture of Ganymede and the eagle in our National Gallery.

> Or sweet Europa's mantle blew unclasp'd
>   From off her shoulder backward borne;
> From one hand droop'd a crocus: one hand grasp'd
>   The mild bull's golden horn.

I quote this as it appears in the earlier editions. In the most recent, the word "blew" in the first line is changed into "blue." The reader may take which he chooses, but I think the picture gains more by the animation and movement of the blowing breeze than by the touch of color. In this instance, the painter would have the advantage of the poet, for with one sweep of the brush he could show the mantle both as blue in color and as blown backward by the wind. When Tennyson tells us that the mantle was blue, he takes the wind out of his picture, and the unclasped mantle threatens to fall down upon the bull's back. Titian may have given the suggestion for this picture also. Round the royal daïs, on which the soul took her seat, were choice paintings of wise men, conspicuous among them Milton, Shakspeare, Dante, and Homer. Plato and Verulam looked down upon her.

At first the soul was joyful and exultant. She sang in feast-ful mirth, feeling herself "lord over nature, lord of the visible earth, lord of the senses five." She rejoiced in her isolation, gazing scornfully on the herds of human swine that darkened the plain. At last she summed up her pride in this magnifi-cent and celebrated verse:

> I take possession of man's mind and deed.
>   I care not what the sects may brawl.
> I sit as God, holding no form of creed,
>   But contemplating all.

So it continued for three years. Then, "lest she should fail and perish utterly," she was struck by Heaven with pangs of hell. She dreaded and loathed her solitude. She scorned herself, then laughed at her self-scorn. She struggled to bethink her of her spacious mansion, her place of strength, her glorious world of intellect, beauty, music, pride.

> But in dark corners of her palace stood
>   Uncertain shapes : and unawares
> On white-eyed phantasms weeping tears of blood,
>   And horrible nightmares.
>
> And hollow shades enclosing hearts of flame,
>   And, with dim-fretted foreheads all,
> On corpses three-months-old at noon she came,
>   That stood against the wall.

Was the imagery of a mind diseased—of a soul tormented by conscience—ever more powerfully delineated ?

> Back on herself her serpent pride had curl'd.
>   " No voice," she shrieked in that lone hall,
> " No voice breaks thro' the stillness of the world :
>   One deep, deep silence all !"
>
> She, mouldering with the dull earth's mouldering sod,
>   Inwrapt tenfold in slothful shame,
> Lay there exiled from eternal God,
>   Lost to her place and name ;
>
> And death and life she hated equally,
>   And nothing saw, for her despair,
> But dreadful time, dreadful eternity,
>   No comfort anywhere.

"She howled aloud, 'I am on fire within !' " There was no reply. For four years the searching agony endured. Then she threw aside her royal robes.

> " Make me a cottage in the vale," she cried,
>   " Where I may mourn and pray.

> " Yet pull not down my palace towers that are
> So lightly, beautifully built:
> Perchance I may return with others there
> When I have purged my guilt."

The essence of the sin was not culture, but the selfishness and aristocraticism of cultured pride; not delight, whether of the senses or of the mind, but delight unshared by others; not abstention from the partisanship of creeds, but contemptuous isolation from those who accept them, and lack of sympathetic appreciation of the truth they contain. Such isolation, such pride, such culture, are indeed damnable.

CHAPTER VI.

TENNYSON AS A PEOPLE'S POET.

IN the Dream of Fair Women and Palace of Art Tennyson dealt with subjects belonging emphatically to what may be called the academic or patrician department of literary production. The fair women whose "star-like sorrows" are written on their "immortal eyes," in the one poem, were, each and all, daughters or wives of kings or mighty chiefs; and the lesson inculcated in the other can hardly have much practical interest for any but persons of elaborate culture, æsthetic sensibility, and high social position. In The Princess, too, the subject, scene, and characters belong to the upper classes, and the various lays of the Round-table are idyls of a king.

At first glance, then, it might seem absurd to call Tennyson in any sense a poet of the people; and yet he has continued from first to last in true poetic sympathy with that wave of democratic feeling and aspiration which passed over the United Kingdom in the days of his early manhood, and which has produced no utterance so melodious as Locksley Hall. The hopes and wishes of the young Liberal in that poem are independent of class distinctions. Listen to his self-delineation:

Yearning for the large excitement that the coming years would yield,
Eager-hearted as a boy when first he leaves his father's field,
And at night along the dusky highway near and nearer drawn,
Sees in heaven the light of London flaring like a dreary dawn;
And his spirit leaps within him to be gone before him then,
Underneath the light he looks at, in among the throngs of men:
Men, my brothers, men the workers, ever reaping something new:
That which they have done but earnest of the things that they shall do.

" Work," " brotherhood "—there are no words more expressive of the kinship of humanity, of the fellowship which is at once noble, rational, and practicable, than these. Mr. Matthew Arnold read us lately an eloquent lecture on the antique precept, " Choose equality and flee greed ;" and there can, I think, be no doubt that, from the days of Menander downward, men have believed that, in some sense or other, social equality was a blessing and a boon, a something to be aimed at and held precious as the finest essence of civilization. But unless we merge all precision of idea in vague flourishes of rhetoric, we must have some understanding as to the nature of the equality in question. Negatively, it cannot be better defined than by pointing out, with Menander and Mr. Arnold, its opposition to greed, selfishness, pride of possession. But when we attempt to define it positively, we are met by the fact, which none but a lunatic will dispute, that, apart from all question of property, no two men, women, or children in the world are equal in respect of capacity, sensibility, or energy. Is there any trait of character which may link us in the bond of a real, and not a merely imaginary equality—an equality attainable by all, and, therefore, presenting a basis on which the brotherhood of mankind might be worked out, not merely as a pleasing fancy, but as a possible fact ?

We may venture, I think, to return an affirmative answer to this question. I see no reason why *mutual consideration* should not become a universal characteristic of men; that is to say, I do not see that any degree of weakness of intellect or will, however extreme, is incompatible with the attainment of this habit. When it becomes so—when a man is literally incapable, whether from meagreness of brain or infirmity of will, of considering any one but himself—then he falls below the human level, and I would no more call him my equal than I should a born idiot. But I can imagine that, in a society in which mutual consideration reached a high point of develop-

ment, the circumstance of there being a wide range of capacities, a wide diversity of traits and characteristics, would tend to
heighten rather than destroy the charm of social intercourse.

It were sheer folly or affectation to deny that a large number of persons are grossly devoid of consideration for others,
and I cannot believe that any true poet could be so flighty a
sentimentalist as to hail these as his brethren. The equality
the true poet desires is the recognition, wherever it occurs, of
that spirit of gentleness and consideration which is the sole
indispensable characteristic of *good* society. This is the true
gentlemanliness, which may be found under the fustian jacket,
and may fail to be found under the imperial purple. Now I
think that Tennyson is peculiarly felicitous in discerning this
badge of the natural knighthood and ladyhood of mankind.
His gardener's daughter is a lady, and yet not a bit too fine for
a real gardener's daughter. His Dora is as generous, gentle,
faithful, modest, affectionate, and simple-hearted as any lady
that ever, from dais or gallery, rained bright influence upon
her knight charging in the lists below; she even has the graciousness, the sweet, winning artfulness, of a lady; for what
could be more exquisitely lady-like than her setting the flower-
wreath on the little boy's head in the wheat-field, in order that
he might be beautiful in his grandfather's eyes? And yet
there is not one word uttered by Dora, not one thing done,
that we do not feel to be entirely natural and appropriate to
the niece of a yeoman. When Burns, in that yearning anticipation of a better future which has visited poetic seers in all
ages, spoke of a time when men should be brothers all over the
world, he must have meant partly that this fine essential manhood would receive social recognition in spite of class distinctions, and partly that the area of noble manhood would be extended, that the ape and tiger would die out of the race, and
that individual and natural selfishness would give place to mutual consideration and a passion for the common advancement.

Meanwhile the best proof that one's sympathies are given not to a class but to mankind is the habit of affectionate and honorable recognition of gentle persons, be their station what it may. In this sense Tennyson has been a Poet of the People.

It seems almost absurd to talk of critically estimating a poem like Dora. The thing is simplicity itself. It contains literally not one similitude, not one metaphor, which might not be used in common discourse by shepherds and husbandmen. Its words are the current coin of our language. There are but two or three words of three syllables, one of these being " consider," another " laborer." The Latin, French, Greek elements of English speech are dispensed with, and the narrative runs along on its German basis. For all this, no poem of Tennyson's strikes me as more essentially poetical, more genuinely imaginative. It is all picture, and yet you see no paint. In this respect it reminds me of Goethe's manner in Hermann and Dorothea, perhaps the most perfect idyl ever written. Neither in the one nor in the other is there a trace of conscious ornamentation—of that sort of adornment which a poetaster might add to the prose framework of his tale to make it pretty; but in Goethe's poem you have all the beauty of vineyards in the glow of sunlight, and in Tennyson's of cornfields and poppies, and in both you have the warm light of honest human faces, and that subtle and sympathetic knowledge of the human heart which enables the poet to penetrate to the deepest sources of laughter and of tears. It must be a flinty heart indeed that can reach the end of Dora unmoved. The pathos is like that of the simple stories of the old Hebrew Bible, the story of Joseph or the story of Ruth. These move and fascinate us in childhood, and the longer we live the more do we love them.

There is exquisitely fine character-painting in the treatment, slight as it looks, of the two women, Dora and Mary. They are not only sharply defined in their individualities, but are types of great contrasted orders among women. Dora is the superior nature, the deeper, the more thoughtful, the more self-sacrificing, of the two ; incapable of coming short in any duty owed either to herself, or to her benefactor, or to the man she loves ; capable of forgiving even the deadliest offence that can be offered to woman, the *injuria spretæ formæ*, the contemptuous disparagement of her beauty, and rejection of her love. Yet we feel that she has her womanly pride, too, and that, if one glance of her eye could enchain William and make her a happy bride, she would not cast it. When her uncle, enraged that his son had married Mary in defiance of him, ordered her not to speak to William or his wife, she "promised, being meek," thinking that the old man would require only to be humored for awhile. "It cannot be," she said to herself; "my uncle's mind will change." But when troubles overtook William, and he passed his father's door day by day heart-broken, then

> Dora stored what little she could save,
> And sent it them by stealth, nor did they know
> Who sent it ; till at last a fever seized
> On William, and in harvest-time he died.

Dora will now obey her uncle no longer. There had been nothing of superstition or slavishness in her obedience, because she felt sure it would be temporary ; but she is quick to blame herself, feeling that it was wrong to countenance even so far the old man's unrighteous anger.

> Then Dora went to Mary. Mary sat
> And look'd with tears upon her boy, and thought
> Hard things of Dora. Dora came and said :
> "I have obey'd my uncle until now,
> And I have sinn'd, for it was all thro' me
> This evil came on William at the first.
> But, Mary, for the sake of him that's gone,
> And for your sake, the woman that he chose,
> And for this orphan, I am come to you:

> You know there has not been for these five years
> So full a harvest: let me take the boy,
> And I will set him in my uncle's eye
> Among the wheat; that when his heart is glad
> Of the full harvest, he may see the boy,
> And bless him for the sake of him that's gone."

The first day the farmer did not see her as she sat with the child; on the second he noticed her, rebuked her sharply, but took the boy.

> "I see it is a trick
> Got up betwixt you and the woman there.
> I must be taught my duty, and by you!
> You knew my word was law, and yet you dared
> To slight it. Well—for I will take the boy;
> But you go hence, and never see me more."

Dora, meekly acquiescent, does not utter one remonstrant word, but at the same time makes no apology for having done what she knows to be right. After weeping in secret, she returns to Mary, and asks to be allowed to live and work with her. But the comparatively commonplace, yet alert and ready-witted Mary, armed with the instinctive wisdom of maternity, has now the advantage. A touch of sacred anger thrills her, and she rebels against the hard old man.

> "This shall never be,
> That thou shouldst take my trouble on thyself:
> And now, I think, he shall not have the boy,
> For he will teach him hardness, and to slight
> His mother; therefore, thou and I will go,
> And I will have my boy, and bring him home;
> And I will beg of him to take thee back:
> But if he will not take thee back again,
> Then thou and I will live within one house,
> And work for William's child, until he grows
> Of age to help us."

This is obviously right, as well as brave and womanly. They set out for the farm. Mary's courage does not fail. She appeals to her father-in-law to take Dora back, and tells him that William died confessing that, though he could not rue marrying Mary, he had done wrong to cross his father, and had prayed God to bless him.

> So Mary said, and Dora hid her face
> By Mary.   There was silence in the room;
> And all at once the old man burst in sobs:
> "I have been to blame—to blame.   I have kill'd my son.
> I have kill'd him—but I loved him—my dear son.
> May God forgive me!—I have been to blame.
> Kiss me, my children."
>
>   Then they clung about
> The old man's neck, and kiss'd him many times.
> And all the man was broken with remorse;
> And all his love came back a hundred-fold;
> And for three hours he sobb'd o'er William's child
> Thinking of William.
>
>   So these four abode
> Within one house together; and as years
> Went forward, Mary took another mate;
> But Dora lived unmarried till her death.

The piece would have been utterly ruined if there had been another fate than this for Dora.   Had she been married, a perfect poem would have become a trivial novelette.   The blunder would have been far worse than making Dinah Morris end her life suckling fools and chronicling small-beer, a desecration of the Methodist Saint Theresa for which I have never been able to stifle a little bit of grudge against George Eliot.   Marriages, however, are the natural climaxes, the final ends of novels, and no *dénouement* could be more in accordance with rule than marriage between the hero and the heroine, especially when the hero was Adam Bede.   Tennyson was under no such temptation to let Dora be absorbed into the mass of commonplace humanity.

Poor Esther Johnson said of Swift that he could write beau-

tifully on a broomstick; but even a broomstick, if one were
permitted to wander in thought to the woods in which it grew,
might seem a likelier subject for poetry than the pecuniary loss
of a city clerk, on which Tennyson has contrived to hang a
powerful and beautiful poem in Sea Dreams. A city clerk is
the hero, his wife, an unknown artist's orphan child, is the heroine; their child Margaret is the personage of next importance
in the story; and the list of characters is completed by a spec-
ulator in mines, whose representations had induced the clerk to
risk his money.

> One babe was theirs, a Margaret, three years old:
> They, thinking that her clear germander eye
> Droopt in the giant-factoried city-gloom,
> Came, with a month's leave given them, to the sea.

The "germander" eye! Some might call this a touch of
pre-Raphaelite conceit or affectation, but I think a poet has a
right to invent color-words for himself when he wants them,
provided only that they are expressive, picturesque, and not too
far-fetched. There is no word in the language that will define
the particular tint of blue which you see not unfrequently in
the eye of an ailing child so well as that which is here applied
by Tennyson. It is the faintly mottled blue of the germander
speedwell—nothing else. As the little flower can be seen in
summer in every English lane, the reference to it can hardly
be called far-fetched.

Reaching the sea-coast, "all sand and cliff, and deep-in-run-
ning cave," on a Saturday, the clerk and his wife went to chapel next morning, and, after sermon,

> Forth they came and paced the shore,
> Ran in and out the long sea-framing caves,
> Drank the large air, and saw, but scarce believed
> (The sootflake of so many a summer still
> Clung to their fancies) that they saw, the sea.

> So now on sand they walk'd, and now on cliff,
> Lingering about the thymy promontories,
> Till all the sails were darken'd in the west,
> And rosed in the east.

There is another reading, fresh and bright, from nature's own page! You stand by the sea, on a southward-looking coast, as the sun goes down. Westward, where the sails come between you and the sunset, they show simply as spots of shade; eastward, where they are farther from the sun than you, they catch the gleam from the west, and every sail is a speck of rose-light. I call that a proper illustration of what the versifier says of our Alfred's "truth of *touch*."

After these experiences, the pair went "homeward and to bed." The wife, who in her Christian tenderness was stronger than her husband, urges him to forgive the man whose "unctuous mouth" had lured him to buy the Peruvian mine shares, and lose the savings of twelve long years. He replies:

> "Forgive! How many will say, 'forgive,' and find
> A sort of absolution in the sound
> To hate a little longer! No; the sin
> That neither God nor man can well forgive,
> Hypocrisy, I saw it in him at once."

He gives his wife an account of his last meeting with the man who had injured him.

> "'My dearest friend,
> Have faith, have faith! We live by faith,' said he;
> 'And all things work together for the good
> Of those'—it makes me sick to quote him—last
> Gript my hand hard, and with 'God-bless-you' went.
> I stood like one that had received a blow.
> I found a hard friend in his loose accounts,
> A loose one in the hard grip of his hand,
> A curse in his God-bless-you: then my eyes
> Pursued him down the street, and far away,
> Amongst the honest shoulders of the crowd,
> Read rascal in the motions of his back,
> And scoundrel in the supple-sliding knee."

Still the woman pleads. She will not grant that the roguery has been made out, and even, if the deception were shown to have been wilful, she would bespeak forgiveness. If he wrongs his friend, he "wrongs himself more," and in "the silent court of justice in his breast," in which he is both judge and jury, he will be condemned. Perhaps, after all, he meant well. The husband remains unconvinced. In that silent court of hers, a man may, he says, be counsel for himself, and then he quotes what he calls an "old satire," but which really is a masterly imitation by Tennyson of our old English satiric style. I am not sure whether it was Dryden or Cowper that he had in view, and I cannot help thinking that he must have been influenced, in composing the lines, by Crabbe. The first line will recall Dryden's "With two left legs and Judas-colored hair."

> "With all his conscience and one eye askew,
> So false, he partly took himself for true;
> Whose pious talk, when most his heart was dry,
> Made wet the crafty crowsfoot round his eye;
> Who, never naming God except for gain,
> So never took that useful name in vain.
> Made Him his catspaw and the Cross his tool,
> · And Christ the bait to trap his dupe and fool;
> Nor deeds of gift, but gifts of grace he forged,
> And snake-like slimed his victim ere he gorged;
> And oft at Bible meetings, o'er the rest
> Arising, did his holy oily best,
> Dropping the too rough H in Hell and Heaven,
> To spread the Word by which himself had thriven."

He asks his wife how she likes this. Her answer honors Tennyson, and is, by implication, one of the noblest tributes ever paid to the heart-wisdom of woman.

> "Nay," she said,
> "I loathe it; he had never kindly heart,
> Nor ever cared to better his own kind,
> Who first wrote satire, with no pity in it."

It is impossible for me to quote the dreams, one dreamed by the clerk, the other by his wife, to which the poem owes its name, and apart from which it might seem an ethically suggestive but somewhat prosaic performance. In one of them—the husband's—the results of speculation are poetically contrasted with those of honest work; in the other—the wife's—there seems to be an imaginative shadowing forth of the general revolutionary movement of these times, and of the battle of Churches and Sects, of creeds and scepticisms, through all which—an echo, shall I say? of the indestructible harmony in her own heart—she hears a note of Divine music. Readers will find much food for musing in these dreams. But we have not quite done with the narrative part of the poem. The wife has seen some one from the town, and has news " later by an hour " than her husband's. She speaks:

> " We *must* forgive the dead."
> " Dead ! who is dead ?"
> " The man your eye pursued.
> A little after you had parted with him,
> He suddenly dropt dead of heart-disease."
> " Dead ? he ? of heart-disease ? what heart had he
> To die of ? dead !"
> " Ah, dearest, if there be
> A devil in man, there is an angel too,
> And if he did that wrong you charge him with,
> His angel broke his heart."

The woman has her triumph. "I do forgive him," says the husband. There is not a nobler heroine in literature than this wife of a city clerk, and I see no reason to believe that there are not many such to be found in London.

In Enoch Arden, Tennyson deals with a subject which might have had charms for Crabbe, but Crabbe would have loaded the shadows too much; in Tennyson's handling the poem is sad but not painful. The hero, Enoch Arden, is beyond rivalry the principal personage in the tale, and his heroism is at once of the loftiest and simplest order. He is an unlucky man, but invincible: his brain is ordinary; morally he is sublime. His duty, however hard it may be, is always clear to him; and, without any consciousness that he is acting heroically, he always proves equal to it. Harder duty, however, has seldom fallen to any man than his.

Enoch Arden, a rough sailor's lad, Philip Ray, the miller's only son, and pretty Annie Lee, played together as children beneath the cliffs that faced the breakers, on the beach of a small seaport town—

> Play'd
> Among the waste and lumber of the shore,
> Hard coils of cordage, swarthy fishing-nets,
> Anchors of rusty fluke, and boats updrawn.

The literal accuracy of these lines is almost comical. Go to Deal and you will see precisely such a shore. Enoch and Philip both love Annie, and the three play at keeping house in a cave which runs in below the cliff. Annie was willing enough to be "little wife to both," but at heart loved Enoch best. He was at first successful; prospered in his fishing, made himself full sailor on board a merchantman, and before he was twenty-one, purchased a boat, and married her. First a daughter, then a son, were born to them, and all things continued to go well with Enoch until he fell from a mast and broke a limb. While he lay recovering, a third son, a sickly one, was born. Meanwhile, some one stepped in and snatched away his trade:

> And on him fell,
> Altho' a grave and staid God-fearing man,
> Yet lying thus inactive, doubt and gloom.
> He seem'd as in a nightmare of the night,
> To see his children leading evermore
> Low, miserable lives of hand-to-mouth,
> And her he loved, a beggar: then he pray'd,
> "Save them from this, whatever comes to me."

"While he prayed," the master of the ship in which he had served heard of his misfortune, and came and offered to take him as boatswain. Enoch consented at once, "rejoicing at that answer to his prayer." He resolved to sell his boat, set Annie up in a little shop stocked "with all that seamen need-ed or their wives," and go on a long voyage. Annie disliked the scheme, was sure that evil would come of it, and entreated him not to go. It was in vain.

> All his Annie's fears,
> Save, as his Annie's, were a laughter to him.
> Yet Enoch, as a brave, God-fearing man,
> Bow'd himself down, and in that mystery
> Where God-in-man is one with man-in-God,
> Pray'd for a blessing on his wife and babes
> Whatever came to him.

Very notable is the stress which the poet lays upon the re-ligion of Enoch. This is an entirely different thing from the virtue of Dickens's poor men, which, except for an enthusiasm about Christmas, dependent chiefly on roast turkey and plum-pudding, has no more connection with Christianity than with the gods of Homer. The fact is that, generally speaking, those of our villagers and sailors who are conspicuous for morality and virtue are religious men. At last Enoch bids Annie farewell.

> "Annie, my girl, cheer up, be comforted.
> Look to the babes; and till I come again
> Keep everything ship-shape, for I must go.
> And fear no more for me; or if you fear,
> Cast all your cares on God; that anchor holds.
> Is He not yonder in those uttermost
> Parts of the morning? if I flee to these
> Can I go from Him? and the sea is His,
> The sea is His: He made it."

Before he went he kissed his two elder children; the sickly one, asleep in his cot, he would not waken.

> But Annie from her baby's forehead clipt
> A tiny curl, and gave it: this he kept
> Thro' all his future; but now hastily caught
> His bundle, waved his hand, and went his way.

The sickly child died. Annie had no success in trade, and but for the delicately tendered help of Philip Ray, would have sunk into poverty. When ten years had gone by and nothing had been heard of Enoch, Philip asked her to marry him. In the twelfth year she became his wife. Enoch, meanwhile, had been wrecked upon a tropic island. There, year after year, with bounteous supply of all his animal wants, but infinite hunger of heart, he remained. The sights and sounds of his home haunted him.

> Once likewise, in the ringing of his ears,
> Tho' faintly, merrily—far and far away—
> He heard the pealing of his parish bells;
> Then, tho' he knew not wherefore, started up
> Shuddering, and when the beauteous, hateful isle
> Return'd upon him, had not his poor heart
> Spoken with That, which being everywhere
> Lets none, who speaks with him, seem all alone,
> Surely the man had died of solitude.

A ship took him off, and he returned to England. So completely was he changed that it was easy for him to live in the same town with Annie and Philip without being discovered. In the darkness he went and looked in at the window, and saw his wife and children in perfect comfort round Philip's hearth. After this peep into the domestic heaven which he had lost, he crept from the garden "out upon the waste." There he fell prone, and prayed.

> "Too hard to bear! why did they take me thence?
> O God Almighty, blessed Saviour, Thou
> That didst uphold me on my lonely isle,
> Uphold me, Father! aid me, give me strength
> Not to tell her, never to let her know."

He had now a new purpose in life, and with heroic fortitude he set himself to carry it out.

> He was not all unhappy. His resolve
> Upbore him, and firm faith, and evermore
> Prayer from a living source within the will,
> And beating up through all the bitter world,
> Like fountains of sweet water in the sea,
> Kept him a living soul.

But he did not live long. When he knew death to be at hand, he told the woman with whom he had lodged, under promise on the Book of secrecy until after his death, who he was, and bade her give Annie the lock of his dead child's hair by which she might know that it had indeed been he, and to tell her that he died blessing her and his children and Philip. Then "the strong, heroic soul" passed away. He had never accused God; he had never unjustly upbraided man; in the long roll of Christian heroes there is not inscribed a truer hero than Enoch Arden.

Such being the justice done by Tennyson to the peasants, clerks, and seamen of England, may we not say that he is, indeed, a Poet of the People?

CHAPTER VII.

THE TWO VOICES.

ONE of the strongest and most widely-diffused prejudices of the English mind is a prejudice against metaphysics; and most Englishmen would, I fancy, agree that, if there is one thing more objectionable than metaphysical prose, it is metaphysical poetry. Nevertheless, a large proportion of the best dramatic and reflective poetry in the English language, if not strictly definable as metaphysical poetry, attests a strong metaphysical turn of mind in its authors. No one can have done more than merely skim the surface of Shakspeare's dramas and sonnets, without feeling that the profoundest metaphysical problems had for him an inexhaustible interest. While the whole complicated tissue of man's material existence—the web of passion and motive, with its ever-shifting colors—lay open to the inevitable glance of his supreme intelligence, he never ceased to ponder, in dumb and baffled amazement, upon the mysteries of man's spiritual life, the secrets of the grave, the relation of the human creature to the universe around him. Hamlet is a born metaphysician—so good a metaphysician, one might be tempted to say, as to be good for nothing else. Prospero is a metaphysician:

> We are such stuff
> As dreams are made on, and our little life
> Is rounded with a sleep.

If we cannot trace the personality of Shakspeare in Hamlet and in Prospero, we may give up all hope of connecting his character with his dramatic impersonations. Not a little of the most beautiful and imaginative English poetry of the present century was written by Shelley and by Coleridge, and these were almost as much metaphysicians as poets; Wordsworth in his highest mood floated naturally away from the summits of his beloved mountains into the blue infinitude of metaphysics; and Byron, shrewd, practical, sarcastic Byron, proves in Manfred and in Cain that he knew the fitness of the highest questions of speculation to become subjects of poetry.   I have no doubt whatever that there is an affinity between the imaginative and the speculative faculties, and that the poet and the metaphysician are brothers.   It would certainly be no extravagant assertion that Plato was as imaginative as Homer.

Tennyson's passion for metaphysics—his feeling of the wonder and mystery of things, and habit of speculative musing—can be traced in his juvenile poems.   In the companion pieces, Nothing Will Die, and All Things Will Die, he gives melodious expression to that antithesis of fixity and of change—of uniformity and of variety—of birth and of death—about which philosophers have disputed for thousands of years.

> When will the stream be aweary of flowing
>   Under my eye?
> When will the wind be aweary of blowing
>   Over the sky?
> When will the clouds be aweary of fleeting?
> When will the heart be aweary of beating?
>   And nature die?
> Never, oh! never, nothing will die;
>   The stream flows,
>   The wind blows,
>   The cloud fleets,
>   The heart beats,
>   Nothing will die.
>   Nothing will die;
>   All things will change.
> Thro' eternity.

Such is the first half of the antithesis.   Change is the sole discernible law of the universe. But the second half of the antithesis remains to be stated. Death, the young metaphysician finds, is as much a reality as change.

> The stream will cease to flow;
> The wind will cease to blow;
> The clouds will cease to fleet;
> The heart will cease to beat;
> For all things must die.

He cannot believe that the world had no beginning, and will have no end.

> The old earth
> Had a birth,
> As all men know,
> Long ago.
> And the old earth must die.

This is feeble metaphysics, if you will, but the verses evince a metaphysical habit of mind.

The highest result as yet attained by any metaphysician is an intelligent ignorance, a confession that we cannot penetrate the veil of appearance. The lines just quoted are among the earliest of Tennyson's metaphysical utterances; the following is one of his latest; and in the last, even more than in the first, he is a wondering inquirer, a wistful ponderer, a confessor of enlightened ignorance.

> Flower in the crannied wall,
> I pluck you out of the crannies;
> Hold you here, root and all, in my hand,
> Little flower—but if I could understand
> What you are, root and all, and all in all,
> I should know what God and man is.

That is to say, all things are linked together; nothing stands in isolation; and we could not know any one thing perfectly without knowing all.

Metaphysical genius, in its real and precious form, is simply

a capacity to observe with nice accuracy a particular order of
facts. The metaphysician goes to the essence and heart of a
thing, looking for a deeper truth than the eye of sense can
discern. Tennyson, for example, gives us a fine instance of
metaphysical observation when, in describing, in Maud, an empty shell, "small and pure as a pearl," he says—

> The tiny cell is forlorn,
> *Void of the little living will*
> *That made it stir on the shore.*

I put into italics the words which fix upon the essential
characteristic of the living shell: it has a will; it stirs on the
shore; it takes, within certain limits, what path it chooses.
By accurate observation, you penetrate to this fact; and when
you clearly realize it, you perceive that, by this living will, the
tenant of the tiny shell is differentiated from all things in the
world that have not life and volition. The ability of Profess-
or Tyndall as an observer of mechanical processes cannot be
questioned; but he seems to me to exhibit, when placed beside such a thinker as Tennyson or such a thinker as Marti-
neau, that order of mind which is expressly *not* metaphysical;
and the point in which his difference from them has been most
conspicuously exhibited is in his failing to perceive that, in a
living will, there is a force which the subtlest energies that act
in crystallization, or the most wide and wayward impulses that
urge star and comet on their way, do not at all resemble. Within certain limits, the little shell,

> Slight, to be crush'd with a tap
> Of my finger-nail on the sand,

is the pilot of its own destiny, the regulator of its own life.
That is more than can be said of the brightest sun in the firmament, or of the most vivacious magnet that quivers, with
motion so life-like, yet not living, toward the Pole. The true

metaphysical genius is displayed in firmly grasping this difference; in remaining unconfused by plausible analogies between
living will and dead matter; in peremptorily realizing that mechanical motion and volitional motion cannot be resolved into
one another, but are essentially distinct.

It is required of all poetry, without exception, that it shall
be lovely and picture-like to the eye, and tuneful to the ear.
These conditions cannot be relaxed in favor of metaphysical poetry. Since, therefore, metaphysical truth is truth in its most
abstract form, it will clearly result that to produce in one and
the same work good metaphysics and delightful poetry is a
matter of extreme difficulty. This difficulty Tennyson has signally vanquished in The Two Voices. It is a compact, closely-
reasoned metaphysical essay on the worth of life and the hope
of immortality, and yet I know no poem of Tennyson's more
variegated in color, more piquantly and brilliantly picturesque,
more truly though gravely melodious.

The first of the Voices opens the dialogue with a recommen-
dation to the poet to commit suicide.

> A still small voice spake unto me,
> "Thou art so full of misery,
> Were it not better not to be?"

The poet replies that he will not destroy what is so wonderful-
ly made. The Voice rejoins that the shuffling off of this mortal coil may open to him new spheres of energy and happiness:

> To-day I saw the dragon-fly
> Come from the wells where he did lie.
>
> An inner impulse rent the veil
> Of his old husk; from head to tail
> Came out clear plates of sapphire mail.
>
> He dried his wings: like gauze they grew:
> Through crofts and pastures wet with dew,
> A living flash of light he flew.

13

The reply of the poet is that man is nature's highest product —the obvious suggestion being that there is no splendid dragon-fly into which the human grub, released by death, is likely to develop. The Voice answers that he is blinded with his pride, that in a boundless universe is "boundless better, boundless worse." As for destroying so fine a piece of work as a man, there would be "plenty of the kind," although he made an end of himself.

> Then did my response clearer fall:
> "No compound of this earthly ball
> Is like another, all in all."

This is undeniable, and the Voice vainly seeks to parry the thrust by jeering at the unimportance of his "peculiar difference" in the sum of things. Now, however, it tries a new tack, and argues that the poet's wretchedness makes him unfit for anything but complaining—

> "Thine anguish will not let thee sleep,
> Nor any train of reason keep;
> Thou canst not think, but thou wilt weep."

The poet declines to shut his life from happier chance. "All the years invent." Every month is enriched with some new development.

> Were this not well, to bide mine hour,
> Tho' watching from a ruin'd tower
> How grows the day of human power?

The Voice retorts that truth is unattainable. He may scale the mountain, but the sacred morning will still gleam above his head.

> "Forerun thy peers, thy time, and let
> Thy feet, millenniums hence, be set
> In midst of knowledge, dream'd not yet.

> "Thou hast not gain'd a real height,
> Nor art thou nearer to the light,
> Because the scale is infinite."

Instead of replying, as I think he might have replied, that the finite mind does not require to grasp the infinitude of truth, but only to go forward from light to light,* the poet evades the difficulty, and takes another line of defence.

> I said, "When I am gone away,
> 'He dared not tarry,' men will say,
> Doing dishonor to my clay."

The voice sees its advantage, and attacks him sharply:

---

* My readers will join with me in thanking the writer of the following letter:

Berlin, S. W., November 10th, 1878.

I have just been enjoying your critical examination of The Two Voices, and re-enjoying the poem itself afterward. I write because I wish to call your attention to a passage in Wordsworth's Prelude to the Excursion, in which he goes farther than you do in your suggestion of an answer to Tennyson's unanswered, and, therefore, as one is led to suppose, almost agreed with Tempter, when he dwells upon the impossibility of the finite ever attaining to an infinite knowledge of truth, and, therefore, upon the uselessness and the misery of trying to press onward and upward. The contrast between the way in which the same thought had affected the two poets struck me strongly years ago, when, with Tennyson's Two Voices enshrined in my heart as a most precious possession, I was reading Wordsworth's Prelude. It was a contrast most fruitful of thought. As perhaps you may not have noticed it, I send you Wordsworth's lines, thinking that when your valuable papers are gathered into a book you may be glad to use them. I am sorry I have forgotten exactly in which part of the Prelude they occur, but I believe it was toward the commencement.

MARY MACK WALL.

> "And deem not profitless those fleeting moods
> Of shadowy exaltation: not for this
> That they are kindred to our purer mind
> And intellectual life; but that the soul,
> Remembering how she felt, but what she felt
> Remembering not, retains an obscure sense
> Of possible sublimity, whereto
> With growing faculties she doth aspire,
> With faculties still growing, *feeling still*
> *That whatsoever point they gain, they yet*
> *Have something to pursue.*"

WORDSWORTH'S *Prelude.*

"This is more vile," he made reply,
"To breathe and loathe, to live and sigh,
Than once from dread of pain to die.

"Sick art thou—a divided will
Still heaping on the fear of ill,
The fear of men, a coward still."

Repulsed here, the poet falls back upon the more hopeful aspects of life, tries to awaken within himself a glow of sympathy with human effort, and recalls the time when he anticipated a life of work and a death of honor.

"In some good cause, not in mine own,
To perish, wept for, honor'd, known,
And like a warrior overthrown:

"Whose eyes are dim with glorious tears,
When, soil'd with noble dust, he hears
His country's war-song thrill his ears:

"Then dying of a mortal stroke,
What time the foeman's line is broke,
And all the war is roll'd in smoke."

This, says the Voice, was the stirring of the young blood—good enough for the moment, but mere illusion. Recurring to the previously urged plea that man cannot read the riddle of the earth or grasp any truth related to the mind, it reiterates its first advice.

"Cease to wail and brawl!
Why inch by inch to darkness crawl?
There is one remedy for all."

The poet is now stung to anger.

"O dull, one-sided Voice," said I,
"Wilt thou make everything a lie,
To flatter me that I may die?"

He refers to the noble lives that have been lived, and maintains that, though the atmosphere of the world is darkened with dust of systems and of creeds, some have achieved calm, and known "the joy that mixes man with heaven." Here occurs that picture of the martyr Stephen which is in Tennyson's loftiest manner.

> "He heeded not reviling tones,
> Nor sold his heart to idle moans,
> Tho' curs'd and scorn'd, and bruised with stones:
>
> "But looking upward, full of grace,
> He pray'd, and from a happy place
> God's glory smote him on the face."

The Voice answers, sullenly, that there were no real grounds of hope in Stephen's case, but that "the elements were kindlier mixed," the circumstances were more than ordinarily fitted to produce illusion.

The poet now suggests that, if he goes hence in quest of truth, he may merely exchange one riddle for a hundred, and that his anguish, "unmanacled from bonds of sense," may become permanent. On this, the Voice, reversing its original argument in favor of suicide, namely, that it might be the door to a life of more splendid activity, tempts him with the prospect of eternal rest in death. Such inconsistency of argument is admirably in keeping with the character of a tempter.

> "Consider well," the Voice replied,
> "His face, that two hours since hath died;
> Wilt thou find passion, pain, or pride?
>
> "Will he obey when one commands?
> Or answer should one press his hands?
> He answers not, nor understands.
>
> "His palms are folded on his breast:
> There is no other thing express'd
> But long disquiet merged in rest."

In several stanzas, equally beautiful and impressive with these, or more so, the Voice argues that death makes an end of a man. The poet calls up his whole strength to reply. If all

is dark, he begins, how are we to know that the dead are dead?
Why, since the victory of death seems so complete, does any
one cherish a doubt upon the subject?

> "The simple senses crown'd his head:
> 'Omega! thou art Lord,' they said,
> 'We find no motion in the dead.'

> "Why, if man rot in dreamless ease,
> Should that plain fact, as taught by these,
> Not make him sure that he shall cease?

> "Who forged that other influence,
> That heat of inward evidence,
> By which he doubts against the sense?"

Here, at last, the poet has opened fire from his main battery.
This is one of the grand arguments on which the advocate of
immortality takes his stand. It is an argument pre-eminently
accordant with modern science and modern philosophy, for no
one can urge it with clearer logic than the evolutionist. Why
is it proper for the bird to fly and for the reptile to crawl?
Because, says the evolutionist, the bird has developed wings.
In like manner, the human creature has developed a faith in
immortality, or, to put it at the lowest, a hope of immortality.
Here and there a few persons, by elaborately educating themselves in the gospel of death, have quenched their hope of life
beyond the grave; but that, throughout all the millions of civilized and semi-civilized humanity, this hope has been evolved,
is just as sure as that a bird has wings. And it adds greatly
to the impressiveness of this hope that it has been evolved, as
Tennyson specially urges, in clear antagonism to the main current of evidence that sense can produce upon the subject.

Having dwelt upon the momentous fact that, in spite of appearance, in spite of the triumph of the worm and the obsti-
nate silence of the dead, we refuse to believe that the spirit of
the deserted house has ceased to exist, the poet names several
circumstances which justify this refusal. Man feels capacities

within him that ask an eternity for bloom and fruitage. There
is in nature something that sends him in yearning search beyond and above nature.

> That type of Perfect in his mind
> In Nature can he nowhere find.
> He sows himself on every wind.

This is simply true, and it would be hard to name a truth of
more importance. In the entire universe, as revealed to man
by his senses, there is nothing perfect; and the central impulse
in all man's noblest striving is derived from the aspiration of
his spirit toward a perfect truth, a perfect beauty, a perfect
happiness, which are exemplified nowhere in the world. Art,
religion, and the impetuous career of the race toward a higher
grade of civilization, depend alike upon the universal imperfection of the material world, and the impossibility that a God-
related spirit, which man is, should be contented therewith.

But I anticipate. The momentous proposition stated respecting man in the foregoing triplet is introductory to the still
more momentous proposition contained in that which comes
next.

> He seems to hear a Heavenly Friend,
> And thro' thick veils to apprehend
> A labor working to an end.

The fount and goal of perfection is God. Being infinite, He
can guarantee the eternal progress of man. Into the vast field
of argument thus opened up the poet does not enter, but, after
indicating by fine imagery that there is more in man's life
than the senses can give account of, defies the Voice to extinguish his hope.

> Heaven opens inward, chasms yawn,
> Vast images in glimmering dawn,
> Half shown, are broken and withdrawn.

*   *   *   *   *

> But thou canst answer not again.
> With thine own weapon art thou slain,
> Or thou wilt answer but in vain.

The force of this reasoning is obvious. The object of the Voice hitherto has been to involve the poet in universal doubt, and if it is legitimate to doubt, it is legitimate to hope. The Voice, therefore, starts a new argument.

> "Where wert thou when thy father play'd
> In his free field and pastime made,
> A merry boy in sun and shade?
>
> *   *   *   *
>
> Before the little ducts began
> To feed thy bones with lime, and ran
> Their course, till thou wert also man."

In one word, "You were nothing before birth, and you will be nothing after death." This is really a formidable argument, and I am not sure that Tennyson's answer is quite so satisfactory as most of his reasonings. If he granted, he says, the thesis that "to begin implies to end," he might still dispute the certainty of his having begun to exist at birth. He might take refuge in Platonic metempsychosis, and suggest that he had been previously embodied. If he has descended from a higher race, he may have hints of his ancestry in gazing up Alpine heights, or yearning toward the stars. Very skilfully he touches upon those strange revealings, with which every one is more or less haunted, of things witnessed in some place or time of which memory has no distinct record.

> Moreover, something is or seems,
> That touches me with mystic gleams,
> Like glimpses of forgotten dreams—
>
> Of something felt, like something here;
> Of something done, I know not where;
> Such as no language may declare.

These strike me as very wonderful stanzas. To express their delicate and subtle meaning in prose would have been too difficult for the great majority of men, and Tennyson expresses it with the utmost possible lucidity in exquisite verse. But the logic of the general argument is not at this point so good as the poetry. It may perplex a captious disputant, but will hardly convince an honest doubter. I think Tennyson might have ventured to buttress it by reference to the Heavenly Friend formerly mentioned, and to the "labor working to an end," which, though "through thick veils," he apprehends in the universe. If, by a process of creative evolution, conducted through uncounted millions of ages, God has matured the spirit, man, until he has been able to look up and see his Father's face, until he has realized his distinctness from matter and his relationship to God, until he has recognized, as the two supreme realities, the finite spirit, man, and the Infinite Spirit, God, then man may entertain a sure and confident hope that no material dissolution will have power to destroy him, and may believe that his Heavenly Friend, who has revealed himself to man as he has *not* revealed himself to the beasts of the field, made him immortal when he capacitated him for worship.

The first Voice, though not confessing itself vanquished, now retires from the conflict. The light of the Sabbath morning breaks upon the poet. He releases the casement and sees the people pressing on to the house of God, where each enters "like a welcome guest." The second Voice is now at his ear. It announces "a hidden hope." This idea of a mystery of hope and promise in the world—veiled from us for good reasons for the present—is one that has dwelt deeply in Tennyson's mind. It appears in the "awful rose of dawn" which God makes himself at the end of the Vision of Sin. The last words in the poem before us are, "Rejoice! Rejoice!"

Such is this extraordinary performance. I have quoted largely, for it would have been quite impossible for me to con-

vey an idea of Tennyson's metaphysical poetry by converting
it into the bald propositions of metaphysical prose.   But I
have not quoted enough to do justice either to the continuity
of the reasoning or to the loveliness of the verse.   The poem
contains nearly 160 stanzas, and I hope that the reader will
turn to it for himself, in order to gather up the missing links
of the argument and the missing jewels of the poetry.*

---

* The following letter, which the Rev. Mr. Kirkman, of St. Stephen's,
Hampstead, kindly permits me to print, needs little introduction. Having
heard, from a common friend, that Mr. Kirkman had talked of my papers
on The Two Voices, and knowing, from the experience of a good many
years, that his remarks were likely to be racy, I asked him to let me have
them in black and white. My readers will, I think, agree with me that
they are suggestive and original.

Hampstead, November 29th, 1878.

I fear such kindly-disposed persons as ——— ——— and you would but
commit the mistake of taking sparrows for nightingales or eagles if you
gave any heed to casual remarks of mine. It is only because I have always been exceedingly interested in The Two Voices that I ventured to criti-
cise your criticisms, which I had so much gratification in reading. I have
often thought of a small volume on that and a few other choice short poems,
because I find nothing more beneficial to the mind, or more pleasing, than
a thorough searching out of all harmonies contained in one such a poem. It
exercises one's ingenuity, and the poet so immensely *agrees with one's self!*
So it is an accident, or else a deep-laid intention, both results of one law
of similar thought in reflective minds free of preconceived notions as fixed
forever, that a vast portion of The Two Voices is almost verbatim *taken
from* (?) Lucretius and Seneca.

The only *two observations* I did *not* go with (in all humility) are (1) the
opening remark about *suicide*. It is not that—or so nakedly that—the
Voice recommends; which would argue that the man was in an *unsound*
state of mind, or bordering on insanity, or IN IT *according to a British jury!*
Then he was unfit to reason. But *we are not* all of us usually under this
impulse; and I suppose Two Voices to be what more or less goes on *in
every reflective mind* in the present day. That is, Hamlet's To be or not to
be!—the general conflict between the value and worthlessness of life. I
should say the Two Voices are the *Intellect* and the *Heart.* Voice No. 2
always, or almost, gives *emotional* replies; the other dry intellectual arguments. Besides, *you cannot help* AGREEING with *Voice No.* 1, only less than
you do with *Voice No.* 2. This must ever be the state of the human mind,
or until far higher stages in this evolution of us and ours! Especially, IM-

MORTALITY *is an emotional longing, and not an intellectual conviction.* And so the argument for it is distinctly conducted by the "*main battery,*" as you call it. We know Cleombrotus for one committed suicide because of his boundless joy at the thought of immortality. But my hesitation No. 2 was about "the elements were kindlier mixed." This is not the *circumstances ;* for they could not be *worse* than in Stephen's case : but it was his *physical and mental construction fed and met by the new Truth in Christ,* which Galen distinctly calls κρᾱσις, and the Latins, after the Greeks, *harmonia.* This is why gentle and lymphatic physical constitutions take life and its problems so gently—

> " Gently comes the world to those
> That are cast in gentle mould "—

and we sanguine constitutions (like your poor servant) *care* too much about truth and its issues, and things in general. But the highest natures *combine* these two peculiarities in a κρασις or ἁρμονια—like *Blake,* Spinoza, Stephen—just the *opposite* of Schopenhauer, *Heine, Swift,* Fichte (?), Carlyle, and those great minds not *kindly* mixed. Forgive my preaching. But, after all, *emotion,* the weakest, yet triumphs, and *its conclusions* of JOY AND TRUST are what gives strength to the intellect, and leads, like the little child leading the bear, or In Memoriam, No. 114.

But I suggest, AS A CHURCHMAN, that *The Two Voices* was evidently a glorious dire (dear) penalty for lying in bed and oversleeping himself on a Sunday morning, and not getting up in time to go to church ! If at 5 *minutes to* 11 those sweet *three* had *looked up at him* in return, and seen him drawing up the blinds in his *chemise-de-nuit,* they would have "*blessed*" him with the advice to come and hear our dear minister, and you will be told all the truth, with the additional advantage of INFALLIBILITY. I am so sorry I troubled you ; but I do heartily appreciate your intense admiration of that which is my first favorite poem.

Yours very sincerely,   J. KIRKMAN.

On this I make but three observations :—First, that the question taken up at the *outset* of the poem is explicitly suicide or not suicide, which question, involving as it does nice ethical, social, and theological considerations, was thought worthy of careful meditation by Shakspeare, Goethe, and Hume ; second, that when I speak of the " circumstances " of Stephen, I mean all the conditions of the case, including, as highly important, those referred to by Mr. Kirkman ; and, third, that I cannot admit the argument from evolution in favor of immortality to be merely emotional.

CHAPTER VIII.

ŒNONE, THE LOTOS-EATERS, ULYSSES, SIMEON STYLITES.

I HAVE dwelt so long upon a few poems that I must guard myself against being supposed to overlook or to underrate a number of pieces which I may not have been able to consider. Many of these are of the very highest excellence, and would repay analysis line by line. Œnone, The May Queen, The Gardener's Daughter, Tithonus, Godiva, The Lotos-Eaters, Ulysses, Lucretius, St. Simeon Stylites, Galahad, The Day Dream, are all, in their widely-varying fashions, masterly.

Œnone was a Nymph of Ida loved by Paris, the son of Priam and Hecuba, King and Queen of Troy, before he decided between the rival goddesses in their strife about the golden apple. Aphrodite, to whom he adjudged the prize, having promised to give him the most beautiful woman in the world to wife, he deserted Œnone, and went to Greece to woo Helen. Tennyson shows us Œnone among the crags of Ida musing upon her sad history and faithless lover. Consummately beautiful as is the poem, it nevertheless illustrates the extreme difficulty, if not impossibility, of effecting a genuine resuscitation of antiquity in modern literature. The same remark applies to Goethe's *Iphigenie auf Tauris*, a work which, in the serenity and tenderness of its tone, recalls Œnone, though its much larger extent and dramatic form preclude minute resemblance. Goethe's heroine is a wise, gentle, blue-eyed, golden-haired German girl; Tennyson's is an English young lady; in both poems the vein of sentiment is distinctively modern. Œnone wails melodiously for Paris without

the remotest suggestion of fierceness or revengeful wrath. She
does not upbraid him for having preferred to her the fairest
and most loving wife in Greece, but wonders how any one
could love him better than she does.

> Most loving is she ?
> Ah me, my mountain shepherd, that my arms
> Were wound about thee, and my hot lips prest
> Close, close to thine in the quick-falling dew
> Of fruitful kisses, thick as Autumn rains
> Flash in the pools of whirling Simois.

A Greek poet would have used his whole power of expression to instil bitterness into her resentful words. The classic
legend, instead of representing Œnone as forgiving Paris,
makes her nurse her wrath throughout all the anguish and terror of the Trojan War. At its end, her Paris comes back to
her. Deprived of Helen, a broken and baffled man, he returns
from the smoking ruins of his native Troy, and entreats Œnone
to heal him of a wound which, unless she lends her aid, must
be mortal. Œnone gnashes her teeth at him, refuses him the
remedy, and lets him die. In the end, no doubt, she falls into
remorse, and kills herself—this is quite in the spirit of classic
legend; implacable vengeance, soul-sickened with its own victory, dies in despair. That forgiveness of injuries could be
anything but weakness—that it could be honorable, beautiful,
brave—is an entirely Christian idea; and it is because this
idea, although it has not yet practically conquered the world,
although it has indeed but slightly modified the conduct of
nations, has, nevertheless, secured recognition as ethically and
socially right, that Tennyson could not hope to enlist the sympathy and admiration of his readers for his Œnone, if he had
cast her image in the tearless bronze of Pagan obduracy.

It is not impossible that our newest school of classical renaissance, guiltless as it is of any tincture of Christian sentiment or sympathy, may restore certain tones of the Pagan

mind more successfully than poets who, like Goethe and Tennyson, have been ethically and emotionally in tune with Christendom.   Such restoration seems to me superfluous, for we
have the actual tones of classic Paganism, fresh, perfect, indestructible, in the books of Homer and Sophocles, of Virgil and
Horace; and, though correct in certain traits of Paganism, the
modern imitation is sure to be false in others, for no modern
poet, however intense may be his rejection of Christ, believes,
as Homer did, in Zeus or Apollo; and the atheistic cynicism
which spurns at Christianity is not likely to sympathize vividly with religion in any form.   I wish English poets were not
so proud, or perhaps I should rather say so conceited.   Goethe
and Schiller, when their fame filled Europe, did not think
themselves too gifted for translation; but young English poets,
whose familiarity with the classics and superb command of
their own language point them out as the men to give us in
English an exact reproduction of the masterpieces of ancient
poetry, seem to think nothing worthy of their talents except
to enter the lists as actual rivals of the Greeks, and try to produce original English poems in their manner.   Mr. Browning
has of late given welcome proof that these remarks do not apply to him, and I trust that his example as a translator will be
followed by younger poets.   One perfectly translated drama
from Sophocles would be worth a hundred tinselly imitations.

Apart from translation, the best way of treating classical
subjects in modern verse is that which was adopted with absolute frankness by Shakspeare, and which has been pursued
less daringly by Goethe and Tennyson—namely, to trust for
effect to the delineation of human nature not as specially modified by the conditions of existence in Greece, but as the poet
sees and knows it in the Germany or the England in which
he lives.   Shakspeare, in Winter's Tale, represents messengers
bringing oracles from the shrine of Apollo at Delphi and Puritans singing psalms to hornpipes.   His stupendous genius can

neutralize even absurdities like this, but no one could safely venture upon such liberties in our day. Goethe and Tennyson, men of academic culture, avoid offending learned readers by freaks of glaring anachronism, and even contrive, by skilful use of classical or semi-classical coloring, to add a peculiar charm to their antique poems; but for their main interest they depend, as truly as Shakspeare depended, upon portraiture of character, exhibition of passion, and beauty of description.

Tennyson's picture of Aphrodite, when she appealed to Paris to give her the apple, is almost too rich and ruddy for a poem in the Greek manner.

> Idalian Aphrodite beautiful,
> Fresh as the foam, new-bathed in Paphian wells,
> With rosy, slender fingers backward drew
> From her warm brows and bosom her deep hair
> Ambrosial, golden round her lucid throat
> And shoulder; from the violets her light foot
> Shone rosy-white, and o'er her rounded form,
> Between the shadows of the vine-bunches,
> Floated the glowing sunlights, as she moved.

The splendor of her beauty overcame Paris as if it had been a vision. The offer of empire and royal power made by Herè, the queen of Olympus; the tender of kingly wisdom, power over himself, and empire of noble manhood, made by Pallas; both these were in a moment swept from his mind by the presence and the glance of Sovereign Love. Aphrodite knew that she was victress before she opened her lips. "A subtle smile in her mild eyes "—she could afford to be mild in the serene intensity of her satisfaction at having triumphed over her sister goddesses—announced her faith in her own irresistibility. She spoke but two or three words and laughed, when Paris handed her the apple, and Œnone saw "great Herè's angry eyes" vanishing into the golden cloud that was to be her chariot through the sky.

In the Lotos-Eaters Tennyson dramatically embodies and expresses a mood of mind very common in the present day, a mood felicitously characterized by Mrs. Barrett Browning in the words "enchanted reverie," a mood in which the weary soul asks whether the gains of life are really worth the toil they cost, and plaintively acquiesces in the conclusion that "there is no joy but calm!" Not one crude, unmelodious, inexpressive, or—so far as I am able to detect—imperfect line occurs in this poem. The imagery is marvellous even for Tennyson, marvellous in its freshness, in its nice accuracy of truth to nature, in its beauty, in its deep appropriateness. The Lotos-land is one in which everything proceeds languidly, pausingly, dreamily.

> A land of streams! some, like a downward smoke,
> Slow-dropping veils of thinnest lawn, did go.

Whoever has seen a stream in its midsummer slenderness of volume, falling down a front of rock divided into steps or ledges, will admit that no words could possibly surpass in descriptive precision these last. The Falling Foss, for example —a small cascade on one of the affluents of the Esk, near Whitby—affords a realization so exact of the "slow-dropping veil of thinnest lawn," that it at once, when I saw it last summer, reminded me of the poem; nor could an officer of the Geological Survey, writing with purely scientific intent, devise a more liberal or a more expressive description. And what imagery could convey the lulling influence of sweet, faint music more movingly than this?

> There is sweet music here that softer falls
> Than petals from blown roses on the grass,
> Or night-dews on still waters between walls
> Of shadowy granite, in a gleaming pass;
> Music that gentlier on the spirit lies
> Than tir'd eyelids upon tir'd eyes.

Equally wonderful are those lines in which, as contrasted with the feverish unrest, with the tumultuous wearing activity, of human existence, the deep quietude of nature's operations in the vegetable world is shadowed forth.

> Lo! in the middle of the wood,
> The folded leaf is woo'd from out the bud
> With winds upon the branch, and there
> Grows green and broad, and takes no care,
> Sun-steep'd at noon, and in the moon,
> Nightly dew-fed; and turning yellow
> Falls, and floats adown the air.
> Lo! sweeten'd with the summer light,
> The full-juiced apple, waxing over-mellow,
> Drops in a silent autumn night.
> All its allotted length of days,
> The flower ripens in its place,
> Ripens and fades, and falls, and hath no toil,
> Fast rooted in the fruitful soil.

And surely the philosophy of sad resignation—the *cui bono*, don't care, *nil admirari* mood, that wants only to rest—the morphia-crave of a generation that has made the circuit of science, art, philosophy, to be told at last by Schopenhauer that life is misery and the universe a failure—never found more appropriate expression than that which follows:

> Let us alone. Time driveth onward fast,
> And in a little while our lips are dumb.
> Let us alone. What is it that will last?
> All things are taken from us, and become
> Portions and parcels of the dreadful past.
> Let us alone. What pleasure can we have
> To war with evil? Is there any peace
> In ever climbing up the climbing wave?
> All things have rest; and ripen toward the grave
> In silence; ripen, fall and cease:
> Give us long rest or death, dark death, or dreamful ease.

In the conclusion of the poem the voyagers agree to " swear
an oath, and keep it with an equal mind," to remain in the
Lotos-land, and " lie reclined on the hills like gods together,
careless of mankind." Then follows a picture of the gods in
their high abodes:

For they lie beside their nectar, and the bolts are hurl'd
Far below them in the valleys, and the clouds are lightly curl'd
Round their golden houses, girdled with the gleaming world:
Where they smile in secret, looking over wasted lands,
Blight and famine, plague and earthquake, roaring deeps and fiery sands,
Clanging fights, and flaming towns, and sinking ships, and praying hands.
But they smile, they find a music centred in a doleful song,
Steaming up, a lamentation and an ancient tale of wrong,
Like a tale of little meaning, tho' the words are strong.

Plagiarism is out of the question, but Tennyson must, I
think, have derived the suggestion of this passage from the
Song of the Fates, repeated by Iphigenie at the end of the
fourth act of Goethe's drama. The gods are therein described
as sitting at golden tables in everlasting feast, or striding along
from peak to peak of the mountains, while, up through gorge
and chasm, steams to them, like light clouds of altar-smoke, the
breath of strangled Titans.* There can be no thought of plagiarism, because Tennyson's treatment is entirely his own. His
substitution of the toiling races of men for the fallen Titans, as
objects of contemplation to the happy gods, adds both to the
sense of reality and to the pathos of the lines; but the coinci-
dence seems too close to have been purely accidental. The
germ, derived from Goethe, may very well have remained in
Tennyson's mind without his recollecting whence it came.

---

*   Sie aber, sie bleiben   Aus Schlünden der Tiefe
        In ewigen Festen   Dampft ihnen der Athem
        An goldenen Tischen.   Erstickter Titanen,
        Sie schreiten vom Berge   Gleich Opfergerüchen,
        Zu Bergen hinüber: Ein leichtes Gewölke.

The only objection which I can conceive taken to this poem
is that it is a linguistic *tour de force*, without adequate motive
—a labored and superlative expression of a mood of over-civil-
ized lassitude, with which the poet has not, and no one ought
to have, true sympathy. I shall not say that this objection is
wholly unreasonable; but a poet is the Æolian harp of his
time, on whose mind every wandering wind of its characteristic
moods may be expected to awaken some tone of music; and
there can be no doubt—the more's the pity—that the melodious effeminacy of the Lotos-Eaters has many to sympathize
with it in these weary days.

Antithetically and grandly opposed to the nerveless sentiment of the Lotos-Eaters is the masculine spirit of the lines on
Ulysses, one of the healthiest as well as most masterly of all
Tennyson's poems. The old sea-king, strong as a fishing-boat
that has battled long with tide and storm, spurns the idea of
rest.

> How dull it is to pause, to make an end,
> To rust unburnish'd, not to shine in use!
> As tho' to breathe were life.

He is far above the weakness of disguising his pride, or pretending not to know that he is a man of men.

> I am become a name;
> For always roaming with a hungry heart
> Much have I seen and known; cities of men
> And manners, climates, councils, governments,
> Myself not least, but honor'd of them all;
> And drunk delight of battle with my peers,
> Far on the ringing plains of windy Troy.

"Delight of battle"—what a superb translation of the *cer-
taminis gaudia* of the Latin poet! The kindly but measure-
less contempt with which old Ulysses regards his universally-
respected son Telemachus has a finer humor in it than Tennyson ever attains elsewhere.

> Most blameless is he, centred in the sphere
> Of common duties, decent not to fail
> In offices of tenderness, and pay
> Meet adoration to my household gods,
> When I am gone.   He works his work, I mine.

Excellent young man!—but what an unspeakable relief it will be never to hear his judicious remarks again.   A wilder set of fellows I have been accustomed to:

>   My mariners,
> Souls that have toil'd, and wrought, and thought with me—
> That ever with a frolic welcome took
> The thunder and the sunshine, and opposed
> Free hearts, free foreheads—you and I are old;
> Old age hath yet his honor and his toil;
> Death closes all: but something ere the end,
> Some work of noble note, may yet be done,
> Not unbecoming men that strove with gods.
> The lights begin to twinkle from the rocks:
> The long day wanes: the slow moon climbs: the deep
> Moans round with many voices.   Come, my friends,
> 'Tis not too late to seek a newer world.
> Push off, and sitting well in order smite
> The sounding furrows; for my purpose holds
> To sail beyond the sunset, and the baths
> Of all the western stars until I die.

Observe how chary Tennyson here is of color.   Compare the roseate glow that pervades Œnone, where the tale is of goddesses contending for the prize of beauty—the wealth of flowers, and clouds delicately creeping among pine-trees, and sunlights floating between shadows of vine-bunches on the rounded form of Aphrodite—with the sharp, smiting, unadorned, laconic phrases of the leader of men.   That will tell us how great a master of *tone* is Tennyson!   We need not quarrel with him for having bestowed those mariners on Ulysses in his old age.   There were, indeed, none such.   They all lay fathom-deep in brine; no Homer, no Athene had paid

regard to *them;* Ulysses returned alone to his isle, the hero
only being of account in the eyes of classic poet or Pagan
goddess. Tennyson's Ulysses is, after all, an Englishman of
the Nelson wars rather than a Greek, and his feeling for his
old salts is a distinctively Christian sentiment. So, indeed, is
his desire for effort, discovery, labor, to the end. It never
would have occurred to Homer that Ulysses could want anything for the rest of his life but pork-chops and Penelope.

Another of Tennyson's memorable and masterly studies of
character is St. Simeon Stylites. Few characters in history
are better deserving of consideration than Simeon of the pillar; for Simeon is typical, as the fewest men are, of an age
and generation. He belonged to the end of the fourth and
first half of the fifth centuries of our era, and was a pattern
Christian of the period. It was characteristic of the pious
men of the time that they utterly perverted Christianity by
overdoing it. Forgetful of St. Paul's divine simplicity and inspired common-sense, of his angry impatience with people that
imposed a yoke upon themselves, observed days and times and
months and years, hesitated to eat what they found in the
market, and fancied that God Almighty could possibly wish
them to do anything with their bodies except keep them clean
and healthy, Simeon and his contemporaries nursed an immoral sanctity by subjecting their bodies to pains and priva-
tions, and rejecting all sorts of natural delights. Simeon was
a Syrian, who, at the early age of thirteen, deserting the useful
vocation of sheep-feeding, entered an austere monastery, and
addressed himself to the worse than useless business of torturing himself into a saint. "After a long and painful novitiate,"
says Gibbon, whose historical accuracy on the subject may be
relied upon, "in which Simeon was repeatedly saved from pious
suicide, he established his residence on a mountain, about thirty
or forty miles to the east of Antioch. Within the space of a
mandra, or circle of stones, to which he had attached himself

by a ponderous chain, he ascended a column, which was successively raised from the height of nine to that of sixty feet
from the ground.   In this last and lofty station, the Syrian
Anachoret resisted the heat of thirty summers, and the cold of
as many winters.   Habit and exercise instructed him to maintain his dangerous situation without fear or giddiness, and successively to assume the different postures of devotion.   He
sometimes prayed in an erect attitude, with his outstretched
arms in the figure of a cross ; but his most familiar practice
was that of bending his meagre skeleton from the forehead to
the feet ; and a curious spectator, after numbering twelve hundred and forty-four repetitions, at length desisted from the
endless account.   The progress of an ulcer in his thigh might
shorten, but it could not disturb, this *celestial* life ; and the patient Hermit expired without descending from his column. . . .
Successive crowds of pilgrims from Gaul and India saluted
the Divine pillar of Simeon ; the tribes of Saracens disputed
in arms the honor of his benediction ; the queens of Arabia
and Persia gratefully confessed his supernatural virtue ; and
the angelic Hermit was consulted by the younger Theodosius in the most important concerns of the Church and State.
The remains were transported from the mountain of Telenissa,
by a solemn procession of the patriarch, the master-general of
the East, six bishops, twenty-one counts or tribunes, and six
thousand soldiers ; and Antioch revered his bones as her glorious ornament and impregnable defence."

Such was the man whose feelings, intentions, hopes—whose
theory of life and general conception of duty and destiny—
Tennyson undertakes to express in Simeon's own words as he
stands or crouches on his pillar.   In the spirit of earnest sympathy, not without a trace of reverence, does the poet enter on
his task, not permitting himself a touch of grotesquerie, and
not in the least inclined, as Gibbon slyly is, to poke fun at
Simeon.   He at once penetrates to the centre of his hero's

scheme of things by grasping his conception of himself as a sinner. These are the opening lines, the speaker being Simeon:

> Altho' I be the basest of mankind,
> From scalp to sole one slough and crust of sin,
> Unfit for earth, unfit for heaven, scarce meet
> For troops of devils, mad with blasphemy,
> I will not cease to grasp the hope I hold
> Of saintdom, and to clamor, mourn, and sob,
> Battering the gates of heaven with storms of prayer,
> Have mercy, Lord, and take away my sin.

The man, remember, had gone in for saintship at thirteen years of age. I am not aware that it has ever been suggested that, before then, he had committed any serious offence. A good-for-nothing shepherd I can well imagine him to have been, but that would not strike him as a sin. The probability, the practical certainty, is that Simeon's sin, as is usual in similar cases, was almost entirely a thing of the imagination, and that there was no definite form of sin, whether of wrong-doing to mankind, wrong-doing to himself, or wrong-doing, in the shape of hatred or indifference, to God—under one or other of which heads all sin that is not mere fantastic imagining must come—of which he could be accused. But you will find that nearly the whole of the false or foolish religiosity in the world—the religiosity that is the shame of religion, pure and undefiled, and that corrupts the best into the worse attribute of man—depends upon a preposterously exaggerated conception of sin. The self-degradation of false humility lies close to spiritual pride, and there is exquisite psychological truth in Tennyson's representation of Simeon, for all his sense of the tons of sin that weigh him down, as reckoning up the claims he has to Divine consideration.

> Bethink thee, Lord, while thou and all the saints
> Enjoy themselves in heaven, and men on earth
> House in the shade of comfortable roofs,

Sit with their wives by fires, eat wholesome food,
And wear warm clothes, and even beasts have stalls,
I, 'tween the spring and downfall of the light,
Bow down one thousand and two hundred times
To Christ, the Virgin Mother, and the saints;
Or in the night, after a little sleep,
I wake: the chill stars sparkle; I am wet
With drenching dews, or stiff with crackling frost.
I wear an undress'd goat-skin on my back;
A grazing iron collar grinds my neck;
And in my weak, lean arms I lift the cross,
And strive and wrestle with Thee till I die;
O mercy, mercy! wash away my sin.

After every paroxysm of self-accusation, the sweet and subtle strain of self-laudation is heard.

I, Simeon of the pillar, by surname
Stylites among men; I, Simeon,
The watcher on the column till the end;
I, Simeon, whose brain the sunshine bakes;
I, whose bald brows in silent hours become
Unnaturally hoar with rime, do now
From my high nest of penance here proclaim
That Pontius and Iscariot by my side
Show'd like fair seraphs.   On the coals I lay,
A vessel full of sin; all hell beneath
Made me boil over.

Nevertheless
            That time is at the doors
When you may worship me without reproach;
For I will leave my relics in your land.
And you may carve a shrine about my dust,
And burn a fragrant lamp before my bones,
When I am gather'd to the glorious saints.

It may seem unreasonable, when we consider how much
Tennyson has given us in this poem, to suggest that he might
have achieved still more if he had endeavored to realize for us

Simeon's connection with the life of his time—to enable us to comprehend a state of society in which the Emperor Theodosius could come to consult this religious maniac on the concerns of Church and State. It was religion of Simeon's kind that brought destruction upon Eastern Christendom. A strong superstition is safer for nations than an infantile religion, and the warrior saints that issued from the Arabian desert trampled into the dust those babyish idolaters that knelt round shrines like Simeon's. Of no creed ever known among men is it so imperiously necessary as it is of Christianity to ask, Of what *sort* is your Christianity? Simeon of the pillar, Oliver Cromwell, John Howard, Dominic the Inquisitor, were all sincere Christians. But a babyish Christianity is the most dangerous of all, and the sturdy atheists that now jostle us on the streets of every city will do to us as Mohammed and his friends did to the worshippers of Simeon Stylites, if the God we reverence is one who sets great store by our genuflections, and is immensely interested in what we have for dinner on Friday.

14

CHAPTER IX.

IN MEMORIAM.

I HAVE just glanced over something I wrote about In Memoriam in 1856, which, as it has been long out of print, as I agree with every word of it, and it strikes me as prettier than what I write now, I shall take the liberty to insert here, if only by way of introduction to further remarks: "The greatest poem, all things considered, that Tennyson ever wrote is In Memoriam. In it the purely æsthetic enthusiasm of the London School has given place to, or rather has obtained a new and grander vitality in, the enthusiasm of life and action. The name of the poem indicates one of the most difficult efforts which can be made in literature. It aims at embalming a private sorrow for everlasting remembrance, at rendering a personal grief generally and immortally interesting. The set eye and marble brow of stoicism would cast back human sympathy; the broken accents and convulsive weeping of individual affliction would awaken no nobler emotion than mere pity; it was sorrow in a calm and stately attitude, sorrow robed in angel-like beauty, though retaining a look of earnest, endless sadness, that would draw generation after generation to the house of mourning. No poet, save one possessed not only of commanding genius, but of peculiar qualifications for the task, could have attempted to delineate a sorrow like this. The genius of Tennyson found in the work its precise and most congenial employment; and the result is surely the finest elegiac poem in the world.

"In whatever aspect we view it, by whatever test we try it,

this poem is great, is wonderful. Very absurdly did those critics talk, who spoke of the grief it contained as not very strong, perhaps not quite sincere, because it was so elaborately sung, and dwelt upon so long. They utterly misconceived the nature of that grief. They applied a general and commonplace rule to an altogether exceptional instance; an instance which might give new canons to criticism, but which might well perplex the old critics. The shadow of death had fallen between two spirits, knit together in close and noble friendship. That friendship had depended for its endurance on the community of lofty and immortal sympathies, of great thoughts, of pure and earnest affections. It was beyond the power of death to bring it to a termination. Death could only cast a veil of shadow between the two friends, and leave the one still on the earthward side to endeavor to pierce its obscurity, to hope for the day of its removal. It was rather a solemnity, a stillness, a composed and majestic mournfulness, that was cast over the life of Tennyson, than a darkening, overpowering distress. It was the silence and sadness of autumn enveloping the glories of summer; it was the melancholy of that aspect of nature, perhaps the loveliest of all, when the year first knows the approach of winter, and welcomes it with a resigned yet mournful smile. The shadow fell everywhere. Amidst the groups of living men, amidst the forms of external nature, there was still its presence, and into all the regions of thought and feeling it came. Everywhere it brought its solemn sadness; only, on the skies of the future, like the shadow of the earth cast up toward immensity, it seemed to kindle brighter lights as it were stars. The maiden combing her golden hair, in expectation of her lover, whose step will not be heard that evening, or at all again, at the door—the bride leaving her father's house—the wife whose husband lives apart from her sympathy, in high and remote regions of thought—the boy-friends of the village green whose paths in after-life lie far asunder—these all move in the

procession of the poem, passing through the shadow of its sorrow.   Nature, too, must mourn with the poet, as Shelley saw
her mourning by the bier of Adonais.   The ocean must sink
into calm around the coming corpse; the gorgeous gloom of
evening must shroud it; and all the tears of morning must fall
over it.   Into the world of thought and meditation the same
solemn influence comes.   The greatest questions on which the
human mind can be engaged, questions relating to the being of
God, to the immortality of the soul, to the limits of knowledge,
to the nature and conditions of future existence, all of which
arise naturally before a mind ever looking beyond the bourne
for the face of a friend, present themselves to the mourner, if,
perchance, he may find any solace or enlightenment in them.
From the simplest scenes of domestic life Tennyson has ascended into the rare atmosphere of metaphysics, and from those
heights of contemplation where he so well can tread, sees the
shadow of his sorrow falling over the filmy clouds.   Nor is this
all.   The shadow of that sorrow fell everywhere, but, as the
poet himself tells us, it was a shadow glory-crowned.   Death
at times takes up the harp of life, as love did in one of Tennyson's earlier poems, and draws from it inspiring music.   The
mighty hopes that make us men, the future glories of humanity, the social joy and tenderness which even on earth shed
a softening radiance over settled sorrow, the encouragement
which a noble heart finds in dwelling on a life honorably finished, in listening to the earnest voices of the dead, all mingle
in the lofty strain.   So perfect is the unity, so mighty the
sweep, of this poem: what more could elegiac poetry be?"

The distinctive character of In Memoriam is determined by
its having been composed, not within the compass of a few
days or weeks, expressly in honor of a deceased friend, like Milton's Lycidas and Shelley's Adonais, but during a number of
years, and apparently without being designed as a single poem.
Poets always write about themselves, and about their time.

Milton, in singing of his friend, tells us how he himself loved to pass his mornings.

> For we were nursed upon the self-same hill,
> Fed the same flock by fountain, shade, and rill;
> Together both, ere the high lawns appeared
> Under the opening eyelids of the morn,
> We drove afield, and both together heard
> What time the gray-fly winds her sultry horn,
> Battening our flocks with the fresh dews of night,
> Oft, till the star, that rose, at evening, bright,
> Toward heaven's descent had sloped his westering wheel.

And the intense Puritanism which occupied Milton's mind, and the minds of a vast proportion of Milton's countrymen, in 1637, appears in his finding or making occasion, in lamenting the fate of drowned Lycidas, to summon St. Peter to rebuke the hireling clergy of the day.

> Last came, and last did go,
> The pilot of the Galilean lake;
> Two massy keys he bore of metals twain
> (The golden opes, the iron shuts amain),
> He shook his mitred locks, and stern bespake:
> "How well could I have spared for thee, young swain,
> Enow of such, as for their bellies' sake
> Creep, and intrude, and climb into the fold.
> Of other care they little reckoning make,
> Than how to scramble at the shearers' feast,
> And shove away the worthy bidden guest;
> Blind mouths! that scarce themselves know how to hold
> A sheep-hook, or have learn'd aught else the least
> That to the faithful herdman's art belongs!"

The hungry sheep, meanwhile, "look up and are not fed" by the recreant shepherds, while "the grim wolf" of Rome "devours apace." The stern Puritan, however, sees the two-edged sword of St. Michael being unsheathed in the background.

> But that two-headed engine at the door
> Stands ready to smite once, and smite no more.

Shelley, too, in describing the poetical mourners round the
bier of Keats, gives us a portrait of himself:

> 'Midst others of less note came one frail form,
> A phantom among men; companionless
> As the last cloud of an expiring storm,
> Whose thunder is its knell; he, as I guess,
> Had gazed on Nature's naked loveliness,
> Actæon-like, and now he fled astray
> With feeble steps o'er the world's wilderness,
> And his own thoughts, along that rugged way,
> Pursued, like raging hounds, their father and their prey.
>
> His head was bound with pansies overblown,
> And faded violets, white, and pied, and blue;
> And a light spear topped with a cypress cone,
> Round whose rude shaft dark ivy-tresses grew
> Yet dripping with the forest's noon-day dew,
> Vibrated, as the ever-beating heart
> Shook the weak hand that grasped it; of that crew
> He came the last, neglected and apart;
> A herd-abandoned deer, struck by the hunter's dart.

But the scheme of In Memoriam permits Tennyson to speak
of himself more than would have been graceful in Milton or
Shelley; almost as much, indeed, as of Arthur Hallam; and to
dwell as long as he pleases upon the characteristics of his time.
In Memoriam, therefore, reflects the second half of the nineteenth century like a mirror. Hallam is not, strictly speaking,
the subject of the poem; he has merely furnished the occasion
and suggestion of it. About one hundred and thirty pieces,
each complete in itself, are knit into a true poetic unity by
being set to one key-note, pervaded with one sentiment, colored
by one feeling, idea, thought. More is not required of any
one of them than that it should have some relation, even
though indirect and distant, to the friendship between Hallam
and Tennyson. They thus become to a very large extent
autobiographical; and their autobiographical interest is higher

than their biographical in the proportion in which Alfred Tennyson is a more important and interesting person than Arthur Hallam. In point of fact, the weakest parts of In Memoriam — and it was impossible that in a poem of such extent there should not be difference in the quality of parts— are those which are devoted exclusively to Arthur. Gifted, noble, and delicate-minded, there is no reason to believe that Tennyson's friend had strength enough to gain, if he had lived, a permanent place in literature. The picture of him in the capacity of oratorical archer, aiming his arrow better than his fellow-debaters, is finely executed.

> And last the master bowman, he
>   Would cleave the mark. A willing ear
>   We lent him. Who, but hung to hear
> The rapt oration flowing free
>
> From point to point, with power and grace
>   And music in the bounds of law,
>   To those conclusions when we saw
> The God within him light his face,
>
> And seem to lift the form, and glow
>   In azure orbits heavenly-wise;
>   And over those ethereal eyes
> The bar of Michael Angelo.

It is unfortunate, in view of this exalted description, that the likeness of Arthur Hallam, published in a recent edition of In Memoriam, should be singularly disappointing. Gentle intelligence and refinement are the highest qualities which you can possibly attribute to the original of such a portrait; the want of any *reserve* of power, any deep thoughtfulness or force, is conspicuous in the face and decisive.

> Heart-affluence in discursive talk
>   From household fountains never dry;
>   The critic clearness of an eye,
> That saw thro' all the Muses' walk.

This we easily believe of the bright youth whose lips wear
an ingenuous smile as he looks on the book in his hand ; but
no such powers can be supposed to slumber under the smooth
features as are attributed to Arthur in the next verse.

> Seraphic intellect and force
>> To seize and throw the doubts of man ;
>> Impassion'd logic, which outran
> The hearer in its fiery course.

Exaggeration, however, on this point was the most venial
of faults in the writer of In Memoriam, and he, I think, must
be base indeed who fails to perceive the inimitable marks of
sincerity and affection in Tennyson's delineation of his friend.
The charm of the autobiographical passages is so exquisite
that every reader wishes there had been more of them, and
they are introduced with a subtle grace and a deep, unconscious modesty, which exclude any suggestion of egotism.
There is more of Tennyson in In Memoriam than of Milton
in Lycidas or of Shelley in Adonais, and yet, judging from
the respective productions, I should say that Tennyson was
less self-centred and egotistical than either Shelley or Milton.

Nothing in the poem is nobler than the introductory stanzas.
They contain a brief presentment of several of the most important ideas that emerge in the course of the work.

> Strong Son of God, immortal Love,
>> Whom we, that have not seen Thy face,
>> By faith, and faith alone, embrace,
> Believing where we cannot prove.

Belief in foundation-truths rests not upon proof drawn out
in articulate logic, but upon convictions, authoritative instincts,
judgments of the reason and the conscience, which are in-
tertwined with the " final, deepest root of the being of man,
whereby he grows out of the invisible, and holds on his God

home." This is one of the main propositions which constitute
the intellectual framework of the poem. The poet proceeds
to express his reverent confidence in God.

> Thou wilt not leave us in the dust:
> Thou madest man, he knows not why;
> He thinks he was not made to die;
> And Thou has made him: Thou art just.
>
> Thou seemest human and Divine,
> The highest, holiest manhood, Thou:
> Our wills are ours, we know not how;
> Our wills are ours, to make them Thine.
>
> Our little systems have their day;
> They have their day and cease to be:
> They are but broken lights of Thee,
> And Thou, O Lord, art more than they.

Immortal Love, the Divine-human Son of God, is Tennyson's
essential conception of the adorable Sovereign of all things.
"The highest, holiest manhood, Thou." High and holy manhood is the best realization for us of the Divine, better than
all the power, the law, the glory of the world. But Sovereign
Love can be seen by faith only. Infinite force is suggested
by the material universe; but there is no voice in the breast
to tell us that force, even though infinite, deserves worship;
not to Power but to Love do we bow down. Love, however,
we cannot *prove* to be infinite. No accumulation of instances
of beneficence in the universe could logically warrant us in
crowding out or ignoring the instances of pain and anguish
which abound; nevertheless the Love, whose apparent shortcoming is the problem, the riddle, the maddening mystery of
the universe, is diviner than the power. Tennyson disguises
no fact in the world of realities. He avoids with innate
repugnance that habit of slurring over the evil in nature, and
dwelling only upon the good, which lends a character of vacuity

14*

to much pulpit declamation, and rightly offends the instinct
for truth, the fidelity to fact, of modern men of science.
Brightness of the sun—blackness of the starless night—they
both are here; and both must be faced, if we are to speak as
honest men.

> Thine are these orbs of light and shade;
>   Thou madest Life in man and brute;
>   Thou madest Death; and lo, Thy foot
> Is on the skull which Thou hast made.

Tennyson never indulges in the unredeemed and imbecile
folly of trying to get rid of the fact of evil by covering it up
in veils of words—to hocus himself by talking of phenomena
and noumena, and by saying that pain and privation, anguish
of body and torture of mind, are not realities, but appearances.
As if a million of industrious and peaceable men, women, and
children perishing by the lingering torments of famine, were
but an optical delusion! As if the locust cloud, hiding the
sky and darkening the earth, were not as real as the rain-cloud,
moving in beauty to the music of the west wind, and dropping
heavenly dew upon the mown grass! Nature, "red in tooth
and claw with ravine," be it what it will, is not unmixed, unqualified, unobstructed benevolence. One truth of transcendent importance is made plain by this fact—namely, that Nature is not God. "Are God and Nature then at strife?" asks
Tennyson, and, finding the question too difficult to answer, be-
takes himself reverently to the prayer of faith and hope.

> I falter where I firmly trod,
>   And falling with my weight of cares
>   Upon the great world's altar-stairs
> That slope thro' darkness up to God,
>
> I stretch lame hands of faith, and grope,
>   And gather dust and chaff, and call
>   To what I feel is Lord of all,
> And faintly trust the larger hope.

I venture to suggest that, by resolute firmness in declaring
that nature is *not* God, the strife between God and nature may
become less appalling. "Strife," indeed, is not the right word
to describe the fact. If nature is imperfect and God alone
perfect, then the result, though looking like strife to us, cannot
really be such. Bacon warned us long since against the mistake that God's works are His very image. The spirit, man,
more nearly related to his Father Spirit than the material universe can be, is entirely at liberty to investigate nature, to
modify the arrangements, to mend the defects, to resist the
laws, of the material universe, in accordance with his own
wants ; and finds an infinitely purer and more faithful revelation of God in his own breast than in the stars of night or the
blue sky of day. So many high-minded and reverent-minded
men in these times profess themselves pantheists, or use language
which seems to me to imply pantheism, that I almost feel constrained to speak with bated breath of the system ; but I cannot help seeing with perfect clearness that, in worshipping the
universe, the pantheist abdicates man's sovereignty over nature,
and annihilates God. Nature is neutral ; neither good nor bad,
neither just nor unjust, neither cruel nor kind ; the wind that
sits laughing in the shoulder of your sail, the wave that rushes
in at the hole opened by a sunken rock, and hurries your ship
and you to the bottom. It is one-sided to speak of nature as
" a stern force to be tamed and mastered," for the balmy air
that nurses the green blade in spring needs no taming, and the
autumn sunshine that ripens the corn needs no mastering. Nature, I repeat, is neutral ; smiles on the battle-field with its miles
of quivering agony, as on the cradle with its sleeping babe. If
you insist upon worshipping it, you are in the eyes of the cool
man of science an idler, in the eyes of the spiritual theist an
idolater. To worship reasonably, you must worship what is
worthy of worship—namely, the " immortal Love," that is different from nature and above nature, that is not dead and un-

conscious, but a Spirit and alive. That which was incarnate in Christ, and which, in measure, is incarnate in every worthy man, we can intelligently worship;—nothing else.

The pantheistic hypothesis of the individual life, as a bubble floating for one moment on the billow of existence and then lost in the All, is explicitly repudiated by Tennyson.

> That each, who seems a separate whole,
>   Should move his rounds, and fusing all
>   The skirts of self again, should fall
> Remerging in the general Soul,
>
> Is faith as vague as all unsweet :
>   Eternal form shall still divide
>   The eternal soul from all beside ;
> And I shall know him when we meet.

Against the idea that man is but a fleeting organism, the product of material forces which made him, and which will dissolve him, the poet protests with impassioned fervor.

> And he, shall he,
> Man, her last work, who seem'd so fair,
>   Such splendid purpose in his eyes,
>   Who roll'd the psalm to wintry skies,
> Who built him fanes of fruitless prayer,
>
> Who trusted God was love indeed,
>   And love Creation's final law—
>   Tho' Nature, red in tooth and claw
> With ravine, shrieked against his creed—
>
> Who loved, who suffer'd countless ills,
>   Who battled for the True, the Just,
>   Be blown about the desert dust,
> Or seal'd within the iron hills ?
>
> No more ? A monster then, a dream,
>   A discord. Dragons of the prime,
>   That tare each other in their slime,
> Were mellow music match'd with him.

> O life as futile, then, as frail !
>> O for thy voice to soothe and bless !
>> What hope of answer, or redress ?
> Behind the veil, behind the veil.

He will not admit that, if the grave were known to be the
end, life would still be precious. The shuddering sense of infinite, inevitable darkness, as it crept over life, ever coming
nearer, would take the light from friendship, and crush the
heart out of love itself.

> O me, what profits it to put
>> An idle case ? If Death were seen
>> At first as Death, Love had not been,
> Or been in narrowest working shut.

With perfect deliberation he records his opinion that, if we
are mocked by the promises of our nature, it were well to fling
back life as a pretended gift, but real burden and cheat.

> I trust I have not wasted breath :
>> I think we are not wholly brain,
>> Magnetic mockeries ; not in vain,
> Like Paul with beasts, I fought with Death ;

> Not only cunning casts in clay ;
>> Let Science prove we are, and then
>> What matters Science unto men,
> At least to me ? I would not stay.

The answer commonly made to this is that the desirability
of a thing is no proof of its being a fact, and that it is childish
to believe in immortality merely because it would be pleasant,
or even because it would be morally beneficial, to be immortal.
But those who thus answer mutilate the argument, and mis-
conceive its scope. It is not upon desirability or upon unde-
sirability, upon pleasantness or unpleasantness, that it depends,
but upon what I may call *genuineness of guarantee*, as predi-
cable of the surmise of immortality. Science recognizes the

trustworthiness of every appetency normally pertaining to the
living thing.   It is in the form of appetency that the announce-
ment is made of results supremely important to the organism.
Hunger is in itself a mere want, but its satisfaction results in
the perpetuation of the individual life.   The genuineness of
the hunger is all we require to know, in order to be justified
in trusting that the administration of food will be beneficial.
So it is in the case of all our appetites and all our passions ;
and we can easily imagine cases in which, though the result of
gratifying a passion had never been experimentally verified, yet
its gratification, simply as such, would be followed by the re-
sulting benefit.   Were two human infants of different sex to be
cast ashore on an uninhabited island, and to grow to maturity,
it would be only by simple obedience, prior to all verification,
of an appetency proper to the human constitution, that mankind could be perpetuated in the island.   This case furnishes
an exact scientific analogue to the argument in favor of immortality used by Tennyson.   The impassioned longing for immortal life is, he virtually alleges—though I am not aware that
he or any one else has stated the case in what I submit to be
its exact scientific form—as proper to the human being as the
passion of sexual love.   It is real, it is normal, it is trustworthy ; and this none the less though the objector may affirm
that it has not been verified by experiment.   Not only poets
and poetical philosophers have rested the defence of a confident
hope of immortality upon its connection with a genuine appetency of our nature, but so rigid and dry a reasoner as Kant.

In Memoriam was written before the publication of Darwin's
Origin of Species, and before the critical elaboration, scarcely
less valuable than the original work, of Darwin's argument by
Huxley.   These date a new epoch in the history of science,
and the doctrine of evolution has been since accepted by a
vast proportion of scientific men.   After having been a chief
subject of discussion in all educated circles for nearly twenty

years, the meaning of evolution is at length beginning to be understood, and I think that, if Tennyson were now composing In Memoriam, he would not add the following stanza to those last quoted.

> Let him, the wiser man who springs
> Hereafter, up from childhood shape
> His action, like the greater ape,
> But I was *born* to other things.

These words have no force except on the supposition that the law of the lower creature remains law for the higher creature that has been developed from it. This is the *reverse* of the fact. If evolution requires the ape to live as a fish, then evolution may require the man to live as an ape: but if evolution pointedly, peremptorily, scientifically requires every creature to conform to the law of that stage of existence to which it has attained—if it is not proper to the frog to swim in the sea or to the bird to crawl on the clay—then evolution *forbids* man to be an ape, and stamps with the signet of its approbation, touches with the sceptre of its authority, every one of those appetencies of the moral nature, those passions of the spiritual life, which distinguish man as man. If, therefore, Tennyson were writing In Memoriam now, and if his acquaintance with the scientific attainment of his time continues as profound and as accurate, *mutatis mutandis*, as it was in 1849, he would, I think, substitute, for the unfortunate stanza about the greater ape, an appeal to those men of science who admit that man has risen to a higher platform of being than the ape's, to acknowledge the trustworthiness of that faith in God and that hope of immortality, which the ape has not, but which, Hume · himself being witness, man *has*, attained to, wherever he is not sunk almost to the brutish level, or has not, let me add, obscured, by fogs of subtle self-sophistication, what Professor Huxley calls the ray that visits his spirit from the "infinite Source of truth."

I know not how many pages I should fill if I were to comment upon every passage in this poem in which light is shed on themes of sacred importance, and I must content myself with noting, in the way of brief, imperfect summary, a few of the main positions taken up by the poet. The Creative Power, the Supreme Life of the universe, is Immortal Love, and this is to be worshipped as God. It is approachable, it is knowable, not by analysis of so-called contrivance in nature, not by consideration of eagle's wing, or dissection of insect's eye, but by listening to the voice of the spirit, inarticulate yet intense, reason and conscience blended in faith, the deep " I have felt my Father's presence " of the heart. The Infinite One cannot be fully known; our systems are but "broken lights" of a truth that is inexhaustible. To rest finally in these, therefore, or to substitute them for the God they partly reveal, is to fall into idolatry. Life beyond the grave is guaranteed by its being the complement of our present life; the want of our spiritual nature; the condition of a right and rhythmic human existence. Progress is the law, hope the privilege, of man's life; nor is the striving onward and upward, or the doubt it necessitates, in any measure sinful, but the reverse, if combined with tenderness of regard for all symbols of the Divine that are the object of sincere worship, and with gracious modesty in touching, more perfectly than before, the hem of God's garment. Man's living will, his own inalienably and freely, rising in the "spiritual rock" of his essential manhood, attests his relationship to God, yet without destruction of his individuality. The mystery of free-will man cannot solve; " our wills are ours, we know not how :" but it is in the exercise of a genuine freedom that he perfects his liberty by conforming it to the law of God; " our wills are ours to make them Thine."

CHAPTER X.

VERY little alteration has been made in the later editions of In Memoriam, and only one piece of three stanzas, embodying a thought suggested by the yew above Arthur Hallam's grave, has been added. In the outset of the poem the "old yew" had been addressed, and the poet had longed for the "stubborn hardihood" of the "sullen tree." The new stanzas, numbered XXXIX., are among the most obscure in the whole compass of In Memoriam.

> Old warder of these buried bones,
>   And answering now my random stroke
>   With fruitful cloud and living smoke,
> Dark yew, that graspest at the stones
>
> And dippest toward the dreamless head,
>   To thee, too, comes the golden hour
>   When flower is feeling after flower;
> But Sorrow fixt upon the dead,
>
> And darkening the dark graves of men,
>   What whisper'd from her lying lips?
>   Thy gloom is kindled at the tips,
> And passes into gloom again.

These verses have an interest as illustrating Tennyson's minute attention to natural facts — an attention almost too minute to be followed by ordinary observers. That a smoke-like dust rises from yew-foliage in spring when struck with a stick — that flower feels after flower in the golden springtime of love — that the bloom of the yew is a kindling of the

tips, as with fine emerald flame, which darkens again into
the deep black-green of the plant's perpetual mourning—are
the facts which he weaves into the symbolism of the poem;
and I suppose he means Sorrow to exult over the tree as
brightening but for a very little time, and then passing "into
gloom again." This may be admirable in respect of truth to
nature, and may afford high delight to those who regard it as
the perfection of poetry to give play to endless subtlety in the
interpretation of imagery into ethics and emotion, but I think
the lines abstruse to a fault.

A slight verbal change has been introduced twice or thrice.
The three concluding stanzas of No. CXIII. prefigure, under a
variety of aspects, the career which Arthur Hallam might have
fulfilled if his life had not been cut short.

> A life in civic action warm,
>   A soul on highest mission sent,
>   A potent voice of Parliament,
> A pillar steadfast in the storm,
>
> Should licensed boldness gather force,
>   Becoming, when the time has birth,
>   A lever to uplift the earth
> And roll it in another course,
>
> With many shocks that come and go,
>   With agonies, with energies,
>   With overthrowings, and with cries,
> And undulations to and fro.

The "many shocks" of the last verse become in recent
editions the "thousand shocks"—a clear improvement, both
because "thousand" is more specific than "many," and because a slight yet real charm is added by the association of
the reader's ideas with Shakspeare's "thousand natural shocks
that flesh is heir to."

"I wake, I rise;" such was the first introduction to No. C.;
it now is, "I climb the hill;" and the appropriateness of the

change is manifest, for from the summit to which the poet climbs can best be seen the "landscape underneath," the various features of which—the gray old grange, the lonely fold, the morass with its whispering reeds, the knoll of ash and hawthorn, the quarry on the hill-side, "haunted by the wrangling daw," the pastoral rivulet winding through the meadow —are detailed in the succeeding stanzas.

More important, as touching, though slightly, on the meaning, and not merely upon its poetical presentation, is the substitution of "sacred wine" for "sacramental wine" in No. XXXVII. "Dear to me," says the poet, "as sacred wine" is all that the dead friend had said. "Sacred" is the larger and more generous word of the two, farther removed than "sacramental" from suggestions of ecclesiastical partisanship.

In No. XXIV. the second stanza used to run as follows:

> If all was good and fair we met,
> This earth had been the Paradise
> It never look'd to human eyes,
> Since Adam left his garden yet.

The later version has been thus modified:

> If all were good and fair we met,
> This earth had been the Paradise
> It never look'd to human eyes,
> Since our first sun arose and set.

One might almost fancy that Tennyson had a grudge against Adam. We saw that, in one of the early poems, he changed him from the "grand old gardener" into the mere "gardener Adam," and here he dismisses him from the verse altogether. The change, however, in the present instance, is for the better. There is no passage within the range of holy writ on which theological ingenuity has more daringly operated than the account of the garden of Eden and the fall of Adam. A particular school of theology has laid so much stress on its doctrine of the Fall, that the latter could scarcely be endorsed without acceptance being virtually intimated of the entire theological scheme elaborated by the school in question; but Tennyson aims, in this poem, at being neither Evangelical nor Ritualist, neither Puritan nor High-Church; he writes in sympathy with the universal religious faith and the universal religious sentiment, in so far as these can be discriminated from all shades of sectarian speciality.   The religion of all the Churches, in so far as it is sincere and of elevating tendency, open to knowledge and reverent in spirit, has his powerful support; but he adopts the catch-words of no party, and speaks bitterly of none.   His religious sympathies are as broad as the face, as deep as the heart, of Christendom; and no better proof could be adduced of his magnanimity and of the generosity and geniality of his nature, than the fact that, son as he is of a clergyman of the State Church, there is not in his works one stanza into which has crept a supercilious or angry reference to Dissent.   The religion of In Memoriam is more comprehensive and in the deepest sense more Christian than it would have been if as Evangelical as Pollok's Course of Time, or as High-Church as Keble's Christian Year.

But there is another reason why the sun was introduced into this verse.   The two stanzas which immediately succeed are these :

> And is it that the haze of grief
>   Makes former gladness loom so great?
>   The lowness of the present state,
> That sets the past in this relief?
>
> Or that the past will always win
>   A glory from its being far;
>   And orb into the perfect star
> We saw not when we moved therein?

A sun seen at a sufficient distance becomes a star; and the harmony of the piece is finely enhanced by the preservation of astronomical imagery throughout, instead of mixing up stars and gardens.

It may be irksome to some of my readers to have their attention directed to linguistic *minutiæ* like these; but poets of culture are critics as well as bards, and it is not uninstructive, nor ought it to be uninteresting, to follow Tennyson's hand in the delicately careful and, on the whole, judicious emendations which he has made upon the earlier editions of this celebrated poem.

CHAPTER XI.

MORE pleasant, however, and in a large sense more profitable also, than the investigation of linguistic niceties, is it to survey In Memoriam in its larger features as they combine into a whole—to consider the articulation of the landscape, its general framework and divisions, its alternations of plain and mountain, of brooding cloud or full sunlight. Mr. Tainsh, in his admirable analysis of the poem, has distinguished a few chronological landmarks which it is useful to keep in view. The first twenty-one pieces are occupied with the period intervening between Arthur's death and burial. In this section of the work the gloom lies deep, though it is at no time oppressive. Sorrow has entered the poet's world, and all nature feels the influence.

> O Sorrow, cruel fellowship,
>   O Priestess in the vaults of Death,
>   O sweet and bitter in a breath,
> What whispers from thy lying lip?
>
> "The stars," she whispers, "blindly run;
>   A web is wov'n across the sky;
>   From out waste places comes a cry,
> And murmurs from the dying sun:
>
> "And all the phantom, Nature, stands—
>   With all the music in her tone,
>   A hollow echo of my own—
> A hollow form with empty hands."

He repels, not without contemptuous anger, the trite condolence that "loss is common to the race."

> That loss is common would not make
>   My own less bitter, rather more:
>   Too common! Never morning wore
> To evening, but some heart did break.
>
> O father, whereso'er thou be,
>   Who pledgest now thy gallant son;
>   A shot, ere half thy draught be done,
> Has still'd the life that beat from thee.
>
> O mother, praying God will save
>   Thy sailor—while thy head is bow'd,
>   His heavy-shotted hammock-shroud
> Drops in his vast and wandering grave.

And yet—such is our human weakness—the community of sorrow is a legitimate theme of condolence.

The voyage of the ship that bears to England the body of Arthur suggests several very beautiful and solemn pieces. With brief, decisive, unerring strokes, like touches of a magic wand, the poet shows us the vessel as it moves onward in the night.

> I hear the noise about thy keel;
>   I hear the bell struck in the night;
>   I see the cabin-window bright;
> I see the sailor at the wheel.

Which is the best of these lays of the returning ship I do not undertake to say, but I can conceive nothing nobler either in feeling, in imagery, or in language than No. XI. I select it for quotation for another reason. It affords illustration of the poet's mastery in two kinds of excellence, rare and precious apart, but far more rare and precious when combined: the first, vividness and truth of local color; the second, breadth. What could be more minutely correct or felicitous in local color than the "pattering" to the ground of the chestnut, or the "twinkle into green and gold" of the gossamers? What could be more magnificently broad than the very next verse, which describes the great English plain sweeping toward the sea, or the verse that portrays the billowy sleep of the ocean?

> Calm is the morn without a sound,
>   Calm as to suit a calmer grief,
>   And only thro' the faded leaf
> The chestnut pattering to the ground:
>
> Calm and deep peace on this high wold,
>   And on these dews that drench the furze,
>   And all the silvery gossamers
> That twinkle into green and gold:
>
> Calm and still light on yon great plain
>   That sweeps with all its autumn bowers,
>   And crowded farms and lessening towers,
> To mingle with the bounding main:
>
> Calm and deep peace in this wide air,
>   These leaves that redden to the fall;
>   And in my heart, if calm at all,
> If any calm, a calm despair:
>
> Calm on the seas, and silver sleep,
>   And waves that sway themselves in rest,
>   And dead calm in that noble breast
> Which heaves but with the heaving deep.

Note that the five stanzas of this glorious poem—for it is a complete poem in itself—constitute a single sentence. To do it justice in reading, one would require to modulate the voice to each change of scene—and there are several—without altering its pitch. As the tone of thought and feeling never changes for a moment, whether it is on the windy wold or on the autumn plain, or on the waves far out at sea, that the poet looks, the appropriateness of this continuity in language, preserved from clause to clause of the great sentence, is beyond question.   The five stanzas sound like one long, rippling swell of cathedral music.

The ship arrives; the grave is dug: and on the ashes of the dead will grow "the violet of his native land."   Arthur Hallam lies in the chancel of Cleveland Church by the Severn.

> There twice a day the Severn fills;
> The salt sea-water passes by,
> And hushes half the babbling Wye,
> And makes a silence in the hills.

Meditating by the grave of his friend, Tennyson next bethinks him of the course of their friendship.   "Through four sweet years" they had walked with each other "from flower to flower, from snow to snow;" in the autumn of the fifth year, the "Shadow feared of man" met them and broke the "fair companionship," bearing Arthur away whither Alfred could not follow, though he walked in haste, and mused that the Shadow was waiting for him "somewhere in the waste." Piece after piece now is filled with the melodious reflections of the poet on the past.   Love had cleft his sorrows in twain, and given half of each to be borne by Arthur. He shrinks, as at a guilty suggestion, from the idea that his affection may die away into indifference.   Nor will he be tempted by the anguish of bereavement to wish that he had never loved.

> I hold it true, whate'er befall;
> I feel it, when I sorrow most;
> 'Tis better to have loved and lost
> Than never to have loved at all.

This is a glimpse of light under the edge of the black cloud; and in the next piece we approach the first Christmas after Arthur's death.   The bells of four hamlets answer each other through the mist on Christmas Eve, and the poet feels that they touch his sorrow with joy, "the merry, merry bells of Yule."   But the season is not as former seasons have been.

> Oh, yet we trust that somehow good
>   Will be the final goal of ill,
>   To pangs of nature, sins of will,
> Defects of doubt, and taints of blood.

No. LXXII. commemorates the first return of the day when Arthur died. The poet has not yet so far triumphed over his sorrow as to discriminate the plaintive melancholy of the autumn wind from the wild howl of misery. It is a day of lashing rain, when the rose pulls sideways and the daisy closes its crimson fringes; but if it had been clear and calm, and if the sunlight had danced in "chequerwork of beam and shade along the hills," it would have been "as wan, as chill, as wild," to the poet as now.

> Lift as thou mayst thy burthen'd brows
>   Thro' clouds that drench the morning star,
>   And whirl the ungarner'd sheaf afar,
> And sow the sky with flying boughs,
>
> And up thy vault with roaring sound
>   Climb thy thick noon, disastrous day;
>   Touch thy dull goal of joyless gray,
> And hide thy shame beneath the ground.

In the interval between the first anniversary of his loss and the second Christmas, he reflects much on the transitory nature of human affairs. The fame that he foresaw has been quenched, and that seems strange in a world in which there is "so much to do." But he believes that "somewhere, out of human view," work may be found for his friend which will be "wrought with tumult of acclaim;" and why repine that he is not on earth to work or to sing, when the lays in which his image is enshrined may be dumb "before the mouldering of a yew?"

> These mortal lullabies of pain
>   May bind a book, may line a box,
>   May serve to curl a maiden's locks;
> Or when a thousand moons shall wane

A man upon a stall may find,
And, passing, turn the page that tells
A grief, then changed to something else,
Sung by a long-forgotten mind.

The second Christmas is not so sad as the first. Over all things broods "the quiet sense of something lost," yet no one shows a token of distress, and long use has dried the tears. There is cheerfulness, accordingly, in the strain in which he greets the new year, and acknowledges the impulse of its young life within him.

Bring orchis, bring the foxglove spire,
The little speedwell's darling blue,
Deep tulips dash'd with fiery dew,
Laburnums, dropping-wells of fire.

O thou, new-year, delaying long,
Delayest the sorrow in my blood,
That longs to burst a frozen bud,
And flood a fresher throat with song.

He recurs to the sentiment that it is better to have loved and lost than never to have loved at all, and in a piece containing about thirty stanzas dwells upon the fact that his grief has not weakened but strengthened him, upon his earnest consciousness that "the sense of human will" demands action from every man, and upon his deliberate resolution to cherish "the mighty hopes that make us men." It will, he feels, be no dishonor to his friend though his heart should glow with new love.

My heart, tho' widow'd, may not rest
Quite in the love of what is gone,
But seeks to beat in time with one
That warms another living breast.

Immediately after this long piece, he lifts up his voice and speaks with veritable rapture. There is no mention of Arthur in the four superb stanzas in which he calls upon the genial

splendor of sunny air to flood his soul with its freshness and joy. The four verses not only constitute a single sentence, but do not contain any punctuating mark except a few commas. The sentence in five stanzas, which I formerly quoted, had several points only less important than the full stop, but there is not even the rest of a semicolon in this long clarion-blast.

> Sweet after showers, ambrosial air,
>   That rollest from the gorgeous gloom
>   Of evening over brake and bloom
> And meadow, slowly breathing bare
>
> The round of space, and rapt below
>   Thro' all the dewy-tassell'd wood,
>   And shadowing down the horned flood
> In ripples, fan my brows and blow
>
> The fever from my cheek, and sigh
>   The full new life that feeds thy breath
>   Throughout my frame, till Doubt and Death,
> Ill brethren, let the fancy fly
>
> From belt to belt of crimson seas
>   On leagues of odor streaming far,
>   To where in yonder orient star
> A hundred spirits whisper "Peace."

The second anniversary of the death is by no means so gloomy as the first. The poet thinks of all those to whom the day comes with memories, whether joyful or sorrowful, calls them "kindred souls," and says that they mourn with him. Before the third Christmas the Tennyson family quit their native Lincolnshire, and their departure affords suggestion for several descriptive lyrics of great beauty.

> Unlov'd, by many a sandy bar,
>   The brook shall babble down the plain,
>   At noon or when the lesser Wain
> Is twisting round the Polar star ;

Uncared for, gird the windy grove,
   And flood the haunts of hern and crake;
   Or into silver arrows break
The sailing moon in creek and cove;

Till from the garden and the wild
   A fresh association blow,
   And year by year the landscape grow
Familiar to the stranger's child;

As year by year the laborer tills
   His wonted glebe, or lops the glades;
   And year by year our memory fades
From all the circle of the hills.

The third Christmas, therefore, is passed in a new land; and now, though grief is not oppressive, Christmas has lost its old associations, and the poet cannot permit it to be devoted to the old mirth. His mood, however, is not that of sorrow, but of pensive hope; and when Christmas-day has stolen quietly by, he bursts out in those jubilant verses, familiar wherever the English language is spoken, that bid the bells of the new year "ring in the Christ that is to be." It is still winter when Arthur's birthday arrives; but though the eaves are fringed with icicles, and the "leafless ribs and iron horns" of the wood make harsh music, the day shall be mirthfully celebrated.

Bring in great logs, and let them lie,
   To make a solid core of heat;
   Be cheerful-minded, talk and treat
Of all things ev'n as he were by;

We keep the day. With festal cheer,
   With books and music, surely we
   Will drink to him, whate'er he be,
And sing the songs he loved to hear.

In the succeeding pieces, to the end of the poem, there is the same crescent glow of hope and strength and joy. Man is to set his foot on nature, and know himself nature's sovereign.

Nature is but "earth and lime;" it dies; "human love and truth" endure. Man has been a giant laboring from his youth; much has he suffered, much also has he conquered; and now his "attributes of woe" are "glories," and the discipline of trouble has but fitted him for higher achievement, if he will

> Arise and fly
> The reeling Faun, the sensual feast;
> Move upward, working out the beast,
> And let the ape and tiger die.

Not inappropriately, and without any break in its pervading and perfect harmony, the work that had death for its suggestion ends with a marriage.

I conceive that this monumental and superlative poem has done more than any literary performance of the nineteenth century to express and to consolidate all that is best in the life of England, its domestic affection, its patriotic feeling, its healthful morality, its rational and earnest religion. Happy the nation whose accepted and greatest poet thus voices its deepest instincts. Let who will adjure Englishmen to galvanize the corpse of Paganism, I shall take my place in the throng of simple folk who listen, well pleased, to the home-bred, heart-felt, honest strains of In Memoriam.

SELDOM has it happened to any author to become, in his own lifetime, a classic to the same extent as Tennyson; and among the many subjects which his works afford to critic, lecturer, and annotator, none, perhaps, yields a richer harvest of remark than his diction. "To describe his command of language," I wrote many years ago, "by any ordinary terms, expressive of fluency or force, would be to convey an idea both inadequate and erroneous. It is not only that he knows every word in the language suited to express his every idea; he can select with the ease of magic the word that above all others is best for his purpose: nor is it that he can at once summon to his aid the best word the language affords; with an art which Shakspeare never scrupled to apply, though in our day it is apt to be counted mere Germanism, and pronounced contrary to the genius of the language, he combines old words into new epithets, he daringly mingles old colors to bring out tints that never were on sea or shore. His words gleam like pearls and opals, like rubies and emeralds. He yokes the stern vocables of the English tongue to the chariot of his imagination, and they become gracefully brilliant as the leopards of Bacchus, soft and glowing as the Cytherean doves. He must have been born with an ear for verbal sounds, an instinctive appreciation of the beautiful and delicate in words, hardly ever equalled. His earliest poems are festoons of verbal beauty, which he seems to shake sportively, as if he loved to see jewel and agate and almondine glittering amidst tropic flowers."

When these words were written the Idyls of the King had

not appeared, and it was only in the Morte D'Arthur that
Tennyson had given earnest of what he was one day to achieve
in the poetic treatment of old British legend; but, though his
later works speak less of the blossom‑time—show less of the
efflorescence and iridescence, and mere glance and gleam, of
colored words—they display no falling off, but rather an ad‑
vance, in the mightier elements of rhythmic speech. He does
not permit that use of compound epithets, in which he exer‑
cises an Elizabethan freedom, to degenerate by frequency into a
mannerism.   The "silver-misty morn," the " wan-sallow plant"
bitten at the root, "the satin-shining palm on sallows in the
windy gleams of March," the "gloomy-gladed " hollow in the
mountain landscape, the "livid-flickering" flash of lightning,
the wave "green-glimmering toward the summit," the "sallow-
rifted glooms" of evening, the "battle-writhen arms " of the
strong knight, are examples of his inventive diction gleaned
from the Idyls.   "Tenderest-touching," " dark-splendid,"
" love-royal," "passion-pale," are single color-words.   Here
and there the language of the Idyls is somewhat weakened by
the too studious courting of an archaic tone, too scrupulous
avoidance of Greek and Latin derivatives, and by the use of
words like " reckling," " roky," " yaffingale," which have no
place in contemporary speech, and were unknown to Johnson.
If we are constrained to admit that, in expressiveness and pict‑
uresqueness, the language not unfrequently reaches the Shak‑
spearian level, we cannot deny that, in variety and wild•forest‑
like freedom, it falls beneath it. No English poet, however,
since Milton, can keep the lists against Tennyson as a master
of language.

The Morte D'Arthur, which now figures as one of the Idyls,
has a history, and to some extent a character, of its own. It
appeared in 1842, and was prefaced by a few admirably graphic
lines, in which it was described as one of twelve Books of an
Epic, condemned by their author to the fire as " faint Homeric

echoes, nothing - worth." Francis Allen had picked this, the eleventh, from the hearth, and kept it for his friend, "the parson Holmes." Whether the eleven Books said to have been burned had any other than an imagined existence, I cannot tell ; but the Morte D'Arthur is much more closely modelled on Homer than any of those Idyls of the King into which it was subsequently fitted. Not only in the language is it Homeric, but in the design and manner of treatment. The concentration of the interest on the hero, the absence of all modernism in the way of love-story or passion-painting, the martial clearness, terseness, brevity of the narrative, with definite specification, at the same time, of detail, are exquisitely true to the Homeric pattern. In some places the language reads like actual translation. Sir Bedivere, when Arthur sent him to cast the brand Excalibur into the mere, gazed upon the jewelled hilt and stood,

> This way and that dividing the swift mind,
> In act to throw.*

That is exactly what Homer would have said. The knight, taking up Arthur to carry him to the barge,

> Swiftly strode from ridge to ridge,
> Clothed with his breath, and looking as he walk'd,
> Larger than human on the frozen hills.
> He heard the deep behind him, and a cry
> Before. His own thought drove him like a goad.

These are, indeed, "Homeric echoes," and they prepare us to find that the few lines which Tennyson has translated from the

---

* I have to thank a correspondent for calling my attention to the fact that this expression, which certainly has a most Homeric sound, is neither more nor less than a literal translation of Virgil's line, *Atque animum nunc huc celerem, nunc dividit illuc.* Tennyson has paid much attention to the Mantuan imitator of Homer. His superb line, What time the mighty moon was gathering light, in Love and Death, is obviously an echo of Virgil's *Luna, revertentes quum primum colligit ignes.*

Iliad are perhaps the finest translation in the language. It will be no digression to quote them here—they cannot be divided.

The Night Bivouac under the Walls of Troy.

So Hector spake; the Trojans roar'd applause;
They loosed their sweating horses from the yoke,
And each beside his chariot bound his own;
And oxen from the city, and goodly sheep
In haste they drove, and honey-hearted wine
And bread from out the houses brought, and heap'd
Their firewood, and the winds from off the plain
Roll'd the rich vapor far into the heaven.
And these all night upon the ridge of war
Sat glorying; many a fire before them blazed:
As when in heaven the stars about the moon
Look beautiful, when all the winds are laid,
And every height comes out, and jutting peak
And valley, and the immeasurable heavens
Break open to their highest, and all the stars
Shine, and the shepherd gladdens in his heart.
So many a fire between the ships and stream
Of Xanthus blazed before the towers of Troy,
A thousand on the plain; and close by each
Sat fifty in the blaze of burning fire;
And eating hoary grain and pulse the steeds,
Fixed by their cars, waited the golden dawn.

ILIAD, VIII. 542–561.

I should pronounce these lines, so far as I am able to judge, quite faultless, but for the omission of the leathern thongs with which the horses were bound to the cars. Homer could no more have forgotten the stout leathern thongs by which all risk of a stampede in the night was avoided, than Carlyle could forget the Spanish snuff on Frederick's blue coat with red facings. If, however, Tennyson took time to translate one of the great Books of the Iliad in this fashion, we might have some experience in England of the fiery enthusiasm with which the Greeks delighted in their Homer.

I have often grudged the devotion of so much of Tenny-son's energy to manipulation of the Arthurian legends. The singer who does not speak to the heart of his own time may be a most entertaining artist, but is not a poetic seer, vested with the authority proper to such. He may delight the eye with forms of beauty moulded as delicately as those of an-tique gems, or please the ear with fairy tales, but he will not be a law-giver in the household. Tennyson has always been aware of this. "Nature," he says, "brings not back the Mas-todon," nor man the modes and habitudes of other times; and his reason for printing the Morte D'Arthur was not because it was Homeric, but because "some modern touches here and there redeemed it from the charge of nothingness." In his final dedication, also, to Queen Victoria, of the Idyls of the King, he is careful to point out that he has not meant the in-terest to be antiquarian, but present and perennial. The poem, he says, is

> New-old, and shadowing Sense at war with Soul
> Rather than that gray King, whose name, a ghost,
> Streams like a cloud, manshaped, from mountain peak,
> And cleaves to cairn and cromlech still.

Having, in addition to the occasional readings of many years, gone again carefully over the whole of the Idyls, I must, for my own part, confess that all grudgings and regrets have melted away in their splendor and fascination; and that, though the subject is liable to objections perhaps unanswera-ble, though the quality of the poetry in some places, owing to this faultiness of subject, sinks from the elevation of epic style, and tends toward the quaint and the archaic, though in some parts we seem to be looking upon exquisite poetic pantomime, and in some upon the fantastic extravagances of religious ma-nia; yet, take them all in all, they form an inestimable addi-tion to English literature.

The Coming of Arthur is a mere introduction to the Books that follow; useful, somewhat tiresome, happily brief. Gareth and Lynette is a tale which Mr. Morris would have handled felicitously; it is dainty reading; but Tennyson seems to me to be in it still only half in earnest. Ingenious readers find profound allegorical meanings in this piece, but I am not sure that those meanings do not belong to them as much as to the poet. At all events, he here sets before us in one or two effective lines the appearance of Arthur's Court when the Round-table was in the beauty of its morning. The "long-vaulted hall" is filled with

> The splendor of the presence of the King
> Throned and delivering doom,

his proudly loyal knights around him. Gareth saw

> In all the listening eyes
> Of those tall knights, that ranged about the throne,
> Clear honor shining like the dewy star
> Of dawn, and faith in their great King, with pure
> Affection, and the light of victory,
> And glory gain'd, and evermore to gain.

Arthur tells Gareth that his knights

> Are sworn to vows
> Of utter hardihood, utter gentleness,
> And, loving, utter faithfulness in love,
> And uttermost obedience to the King.

We are thus enabled to form an idea of Arthur's scheme of beating his foes and ennobling his subjects, by means of a brotherhood of dauntless and heroic knights constituting the Round-table; which idea accompanies us throughout the successive Books of the poem. All this is real enough; but the notion of Gareth, a prince by birth, serving as a kind of male Cinderella, and the character of his adventures in subduing the absurd creatures against whom he fights in the interest of Ly-

nette, throw us back into fairy-land. The portrait of Lynette
is brightly touched:

> A damsel of high lineage, and a brow
> May-blossom, and a cheek of apple-blossom,
> Hawk-eyes; and lightly was her slender nose
> Tip-tilted like the petal of a flower.

Quite in keeping with her tip-tilted nose and hawk-eyes are
her petulant, testy ways with her true knight, whom, on account of his apprenticeship in the kitchen, she haughtily repels,
holding her tip-tilted nose with finger and thumb when he
comes near, by way of hinting that he brings with him airs
from the lower regions.

Geraint and his submissive Enid are more real than Gareth
and his intractable Lynette, and memorable lines occur here
and there in the Book, as those spoken of the villagers by Geraint, to which Tennyson calls our attention by giving them,
with slight modification, twice over:

> They take the rustic murmur of their bourg
> For the great wave that echoes round the world.

In the morbid suspicion and crazy jealousy of Geraint, we
are probably intended to discern the first adumbration of those
clouds and storms which are gradually to blot out the whole
glory of the Round-table. The existence of mortal taint is
fully revealed in the next Book, which contains the triumph of
Vivien over Merlin. In respect of power Tennyson has never
surpassed the description of the guilty loves of Merlin and
Vivien. Byron has done nothing in passion-painting to equal
this piece; and those critics who say that Tennyson writes for
women, whereas Byron wrote for men, might learn from it
that it is not because he is unable to depict the unhallowed
raptures of desecrated love that Tennyson has shunned subjects which attracted Byron, but because he is still more at

home in those loftier regions where Byron's footing was infirm.

Elaine, or, as the Book is now called, Lancelot and Elaine, though less epical than Guinevere—not so sustained and severe in grandeur—must be classed as one of the mountain-summits of English poetry. The portrait of Lancelot is in some respects a higher because a more difficult achievement than the portrait of Arthur. In Lancelot's delineation Tennyson gives renewed expression to some of those fundamental ideas which run through all his writings, especially to the idea that sin is not the normal, the healthful state for man, and that no true man can in sin be permanently happy. In the hands of Byron, Lancelot would have been a gay and godless Lothario, a brilliant but commonplace man of the world; in the hands of Tennyson he is a hero who, though he has swerved from virtue, is at heart as heroic, as deeply in sympathy with righteousness and honor, as Arthur himself. The pure Gretchen instinctively shrank from the diabolic presence of Mephistopheles; but the pure and sweet Elaine was sensible of no badness in Lancelot, and, before she fully saw his face, was won by the music of his voice.

> The lily maid Elaine,
> Won by the mellow voice before she look'd,
> Lifted her eyes, and read his lineaments.
> The great and guilty love he bare the Queen,
> In battle with the love he bare his lord,
> Had marr'd his face and mark'd it ere his time.
> Another sinning on such heights with one,
> The flower of all the west and all the world,
> Had been the sleeker for it: but in him
> His mood was often like a fiend, and rose
> And drove him into wastes and solitudes
> For agony, who was yet a living soul.
> Marr'd as he was, he seemed the goodliest man
> That ever among ladies ate in hall,
> And noblest, when she lifted up her eyes,

However marr'd, of more than twice her years,
Seam'd with an ancient sword-cut on the check,
And bruised and bronzed, she lifted up her eyes
And loved him, with that love which was her doom.

I cannot trust my own words to describe what it was in
Arthur that caused him to be unsatisfying to Guinevere, and
must quote Tennyson's. The Queen speaks to Lancelot:

She broke into a little scornful laugh:
"Arthur, my lord, Arthur, the faultless King,
That passionate perfection, my good lord—
But who can gaze upon the sun in heaven?
He never spake word of reproach to me,
He never had a glimpse of mine untruth,
He cares not for me: only here to-day
There gleam'd a vague suspicion in his eyes:
Some meddling rogue has tamper'd with him—else
Rapt in this fancy of his Table Round,
And swearing men to vows impossible,
To make them like himself; but, friend, to me
He is all fault who hath no fault at all;
For who loves me must have a touch of earth;
The low sun makes the color: I am yours,
Not Arthur's, as ye know, save by the bond."

It is Guinevere who suggests to Lancelot the disguise out of
which comes all the trouble of Elaine; and the evolution of
the tale until Elaine's death is more like that of an exquisite
novelette than like the progress of an epical narrative. Lancelot, in order that, as the Queen has advised, he may joust without being known, leaves with Elaine his shield, taking instead
that of one of her brothers, and humoring the girl by consent-
ing to wear her sleeve on the borrowed shield in the combat.
He is wounded in the lists, and retires into the concealment
of a hermit's cave to be healed. Arthur sends Gawain, one
of his knights, in quest of Lancelot. Gawain takes with him
the sleeve that had been·worn by Lancelot, and finds not the

knight, but Elaine, who recognizes the sleeve, and tells him that
she had given it to Lancelot.   Gawain, a worthless, mischief-
making fellow, leaves with her the sleeve, tells her to seek
Lancelot, and hurries off to spread about the court what he believes to be the true tale of Lancelot's illicit love.   The court
gossips seize upon it with eager delight, and the palace buzzes
with the scandal.

>   One old dame
> Came suddenly on the Queen with the sharp news.
> She, that had heard the noise of it before,
> But sorrowing Lancelot should have stoop'd so low,
> Marr'd her friend's aim with pale tranquillity.
> So ran the tale like fire about the court,
> Fire in dry stubble a nine-days' wonder flared;
> Till e'en the knights at banquets twice or thrice
> Forgot to drink to Lancelot and the Queen,
> And pledging Lancelot and the lily maid
> Smiled at each other, while the Queen, who sat,
> With lips severely placid, felt the knot
> Climb in her throat, and with her feet unseen
> Crush'd the wild passion out against the floor
> Beneath the banquet, where the meats became
> As wormwood, and she hated all who pledged.

Will any one say that the writer of these lines does not
know human nature as well as Byron?

Of course protestations are of no avail—and in fact Lancelot is not the man to protest much—to convince Guinevere
that he does not love Elaine.   Meanwhile the girl is dying for
him.   The scene in which Guinevere, having received from
Lancelot the diamonds which she believes him to have intended
for Elaine, casts them into the river, is far beyond Byron, and
would not disgrace Goethe.   Hardly has she dropped the jewels, when the dead Elaine, in a barge steered upon the tide by
the dumb servitor of the house, comes into sight.

>   All up the marble stair, tier over tier,
>   Were added mouths that gaped, and eyes that ask'd

"What is it?"   But that oarsman's haggard face,
As hard and still as is the face that men
Shape to their fancy's eye from broken rocks
On some cliff-side, appall'd them, and they said,
"He is enchanted, cannot speak—and she,
Look how she sleeps—the Fairy Queen so fair!
Yea, but how pale! what are they? flesh and blood?
Or come to take the King to fairy-land?
For some do hold our Arthur cannot die,
But that he passes into fairy-land."

 While thus they babbled of the King, the King
Came girt with knights; then turn'd the tongueless man
From the half-face to the full eye, and rose
And pointed to the damsel, and the doors.
So Arthur bade the meek Sir Percivale
And pure Sir Galahad to uplift the maid;
And reverently they bore her into hall.
Then came the fine Gawain and wonder'd at her,
And last the Queen herself, and pitied her:
But Arthur spied the letter in her hand,
Stoopt, took, brake seal, and read it; this was all:
"Most noble lord, Sir Lancelot of the Lake,
I, sometime call'd the Maid of Astolat,
Come, for you left me taking no farewell,
Hither, to take my last farewell of you.
I loved you, and my love had no return,
And therefore my true love has been my death.
And therefore to our Lady Guinevere,
And to all other ladies, I make moan.
Pray for my soul, and yield me burial.
Pray for my soul thou too, Sir Lancelot,
As thou art a knight peerless."
       Thus he read,
And ever in the reading, lords and dames
Wept, looking often from his face who read
To hers which lay so silent, and at times,
So touch'd were they, half-thinking that her lips,
Who had devised the letter, moved again.

The glory is now departing from the Round-table.   The

hysterical adventures detailed in The Holy Grail do little to recall it. The tragical failure of Pelleas, whose story is perhaps
the most poignantly sad in all the Idyls, to live the life and
perform the service of a true knight, shows that the catastrophe
is hastening on. In The Last Tournament it has almost come;
and in Guinevere the heaven is clothed with sackcloth. It
would probably be held by a majority of competent critics that
the greatest triumph of Tennyson's art has been attained in the
conception and execution of the group of Arthur and Guinevere as they met at Almesbury. Then at last she gives him all
her heart, not only owning him superior to Lancelot, but loving him better, and feeling that he, not Lancelot, had loved her
best. The cloudy battle in the west, and the passing away of
Arthur, are the appropriate conclusion of the poem after this
mighty Book. The "moanings of the King" in his tent, heard
by Sir Bedivere as they were on their way to the final conflict,
sum up Arthur's reflections on the general tragedy of the poem.

> I found Him in the shining of the stars,
> I mark'd Him in the flowering of His fields,
> But in His ways with men I find Him not.
> I waged His wars, and now I pass and die.
> O me! for why is all around us here
> As if some lesser god had made the world,
> But had not force to shape it as he would,
> Till the High God behold it from beyond,
> And enter it, and make it beautiful?
> Or else as if the world were wholly fair,
> But that these eyes of men are dense and dim,
> And have not power to see it as it is:
> Perchance, because we see not to the close;—
> For I, being simple, thought to work His will,
> And have but stricken with the sword in vain;
> And all whereon I lean'd in wife and friend
> Is traitor to my peace, and all my realm
> Reels back into the beast, and is no more.
> My God, thou hast forgotten me in my death:
> Nay—God my Christ—I pass but shall not die.

Here, as everywhere, Tennyson refuses to throw any hues of softening optimism over the world; here, as everywhere, he refuses to accept the devil's creed of pessimism, or to quench the light of hope on the far horizon. The same combination of ideas is presented in the Vision of Sin. Of this poem he has vouchsafed no word of explanation, though it might be thought that a hint with reference, at least, to its central intention was more requisite than in connection with the Palace of Art, where just so much of defining light is granted in the prefatory lines as suffices to bar the reader from random speculation. I see no reason to doubt, however, that the interpretation commonly given of the Vision of Sin is correct.

The hero is first seen as a youth riding a horse with wings, "that would have flown, but that his heavy rider kept him down." That is to say, the earth-ward and death-ward cleaving gravitation of the lower nature—selfishness, sensuality—prevents the celestial particle in him from asserting its power. "A child of sin," therefore, emerging from a palace-gate, leads him by the curls, an easy victim, into the interior, where a company, "with heated eyes," lie between paroxysms of dissipation, "languid shapes, by heaps of gourds, and skins of wine, and piles of grapes." De Quincey's Confessions of an Opium-eater might throw some light upon the experiences of these revellers. The excitement that inthralls them begins in "low voluptuous music," which passes through various changes, and acts by its sound upon a mysterious fountain showering "sleet of diamond-drift and pearly hail."

> Then the music touch'd the gates and died ;
> Rose again from where it seem'd to fail,
> Storm'd in orbs of song, a growing gale ;
> Till thronging in and in, to where they waited,
> As 'twere a hundred-throated nightingale,
> The strong tempestuous treble throbb'd and palpitated ;
> Ran into its giddiest whirl of sound,

Caught the sparkles, and in circles,
Purple gauzes, golden hazes, liquid mazes,
Flung the torrent rainbow round:
Then they started from their places,
Moved with violence, changed in hue,
Caught each other with wild grimaces,
Half-invisible to the view,
Wheeling with precipitate paces
To the melody, till they flew,
Hair, and eyes, and limbs, and faces,
Twisted hard in fierce embraces,
Like to Furies, like to Graces,
Dash'd together in blinding dew:
Till, kill'd with some luxurious agony,
The nerve-dissolving melody
Flutter'd headlong from the sky.

Meanwhile,
                    far withdrawn
          Beyond the darkness and the cataract,
          God made Himself an awful rose of dawn,
          Unheeded.

There can be no question that the preceding passage describes the frenzied revelry of godless passion. But God's curse—the curse of old age, and expiring strength, and deadly ennui — in form of "a vapor heavy, hueless, formless, cold," steals ever nearer to the frantic crew. They do not heed it, and the poet in his dream "would have spoken" and "warned that madman," the youth who had been enticed by the child of sin, "ere it grew too late;" but, "as in dreams," he could not. The creeping vapor reached the palace-gate, and then his dream was broken; and though, in the next line, it "linked again," a considerable number of years must have gone by in the interval. For now the youth has become

          A gray and gap-toothed man, as lean as death,
          Who slowly rode across a wither'd heath,
          And lighted at a ruin'd inn.

The ruined inn—the "Dragon on the heath"—is all that remains of the palace of pleasure of his early days. There is now no music in its courts, no enchanting daughters and sons of Belial to dance with. The hostler is wrinkled, grim, and thin; the bar-maid "bitter" and "waning fast;" the waiter slipshod, lank, and sour. These are fit companions for the gap-toothed skeleton who has just life enough to remember that his youth, in its madness of passion, was "half-divine." Having chosen ignobleness, he has lost the capacity to believe in nobleness, and, like every cynic, takes refuge from his self-contempt in fiercely asserting that all men are contemptible. His mirth is the joyless mirth that is forced into dreary uproariousness by wine.

> Fill the cup, and fill the can:
>   Have a rouse before the morn:
> Every moment dies a man,
>   Every moment one is born.
>
> We are men of ruin'd blood;
>   Therefore comes it we are wise.
> Fish are we that love the mud,
>   Rising to no fancy-flies.
>
> Name and fame! to fly sublime
>   Through the courts, the camps, the schools,
> Is to be the ball of Time,
>   Bandied by the hands of fools.
>
> Friendship!—to be two in one—
>   Let the canting liar pack!
> Well I know, when I am gone,
>   How she mouths behind my back.
>
> Virtue!—to be good and just—
>   Every heart, when sifted well,
> Is a clot of warmer dust,
>   Mix'd with cunning sparks of hell.

His contempt, except for himself, is partly affected; his hatred for his fellow-men is genuine. No more intense or re-

lentless hatred dwells in the human breast than that of the
thoroughly bad man for every one who, tacitly or expressly,
claims to be better than himself. As our cynic scorns friendship, love, religion, so he has no trust in freedom or in patriotism.

> Drink, and let the parties rave:
>   They are fill'd with idle spleen;
> Rising, falling, like a wave,
>   For they know not what they mean.
>
> He that roars for liberty
>   Faster binds a tyrant's power;
> And the tyrant's cruel glee
>   Forces on the freer hour.

He calls on the dead to arise and dance with him, and welcomes, as they come "trooping from their mouldy dens," the
fleshless spectres.

> Drink to Fortune, drink to Chance,
>   While we keep a little breath!
> Drink to heavy ignorance!
>   Hob-and-nob with brother Death!

He does not believe even in his own scoffing.

> Youthful hopes, by scores to all,
>   When the locks are crisp and curl'd;
> Unto me my maudlin gall
>   And my mockeries of the world.

The last line of this ghastly chant, "Yet we will not die
forlorn," seems to show that the light of his spirit is not wholly extinguished. Another break now occurs in the dream,
long years again elapse, and the scene, when it reappears in the
vision, has undergone further change.

> Below were men and horses pierced with worms,
> And slowly quickening into lower forms;
> By shards and scurf of salt, and scum of dross,
> Old plash of rains, and refuse patch'd with moss.

A few lines now follow, in which, I suppose, could we but be sure of their interpretation, the riddle of the poem may be read.

> Then some one spake: "Behold! it was a crime
> Of sense avenged by sense that wore with time."
> Another said: "The crime of sense became
> The crime of malice, and is equal blame."

Mr. Shepherd tells me that, in a volume of Selections from Tennyson, published in 1865, there were inserted, at this point, these two lines—

> Another answer'd: "But a crime of sense?
> Give him new nerves with old experience."

These are excluded from the collected edition of 1878, but they are suggestive, and will interest our physiological school of moralists. With them, we have four; without them, three, opinions from Tennyson upon the case of the sinner. The last of the four, and a few lines which must be taken as the poet's declinature to pronounce decisively upon his hero's fate, while refusing to say that there was no hope, conclude the poem.

> And one: "He had not wholly quench'd his power;
> A little grain of conscience made him sour."
> At last I heard a voice upon the slope
> Cry to the summit, "Is there any hope?"
> To which an answer peal'd from that high land,
> But in a tongue no man could understand;
> And on the glimmering limit far withdrawn
> God made Himself an awful rose of dawn.

Still more difficult than the Vision of Sin is the short poem, of which even the name is mysterious, The Voice and the Peak. If it is a reasonable objection to a poem that, read with the utmost deliberation to an educated audience, it would certainly fail to convey to them a definite and distinct meaning, or even to make them sure that they had followed the

lines of suggestion in which the poet intended their ideas to
move, then this poem is objectionable. I presume, however,
that the main drift of its imagery, which as imagery is glorious, must be, when interpreted into a logical proposition, that,
amidst the changes, however extended they may be, of nature,
the spirit of man will endure.

> The peak is high, and flush'd
>   At his highest with sunrise fire;
> The peak is high, and the stars are high,
>   And the thought of a man is higher.

The lines entitled the Higher Pantheism are, to me at least,
tantalizing.   Some of them strike one as explicitly pantheistic.

> The sun, the moon, the stars, the seas, the hills, and the plains—
> Are not these, O soul, the Vision of Him who reigns?
> Is not the Vision He? tho' He be not that which He seems?
> Dreams are true while they last, and do we not live in dreams?

Nature is not a vision, but a fact; fact or vision, we know
nothing of it except as it seems; and it is pure, gratuitous,
impertinent, and useless fancy to suggest that it is, or can be,
anything but what it seems.   Nor is nature God.   The vision
is not He.   And we do not live in dreams in any sense corresponding to that in which we live in the world revealed to us
by our senses.   Those of my readers who may have cared to
wade through my articles on Hume, in the *Literary World*,
know that these are not, with me, random assertions, but that
I have taken pains to ascertain the truth of what I say.   I
shall not, however, allege that Tennyson intends these lines to
be pantheistic, for some which follow are irreconcilable with
the pantheistic theory.

> Speak to Him thou for He hears, and Spirit with spirit can meet—
> Closer is He than breathing, and nearer than hands and feet.

These words, ineffable in their beauty, their tenderness, and

their depth, admit of no pantheistic interpretation. If pantheism means anything, it means that speaking to God is scientifically equivalent to speaking to the wind or the sea. If the
personality of the Spirit, God, and of the spirit, man, is distinctly posited, as in these lines, then the vague lines previously quoted, and many others that sound pantheistically in the
piece, may possibly be capable of an interpretation consistent
with spiritual theism.

Entirely in harmony with this conclusion are the two brief
but noble poems, Wages and Will. The thesis, or rather the
reverent suggestion, of the first is that God, having revealed
Himself to us—having taken us into His service in the universal battle of light against darkness—would act with strange
and cruel unfairness if He extinguished finally the aspirations
and energies He has awakened.

> The wages of sin is death: if the wages of Virtue be dust,
> Would she have heart to endure for the life of the worm and the fly?
> She desires no isles of the blest, no quiet seats of the just,
> To rest in a golden grove, or to bask in a summer sky:
> Give her the wages of going on, and not to die.

Since Milton penned his sonnets, the grandeur of spiritual
manhood, the majesty of moral strength, have not found state-
lier expression than in Tennyson's lines on Will. By this term
he means the sovereign faculty by which man decides for the
right; and he describes the inexpugnable fortitude, the Divine
peace, of the man who maintains it in its legitimate authority.

> O well for him whose will is strong!
> He suffers, but he will not suffer long;
> He suffers, but he cannot suffer wrong.

He will not suffer long, because, as his pain can be but
physical, there is an obvious term to it, either through restoration to health or death. He *cannot* suffer wrong: for not the
smallest particle of suffering can reach him, shielded as he is

by the proudly placid consciousness that injustice, in relation
to him on whom it is inflicted, is, strictly estimated, nothing at
all.   Brand him, lash him, crucify him; he pities you, not
himself.

> But ill for him who, bettering not with time,
> Corrupts the strength of heaven-descended Will,
> And ever weaker grows thro' acted crime,
> Or seeming-genial venial fault,
> Recurring and suggesting still !

How shrewdly practical, how penetrating and priceless, is
moralizing like this !   The merchandise of it is better than the
merchandise of silver, and the gain thereof than fine gold.

No reader, I trust, will imagine that, because I have not
touched upon many of Tennyson's poems, I overlook or underrate them.   The poems descriptive of the Lincolnshire Farmer,
old style and new style, attest immense dramatic power, and
run over with broad and racy humor.   The Princess is admirable as a serio-comic poem, and contains some of the finest
songs ever penned.   The poetry connected, directly or indirect-
ly, with his position as Laureate, is unequal, but it is incomparably superior to any poetry of its class.   The Gardener's
Daughter, Tithonus, Lucretius, are all, in their widely-varying
manners, excellent.   The " wicked broth " that killed Lucretius
has been thought superbly imaginative ; but it has always, I
confess, suggested to my mind unprincipled plum-pudding.

Take him for all in all, Tennyson must, I think, be pronounced the greatest poet of his time.   Victor Hugo is indeed
a colossal genius, wider in his range than Tennyson, who has
not succeeded in the acting drama, but his touch is too pano-
ramic for poetic art of the highest order; and Browning, though
he has power of intellect and imagination sufficient for ten
poets, is far from Tennyson's equal in literary form.

JOHN RUSKIN.

CHAPTER I.

AFTER the great artist, the great critic. For half a century before John Ruskin was born (February, 1819), the art which delineates nature's beauty, whether with pen or with pencil, had been gloriously at work in Great Britain. Cowper and Burns had leaped back to nature, flinging from them, by the mere expanding energy of their manhood and genius, the traditions of the artificial schools, whose intellectual sovereign is Pope; and so sweet and strange and enchanting was the charm which nature lent them, that poets and painters hastened to follow their example. Scott, in simple boy-like enjoyment of morning clouds and breezy hills, of sward begemmed with dewdrops and torrents flashing in keen lightnings down the gorge; Byron, with less depth and sincerity of love for nature than Scott, but a more fiery and imaginative sympathy for her sterner aspects and moods, for the throbbing of the earthquake and the answering of mountain to mountain in the thunderstorm; Keats, with a town - bred boy's ecstasy, almost sickly in its yearning intensity, over every glimpse of green leafage "sprouting a tender boon for nibbling sheep;" Wordsworth, looking upon himself as a poet-seer, hierophant of the sacredness and the mystery of nature, watching the shadow of the daisy on the stone, and listening to the syllables of the brook in the wood; Shelley, exulting in the beauty of the world and casting over it the light of a loftier idealization than that of any of the others; these, and not these alone, but Campbell, and Hogg, and Christopher North, had filled their works with landscape description, and had made their readers familiar with

the countless changes of nature's grandeur and loveliness, from
the purpling of the lake at dawn to "the lustrous gloom of
leaden-colored even."

The painter had followed in the wake of the poet, or had
accompanied him, sharing a common inspiration.   Gainsbor-
ough, writing in color, was as true a poet as ever lived, and
stood somewhat in the same relation to our recent school of
landscape-painting as Cowper and Burns to our recent school
of landscape-poetry.   But it was the English Water-color
School of painting that was pre-eminently the school of landscape.   No other school known to the historian of art ever did
so much to show what the forms and hues of nature really are;
what witchery of grace, what eye-music of delicately woven
lines, there is among the forest boughs; with what splendor,
"ensaffroning the whole hill-side," the sun can flood the air
when near his setting; in one word, what beauty and comeli-
ness this dwelling-place of man has received from the hand of
its Maker.   When we recollect Who it was that declared the
loveliness of the lily of the field to excel that of Solomon in
all his glory, we may be prepared to recognize a natural sacredness in the art that concerns itself with the trees and the flowers; and cannot but feel an appropriateness in the indisputable fact that the English school of landscape is distinguished
by a vestal purity of feeling and association, placing it, in moral
respects, almost on a level with the art of Angelico.   Or why
should I say "almost" on a level?   Why should I not dare
to be just to my own time, and affirm that the school of landscape-painting, which has flourished in Great Britain, occupies
a *higher* moral level than that of Angelico?   The art of Angelico, with its mawkish saints, its monastic quaintnesses, its en-
ervating air of simpleton piety and nursery innocence, is un-
healthy, and, to the extent of its unhealthiness, unholy.   Without purism, without sectarianism, the landscape art of England
is delicately reverent of all manly religion, all home-bred virtue,

and as wholesome in its influence as the grass of the mountains and the rain of the sky.

The English Water-color School was just strong enough to furnish him with the instruments of his art, when there appeared in England one of those men of unique and transcendent powers, who are seldom born except at intervals of centuries—J. M. W. Turner. He stood in much the same relation, in respect of comprehensiveness and energy of genius, to the other landscape artists of his day, in which Shakspeare stood to the other dramatists of the Elizabethan age. The dramatists contemporary with Shakspeare were great—greater than any who have succeeded them in England—but none of them approached the greatness of Shakspeare. Prout, Fielding, Cotman, Crome, Bonington, Constable, Calcott, De Wint, and many others, contemporary with Turner, were admirable landscapists, but none was equal, none was second, to him. It was in vindication of Turner against the depreciation of reviewers that Ruskin wrote his first great book; and it then became apparent that, in addition to the English poets who had described nature in melodious verse, and the English painters who had depicted nature in expressive color, an English critic of the first order had arisen, whose prose revealed the subtlety and the opulence of nature's beauty with an imaginative splendor equalling that of the poet, and a precision and graphic power hardly inferior to those of the painter.

Mr. Ruskin has sprinkled over his writings a good many intimations, all deeply interesting, as to his infancy and youth. "The first thing," he writes, "which I remember, as an event in life, was being taken by my nurse to the brow of Friar's Crag on Derwentwater; the intense joy, mingled with awe, that I had in looking through the hollows in the mossy roots, over the crag, into the dark lake, has associated itself more or less with all twining roots of trees ever since." Two other things he remembers as being, "in a sort, beginnings of life:

16*

crossing Shapfells (being let out of the chaise to run up the hills), and going through Glen Farg, near Kinross, in a winter's morning, when the rocks were hung with icicles." When he came near mountains he had a pleasure, from the earliest time he can recollect until he was eighteen or twenty, "infinitely greater" than he has since found in anything; "comparable for intensity only to the joy of a lover in being near a noble and kind mistress, but no more explicable or definable than that feeling of love itself."

The correctness of these reminiscences is proved in those verses which, from the years of earliest boyhood until he reached the age of twenty-six, he continued to produce. He prints in The Queen of the Air "one of many" of his childish rhymes, "written on a frosty day in Glen Farg, just north of Loch Leven," when he had almost completed his ninth year.

> Papa, how pretty those icicles are,
> That are seen so near, that are seen so far;
> Those dropping waters that come from the rocks,
> And many a hole, like the haunt of a fox.
> That silvery stream that runs babbling along,
> Making a murmuring, dancing song.
> Those trees that stand waving upon the rock's-side,
> And men, that, like spectres, among them glide,
> And water-falls that are heard from far,
> And come in sight when very near.
> And the water-wheel that turns slowly round,
> Grinding the corn that requires to be ground—
> And mountains at a distance seen,
> And rivers winding through the plain.
> And quarries with their craggy stones,
> And the wind among them moans.

What a great deal the little fellow manages to get into his lines! And is not his observation nice? are not his epithets happy? Every one who has approached a water-fall through woodland must remember how long he has heard it sounding through the trees, and how often he was disappointed when he thought that, after the next clump of foliage, it would surely open on him.

The landscape described in these lines is not, however, necessarily mountainous; the wheel grinding the corn suggests rather that it is not far from the lowlands; but Ruskin's general love of nature concentrated itself, in later boyhood, into that passion for mountains which we have already found attested in his own words. I am privileged to possess a small volume in which his early poems were printed for circulation among his relatives and friends. They form, in a striking degree, an autobiographical introduction to his prose works. The first in the series, written when he was fourteen, expresses the lyric passion and longing of the writer for mountains. This is the first verse:

> I weary for the torrent leaping
> From off the scaur's rough crest;
> My muse is on the mountain sleeping,
> My harp is sunk to rest.

It is profoundly touching, at the present moment, to find that already he has been impressed by Coniston.*

> The crags are lone on Coniston,
> And Loweswater's dell;
> And dreary on the mighty one,
> The cloud-inwreathed Scawfell.

The hand of the great describer is now beginning to make itself still more distinctly felt than in the Glen Farg verses.

> I long to tread the mountain-head
> Above the valley swelling;
> I long to feel the breezes sped
> From gray and gaunt Helvellyn.

---

* At the time when these words were written Mr. Ruskin lay dangerously ill at Brantwood, Coniston.

> I love the eddying circling sweep,
>   The mantling and the foam
> Of murmuring waters, dark and deep,
>   Amid the valleys lone.

The boy who wrote this last verse was father of the man that could do justice to the rich, brown, transparent water, circling and wreathing in long eddies, under the high cliff in Turner's Bolton Abbey! The closing verse in the poem goes far to explain why Ruskin became the greatest literary delineator of mountains in Europe.

> There is a thrill of strange delight
>   That passes quivering o'er me,
> When blue hills rise upon the sight
>   Like summer clouds before me.

In these boyish poems we meet, as is usual in juvenile poetry, with many echoes from the poets in whom the boy delights. The influence of Scott is traceable everywhere, in light sunny sketching of landscape, and vivid observation of man and his works. In a fragment from a metrical journal recording the occurrences of what seems to have been Ruskin's first visit to the Continent, we find him looking from the crest of Ehrenbreitstein upon the city of Coblentz, the junction of the Rhine and the Moselle, the old stone bridge, the bridge of boats, and the rafts of pine-wood floating down the river.

> We climbed the crag, we scaled the ridge,
> On Coblentz looked adown ;
> The tall red roofs, the long white bridge,
> And on the eye-like frown
> Of the portals of her palaces,
> And on her people's busy press.
> There never was a fairer town,
> Between two rivers as it lay,
> Whence morning mist was curling gray
> On the plain's edge beside the hill:
> Oh ! it was lying calm and still

In morning's chastened glow:
The multitudes were thronging by,
But we were dizzily on high,
And we might not one murmur hear,
Nor whisper tingling on the ear,
From the far depth below.

The bridge of boats, casting across the impetuous stream its " one dark bending line," not only pleases his eye, but suggests a few of those moral reflections to which boy minstrels are prone.

The feeble bridge that bends below
The tread of one weak man—
It yet can stem the forceful flow,
Which naught unyielding can.
The bar of shingle stems the sea,
The granite cliffs are worn away;
The bending reed can bear the blast,
When English oak were downward cast;
The bridge of boats the Rhine can chain,
Where strength of stone were all in vain.

The descriptive references to the felling of the trees for the raft, which is to go like a sailing island from the mountain to the sea, are picturesque and felicitous.

The Schwartzwald pine hath shed its green,
But not at autumn's frown;
A sharper winter stripped them there—
The tall straight trunks are bald and bare:
The peasant, on some Alpine brow,
Hath cut the root and lopped the bough;
The eagle heard the echoing fall,
And soared away to his high eyrie;
The chamois gave his warning call,
And higher on the mountain tall
Pursued his way unweary.

The following description of a forest-glade is still more carefully elaborated, and still more boldly imaginative.

'Twas in the hollow of a forest dim,
Where the low breezes sang their evening hymn,
As in a temple by thick branches aisled,
Whose leaves had many voices, weak or wild;
Their summer voice was like the trooping tread
Of fiery steeds, to meteor battle bred;
Their autumn voice was like the wailing cry
Of a great nation, bowed in misery;
The deep vast silence of the winter's wood
Was like the hush of a dead multitude.
And, in the centre of its summer shade,
Opened a narrow space of velvet glade,
Where sunbeams, through the foliage slanting steep,
Lay, like a smile upon the lips of sleep.
And dew, that thrilled the flowers with full delight,   .
Fell from the soft eyes of the heaven by night;
And richly there the panting earth put on
A wreathèd robe of blossoms wild and wan:
The purple pansies glowed beneath unseen,
Like voiceless thoughts within a mind serene;
The passioned primrose blessed the morning gale,
And starry lilies shook in their pavilions pale.

Can these lines fail to remind any reader of Endymion of
the delicate fingering of Keats? The lines on the voices of
the forest leaves are worthy of any poet, and are wonderful for
a poet of seventeen.

It has often been remarked that the poetry of happy boyhood is apt to be sad, and there is in Ruskin's no lack of melancholy tones, frequently with something in them to remind
us of Byron, yet never approaching either the sentimentality
or the theatricality of Byron's stage manner. The following
is too manifestly sincere, too quietly beautiful, to have been
written by his lordship, and yet there is something in the lines
that reminds one of Byron:

THE LAST SMILE.

She sat beside me yesternight,
With lip and eye so sweetly smiling,

So full of soul, of life, of light,
So beautifully care-beguiling,
That she had almost made me gay,
Had almost charmed the thought away
(Which, like the poisoned desert wind,
Came sick and heavy o'er my mind),
That memory soon mine all would be,
And she would smile no more for me.

Quite unmistakably, in the following Spenserian stanza, descriptive of a dream, is heard the music of Shelley :

And yet it was a strange dim dream:
I drifted on a mute and arrowy stream,
Under the midnight, in a helmless boat
That lay like a dead thing cast afloat
On the weight of the waves; I could feel them come,
Many and mighty, but deep and dumb;
And the strength of their darkness drifted and drew
The rudderless length of that black canoe,
As the west wind carries a fragment rent
From a thunder-cloud's uppermost battlement.

But though his early verses bear witness to his enthusiastic study of the poets of his time, they are by no means void of true originality. Not only do they display powers of description hardly paralleled by any poet of his years, but reveal no ordinary power of thought and insight, and are sometimes curiously prophetic of his career. It is startling to find, in a poem written when he was seventeen, lines which might serve as texts for chapters, almost for volumes, written when his fame had made the tour of the world.

There's but one liberty of heart and soul,
A thing of beauty, an unfelt control,—
A flow, as waters flow in solitude,
Of gentle feeling, passioned, though subdued,
When Love, and Virtue, and Religion join
To weave their bonds of bliss, their chains divine,

And keep the heaven-illumined heart they fill
Softly communing with itself, and still,
In the sole freedom that can please the good,
A mild and mental, unfelt servitude.

Several of the poems were composed when he had attained
the ripe age of twenty-five or twenty-six, and in these can be
discerned not merely the prophecy of his power, but not a
little of its manifestation. This remark applies particularly
to descriptive passages on the Alps, which read like pieces of
Ruskinian prose finely versified. He looks toward the mountains from Marengo, and speaks:

The glory of the cloud—without its wane;
The stillness of the earth—but not its gloom;
The loveliness of life—without its pain;
The peace—but not the hunger of the tomb!
Ye pyramids of God! around whose bases
The sea foams noteless in his narrow cup;
And the unseen movements of the earth send up
A murmur which your lulling snow effaces
Like the deer's footsteps.   Thrones imperishable!
About whose adamantine steps the breath
Of dying generations vanisheth,
Less cognizable than clouds; and dynasties
Less glorious and more feeble than the array
Of your frail glaciers, unregarded rise,
Totter, and vanish.

Some lines on Mont Blanc, when he revisited it in 1845,
have a solemn tenderness befitting a psalm or hymn.

Oh, mount beloved! mine eyes again
Behold the twilight's sanguine stain
    Along thy peaks expire;
Oh, mount beloved! thy frontier waste
I seek with a religious haste,
    And reverent desire.

Having referred to the worship which God "wins" from
the lowlier creatures, "the partridge on her purple nest, the

marmot in his den," he cries out in stern lamentation over the contrast to their "purer praise" afforded by that found upon the lips of men.

> Alas for man! who hath no sense
> Of gratefulness nor confidence,
>   But still rejects and raves;
> That all God's love can hardly win
> One soul from taking pride in sin,
>   And pleasure over graves.

He checks himself, however, with a reflection which affects me with a sense of amazed pain, for again and again has the same occurred to me while reading his fiery invectives, hurled, in these last years, against men who, faultily it might be, yet with sincere intention to speak truth and do good, have written what displeased him on social questions.

> Yet let me not, like him who trod
> In wrath, of old, the mount of God,
>   Forget the thousands left;
> Lest haply, when I seek His face,
> The whirlwind of the cave replace
>   The glory of the cleft.

Already he had looked with bitter sorrow into the mystery of evil, and found "worse treachery on the steadfast land than variable sea."

> The treachery of the deadly mart
>   Where human souls are sold;
> The treachery of the hollow heart
>   That crumbles as we hold.

In short, we have in these poems, as in a mirror, the faintly shadowed outline of all that Ruskin was to be. Their qualities are stateliness and chastened magnificence of language, burning purity of feeling, and elevation of thought. The most comprehensively characteristic, perhaps, of all the pieces, is one written when he was twenty-three. No man is perfectly true to his own ideal; but when we look along the records of Ruskin's

life, we can affirm that it has, on the whole, been pervaded with
the spirit, the sentiment, the principles, of these noble verses:

CHARITIE.

The beams of morning are renewed,
   The valley laughs their light to see;
And earth is bright with gratitude,
   And heaven with Charitie.

Oh, dew of heaven! Oh, light of earth!
   Fain would our hearts be filled with thee,
Because nor darkness comes, nor death
   About the home of Charitie.

God guides the stars their wandering way,
   He seems to cast their courses free;
But binds unto himself for aye,
   And all their chains are Charitie.

When first he stretched the signed zone,
   And heaped the hills, and barred the sea,
Then wisdom sat beside His throne,
   But His own word was Charitie.

And still through every age and hour,
   Of things that were and things that be,
Are breathed the presence and the power
   Of everlasting Charitie.

By noon and night, by sun and shower,
   By dews that fall and winds that flee,
On grove and field, on fold and flower,
   Is shed the peace of Charitie.

The violets light the lonely hill,
   The fruitful furrows load the lea;
Man's heart alone is sterile still,
   For lack of lowly Charitie.

He walks a weary vale within,
   No lamp of love in heart hath he;
His steps are death, his thoughts are sin,
   For lack of gentle Charitie.

Daughter of heaven! we dare not lift
  The dimness of our eyes to thee:
Oh! pure and God-descended gift!
  Oh! spotless, perfect Charitie.

Yet forasmuch Thy brow is crossed
  With blood-drops from the deathful tree,
We take Thee for our only trust,
  Oh! dying Charitie.

Ah! Hope, Endurance, Faith—ye fail like death,
  But Love an everlasting crown receiveth;
For she is Hope, and Fortitude, and Faith,
  Who all things hopeth, beareth, and believeth.

For reasons into which it is needless to inquire, Ruskin decided that he would not come before the world as a poet. His fame, however, has been too much for him; Mr. Shepherd's Bibliography of Ruskin states where each of his poems is to be obtained; and whoever chooses to ransack the British Museum can have a sight of them. The volume in which most of them are collected is to be had, though seldom, in the book market. These facts make it absolutely certain that, if he does not appropriate them to himself by publication during his lifetime, some bookseller will publish them when he is dead. Surely it were best that he should publish them himself, stating how they fit into the story of his life, and what part they played in the development of his genius and the formation of his character. Information of this kind he has frequently given, and I, for one, have always prized and enjoyed the dainty morsels. The poems would give pleasure to many, and hurt or offend none, and could not possibly impair the reputation of Mr. Ruskin. They do not satisfy him; but if the satisfaction of authors, not the innocent pleasure of readers, is to be the rule of publication, vanity will publish everything, and pride will publish nothing.

CHAPTER II.

THE work on Modern Painters, dedicated to the Landscape Artists of England, on which Ruskin's fame as an author was first reared, and on which it still principally rests, originated, as he tells us in the preface to the first edition, "in indignation at the shallow and false criticisms of the periodicals of the day" on the works of J. M. W. Turner. I am desirous, in these after-dinner talks about "my very noble and approved good masters," to avoid questions which might lead into the waters of controversial discussion; but it will be impossible to comprehend the literary career of Mr. Ruskin, unless we attain some clearness of idea respecting the necessity for that vindication of Turner which called him into the field.

He has maintained in all his books that Turner was treated with gross injustice by his contemporaries. It is not true, however, that he has never given any other reason for writing on art than the compulsion under which he felt to defend Turner. In the preface to which I have just referred, he particularly fences himself against being supposed to be actuated merely by a desire to vindicate Turner's reputation. "No zeal," he says, "for the reputation of any individual, no personal feeling of any kind, has the slightest weight or influence with me. The reputation of the great artist to whose works I have chiefly referred, is established on too legitimate grounds among all whose admiration is honorable, to be in any way affected by the ignorant sarcasms of pretension and affectation." He wrote, he adds, to correct the taste of the public,

misdirected by the same critics who attacked Turner. These
taught their readers to look with contempt upon "the most
exalted truth, and the highest ideal of landscape, that this or
any other age has ever witnessed." The two motives—to vindicate Turner and to purify the public taste—were blended
in Ruskin's original impulse to write, and have been blended
in all he has published on landscape art. He has sometimes,
however, forgotten the fact. In the fifth volume of Modern
Painters he says expressly that his books arose "not in any
desire to explain the principles of art, but in the endeavor to
defend an individual painter from injustice." This is, of
course, irreconcilable with the denial, in his earliest preface,
that "zeal for the reputation of any individual," or "personal
feeling of any kind," had "the slightest weight or influence"
with him; but the slip of memory is of no great importance.

Whatever were Ruskin's motives in writing or publishing,
he has always, I repeat, declared Turner to have been treated
with cruel injustice by his contemporaries. He told an Edinburgh audience in 1853 that, until seventy years old, the great
artist never met with "a single word or ray of sympathy;"
that "from the time he knew his true greatness all the world
was turned against him;" that "no one understood him, no
one trusted him, and every one cried out against him;" that
every voice he heard from the human beings around him was
raised, year after year, through all his life, only in condemnation of his efforts and denial of his success.

Such statements are at first sight positively bewildering.
To any one who has the slightest acquaintance with the history of art in England during the life of Turner, certain facts
occur which, interpret them as we may, are indisputable, and
which appear to be in absolute contradiction to Mr. Ruskin's
words. Turner was elected an Associate of the Royal Academy at the extraordinarily early age of twenty-four, a Royal
Academician at twenty-seven; he exhibited about two hundred

pictures at the Royal Academy; he was engaged in illustrating the works of the most eminent writers of his time, taking precedence in that department of all contemporary artists, many of whom were men of great genius. Rogers, the poet, a leader in criticism and in society, chose him to illustrate his books; and Sir Walter Scott, avowedly preferring Thomson of Duddingstone, nevertheless bowed to the ruling fashion in having both his poetry and his prose illustrated by Turner. Artists enthusiastically recognized his power. His pictures in oil and in water-color afforded occupation to a number of the ablest engravers that ever lived. He sold vast numbers of pictures, refused large sums for others, and died worth something like £100,000. These being unvarnished and undisputed facts, some explanation is obviously necessary before Mr. Ruskin's statements in the Edinburgh Lectures can be accepted as true, or, indeed, can be understood. Such explanation, however, is at hand.

In the first place, though Turner did, at a very early period, obtain as much recognition as the academic authorities could accord him, he was for many years a struggling man. Buyers of pictures formed then a small class compared with buyers of pictures now, and of those who bought pictures only a small proportion cared for landscape. It is certain that, until within a few years of his death, the prices he obtained for pictures were insignificant compared with those now obtained by third or fourth rate men, and that some of those schemes upon which he set his heart were pecuniary failures. Conspicuous among these was the world-famous *Liber Studiorum*. He began the publication of this work when he had been five years a Royal Academician; and for twelve years, during which his genius retained the freshness of youth, but displayed the full power of manhood, he tried to make it succeed. Five pieces appeared in each issue, the price of the five, in their finest state, being twenty-five shillings. They were mezzotint engravings, in a rich brown, executed from his drawings and under his direction, and, in large part, etched by his own hand. They are the noblest landscape compositions in the world, the corresponding works of Claude, which till then reigned supreme, having been confessedly dethroned by them. But in opulent England he could not find encouragement enough to support him in the enterprise. "Five of the finest works of his genius," says Mr. Frederick Wedmore, a recent writer on the subject, "were to be bought of him for five-and-twenty shillings; and, for years, splendid impressions of them lay rotting in the chambers in Queen Anne Street." It ought to be recollected also that Turner was excessively penurious in his habits, spending no more than would keep body and soul together with some show of respectability, so that the large total of his fortune may have been due not more to the prices he got than to strenuous saving.

Most important, perhaps, of all, with a view to appreciating the whole of Mr. Ruskin's case in alleging Turner to have been an ill-used and underrated man, is the consideration that Turner's genius did, in some respects, reach its supreme development after he was sixty years of age, and that Ruskin was almost alone, not indeed in believing his power to be still great, but in believing it to be greater than it ever was. In the epilogue to Mr. Ruskin's Notes, on his own Turner drawings, the story of Turner's artistic activity after he was sixty-five is told in minute detail, and with a spice of delightful humor.

In 1840, Turner, then sixty-five, entered on that latest phase of his activity which Mr. Ruskin calls his sunset time. He then, Mr. Ruskin goes on to say, "quitted himself of engraver work," and revisited his Alpine haunts, not so much to draw for other people as to gratify his own untrammelled sense of beauty. He returned to London in the winter of 1841, bringing with him an immense number of sketches. Of these he

chose ten, embodying his ultimate ideal of landscape beauty.
To work up the ten into finished pictures in water-color, tech-
nically called drawings, would be a labor of love. He executed
four, and took them, by way of specimen, to Mr. Griffiths, then
his favorite dealer. "The Pass of the Splugen"—I now quote
from Mr. Ruskin—"A red Righi, and a blue Righi, and a blue
Lake Lucerne. 'And,' says Mr. Turner to Mr. Griffiths, 'what
do you think you can get for such things as these?' So says
Mr. Griffiths to Mr. Turner, 'Well, perhaps, commission included,
eighty guineas each.' Says Mr. Turner to Mr. Griffiths, 'Ain't
they worth more?' Says Mr. Griffiths to Mr. Turner (after
looking curiously into the execution, which you will please note
is rather what some people might call hazy), 'They're a little
different from your usual style—(Turner silent, Griffiths does
not push the point)—but—but—yes, they are *worth* more, but
I could not get more.'"

Mr. Ruskin believes that Turner expected each picture to
fetch one hundred guineas, inclusive of ten per cent. commission. Here, then, was a disappointment to begin with. But
Griffiths was by no means sure that he could find buyers even
at eighty guineas. The style was somewhat changed, the artist
was sixty-five, and his reputation had just, says Mr. Ruskin, been
"pretty nearly overthrown by *Blackwood's Magazine.*" However, "Griffiths did his best. He sent to Munro, of Novar,
Turner's old companion in travel; he sent to Mr. Windus, of
Tottenham; he sent to Mr. Bicknell, of Herne Hill; he sent to
my father and me." After the utmost exertion, Griffiths could
get orders for no more than nine drawings. Turner executed
the ten, giving Griffiths the tenth for his commission. In
1842, therefore, Turner, assisted by a skilful and thoroughly-
informed dealer, was able to get, for ten of the most elaborate
water-color pictures he had ever executed in his life, seven hundred and twenty guineas clear. If you will walk round any
water-color exhibition, in the London season, and observe how

many commonplace drawings, by men making no pretence to
genius, are priced at more than seventy-two guineas, you may
be able to appreciate the significance of this fact as illustrating Ruskin's assertion that Turner did not get justice in his
own lifetime.

And more is to be told. In 1843, Turner offered to do ten
more drawings on the same terms. But this time Griffiths
was baffled. Ruskin prevailed on his father to order two, and
Munro, of Novar, took three; in all England, Griffiths could
not get another bid. "Turner," says Ruskin, "was angry, and,
therefore, partly ill." He was not too proud to do the five,
"but said it was lucky there were no more to do." There was
intense bitterness in that remark of Turner's. It went to his
heart to know that there were but two men in England (both of
them Scotch) who would give eighty guineas for the loveliest
things he could put upon paper, out of which eighty guineas
eight must go to the hard-wrought Griffiths. And what, as
tried by the time-test of forty-five years, was the value of those
all but unsalable drawings? One of the three which Munro
had taken was Kussnacht, on the Lake of Lucerne. It was
sold on the 6th of April, 1878, in London, for £1018 10s.
The town sits on the lake in radiance of beauty, like one great
crystal of opal, or of snow, on a mirror of amethyst. To have
seen it—to have hung it up in the hall of imaginative memory
—is to have become richer for evermore. And for that glorious work of art old Turner, assisted by the sleuth-hound Griffiths, warranted to track any Turner enthusiast in England and
bleed him, could get, in 1843, but seventy-two guineas. One
of the ten executed in 1842—the Zurich—was sold at the same
time with the Kussnacht for £1260. Another was the Pass
of the Splugen. Ruskin, when he saw it in 1842, made up his
mind that it was "the noblest Alpine drawing Turner had ever
till then made." I am under the impression that Ruskin had
not at that time seen the Farnley Turners, among which, in

17

my humble opinion, is to be found rock drawing finer than in
the Pass of the Splugen.   Be that as it may, Ruskin, owing to
his father's absence on business, could not get the Splugen in
1842, and Munro had it; but a few of Ruskin's friends bethought them of his admiration for it, and, at the sale just
mentioned, they bought it for a thousand guineas to present to
him.   That was a pleasant kind of thing to do.

Such experiences as these go far to acquit Mr. Ruskin of in-
accuracy or exaggeration in his statements as to the neglect of
Turner by his contemporaries, and as to his painful consciousness of working without appreciation.   Turner was aware of
his greatness.   He had deliberately measured himself against
master after master among celebrated landscape painters, and
had conquered all with whom he coped.   Mr. Ruskin tells us
that he was sensitively alive to criticism.   We can therefore
understand and sympathize with that "indignation" with which
the critic witnessed the derision poured upon the efforts of a
man who was still mighty, and who, even if his right hand
were losing its cunning, had done so much with it in the days
of his strength to shed lustre upon England, that he deserved
respect in his closing years.

Mr. Ruskin is not only a man of great genius, which implies intense activity of thought, and, in most cases, inventive
changefulness and progress of opinion, but a man of impassioned feeling.   It is impossible that his statements at one
period should be mere stereotype repetitions of his statements
at another.   Of Turner he has spoken in a variety of ways,
startling us, at one time, by the transcendency of his admiration, at another by the almost equally audacious length he goes
in affirming defects.   I shall quote the two extremes of his estimate of Turner, and add those few words, recently printed,
which seem to indicate the final rest of his judgment in a
golden mean equally remote from both.   The first is from the
Edinburgh Lectures.

His Estimate of Turner in 1853.

I tell you the truth which I have given fifteen years of my life to ascertain, that this man, this Turner, of whom you have known so little while he was living among you, will one day take his place beside Shakspeare and Verulam, in the annals of the light of England. Yes: beside Shakspeare and Verulam, a third star in that central constellation, round which, in the astronomy of intellect, all other stars make their circuit. By Shakspeare humanity was unsealed to you; by Verulam the *principles* of nature; and by Turner her *aspect*. All these were sent to unlock one of the gates of light, and to unlock it for the first time. But of all the three, though not the greatest, Turner was the most unprecedented in his work. Bacon did what Aristotle had attempted; Shakspeare did perfectly what Æschylus did partially; but none before Turner had lifted the veil from the face of nature; the majesty of the hills and forests had received no interpretation, and the clouds passed unrecorded from the face of the heaven which they adorned, and of the earth to which they ministered.

In 1869 Mr. Ruskin published a volume on the Greek myths of cloud and storm, entitled The Queen of the Air. In it we find a historical parallel drawn between Luini, an Italian painter, born in the second half of the fifteenth century, and Turner. In order to understand what is said about Turner, we must read part of what is said about Luini, which we may do with the less reluctance, because Mr. Ruskin never wrote more beautifully.

Turner and Luini.

Luini has left nothing behind him that is not lovely; but of his life I believe hardly anything is known beyond remnants of tradition, which murmur about Lugano and Saronno, and which remain ungleaned. This only is certain, that he was born in the loveliest district of North Italy, where hills and streams and air meet in softest harmonies. Child of the Alps, and of their divinest lake, he is taught, without doubt or dismay, a lofty religious creed, and a sufficient law of life, and of its mechanical arts. Whether lessoned by Leonardo himself, or merely one of many, disciplined in the system of the Milanese school, he learns unerringly to draw—unerringly and enduringly to paint. His tasks are set him, without question, day by day, by men who are justly satisfied with his work, and who accept it without any harmful praise or senseless blame. Place, scale,

and subject are determined for him on the cloister wall or the church
dome; as he is required, and for sufficient daily bread, and little more,
he paints what he has been taught to design wisely, and has passion to
realize gloriously; every touch he lays is eternal, every thought he conceives is beautiful and pure; his hand moves always in radiance of
blessing; from day to day his life enlarges in power and peace; it
passes away cloudlessly, the starry twilight remaining arched far against
the night.

Oppose to such a life as this that of a great painter amidst the elements
of modern English liberty. Take the life of Turner, in whom the artistic
energy and inherent love of beauty were, at least, as strong as in Luini;
but, amidst the disorder and ghastliness of the lower streets of London,
his instincts in early infancy were warped into toleration of evil, or even
into delight in it. He gathers what he can of instruction by questioning
and prying among half-informed masters; spells out some knowledge of
classical fable, educates himself, by an admirable force, to the production
of wildly majestic or pathetically tender and pure pictures, by which he
cannot live. There is no one to judge them or to command him; only
some of the English upper classes hire him to paint their houses and
parks, and destroy the drawings afterward by the most wanton neglect.
Tired of laboring carefully, without either reward or praise, he dashes out
into various experimental and popular works, makes himself the servant
of the lower public, and is dragged hither and thither at their will; while
yet, helpless and guideless, he indulges his idiosyncrasies till they change
into insanities; the strength of his soul increasing its sufferings and giving force to its errors; all the purpose of life degenerating into instinct,
and the web of his work wrought, at last, of beauties too subtle to be understood, his liberty, with vices too singular to be forgiven—all useless,
because magnificent idiosyncrasy had become solitude, or contention, in
the midst of a reckless populace, instead of submitting itself in loyal harmony to the Art laws of an understanding nation. And the life passed
away in darkness; and its final work, in all the best beauty of it, has already perished, only enough remaining to teach us what we have lost.

Few things from the pen of Ruskin have surprised me more
than this passage. I have never been able to endorse it, nor
can I believe that Ruskin would have written it, had he not at
the moment been in a state of fierce and, I think, unreasonable
indignation against "liberty" as opposed to "law." Finally,

in 1878, he speaks quietly, moderately, rightly, of Turner. I quote the decisive words.

THE FINAL ESTIMATE.

He produced no work of importance till he was past twenty; working constantly, from the day he could hold a pencil, in steady studentship, with gradually-increasing intelligence, and, fortunately for him, rightly-guided skill. His true master was Dr. Munro: to the practical teaching of that first patron, and the wise simplicity of water-color study in which he was disciplined by him and companioned by Girtin, the healthy and constant development of the youth's power is primarily to be attributed. The greatness of the power itself it is impossible to over-estimate. As in my own advancing life I learn more of the laws of noble art, I recognize faults in Turner to which once I was blind; but only as I recognize also powers which my boy's enthusiasm did but disgrace by its advocacy.

I am disposed to think that, in the same amount of space, Ruskin has never said anything so true, so pertinent, so inform-ing, of Turner, as what we have in these lines.

CHAPTER III.

RUSKIN has sometimes appeared to prefer the name of artist to that of author; and during a few weeks, at the close of the exhibition of his Turner drawings in Bond Street in 1878, he placed beside these a series of his own, amply representing his claim to the designation. An admirable opportunity was thus obtained by students of Ruskin and of Turner for comparing their works, and forming a clear, comprehensive, definite opinion as to the relation in which the great critic stands to the great artist.

What is art? A good many years ago I had occasion to consider this question very carefully, and I stated the result in an essay on the Elementary Principles of Criticism. Working upon lines which had been followed to a certain point by Professor Masson, and by that acute and far-seeing critic, the late Mr. Brimley, of Cambridge, I pronounced art, in its essential nature, to be a "mimic creation" of man's, the product of those instincts which urge him to imitate nature, and still more to make use of her forms and colors to create organic unities of his own. The imitative and the creative instincts are distinguishable, and even admit of being developed at the expense of each other; but it is seldom, perhaps it is never, practicable to discriminate them in the producing impulse of art, or to assign to each its part in a poem or a picture. In the harmonious union of the two—imitation, the lower, ministering to creation, the higher—the artist finds the ruling principle of his method of work; and the genuine art-product—the true picture, the living poem—exhibits imitation and creation, what the artist finds in nature, and what he gives to nature, indissolubly blended. Whether, however, we dwell upon the imitative element or upon the creative element in art, stress is to be laid upon the *appropriation* to man of the art - product. He delights in it first of all, and he delights in it last of all, not because it records for him any fact in nature (then he were a natural historian), not because it reveals to him any secret of nature (then he were a man of science), but because it is the child of his soul, the Pallas of his brain. The *differentia* of art—that which it shares neither with science nor with religion —is thus ascertained; and when this has been done, it becomes a simple matter to classify the several fine arts by the materials with which they work, sculpture employing light and shade, music clothing itself in sound, poetry making use of language, painting rejoicing in color.

"This theory," I wrote twenty years ago, "finds a *prima facie* vindication in its applicability to practical problems." In the interval I have always, more or less, been studying art, and I have never found the theory fail me. I have studied the art of Turner more closely and constantly than that of any other artist, and I have arrived at the conviction—a conviction which deepened with every year of increasing knowledge— that, on the whole, Turner's education in art and practice of art were perfect, and that his works are expressive illustrations, and authoritative, monumental examples, of what art ought to be.

In Turner's works there is always implicit recognition of man's sovereignty over nature; there is always the transforming touch by which nature becomes art. This vital element may be seen on a small scale or on a great; in the few strokes of the hand by which the line-harmonies of two or three laurel leaves are abstracted and fixed, or in the serene might of imagination by which the cliffs and ash-trees of Bolton Abbey are dowered with new and immortal beauty. But it is never

absent.   Turner executed not one literal transcript from nature
in his life.

Ruskin, in his earliest drawings, walked in the same track
with Turner.   Nothing ever interested me more in connection
with art than the discovery of this fact.   I had seen, previously to last summer, many of the drawings made by Ruskin after
he was grown up; and from these I had absolutely convinced
myself that, in his maturity, he had worked on a quite different
method from Turner's ; but the drawings of his boyhood I first
saw in Bond Street last year; and it was for me a revelation,
startling in its suddenness, yet infinitely corroborative of my
fundamental opinions respecting both Turner and Ruskin, to
find that, until he reached a certain stage in his development,
Ruskin had worked on the principles of Turner.   So much
alike, or akin, is there in their early drawings, that Ruskin
thinks it necessary to guard himself against the suspicion of
copying.   "It might easily be thought," he says, "that I was
partly imitating Turner's sketches in the foregoing series.   But
I never saw a Turner sketch till 1842."   No idea of conscious
imitation on Ruskin's part would have occurred to me ; his
drawings bear, quite distinctly, the stamp of his own genius and
personality ; but they are akin to Turner's in this, that they
are not mere transcripts from nature, or records of fact, but imbued with the appropriating, transforming, vitalizing spirit of art.

What, then, is the reason why Ruskin did not grow into an
artist whose achievement, as a whole, might bear comparison
with that of Turner ?   The answer is distinctly given in these
drawings.   Ruskin abandoned the path along which Turner,
steadily advancing, rose upward until he reached the summit
of the mountain.   At a point indicated in these drawings, a
point on which he himself lays his finger, Ruskin struck into a
path of his own, and has since, with indomitable energy, been
scaling precipices of shingle, grasping here a tuft of star-like
flowers, there a jut of purple rock, but never striking again

into the only path that could lead to the heights of art. Circumstances which he could not overrule contributed to this result. His friends "were minded" to make him a poet, a bishop, or a member of Parliament. His heart, moreover—and this is a cardinal point—was divided between geology and art. The artistic impulse and the scientific impulse being generically different—belonging to contrasted types of mind—are practically irreconcilable, except when the strength of both is mediocre. Science killed art in Goethe. When he wrote the first part of Faust, he was a mighty dramatic artist; when he wrote the second, he was a philosopher and man of science: to pass from the one part to the other is to sail from the river Jordan into the Dead Sea. Ruskin in his youth desired to put his "whole strength into drawing and geology." It is profoundly to be regretted that he was not allowed to do so; in that case he would probably have been the greatest artist that ever was a great geologist, and the greatest geologist that ever was a great artist: but it is in the highest degree improbable that, with allegiance divided between art and science, he would have been so great an artist as Turner. At all events, I am able to point to early work of Ruskin's which, in method, was sound; to point, on the other hand, to work of which the method was fatal to art production; and to specify approximately the time when, and the immediate occasion why, the change took place.

His Stirling drawings of 1838 are true art-work. The boy looks upon the landscape; thrills with its beauty; resolves to make a picture of it; shows his castle standing out boldly against the sky; takes from nature what he wants; puts the sign-manual of his own invention on everything; and is glad and proud in what, with all its imperfection, is his own, and a work of art. The "Study outside the south gate of Florence," marked "25. R. (B.)" in the exhibition of last summer, seems to have been executed about four years later than the drawings

17*

of Stirling Castle; and in it the change is complete. In all
the work of Turner that ever I saw—in all the work of Leonardo, of Titian, of Claude, of Rembrandt, nay, of Gainsbor-
ough, of Constable, of any and every man that has gained high
distinction in art—I never saw one like this. The subject is a
great group of tree-stems and foliage; the drawing, executed
in sepia, attests a strength of hand and a truth of graphic
touch transcending, I have no doubt, by a great deal, what he
was capable of when he executed the Stirling Castle; but now,
vehement in passionate realization, he strives to set down every fact in the scene before him, every tree-stem with its mark-
ings, every leaf with its lines and lights. In the drawing there
is proof of splendid power; but the whole is scattered, incom-
plete, without unity, without end. The work is not a picture.
Ruskin no longer paints his impression of what he sees; no
longer puts forth a reverent hand to God's quarry, and takes of
its stones to rear his cottage, small, it may be, yet his own, and
to be regarded by him with honorable pride: he attempts to
tear up and carry with him the quarry itself, to exhaust, on his
paper, the truth of nature, a thing which no man will do, were
he Hercules and Samson in one; a thing which no man can
persistently attempt to do, without destroying his power to
produce works of art.

    The date of the change I take to have been 1842. In that
year, Ruskin tells us, he formed a "resolute determination" to
have "ever so small a bit" of his work "right," "rather than
any quantity wrong." This, of course, would have been unob-
jectionable if by "right" he had meant right in relation to
the requirements of his picture as a whole, right in the sense
in which alone rightness can be predicated of any part of a
work of art. But I cannot look at that drawing of the trees
at Florence without seeing that what he meant by "right"
was literal accordance with the facts of nature; and, since nature is inexhaustible by human hand, he who resolves to have

every bit of his picture right in this sense will paint *bits* of nature, and no pictures, all the days of his life. "Serious botanical work," adds Mr. Ruskin, "began that same year in the Valley of Chamouni, and a few careful studies of grass-blades and Alpine-rose bells ended my Proutism and my trust in drawing things out of my head, forever." The grass-blades were very exquisite, the Alpine-rose bells very beautiful, but the price of them was *too* great.

"I have always felt," said Ruskin in one of his Mornings in Florence, "that, with my intense love of the Alps, I ought to have been able to make a drawing of Chamouni, or the vale of Cluse, which should give people more pleasure than a photograph; but I always wanted to do it as I saw it, and engrave pine for pine, and crag for crag, like Albert Dürer. I broke my strength down for many a year, always tiring of my work, or finding the leaves drop off, or the snow come on, before I had well begun what I meant to do. If I had only *counted* my pines first, and calculated the number of hours necessary to do them in the manner of Dürer, I should have saved the available drawing-time of some five years, spent in vain effort. But Turner counted his pines, and did all that could be done for them, and rested content with that." He refers elsewhere in pathetic terms to another of his drawings "colored only in a quarter of it before the autumn leaves fell—then given up—cut into four—now pasted together again to show how it was meant to be."

Does Ruskin, as a critic, hold that his early method—which continued to be Turner's method to the end—was artistically right, and the method he subsequently pursued artistically wrong? Or does he believe that the second method is intrinsically sound, and, with genius enough, might produce nobler art than the first?

A good deal might be said on each side of this very important question. A debater who chose to maintain that Ruskin

views art as fundamentally a thing of memory and transcript
might buttress his case by formidable arguments. He might
quote the many passages in which Ruskin declares art to be
the expression of man's delight in the works of God, apparently overlooking or denying the deeper truth that art is the
expression of man's delight in his *own* work, and of his incapacity to be completely satisfied with any work of nature. He
might refer to Ruskin's vehement patronage of the pre-Raphaelites, a coterie infected, beyond question, though not in the persons of all its members, with the deadly heresy of literalism.
He might dwell upon Ruskin's insatiable demand for accuracy
—a demand which has strengthened with his years; upon his
habit of laying much stress on truth, and saying comparatively little of beauty; upon that chapter in Modern Painters in
which he speaks of a series of windows opening on lovely Alpine landscapes, and seems to suggest that, if these views could
be transferred, line for line and tint for tint, to canvas, they
would be superlative works of art. But the maintainer of the
opposite hypothesis—namely, that Ruskin recognizes the supremacy of imagination in art, and looks upon nature as but
furnishing the materials of artistic creation—might also bring
into the field an imposing array of arguments. While insisting upon fidelity to nature, Ruskin has always reserved his
highest praise for imagination. Those of the pre-Raphaelites
whom he liked best have handled nature imaginatively, and
few more imaginative pictures could be named than Millais's
Autumn Leaves and Hunt's Light of the World. When the
pre-Raphaelites, as a school, failed in imagination, he threw them
off. Turner, whom he exalts above all landscape-painters, never, as I said before, executed a literal transcript from nature in
his life. Even in that ticklish tenth chapter in the third volume of Modern Painters, Ruskin teaches that there is something in art which nature does not possess—a subtle element
derived from humanity; that imagination has a "creative func-

tion;" and that "the substantial presence even of the things which we love the best will inevitably and forever be found wanting in *one* strange and tender charm, which belonged to the dreams of them."

The second of these answers to our question is, I think, correct. Ruskin has strained the resources of language to give emphasis to his inculcation of truth to fact and fidelity of representation; but this is because he holds that imagination feeds on fact, not on fancy; on truth, not on falsehood; and whenever he is called upon to discriminate between the materials with which art works, and the powers of invention and imagination which breathe into these materials a new life, he assigns the throne to the last. Ruskin has himself warned us that "useful truths" are "eminently biped," and we must be on our guard against concluding that, because he vehemently claims attention to one of the two legs of a truth, he is denying the existence of the other. His practical procedure as a critic of pictures accords with the position that he owns the supremacy of imagination in art. We may talk on theory for weeks, and yet attain to no certainty that we know each other's meaning, until we exemplify it by specification of instances. Ruskin has denied to recent landscapes by Brett and Millais the name of works of art, on the ground of their lack of imagination. There is no doubt that, as executive draughtsmen, Brett and Millais are among the most consummate of their time, and if literal transcript from nature were Ruskin's idea of perfect art, he would have been in ecstasies over their work. For my part, I see more imagination in Brett's rock and sea, and in Millais's hill and field, than suffices to entitle them, in my opinion, to be classed as works of art; but all the more convincing on this account, as evidence that Ruskin is no literalist in art, is his estimate of them as mere illustrations in topography or natural history.

One other question as to the nature of Ruskin's teaching

must be faced. What is to be the governing principle in the
education of artists? Is imagination, in the scholar as well as
in the master, in the young artist as well as in the old, to be
allowed to touch nature with the transforming or transfiguring
sceptre of sovereignty? Ruskin's answer to this question must,
I fear, be allowed to be negative. "From young artists," he
says, "nothing ought to be tolerated but *bona fide imitation* of
nature. .... Their duty is neither to choose, nor compose, nor
imagine, nor experimentalize; but to be humble and earnest in
following the steps of nature, and tracing the finger of God. ....
They should go to nature in all singleness of heart, and walk
with her laboriously and trustingly, having no other thoughts
but how best to penetrate her meaning, and remember her instruction; rejecting nothing, selecting nothing, and scorning
nothing; believing all things to be right and good, and rejoicing always in the truth. Then, when their memories are stored
and their imaginations fed, and their hands firm, let them take
up the scarlet and the gold, give the reins to their fancy, and
show us what their heads are made of." If this, which was
written many years ago, means only that students and young
artists—nay, artists of every age—ought to work from nature
constantly and faithfully, that conscious invention in young
men is generally conceit or insolence, that imagination cannot
work without materials, and that, in the logical order, accumulation of materials comes before the imaginative use of them, I
assent to it, every word; and this is, perhaps, all that Ruskin
would now affirm. But appealing to the studies of Leonardo
da Vinci on the one hand, and to the studies and sketches of
Turner on the other, I am quite sure that the art-student works
imaginatively from the first, works imaginatively even when he
is gathering the materials for invention, and can never, except
at the risk of stifling his imagination, break himself to slavish
imitation. Above all, he must from the first learn *to reject*.
Unless he rejects decisively, promptly, by art-instinct, he will

either execute *fac-similes* of little bits of nature all his life, or will wrestle with nature on a large scale, and, like the man that wrestled with God, will go a cripple to his grave. Of all the lessons — and they are not to be numbered — derivable from Turner's course as a student, none, I think, is more impressive or more important than the magnificent ease, the absolute decision, with which he takes from nature what he wants, and lets the rest alone. I cannot but believe that if Turner had not been an imaginative student, he would never have been an imaginative master. Students who work in their youth as slaves will not take up the scarlet and the gold at all. Having forced themselves for ten or twenty years to draw as botanists or as *fac-simile* makers, they will find imagination stiff and cold, her dead hand capable, indeed, of manufacture, but powerless to create.

It was, then, I must conclude, fatal to Ruskin's prospects as an artist, that "serious botanical work," and a frenzy of admiration for grass-blades and Alpine-rose bells, made him break the neck of his imagination; but with deliberate and entire acquiescence, I note his remark, "The power of *delineation* natural to me only became more accurate." It has not only been exquisitely accurate in transcript from nature, but has been guided by a poetically tender and delicate choice of natural objects to be delineated, and almost all that it has yielded us is beautiful. Ruskin's "Wild strawberry blossom, *one* of the weeds of such a rock, painted as it grew," is a ravishing glimpse of "nature's naked loveliness." It would have made Shelley weep for joy. The pale, tiny flower, frail in its whiteness, unites in simple harmony with the green and gray and russet-ruby in leaf, crag, tendril, making up a gem of beauty which we take to ourselves at once and forever, to wear next the heart "for fear our jewel tine." Not with the pen alone, but with the brush and the pencil, has Ruskin been a revealer of nature's sweet and subtle beauty; and his productions, if not in the strict sense works of art, are precious and unique.

CHAPTER IV.

WHATEVER he may call himself, it is as a painter of nature with words that Ruskin is named with enthusiasm wherever men speak the English tongue. It has been through his books, not through his pictures, that he has mainly influenced his generation, and sent that wave of passionate enthusiasm for nature into ten thousand young hearts, which has shown itself in the fresh, impetuous, exulting, and sometimes weak and affected naturalism of our recent schools. Nor has its influence been confined to the schools or the coteries of pictorial art. It has told upon literature; it has been felt in social life; it has penetrated into quarters in which pictures are scarcely known. The class directly influenced by Turner's pictures has been small compared with that influenced by Ruskin's books.

Some twenty years ago, I had occasion to state, in print, my estimate of the value and importance of Ruskin's word-painting of nature. The passage was received by some with ridicule as mere enthusiastic extravagance; but I have never seen cause to modify it; and I have the more satisfaction in recurring to it now, because I wish to say that, however much I may have disagreed with some of his recent opinions, I have never harbored a doubt as to the greatness and the splendor of his service in delineating the facts of nature.

·After an introductory word or two upon the ministry of mind to mind, so that an original thinker inspires multitudes with thought, and " the delight first felt in a single breast is communicated by sympathy, and thrills through a thousand," I proceeded as follows: "A man gifted with pre-eminent sensibility to nature's beauty, with pre-eminent ability to perceive nature's truth, lends a voice to the hills, and adds a music to the streams; he looks on the sea, and it becomes more calmly beautiful; on the clouds, and they are more radiantly touched; he becomes a priest of the mysteries, a dispenser of the charities of nature; and men call him poet. Ruskin stands among a select and honored few who have thus interpreted nature's meaning, and conveyed her bounty to mankind. He has spoken with a voice of fascinating power of those pictures which never change, yet are ever new; which are old, yet not dimmed or defaced; of the beauty of which all art is an acknowledgment, of the admiration of which all art is the result, but which, having hung in our view since childhood, we are apt to pass lightly by. He has reminded us that morning, rosy-fingered as in the days of Homer, has yet a new and distinct smile at each arising; and that, as she steps along the ocean, its foam is still wreathed into new broideries of gold and roses. He has shown us, by evidence which none can resist, that no true lover ever trysted with Spring by her own fountains or in her own woods, without seeing some beauty never seen before. At his bidding we awake to a new consciousness of the beauty and grandeur of the world. We have more distinct ideas as to what it is; we know better how to look for it. Summer has for us a new opulence and pride; Autumn—which is Summer meeting death with a smile—a new solemnity and a more noble sadness. Even to Winter we learn to look for his part in nature's pageantry, in nature's orchestral beauty; we find a new music in his storms, a new majesty in his cataracts, a more exquisite pencilling in his frost-work." There are multitudes now who, without fear of ridicule, would apply these words to Ruskin, and declare that he had either opened their eyes to the grandeur and loveliness of nature, or enabled them to see more of the beauty than they had ever seen before; but there were not so many twenty years ago.

In order to understand and appreciate Ruskin's descriptions, we must exactly apprehend the object with which they were produced. They were intended to vindicate Turner's *knowledge*, not his art—to prove that he knew more, and recorded more, of the facts of nature than any other painter. The critics, Ruskin tells us, had denied that Turner could draw. They alleged that they saw less of nature in Turner's pictures than in those of other men. Ruskin met them on the issue of fact, putting aside or postponing questions respecting the use Turner had made of his facts in creating imaginative pictures. The mistake of the critics, judging as they did by Turner's latest works, was hardly surprising, inasmuch as the intense imaginative brilliancy of Turner's final manner hid the accurate realism that lay beneath. If you see the Lake of Lucerne and its encompassing mountains, rendered in perfect harmony of rose-light and blue, looking as if the whole were one finely-veined jewel, you are apt to think that the work is but an abstract harmony of color, such as might be seen in a prism, and to overlook the veracity of mountain line, the faultless rightness of lake surface, which no man in Europe except Turner could have given with the same consummate truth. I heard a man in the crowd, at the exhibition of the Novar Turners, making this very comparison of the Lucerne to the color of a prism, and pooh-poohing the work in consequence. What this man wanted was an instructor who could lift the veil of imaginative radiance from Turner's drawing, and show him the truth lying below. This was what Ruskin undertook to do; and therefore, whatever quality his descriptions might lack, they were bound, if fitted to serve their purpose at all, to be literally true to nature. Hence their unparalleled accuracy. There is a more minute and extensive knowledge in them than can be claimed for the corresponding word-pictures, either of descriptive poets, like Tennyson, Shelley, Scott, Keats, and Wordsworth, or of authors who elaborately describe nature in prose, like Jean Paul Richter and Christopher North. He has such a knowledge of nature as Tennyson would have had if he had devoted himself to landscape-painting; and he has a command of words such as only the greatest authors, prose or poetical, have possessed. He says modestly that no description of his is worth four lines of Tennyson; but highly as I prize Tennyson's descriptions, I cannot assent to that. Tennyson is faultlessly true, but his knowledge is not so wide as Ruskin's.

It is in the extent combined with the precision of his observation, and the unprecedented tenacity with which he has stored up in memory the record of what he has seen, that Ruskin stands alone. You are apt, when you read his account of one series of natural appearances, to conclude that he must have devoted all his time and all his attention to that particular series. Listen to his description of the sea, and you figure him as standing for hours on the sea-shore, or on some pier-head above the line of breakers, watching the waves in their race up the beach, and the backward flow of the recoiling billow, its surface "marbled" by the foam, which has partly entered into its substance and shows in it like the air in effervescing wine, and partly floats upon it, opening into "oval gaps and clefts." Again and again, as you read Ruskin's descriptions of the sea, you exclaim—if you have yourself been a haunter of the shore, a watcher of the waves from pier-head, cliff, or deck—"Ah, I have seen that!" In the first volume of Modern Painters, he criticises, in a single sentence, the treatment of the sea by the Dutch school, and we cannot but feel, as we read it, that, though he by no means recognizes the whole merit of Vandevelde and his fellows, who painted gray quiet sea and drooping sails with what seemed, I believe, to Turner, the highest possible perfection, he has acquired a far more thorough acquaintance with the sea in motion and in sunlight—with all that is the sea's peculiar glory—than those wonderful and indomitable Hollanders. "Foam," he says, "appears to me to curdle and cream on the wave sides, and to fly flashing from their crests, and not to be set astride upon them like a peruke; and waves appear to me to fall, and plunge, and toss, and nod, and crash over, and not to curl up like shavings; and water appears to me, when it is gray, to have the gray of stormy air mixed with its own deep, heavy, thunderous, threatening blue, and not the gray of the first coat of cheap paint on a deal door; and many other such things appear to me, which, as far as I can conjecture by what is admired marine painting, appear to few else."

To point out wherein artists have misrepresented nature is an important part of the duty of a critic, but it is a more difficult part of his duty to discover, in the works of an artist, who is misrepresented or misunderstood, instances of truth to nature which escape the common eye. Nothing is more likely to strike the careful and observant painter, who makes it his business to watch nature, and who perpetually witnesses effects which none but a watcher of nature will notice, with despair than to find, when he has recorded his original and exquisite observation, either that no one discovers him to have done anything unusual, or that some critic, ignorant, impudent, and unfeeling, sure only that *he* never saw the effect in question, accuses him of painting falsely. It is in pointing out unnoticed truths in Turner's works, and thus, at one and the same moment doing justice to the artist, and revealing nature to his readers, that Ruskin affords a sovereign example to critics. I must quote a passage to illustrate this statement, but it is difficult to select one which admits of being separated from the context. In that which I have chosen, the opening sentences form part of a comprehensive criticism of Turner's water-color picture of Laugharne Castle.

SEA WAVES.

In the distance of this grand picture, there are two waves which entirely depart from the principle observed by all the rest, and spring high into the air. They have a message for us which it is important that we should understand. Their leap is not a preparation for breaking, neither is it caused by their meeting with a rock. It is caused by their encounter with the recoil of the preceding wave. When a large surge, in the act of breaking, just as it curls over, is hurled against the face either of a wall or of a vertical rock, the sound of the blow is not a crash, nor a roar, it is a report as loud as, and in every respect similar to, that of a great gun, and the wave is dashed back from the rock with force scarcely diminished, but reversed in direction; it now recedes from the shore, and at the instant that it encounters the following breaker, the result is the vertical bound of both which is here rendered by Turner. Such a recoiling wave will proceed out to sea through ten or twelve ranges of following breakers, before it is overpowered. The effect of the encounter is more completely and palpably given in the Quillebœuf, in the Rivers of France. It is peculiarly instructive here, as informing us of the nature of the coast and the force of the waves far more clearly than any spray about the rocks themselves could have done. But the effect of the blow at the shore itself is given in the Land's End and Tantallon Castle. Under favorable circumstances, with an advancing tide, under a heavy gale, where the breakers feel the shore underneath them a moment before they touch the rock, so as to nod over when they strike, the effect is nearly incredible except to an eye-witness. I have seen the whole body of the wave rise in one white, vertical, broad fountain, eighty feet above the sea, half of it beaten so fine as to be borne away by the wind, the rest turning in the air when exhausted, and falling back with a weight and crash like that of an enormous water-fall. This is given in the vignette to "Lycidas;" and the blow of a less violent wave among broken rocks, not meeting it with an absolute wall, along the shore of the Land's End. This last picture is a study of sea, whose whole organization has been broken up by constant recoils from a rocky coast. The Laugharne gives the surge and weight of the ocean in a gale, on a comparatively level shore; but the Land's End, the entire disorder of the surges when every one of them, divided and entangled among promontories as it rolls in, and beaten back part by part from walls of rock on this side and that side, recoils like the defeated divisions of a great army, throwing all behind it into disorder, breaking up the succeeding waves into vertical ridges, which in their turn, yet more totally shattered upon the shore, retire in more hopeless confusion, until the whole surface of the sea becomes one dizzy whirl of rushing, writhing, tortured, undirected rage, bounding, and crashing, and coiling in an anarchy of enormous power; subdivided into myriads of waves, of which every one is not, be it remembered, a separate surge, but part and portion of a vast one, actuated by internal power, and giving in every direction the mighty undulation of impetuous line which glides over the rocks and writhes in the wind, overwhelming the one and piercing the other with the fury and swiftness of a sheet of lambent fire.

What Ruskin did for Turner in respect of the sea he did for him in respect of every other province of nature which enters into the domain of landscape art: the sky with its clouds; the forest with its grouped or single trees, its capricious beauty of branch and infinite variation of foliage; the river with its every change and humor from the fountain to the sea; the mountains, great and small, from the little hills of

> Most gentle dimplement,
> (As if God's finger touched but did not press
> In making England!)

to the colossal ranges of Switzerland, great cities on their flanks, and furrowed by rivers which water half a continent. Long and constantly as I have read his works, I should have difficulty in saying whether it is in describing clouds, or hills, or rivers, or trees, or waves that he is most successful. His eloquence, perhaps, reaches its climax in the description of mountains, "their gates of rock, pavements of cloud, choirs of stream and stone, altars of snow, and vaults of purple traversed by the continual stars." There is a piece of mountain and cloud description in the first volume of Modern Painters which, though long, I shall place before my readers, because it is in all respects characteristic of Ruskin in his first period of developed strength.

From Dawn to Dawn in the Alps.

Stand upon the peak of some isolated mountain at daybreak, when the night mists first rise from off the plains, and watch their white and lake-like fields, as they float in level bays and winding gulfs, about the islanded summits of the lower hills, untouched yet by more than dawn, colder and more quiet than a windless sea under the moon of midnight; watch when the first sunbeam is sent upon the silver channels, how the foam of their undulating surface parts and passes away, and down under their depths the glittering city and green pasture lie like Atlantis between the white paths of winding rivers; the flakes of light falling every moment faster and broader among the starry spires, as the wreathed surges break and vanish above them, and the confused crests and ridges of the dark hills shorten their gray shadows upon the plain. Has Claude given this? Wait a little longer, and you shall see those scattered mists rallying in the ravines, and floating up toward you, along the winding valleys, till they couch in quiet masses, iridescent with the morning light, upon the broad breasts of the higher hills, whose leagues of massive undulation will melt back and back into that robe of material light, until they fade away, lost in its lustre, to appear again above, in the serene heaven, like a wild, bright, impossible dream, foundationless and inaccessible, the very bases vanishing in the unsubstantial and mocking blue of the deep lake below. Has Claude given this? Wait yet a little longer, and you shall see those mists gather themselves into white towers, and stand like fortresses along the promontories, massy and motionless, only piled every instant higher and higher into the sky, and casting longer shadows athwart the rocks, and out of the pale blue of the horizon you will see forming and advancing a troop of narrow, dark, pointed vapors which will cover the sky, inch by inch, with their gray net-work, and take the light off the landscape with an eclipse which will stop the singing of the birds and the motion of the leaves, together; and then you will see horizontal bars of black shadow forming under them, and lurid wreaths create themselves, you know not how, along the shoulders of the hills; you never see them form, but when you look back to a place which was clear an instant ago, there is a cloud on it, hanging by the precipices, as a hawk pauses over his prey. Has Claude given this? And then you will hear the sudden rush of awakened wind, and you will see those watch-towers of vapors sweep away from their foundations, and waving curtains of opaque rain let down to the valleys, swinging from the burdened clouds in black bending fringes, or pacing in pale columns along the lake level, grazing its surface into foam as they go. And then, as the sun sinks, you shall see the storm drift for an instant from off the hills, leaving their broad sides smoking, and loaded yet with snow-white, torn, steam-like rays of capricious vapor, now gone, now gathered again, while the smouldering sun, seeming not far away, but burning like a red-hot ball beside you, and as if you could reach it, plunges through the rushing wind and rolling cloud with headlong fall, as if it meant to rise no more, dyeing all the air about it with blood. Has Claude given this? And then you shall hear the fainting tempest die in the hollow of the night, and you shall see a green halo kindling on the summit of the eastern hills, brighter—brighter yet, till the large white circle of the slow moon is lifted up among the barred clouds, step by step, line by line; star after star she quenches with her kindling light, setting in their stead an army of pale, penetrable, fleecy wreaths in the heavens, to give light upon the earth, which move together, hand in hand, company by company, troop by troop, so measured in their unity of motion that the whole heaven seems to roll with them, and the earth to reel under them. Ask Claude, or his brethren, for that. And then wait yet for one hour, until the east again becomes purple, and the heaving mountains, rolling against it in darkness, like waves of a wild sea, are drowned one by one in the glory of its burning; watch the white glaciers blaze in their winding paths about the mountains, like mighty serpents with scales of fire: watch the columnar peaks of solitary snow, kindling downward, chasm by chasm, each in itself a new morning; their long avalanches cast down in keen streams brighter than the lightning, sending each his tribute of driven snow, like altar-smoke, up to the heaven: the rose-light of their silent domes flushing that heaven about them and above them, piercing with purer light through its purple lines of lifted cloud, casting a new glory on every wreath as it passes by, until the whole heaven, one scarlet canopy, is interwoven with a roof of waving flame, and tossing, vault beyond vault, as with the drifted wings of many companies of angels: and then, when you can look no more for gladness, and when you are bowed down with fear and love of the Maker and Doer of this, tell me who has delivered his message unto men!"

In his recent books Mr. Ruskin has pooh-poohed the first volume of Modern Painters, and in a note appended to the above passage in a volume of selections from his works, lately published, he laughs genially at his former self, observing upon the uncomfortable or non-existent arrangements for breakfast and dinner, during this contemplation, at least twenty-four hours long, of Alpine phenomena. But, in truth, that great first volume was not only the basis of his fame, but authoritatively displays the foundation on which the general achievement of his life was reared. The thorough and comprehensive acquaintance with nature which it reveals prepared him for all he has done. It is one of those first books which the authors who produced them have subsequently referred to with depreciation, but which the world has, with just obstinacy, continued to admire. Goethe lived to think very little of Werther, Schiller to smile at the extravagance of The Robbers; but the world thinks, and thinks rightly, that Werther, whatever its defects, is worth more than the second part of Faust; and Schiller certainly never showed more magnificent imaginative strength than in the character of Karl Moor, the love-song of Amelia, and the meeting of Brutus and Cæsar in the land of ghosts. By a sure instinct the heart of the world has taken to those books, which have on them the glory and freshness of the morning, the artless exuberant splendor of genius in its dawn.

18

CHAPTER V.

IN the second volume of Modern Painters Ruskin propounded the theory that beauty in nature, except in so far as it is the manifestation of happy life in organic things, is typical of moral perfection, and emblematic of the attributes of God. This volume was written when he was strongly under the influence of Hooker, whose long, melodious periods are its model in style, and whose reverent enthusiasm of Christian faith, hope, and charity is its pervading spirit. In the preceding volume we had the facts of nature. This volume adds their consecration through the Divine light falling on them. It will be worth our while to follow Ruskin's finger as he traces that light. He first specifies the fact or quality of natural beauty, and then specifies its typical significance.

Infinity, as suggested by many aspects of nature — by the traceless delicacy of curvature in lines of mountain undulation and of forest branches—by the light on distant horizons—by "the still small voice of the level twilight behind purple hills, or the scarlet arch of dawn over the dark troublous-edged sea" —is, for him, the type of Divine incomprehensibility. He points out that the power of such distances upon the mind does not depend on richness or splendor of color. "In the blue of the rainy sky, in the many tints of morning flowers, in the sunlight on summer foliage and field, there are more sources of mere sensual color-pleasure than in the single streak of wan and dying light. It is not, then, by nobler form, it is not by positiveness of hue, it is not by intensity of light (for the sun itself at noonday is effectless upon the feelings), that this strange distant space possesses its attractive power. But there is one thing that it has, or suggests, which no other object of sight suggests in equal degree, and that is—Infinity. It is of all visible things the least material, the least finite, the farthest withdrawn from the earth prison-house, the most typical of the nature of God, the most suggestive of the glory of his dwelling-place." The expression of infinity he alleges to be an unfailing characteristic of noble and joy-giving art. " If there be any one grand division by which it is at all possible to set the productions of painting, so far as their mere plan or system is concerned, on our right and left hands, it is this of light and dark background, of heaven light or of object light." He knows no " truly great painter " of any time who did not take " the most intense pleasure " in his luminous distances; nor is he aware that, except in the case of Rembrandt—" and then under peculiar circumstances only "—the use of dark backgrounds was associated with high power of intellect. The great Florentines—Giotto, Angelico, Perugino, Raphael in his early period, the great Venetians—Carpaccio, John Bellini, Giorgione, Titian, Tintoret, rejoiced in distant open sky and clouds on remote horizons touched with white sunlight; and the grand tradition of luminous distance was handed on to Claude, Gasper Poussin, and the modern masters of landscape. I do not remember that Ruskin has said, but he might have said with perfect truth, that no artist ever more deeply felt the value of distant light in landscape than Turner, and that no landscapes are comparable with his for the suggestion of infinity. Ruskin is careful to say that he does not narrowly require his reader to accept his interpretation of nature's facts into their Divine or moral analogies; and I confess that the rose of dawn on the horizon of stormy sea, and the pale gleam beneath the skirts of the thunder-cloud, and other landscape aspects which beckon us on toward the infinite, seem to me to suggest not only the Divine

incomprehensibility but the Divine kindness, never letting hope
be extinguished in the world, or leaving man to the conviction
that earth is his eternal grave. Interpret it as we may, there
can be no doubt that a power to touch that mightiest chord
in the human breast which vibrates in response to the infinite
is a characteristic of the greatest art.

Unity, in nature and in art, he takes to be typical of the
Divine comprehensiveness. Separation, isolation, "self-depend-
ence," are indications of imperfection; connection and brotherhood are significant of perfection in the things combined, and
"typical of that unity which we attribute to God." It is a
unity not of absolute oneness, but of universality—the indwell-
ing spirit of a vast comprehensiveness. It is the unity, in human creatures, of sympathy, of mutual help, of affection; their
coworking and army fellowship; their delight in receiving
and imparting benefits. It is not "the dead and cold peace
of undisturbed stones and solitary mountains; but the living
peace of trust, and the living power of support; of hands that
hold each other and are still." The unity of matter, in its
noblest form, is exemplified in the human body, the temple
of the human spirit; in its lower forms, it is "the sweet and
strange affinity which gives" to matter "the glory of its orderly elements, and the fair variety of change and assimilation
that turns the dust into the crystal, and separates the waters
that be above the firmament from the waters that be beneath."
It is in obedience to this law that winds and waves move in
companies, that nature's forms and forces work, and walk,
and cling together. The presence of unity always inspires
order and beauty, and if it be totally absent there is no beauty.
"The appearance of some species of unity is, in the most
determined sense of the word, essential to the perfection of
beauty in lines, colors, or forms." Out of the necessity of
unity arises that of variety, for unity without variety would
be dead uniformity. He urgently inculcates that variety

for its own sake, mere novelty and changefulness, can claim no place in art. "It will be found that they are the weakest-minded and the hardest-hearted men that most love variety and change." The noble variety is that "which accomplishes unity, or makes it perceived." When it performs this service "its operation is found to be very precious" in connection with unity of subjection, unity of sequence, unity of membership; "for although things in all respects the same may, indeed, be subjected to one influence, yet the power of the influence, and their obedience to it, are best seen by varied operation of them on their individual differences; as in clouds and waves there is a glorious unity of rolling, wrought out by the wild and wonderful differences of their absolute forms, which differences, if removed, would leave in them only multitudinous and petty repetition, instead of the majestic oneness of shared passion." In great works of art the most impressive and sublime effects are produced when specialities of passion and character are represented as under the influence of one great thought. In a fresco by Angelico, for example, we behold the spirits in prison listening to Christ, each individualized, yet "the intense, fixed, statue-like silence of ineffable adoration" imprinting one solemn thought on the faces of all, as they kneel "side by side, the hands lifted, and the knees bowed, and the lips trembling together." Unity in variety, both in nature and in every kind of art, from groups in sculpture to airs in music, is an indispensable element of power and beauty.

Repose, a third constituent of beauty, he views as typical of Divine permanence. "As opposed to passion, change, fulness, or laborious exertion, repose is the especial and separating characteristic of the eternal mind and power. It is the 'I am' of the Creator opposed to the 'I become' of all creatures; it is the sign alike of the supreme knowledge which is incapable of surprise, the supreme power which is incapable of labor, the

supreme volition which is incapable of change; it is the stillness of the beams of the eternal chambers laid upon the variable waters of ministering creatures." Having noted the impressive influence upon the mind of the appearance of quiet
permanence in massy forms of crag and mountain, and "the
lulling effect of all mighty sight and sound," he points out
with finest accuracy of observation that repose, in rocks, in
stones, in trees, demands for its expression "the implied capability of its opposite, energy." Having seen a great rock
bounding down the mountain-side, we feel its repose as it rests
immovably in the fern. Scattered rocks may fail to impress
us, but we are sensible of their restfulness when Wordsworth
tells us that they "lie couched around us like a flock of sheep."
True repose is not that of the bough, hewn square for threshold or lintel, but that of the living branch, bearing with queen-
like ease its drapery of leaf and blossom in the summer air.

Then follows one of those passages, not uncommon in this
volume, which require but the form of verse to be recognized
as Christian hymns replete with elevated and lovely poetry.
The passage is peculiarly endeared to me, for it was on it my
eye fell when, in a bookseller's shop in Edinburgh, I for the
first time took a volume of Ruskin's into my hand.

THE REPOSE OF FAITH.

But that which in lifeless things ennobles them by seeming to indicate
life, ennobles higher creatures by indicating the exaltation of their earthly
vitality into a Divine vitality; and raising the life of sense into the life
of faith: faith, whether we receive it in the sense of adherence to resolution, obedience to law, regardfulness of promise, in which from all time it
has been the test, as the shield, of the true being and life of man; or in
the still higher sense of trustfulness in the presence, kindness, and Word
of God, in which form it has been exhibited under the Christian dispensa-
tion. For, whether in one or other form—whether the faithfulness of
men whose path is chosen and portion fixed, in the following and receiving
of that path and portion, as in the Thermopylæ camp; or the happier
faithfulness of children in the good giving of their father, and of subjects

in the conduct of their King, as in the "Stand still and see the salvation of God" of the Red Sea shore—there is rest and peacefulness, the "standing still," in both, the quietness of action determined, of spirit unalarmed, of expectation unimpatient: beautiful even when based only, as of old, on the self-command and self-possession, the persistent dignity or the uncalculating love, of the creature; but more beautiful yet when the rest is one of humility instead of pride, and the trust no more in the resolution we have taken, but in the hand we hold.

Repose he pronounces "the most unfailing test of beauty," and says "that all art is great in proportion to the appearance .of it." We may trust to it to lead us to the mightiest masters. By its light "three colossal images are seen standing up side by side, looming in their great rest of spirituality above the whole world-horizon—Phidias, Michael Angelo, and Dante; and then, separated from their great religious thrones only by less fulness and earnestness of faith, Homer and Shakspeare." Universally in art you may apply the test of repose, to unveil the good, and detect the bad. "Everything of evil is betrayed and winnowed away by it; glitter, confusion, or glare of color; inconsistency of thought; forced expression; evil choice of subject; redundance of materials, pretence, overcharged decoration, or excessive division of parts; and this in everything. In architecture, in music, in acting, in dancing, in whatsoever art, great or mean, there are yet degrees of greatness or meanness entirely dependent on this single quality of repose." As an instance of treatment in which the law of repose is disregarded, he names the famous group of Laocoon struggling convulsively with the serpents; and, as an instance of its perfect observance, the Theseus of the Elgin marbles. But the most deeply impressive, and at the same time most delicately and richly instructive, of the illustrations he gives of repose in art is that which follows: "In the Cathedral of Lucca, near the entrance-door of the north transept, there is a monument by Jacopo della Quercia to Ilaria di Caretto, the wife of Paolo Guinigi. She is lying on a simple couch, with a hound at her feet; not on the side, but with the head laid straight and simply on the hard pillow, in which, let it be observed, there is no effort at deceptive imitation of pressure. It is understood as a pillow, but not mistaken for one. The hair is bound in a flat braid over the fair brow, the sweet and arched eyes are closed, the tenderness of the loving lips is set and quiet; there is that about them which forbids breath; something which is not death nor sleep, but the pure image of both. The hands are not lifted in prayer, neither folded; but the arms are laid at length upon the body, and the hands cross as they fall. The feet are hidden by the drapery, and the forms of the limbs concealed, but not their tenderness."

Symmetry, the quality of beauty next considered, is somewhat dubiously pronounced to be the type of Divine justice. On this quality of beauty and symbol of moral perfection he says comparatively little. He will not dogmatically affirm that the charm of symmetry is due to its expressing abstract justice, but asserts "that it is necessary to the dignity of every form." Its nature is to be distinguished from that of proportion. "Symmetry is the *opposition* of *equal* quantities to each other; proportion the *connection* of *unequal* quantities with each other. The property of a tree sending out equal boughs on opposite sides is symmetrical; its sending out shorter and smaller toward the top, proportional. In the human face, its balance of opposite sides is symmetry; its division upward, proportion." The agreeableness of symmetry is felt in the balance and arrangement of the opposite stars or sides in ornamental designs; "which orderly balance and arrangement are essential to the perfect operation of the more earnest and solemn qualities of the Beautiful, as being heavenly in their nature, and contrary to the violence and disorganization of sin; so that the seeking of them, and submission to them, are characteristic of minds that have been subjected to high moral discipline, and constant in all the great religious painters, to the

degree of being an offence and a scorn to men of less tuned
and tranquil feelings." All who are acquainted with the works
of the old religious painters of Italy, Giotto, Perugino, Angelico, must recollect how saint balances saint on opposite sides
of the composition; "if there be a kneeling figure on one side,
there is a corresponding one on the other; the attendant angels beneath and above are arranged in like order." By skilful
violations of symmetry artists may heighten the expression of
passion and produce sublime pictures, "but they lose propor-
tionately in the Diviner quality of beauty." I would venture
to suggest that symmetry, though an infallible test of the presence of art, belongs to art rather in its initial than in its higher
stages. The savage is becoming an artist so soon as he delights
in arranging lines in symmetrical patterns or in matching colors. Symmetry prevails in the old art of Italy, both because
it promotes solemnity, and because the old art of Italy, being
completely subordinate to religion, was, as art, in a state of infancy and imperfection. The immediate perception of symmetry in a picture—its prominence and unmistakability—mark
the work as too stiff and quaint to possess the higher attributes
of beauty. The symmetry that is most precious in art is always unsymmetrical—the right measure of deviation from obvious and absolute symmetry being the secret of genius, not
definable in words.

Purity, the fifth element of typical beauty, symbolizes Divine
energy. Believing that our ideas of impurity "refer especially
to conditions of matter in which its various elements are placed
in a relation incapable of healthy or proper operation, and
most distinctly to conditions in which the negation of vital or
energetic action is most evident, as in corruption and decay of
all kinds," he supposes "that pureness is made to us desirable,
because expressive of that constant presence and energizing of
the Deity by which all things live and move, and have their
being; and that foulness is painful as the accompaniment of

disorder and decay, and always indicative of the withdrawal of
Divine support." In human life outward foulness goes "with
mental sloth and degradation, as well as with bodily lethargy
and disease," and freshness and purity belong to every healthy
organic frame, as to "the young leaves when first their inward
energy prevails over the earth, pierces its corruption, and
shakes its dust away from their own white purity of life."
Last of all, "with the idea of purity comes that of spirituality;
for the essential characteristic of matter is its inertia, whence,
by adding to it purity or energy, we may in some measure
spiritualize even matter itself." These are beautiful and suggestive ideas, worthy of careful meditation, but Ruskin does
not give us particular instances by which to define their application to painting. I shall not undertake to supply the
want, but I think that if we recall the loveliest faces we have
seen from the hand of Reynolds, and the loveliest landscapes
we have seen from the hand of Turner, we shall feel that the
pure glow of the one and the bright vivacity of the other are
connected with the expression of strenuous life in man and in
nature. Turner's supremacy among landscape-painters depended, next to his imaginative invention, on his power of showing
the *light* on the leaf and the *life* in the branch.

The list of symbolic elements of beauty is closed with moderation, the type of Divine government by law. Ruskin holds
that, in contemplating lines and colors, we may trace "an un-
dercurrent of constantly agreeable feeling, excited by the appearance in material things of a self-restrained liberty; that is
to say, by the image of that acting of God with regard to all
His creation, wherein, though free to operate in whatever arbitrary, sudden, violent, or inconstant ways he will, he yet, if
we may reverently so speak, restrains in himself this his omnipotent liberty, and works always in consistent modes, called
by us laws." Whether he succeeds or fails in pointing out an
element or influence of restraint in nature, he has no hesitation

in pronouncing moderation a primary law of art, and dwells with eloquent enthusiasm on its importance. " I have put this attribute of beauty last, because I consider it the girdle and safeguard of all the rest, and in this respect the most essential of all ; for it is possible that a certain degree of beauty may be attained even in the absence of one of its other constituents, as sometimes in some measure without symmetry or without unity. But the least appearance of violence or extravagance, of the want of moderation and restraint, is, I think, destructive of all beauty whatsoever in everything—color, form, motion, language, or thought : giving rise to that which in color we call glaring, in form inelegant, in motion ungraceful, in language coarse, in thought undisciplined, in all unchastened ; which qualities are in everything most painful, because the signs of disobedient and irregular operation." In the essential beauty of moderation he finds the reason why curves which approach the straight line are more beautiful than those which fall into "wide and far license of curvature," and why the "pure and severe" curves of the draperies in religious pictures are beautiful. In color rose is lovelier than red ; gray-green, "or such pale green and uncertain as we see in sunset sky and in the clefts of the glacier and the chrysoprase," is more beautiful than the strong green of summer foliage. "The very brilliancy and real power of all color is dependent on the chastening of it, as of a voice on its gentleness, and as of action on its calmness, and as all moral vigor on self-command. And therefore," says Mr. Ruskin, in conclusion, "as that virtue which men last, and with most difficulty attain unto, and which many attain not at all, and yet that which is essential to the conduct and almost to the being of all other virtues ; since neither imagination, nor invention, nor industry, nor sensibility, nor energy, nor any other good having, is of full avail without this of self-command, whereby works truly masculine and mighty are

produced, and by the signs of which they are separated from
that lower host of things brilliant, magnificent, and redundant,
and farther yet from that of the loose, the lawless, the exaggerated, the insolent, and the profane; I would have the necessity of it foremost among all our inculcating, and the name of
it largest among all our inscribing, in so far that, over the doors
of every School of Art, I would have this one word, relieved
out in deep letters of pure gold—Moderation."

There is room for debate as to the strictly scientific value,
whether æsthetic or theological, of this doctrine of typical
beauty. It is not in nature but in man that we have the most
vivid revelation of God—in his image, not in his works. If
the worship of God's visible works, instead of his invisible and
immaterial essence, is what all the greatest seers of human history have denounced as the cardinal sin, idolatry, ought we not
to be on our guard against any such sentiment of reverence, in
contemplating the aspects of nature, as is legitimately suggested by the beauty of moral perfection? On the other hand,
though we may refuse to admit that nature is either God, or
the image of God, or the immediate operation of God, we cannot altogether disconnect nature from the Creator, or hesitate
to admit that it is what it is by Divine ordinance. This consideration furnishes, perhaps, a sufficient basis for Ruskin's
scheme. The habit of dwelling with feelings of grateful adoration on the beautiful and benignant aspects of nature, as
proofs of the benignity and glory of the Maker, has characterized devout minds from the days of Job and of David. "The
fact," says Ruskin, "of our deriving constant pleasure from
whatever is a type or semblance of Divine attributes, and from
nothing but that which is so, is the most glorious of all that
can be demonstrated of human nature; it not only sets a great
gulf of specific separation between us and the lower animals,
but it seems a promise of a communion, ultimately deep, close,

and conscious, with the Being whose darkened manifestations we here feebly and unthinkingly delight in."

At all events, the chapters in which this theory is expounded are cantos of a prose poem, deficient neither in color nor in melody, upon the Divine beauty of nature and its reflection in art.

CHAPTER VI.

THE second volume of Modern Painters was published in
1846. With its appearance closed what we may mark
off as the first period of Ruskin's literary production and critical activity. The third volume was not issued until 1856, and
in the ten intervening years he had completed very important
undertakings in other departments.

In 1849—for the accuracy of this and of many other of the
dates mentioned I depend upon Mr. R. H. Shepherd's Bibliography of Ruskin—appeared The Seven Lamps of Architecture.
The volume contained "illustrations, drawn and etched by the
author;" and from this time forward, Ruskin, the draughtsman,
figured in his books almost as prominently as Ruskin, the critic. There are some who have viewed this circumstance with
very qualified satisfaction, and I must own myself of the number. Though deriving much enjoyment from the products of
his pencil, I have looked with jealousy on its encroachments
upon the province of his pen. The title of the new work was
also prophetic. It was one of the first of those symbolical
designations which he has so frequently adopted for his books
—The Stones of Venice, The Queen of the Air, Sesame and
Lilies, The Crown of Wild Olive, Ethics of the Dust, Fors
Clavigera. The "lamps" of architecture are the characteristics which good architecture should possess, the spirit in which
good architecture is produced, the moral perfections which
good architecture should illustrate; in short, the principles

which are safeguards against error and sources of success in architectural art. A chapter is devoted to each lamp.

The first is the lamp of Sacrifice. Its light is shed chiefly upon buildings raised for devotional purposes. He maintains that, as the Hebrews were enjoined to honor God with their substance, so, in Christian churches, noble and costly workmanship ought to be one attestation of the sincerity of our worship. Better it is, indeed, to have poor churches than none; but the question is whether wealth shall be spent in the service of our own pride or in adorning the temple of God. "I do not understand the feeling which would arch our own gates and pave our own thresholds, and leave the church with its narrow door and foot-worn sill; the feeling which enriches our own chambers with all manner of costliness, and endures the bare wall and mean compass of the temple."

The second is the lamp of Truth. Its light burns and purges away all falsity and pretence in the use of materials, whether as to their quality or their quantity. Our architecture becomes mean through "petty dishonesties." The first step toward greatness is to discard these. "We may not be able to command good, or beautiful, or inventive architecture; but we *can* command honest architecture: the meagreness of poverty may be pardoned, the sternness of utility respected; but what is there but scorn for the meanness of deception?"

The third is the lamp of Power. It is opposed to puny precision and frivolous accuracy. Our streets are so poor and cramped that there is no hope for our cathedrals. "Until that street architecture of ours is bettered, until we give it some size and boldness, until we give our windows recess, and our walls thickness, I know not how we can blame our architects for their feebleness in more important work; their eyes are inured to narrowness and slightness: can we expect them at a word to conceive, and deal with, breadth and solidity?"

The fourth is the lamp of Beauty, and in the chapter devoted to its illustration he maintains that, in architecture, "all most lovely forms and thoughts" are directly taken from natural objects. The fifth is the lamp of Life; and the gist of the chapter allotted to it is, that "to those who love architecture, the life and accent of the hand are everything." If there is vitality, a thousand shortcomings are venial; if there is mechanism, the utmost completeness and precision are but the formalism of death. This, of course, applies most obviously to the sculptured ornaments of buildings; but there may be dulness and deadness in an entire architectural design. Always there ought to be vivid life. The sixth is the lamp of Memory. He would have all public edifices to be records of national life; all ordinary dwelling-houses to be homes endeared to their owners by sacred and sweet associations. He suggests that blank stones might be left in places about the house, to be inscribed, after the occupant's death, with a summary of his life and experience. He is sorrowfully aware, however, that this proposal could not well be carried out in "the crowded tenements" of our "struggling and restless population." The seventh is the lamp of Obedience. This is a subject which has always stirred his enthusiasm to its depths. Obedience is, for him, that principle to which "polity owes its stability, life its happiness, faith its acceptance, creation its continuance." He pleads with passionate intensity for the enforcement of an established type of architecture "from the cottage to the palace, and from the chapel to the basilica, and from the garden fence to the fortress wall," declaring, in the most positive terms, that architecture must languish "in the very dust," until "a universal system of form and workmanship be everywhere adopted and enforced." If this is impossible for other arts as well as architecture, "English art is impossible."

In 1851 Mr. Ruskin came before the public in a character assumed for the first and—as seems probable—for the last time —that, namely, of an author of fiction. Written for a little girl, The King of the Golden River, or the Black Brothers, is one of the best children's books I know. It reads capitally as a story, and yet it has very deep meanings. The boy-hero, oppressed and beaten by his morally and physically swarthy brothers, encounters a series of adventures of a fantastic and entertaining kind, with due intermixture of the fairy element. The brothers are much too economical farmers to let a black-bird exist on their land, and starve and kick their brother by way of curing him of the soft-heartedness that would allow a perishing wanderer to warm himself at the fire, or even—climax of atrocity—to eat a small slice of mutton. In the long run, the hard-hearted economy of the farmers does not make them rich, and the soft-hearted kindness of their brother does not make him poor; and my readers will probably surmise that the bullion commended in the tale is not that which comes to the mint, but that which glows in the fruit of autumn orchards, or rustles in the leaf-gold of the cornfield. The little volume is illustrated by Doyle with a genial piquancy, a bright and heart-felt felicity, which proves that he loved his work.

In 1851 he published the first volume, in 1853 the second and third volumes, of The Stones of Venice. The first had as sub-title, The Foundations; the second, The Sea Stories; the third, The Fall. These indicate sufficiently the contents of the volumes, which comprise an account not only of the architect-ure, but, to a considerable extent, of the history of Venice. In massive power, and in richness, vividness, and poetical expres-siveness of description—in comprehensiveness of treatment and unity of effect—this work is one of the prose masterpieces of the century. In symmetry of workmanship it surpasses the Modern Painters, though not equalling it in variety and brilliance.

In November, 1853, Ruskin delivered in Edinburgh four Lectures on Architecture and Painting, which were soon after published in London. In them he still appears as the cham-

pion of Gothic architecture, the uncompromising denouncer of
Greek. Gothic he represents as the architecture of common-
sense and universal convenience, and gives one advice to the
people of Edinburgh so simple, so comprehensive, so wise that,
if it could be but boldly acted upon, all nonsense and affectation would be knocked out of our theories and our habits of
building, and we should begin to have houses, churches, and
public edifices that we could honestly call our own. "Find out
what will make you comfortable, build that in the strongest
and boldest way, and then set your fancy free in the decoration
of it." In these lectures he extolled the pre-Raphaelites, proph-
esying that the young men would carry everything before them.
"On their works such a school will be founded as shall justify
the third age of the world's civilization, and render it as great
in creation as it has been in discovery."

A notable characteristic of all these writings of Ruskin—
stamped on them in strong relief until after the publication of
the three volumes of The Stones of Venice—is the earnestness
and Biblical simplicity of their religion. His father and mother, especially the latter, were fervently devout persons, of the
Evangelical school, which in Ruskin's early days had not lost
its intellectual prestige, or, to speak more strictly, had never
been thought, by itself or by others, to stand in need of intellectual prestige. With the ingenuous passion of an affectionate, trustful, dutiful boy, whose home had been for him a temple, he accepted loyally, as beyond all dispute, the creed he
learned at his mother's knee. The Bible was the very voice of
God, infallible and alone infallible; the Church of Rome was
the great and subtle apostasy; the honor, wealth, stability of
England depended on her faithfulness to the principles of Protestantism. In books which carried his name throughout the
world of culture, he quoted from Dr. Croly and from his own
father passages in which the emancipation of the Roman Catholics was spoken of as fraught with ruin to Great Britain.

With the religious principles—in all essentials—of the Puritans, Ruskin had also their courage, and was as frank as Milton. He shrank not from calling the laws of painting and of architecture God's laws, or from buttressing his arguments with texts. " We treat God," he says, in the introduction to The Seven Lamps of Architecture, " with irreverence by banishing him from our thoughts, not by referring to his will on slight occasions. His is not the finite authority or intelligence which cannot be troubled with small things. There is nothing so small but that we may honor God by asking his guidance of it, or insult him by taking it into our own hands; and what is true of the Deity is equally true of his Revelation. We use it reverently when most habitually; our insolence is in ever acting without reference to it, our true honoring of it is in its universal application. I have been blamed for the familiar introduction of its sacred words. I am grieved to have given pain by so doing; but my excuse must be my wish that those words were made the ground of every argument and the test of every action." He told his Edinburgh audience that he thought it unlikely that iron and glass would ever become important elements in architectural effect, because in that case the illustrations of the Bible would no longer be clear and intelligible. He traced, in a passage full of beauty and truth, the "delight in natural imagery" manifested in the books of Scripture, and alleged that, as Christianity had brought the love of nature into Paganism, so the return of Paganism, at the Renaissance, had destroyed this love of nature. The Evangelical, as distinguished from the High-Church and Broad-Church parties, may claim all Ruskin's writings, until he was nearly forty, as their own, and no other religious school can point to a literary monument of even approximate splendor. It must be added that, in works published after 1860, he has referred to the Evangelical school with deepening bitterness. He would say, I think, that the ultra-Protestants and Puritans of the day had learned to

keep their Bible for theological purposes; that, when he quoted
Scripture about architecture or painting, they smiled at his
simplicity; and that, when he made the New Testament a manual of political economy, they laughed at him outright; and
that therefore he turned from them in sorrowing contempt.

In 1856 appeared two additional volumes of Modern Painters. The third treats " Of Many Things," and it is manifest
at a glance that Ruskin has, to some extent, left the lines
which he had marked out for himself in the earlier volumes.
He frankly tells the reader that he will no longer be "so laboriously systematic." Cherries are cherries, whether gathered by
handfuls from the branch or tied upon sticks by the old wom-
en of Pomona with a view to their becoming impressive in the
eyes of customers. " I purpose henceforth to trouble myself
little with sticks or twine, but to arrange my chapters with a
view to convenient reference, rather than to any careful division of subjects, and to follow out, in any by-ways that may
open, on right hand or left, whatever question it seems useful
at any moment to settle." Accordingly the volume contains
eighteen essays, labelled chapters, on " many things " of great
importance connected with art, but which would have been of
pretty nearly the same value— an extremely high value — although the two preceding volumes of Modern Painters had not
gone before them, and although the two succeeding volumes
of Modern Painters had not come after them. Of the eighteen
essays, the five devoted to the discussion of the Ideal in art are
perhaps the most valuable. The false ideal is investigated under the opposite types of the religious and the profane, the
true under the successive phases of purism, naturalism, and the
grotesque. The treatment might have been more strictly logical if the naturalist ideal had been viewed not merely as a
phase of the true ideal, but as the only true ideal—the one imaginative and perfect art—purism and grotesquerie, even of the
best kinds, being considered as deviations from the right path.

The defect is, however, but formal, and the substantial doctrine of these five chapters is that the central and highest art is that which, " accepting the weaknesses, faults, and wrongnesses in all things that it sees, so places and harmonizes them that they form a noble whole, in which the imperfection of each several part is not only harmless, but absolutely essential, and yet in which whatever is good in each several part shall be completely displayed." This may, or may not, be a satisfactory definition of the mode in which imagination uses reality in producing the highest art; but it is essentially right in recognizing the element of imagination as indispensable to its production.

The third volume of Modern Painters, unlike its two predecessors, is pictorially illustrated; and very noble the illustrations are. In the preface a few important remarks occur on the relation between executive faculty and critical judgment. "It is probable," says Ruskin, "that the critical and executive faculties are in great part independent of each other;" but he adds " that a certain power of drawing is *indispensable* to the critic of art." In this I am quite sure that he errs. The man who can draw will, I admit, have a practically immeasurable advantage over the man who cannot draw, in discerning between good execution and bad, in seeing that one line is delicately and rightly, another line coarsely and wrongly, drawn; but if there is one law more than another capable of absolute demonstration in respect of all arts whatever, I believe it to be the law that, in feeling the power, or appreciating the value, of works of art, no acquaintance of their methods of production is necessary. Accurate perception, true and comprehensive sensibility — refinement, imagination, sympathy, intelligence— are indispensable to a right judgment in art; but acquaintance with the methods of art, skill or practice in the execution of art, are not wanted. This rule is universal. The critic's question *never* is how the work of art has been produced; it *always* is whether the work of art is in itself beautiful, great, impres-

sive. From culinary art upwards this holds good. The critic
of a pudding is not a cook, but an epicure. The critic of a
coat is not a tailor, but a man of taste and fashion. The critic
of art is not one who can delineate forms or lay on colors, but
one who has an eye and a heart for the permanent beauty, the
perennial sweetness and light, the ideal loveliness, that is less
gaudy and more glorious than the trimnesses of fashion or the
brilliant piquancies of mode. It is just as unreasonable to say
that I cannot intelligently admire the clouds in a drawing by
Turner of the dawn because I cannot draw clouds, as it would
be to say that I cannot admire the clouds of actual morning,
because I cannot tell how God touches their wings with gold
and their heads with crimson as they fly along the sea. Nor
do we say anything inconsistent with this fundamental canon
of art-criticism when we admit that a subtle, intense, and exquisite charm will be felt in masterly workmanship by those
who have themselves done enough in drawing or painting to
appreciate the supreme difficulty and rarity of consummate
artistic execution. There is a thrilling delight, practically, I
suppose, confined to those who have some skill, or who have
long tried to attain some skill, in drawing, experienced in looking at leaves and fruit by Leonardo da Vinci, at mills and faces
by Rembrandt, at ship-tackling and gray seas by Willian Vandevelde, at Paul Potter's neighing horse, at Turner's tree
branches, or at the lightning-like touches of Landseer's pencil,
when, evidently in a few minutes, he realizes the twinkling
movements and separate individualities of a score of deer trot-
ting away in perspective. In point of fact, it is because this
charm is so powerful as to be commonly irresistible, and thus
to divert the attention from the meaning and soul and ideal
beauty of art, that the critic requires to be on his guard against
it. It is hardly conceivable that Bentley could have failed so
egregiously as a critic of Paradise Lost if he had not been
mighty as a grammarian.

In the fourth volume of Modern Painters Ruskin pushes on his illustration of Turner in a succession of valuable chapters on Turnerian picturesque, Turnerian topography, Turnerian light, and Turnerian mystery. The main contents of the volume, however, consist of an investigation of mountain beauty in a number of chapters, in which the writer claims attention almost as much in character of geologist as of art-critic. It concludes with two chapters, one on the mountain gloom, the other on the mountain glory, in which the poetic richness and splendor and modulation of the language transcend, perhaps, any previous efforts of Ruskin, while their searching and terrible glances into the human toil and pain that are untouched amidst the magnificence of nature's pageantry give earnest of a more tragic power, and a more strong and strenuous and unflinching determination to look into the very fact of things, than he had yet revealed.

Four years—1856–1860—elapsed between the publication of the fourth and that of the fifth and last volume of Modern Painters. In the interval Ruskin issued his Elements of Drawing, one of the most delightful as well as practically serviceable of all his books. In some points, as he now sees, its teaching is not safe. It attaches less importance to outline than is assigned it in The Laws of Fesole, which embody his latest views on drawing. The illustrative sketch given of a boat—a nice and even subtle bit of pen-work—is, comically enough, a boat turned outside in, the framing ribs, on which the planks are nailed, being exposed to view. But as a sketcher's companion the book is beyond all rivalry. Not only is its instruction lucid and simple, but it is made vividly fascinating, by the author's catching enthusiasm for the beauty of that nature to which he sends the student. In the chapter on color and composition, there is a survey of the principles of composition—essentially, therefore, of the principles of art-criticism—so comprehensive in its brevity, so right in its simplicity, so sound

and sure in its teaching, that I know not where, within the
whole compass of his works, he has stowed away so much of
sterling treasure within so small a space.

The fifth volume of Modern Painters somewhat hurriedly
concludes the Book. "Feebly and faultily," says Ruskin,
after mentioning the drawbacks under which he had worked,
"yet as well as I can do it under these discouragements, the
book is at last done." During the seventeen years in which
he had been engaged upon it, he had experienced "oscillations
of temper and progressions of discovery," but he warns the
reader against inferring that the book is worse on that account.
"All true opinions are living, and show their life by being capable of nourishment; therefore of change. But their change
is that of a tree—not of a cloud." In the "main aim and
principle of the book" there had been no change. "It declares the perfectness and eternal beauty of the work of God;
and tests all work of man by concurrence with, or subjection
to that."

The fifth volume formally completes the framework of the
book as originally outlined. It contains four Parts: Of Leaf
Beauty; Of Cloud Beauty; Of Ideas of Relation, under the
head of formal invention; Of Ideas of Relation, under the
head of spiritual invention. These, however, are not treated
on the same scale as the divisions of the subject handled in
the earlier volumes, and the author is sensible that there has
been a certain amount of huddling up in the completion of
the author's scheme. The materials accumulated were not, he
found, reducible to a single volume, and he contemplated the
treatment in separate books of questions suggested by the section on vegetation, and of questions suggested by the section
on the sea.

These are grave omissions. Nevertheless, the volume is one
of abounding and intense interest, replete with genius. Here,
finally, Ruskin pronounces against the pre-Raphaelites. In the

fourth volume, he had schooled them sharply, talking, as he had made others afraid to talk, with almost contemptuous anger, of their sitting down " to sacrifice the most consummate skill" on studies of duck-pond weeds, of their leaving "all of lovely and wonderful" to be painted by vile incompetence, and of their forcing us to behold "nettles and mushrooms, which were prepared by nature eminently for nettle porridge and fish sauce, immortalized by art as reverently as if we were Egyptians, and they deities." In the fifth volume he expresses himself more calmly because he has lost hope. He has conclusively ascertained "that they were almost destitute of the power of feeling vastness, or enjoying the forms which expressed it. A mountain or great building only appeared to them as a piece of color of a certain shape. The powers it represented, or included, were invisible to them. In general they avoided subjects expressing space or mass, and fastened on confined, broken, and sharp forms; liking furze, fern, reeds, straw, stubble, dead leaves, and such like, better than strong stones, broad-flowing leaves, or rounded hills : in all such greater things, when forced to paint them, they missed the main and mighty lines; and this no less in what they loved than in what they disliked; for though fond of foliage, their trees always had a tendency to congeal into little acicular thorn-hedges, and never tossed free." Great composers, on the other hand, "not less deep in feeling, are in the fixed habit of regarding as much the relations and positions, as the separate nature, of things; reap and thresh in the sheaf, never pluck ears to rub in the hand ; fish with net, not line, and sweep their prey together within great cords of errorless curve." So that the inarticulate instinct of the world, which, while acknowledging the greatness and pathos of such exceptional works as Millais's Autumn Leaves and Holman Hunt's Light of the World, pronounced inexorably against the affectations, and conceits, and cliquish sectarianisms of the brethren, had

19

been in the right, after all; and the prophecy of the Edinburgh Lectures had failed !*

Less gracefully opulent and easy—less boy-like in freshness and careless magic of fascination, and lavish sowing of the page with orient pearl—than the first volume, the fifth displays no failure in real power of eloquence, rather is it more concentrated and commanding. Yet its power touches me less than its tenderness. That poetry which welled up in Ruskin's youth now makes music of finest sympathy—delicate and deep as Wordsworth's best—as we wander with him through glades of pine. He gives life to the trees and buds and leaves. The young pines, delicate in their beauty, human in their fellowship, "follow each other along the soft hill-ridges, up and down." In exalting his dearest pines, he cannot help doing some injustice to other trees. "Lowland trees may lean to this side and that, though it is but a meadow breeze that bends them, or a bank of cowslips from which their trunks lean aslope. But let storm and avalanche do their worst, and let the pine find only a ledge of vertical precipice to cling to, it will nevertheless grow straight. Thrust a rod from its last shoot down the stem; it shall point to the centre of the earth as long as the tree lives." This of course is not the case. All trees grow straight, and every stem points to the centre of the world. There is in this respect no peculiarity in pines.

This volume, as well as the third and fourth, is enriched with pictorial illustrations of great interest and value, a large proportion of them from Ruskin's own hand. These vary in excellence. The best, I think — though many of the cloud drawings are superb—is in the fourth volume, numbered 46, The Buttresses of an Alp. The long ridge of mountain, rising as it retreats, along which we feel that we could walk mile after mile, with its steeps of precipice, wrinklings of rain

* See p. 426.

course, and bossy work of woodland, is altogether masterly. The mountain recalls Turner, the foreground Dürer, but the work is Ruskin's own, and he is worthy to stand between those two sons of the mighty. Having said which I think Ruskin's best drawing, I shall say also which I think his worst. It is surely that in the fifth volume, numbered 84, and named Peace. This is the weakest bit of draughtsmanship I have ever seen from Ruskin's hand. It has some fine quality, or it could not be his; but the ineffectuality of literalism is written on its counted stones, and wriggling bits of iron, and lifeless trees.

Modern Painters has, questionless, its shortcomings and defects; but less cannot be said of it than that it is one of the monumental books of the century, one of the imperishable masterpieces of English literature. Its teaching on art is in the main, in so far as I can satisfy myself on that point by long years of study and consideration, right. But more important, or at least more influential than its express teaching on art, is that passion of enthusiasm for nature's beauty with which it vibrates from its first page to its last. Goethe and others may have spoken with as much accuracy of the laws and principles of painting; but Ruskin took up the art of his country and laid it on the bosom of its mother, nature, to rise inspired with new ardor, braced with new strength, and to begin anew to scale the heights of the ideal.

CHAPTER VII.

IN the fifth volume of Modern Painters, Mr. Ruskin declared that the distinctive character of his books on art is "their bringing everything to a root in human passion or human hope." This speciality of his writings—their supreme interest in humanity—he alleged to have been, "of all their characters, the one most denied." Not a few, I dare say, were surprised to hear that Mr. Ruskin's interest in humanity exceeded his interest either in the taste of the public, the reputation of Turner, or the abstract principles and particular facts of beauty; but I cannot charge myself with having failed to recognize that intense and rugged sympathy with his kind which led him to dwell with a glow of affectionate wonder on "the fisherman's boat and the grimy practicality of the collier brig," and the brave hearts tossing in them at the mercy of wind and wave, and which made him rejoice in the Gothic workman, as he struck from the stone rude semblances of flower and flame, incomparably more than in the Greek slave, though he moulded a capital that would give the law of beauty for thousands of years. The subtlest essence of Mr. Ruskin's originality is connected with the two passions which, to his own consciousness, may have seemed to work in harmony, but which, to the world of hasty readers, appeared often to contend with each other for the mastery—namely, love of man and love of landscape beauty. In a description of what he saw and felt in looking upon a pine forest in the Jura, he presents to us these two passions in their harmonious action. Believing the key to a great deal that has caused perplexity and offence in his writings on political economy to lie in this twofold characteristic, I shall quote the passage.

NATURE AND MAN.

Among the hours of his life to which the writer looks back with peculiar gratitude, as having been marked by more than ordinary fulness of joy or clearness of teaching, is one passed, now some years ago, near time of sunset, among the broken masses of pine forest which skirt the course of the Ain, above the village of Champagnole, in the Jura. It is a spot which has all the solemnity, with none of the savageness, of the Alps; where there is a sense of a great power beginning to be manifested in the earth, and of a deep and majestic concord in the rise of the long, low lines of piny hills; the first utterance of those mighty mountain symphonies, soon to be more loudly lifted and wildly broken along the battlements of the Alps. But their strength is as yet restrained, and the far-reaching ridges of pastoral mountain succeed each other, like the long and sighing swell which moves over quiet waters from some far-off stormy sea. And there is a deep tenderness pervading that vast monotony. The destructive forces and the stern expression of the central ranges are alike withdrawn. No frost-ploughed, dust-encumbered paths of ancient glacier fret the soft Jura pastures; no splintered heaps of ruin break the fair ranks of her forests; no pale, defiled, or furious rivers rend their rude and changeful ways among her rocks. Patiently, eddy by eddy, the clear green streams wind along their well-known beds; and under the dark quietness of the undisturbed pines there spring up, year by year, such company of joyful flowers as I know not the like of among all the blessings of the earth. It was spring-time, too; and all were coming forth in clusters crowded for very love; there was room enough for all, but they crushed their leaves into all manner of strange shapes only to be nearer each other. There was the wood-anemone, star after star, closing every now and then into nebulæ; and there was the oxalis, troop by troop, like virginal processions of the Mois de Marie, the dark vertical clefts in the limestone choked up with them as with heavy snow, and touched with ivy on the edges—ivy as light and lovely as the vine; and, ever and anon, a blue gush of violets, and cowslip bells in sunny places; and, in the more open ground, the vetch, and comfrey, and mezereon, and the small sapphire buds of the polygala Alpina, and the wild strawberry, just a blossom or two, all showered amidst the golden softness of deep, warm, amber-colored moss. I came out presently on the edge of the ravine: the solemn murmur of its waters rose suddenly from beneath, mixed with the singing of the thrushes among the pine boughs; and, on the opposite side of the valley, walled all along as it was by gray cliffs of limestone, there was a hawk sailing slowly off their brow, touching them nearly with his wings, and with the shadows of the pines flickering upon his plumage from above; but with a fall of a hundred fathoms under his breast, and the curling pools of the green river gliding and glittering dizzily beneath him, their foam-globes moving with him as he flew.   It would be difficult to conceive a scene less dependent upon any other interest than that of its own secluded and serious beauty; but the writer well remembers the sudden blankness and chill which were cast upon it when he endeavored, in order more strictly to arrive at the sources of its impressiveness, to imagine it, for a moment, a scene in some aboriginal forest of the New Continent. The flowers in an instant lost their light, the river its music; the hills became oppressively desolate; a heaviness in the boughs of the darkened forest showed how much of their former power had been dependent upon a life which was not theirs, how much of the glory of the imperishable, or continually renewed, creation is reflected from things more precious in their memories than it, in its renewing.   Those ever-springing flowers and ever-flowing streams had been dyed by the deep colors of human endurance, valor, and virtue; and the crests of the sable hills that rose against the evening sky received a deeper worship, because their far shadows fell eastward over the iron wall of Joux and the four-square keep of Granson.

Here we have, first, impassioned love of beauty; and, secondly, love, also profound and impassioned, for mankind.   If the spirit of beauty received only the second homage of his heart, which we just now found him expressly asserting, his was an intense and energetic vassalage for all that; and whenever the spirit of modern improvement, real or so-called, the spirit of modern invention, of industry, of material progress, blasted with the furnace-breath of its engines the fields, the hills, the woods, the secluded ruins, which were in his eyes sacred to the spirit of beauty, he cried out against it with the bitterness of a Hebrew prophet seeing the abomination of desolation carried into the holy place.   Hence, to those who have not deeply and sympathetically, nay, to some extent indulgently, studied Mr. Ruskin's books, he may sometimes appear cynically indifferent to human happiness, or, at least, incapable of sympathizing with it on a large scale when it is accompanied with any drawbacks offensive to a cultivated æsthetic faculty. The *mere* fact that many were made glad, irrespective of the quality of their enjoyment, even when it was innocent and healthful, has not been enough for him. He has had no reverence for those acclamations of gratified myriads which believers in the religion of humanity, from its highest form, as taught by the Divine Man, to its mutilated but, in some respects, genuine form as taught by Comte, must regard as having in them accents of the voice of God. The Great Exhibition of 1851 did not come up to his æsthetic ideal, and the fact that it gave pleasure to hundreds of thousands did not procure for it favor in his eyes. He has always, and bitterly, sneered at the Crystal Palace, regardless of what I may be allowed to call the appealing smile of not very elevated but certainly genuine satisfaction on the faces of millions of men, women, boys, girls, and little children, whom it has made, for a few hours at least, extremely happy. He has inveighed with blistering scorn against the long lines of suburban London streets and "villas," inhabited by the lower middle classes of the metropolis, without its ever seeming to occur to him that in those not very bright or variegated abodes, with their little bits of gardens, thousands of honest fellows, Bob Cratchits and Tom Pinches, busy all day in city offices, snatch a little fresh air in the mornings and evenings, toss their babies, kiss their wives, and lead a perhaps not very refined, but honest, healthy, manly, enjoyable existence.

In all this I must frankly confess my disagreement with Mr. Ruskin. I own to recognizing a kind of sacredness in human joy, even when it can give no account of itself that will pass muster with men of taste and culture. But what I want to call attention to is the fact that, for more than forty years, Mr. Ruskin has beheld what was, in his eyes, the choicest and most precious beauty destroyed by that outburst and advance of ma-

terial prosperity with which are inseparably associated in his
mind our Great Exhibitions, our Crystal Palaces, our increase
of population, our enormous production of urban architecture.
Nearly thirty years have passed since, in the second volume of
Modern Painters, he complained that the iron roads were "tearing up the surface of Europe, as grape-shot do the sea," their
great net "contracting all its various life, its rocky arms and
rural heart, into a narrow, finite, calculating metropolis of manufactures," and that there was "not a monument throughout
the cities of Europe," speaking "of old years and mighty people," but was "being swept away to build *cafés* and gaming-
houses." In a note he gave a long list of instances of destruction : inestimable relics of mediæval architecture removed to
make room for warehouses, ancient churches used as smithies,
frescoes knocked to pieces by bricklayers, pictures by Giotto
with beams of roofs thrust into them, canvases of Tintoret with
the rain pouring through them. The sensation with which
this kind of thing affected Ruskin can be described only by the
word anguish, and it has been an anguish protracted through
more than forty years. He could not recognize as happiness—
or if as happiness, then only as the degrading happiness of the
brutish person or the fool—that material prosperity and stolid
satisfaction which he connected with the destructive agencies.

Nor was it only the works of man that were inundated and
wrecked by the advancing wave of industrial energy ; the loveliest nooks of God's earth were also desecrated. "Twenty
years ago," he cries out, in the preface to The Crown of Wild
Olive, published in 1866, "there was no lovelier piece of lowland scenery in South England, nor any more pathetic in the
world, by its expression of sweet human character and life,
than that immediately bordering on the sources of the Wan-
dle, and including the lower moors of Addington, and the villages of Beddington and Carshalton, with all their pools and
streams. . . . With deliberate mind I say that I have never

seen anything so ghastly in its inner tragic meaning—not in Pisan Maremma—not by Campagna tomb—not by the sand-isles of the Torcellan shore—as the slow stealing of aspects of reckless, indolent, animal neglect, over the delicate sweetness of that English scene: nor is any blasphemy or impiety—any frantic saying or godless thought—more appalling to me, using the best power of judgment I have to discern its sense and scope, than the insolent defiling of those springs by the human herds that drink of them." Three years later we have The Queen of the Air, and in the preface he renews his complaint. "This first of May, 1869, I am writing where my work was begun thirty-five years ago, within sight of the snows of the higher Alps. In that half of the permitted life of man, I have seen strange evil brought upon every scene that I best loved, or tried to make beloved by others." The light of the "pale summits" had become "umbered and faint;" the air which once "inlaid the clefts of all their golden crags with azure" was "defiled with languid coils of smoke, belched from worse than volcanic fires." The once crystalline waters were "dimmed and foul." "These," he says, "are no careless words—they are accurately, horribly true. . . . The light, the air, the waters, all defiled!"

It is not necessary that we should agree with Mr. Ruskin as to the extent to which railway lines have defaced the scenery of Europe and factory smoke blurred and blasted it, but it cannot be reasonably denied that his representations have a broad basis in fact; and if this be so, it is natural that he should feel it deeply. He is so organized that an offence to beauty affects him as with a pang of literal pain, and it is equally certain that he never thinks of this pain as selfish, but attaches to it a moral quality, as if it were the sting of an æsthetic conscience—as if the duty were imposed upon him of protesting against the destruction of beauty as a sacrilege and a sin. His own countrymen, the foremost manufacturers and traders of the world, he

18*

regards as ringleaders in the work of profanation, and with
seer-like fury hurls his anathemas upon them. "You have put
a railroad bridge over the fall of Schaffhausen. You have tun-
nelled the cliffs of Lucerne by Tell's chapel; you have destroyed the Clarens shore of the Lake of Geneva; there is not
a quiet valley in England that you have not filled with bellowing fire; there is no particle left of English land which you
have not trampled coal ashes into, nor any foreign city in which
the spread of your presence is not marked among its fair old
streets and happy gardens by a consuming white leprosy of
new hotels and perfumers' shops." His denunciations reached
a climax when he proposed that the Manchester Corporation
should be drowned in the Lake of Thirlmere, which they intended to violate. That capital and competition, manufactures
and machinery, are at the root of all this mischief, he is profoundly convinced; and machine-labor of all but the simplest
kinds, machine-labor, especially, which is dependent upon fire,
he regards with peculiar detestation as incapacitating the eye
for the perception, the hand for the production, of beauty universally, whether in nature or in art.

The malady of the age being thus deep and malignant, the
remedy which Mr. Ruskin would apply is correspondingly thorough. The nature of the remedy he has explained in a large
number of treatises, which, with hardly an exception, I have
studied, but I would not have my readers understand me to
speak of it with absolute confidence, or to affirm that Mr. Ruskin would unreservedly endorse my account of it.

To me, after long pondering, the most comprehensively just
and accurate way to describe his scheme of reform is as a
system of communism, purporting to be in harmony with, if
not expressly based upon, Christianity, dissociated from all violent and revolutionary methods of propagation, and practically worked out in obedience to the laws of order, beauty, and
righteousness. I have no evidence that Mr. Ruskin would ac-

cept the word "communism," and many passages might be gleaned from his works in which he points out that forcible interference with the existing distribution of property would be sheer folly, worse than useless to the body of the people. When I say that he teaches communism, I mean that he proposes what he deems to be an explicit, honest, thoroughgoing adoption of Christ's rule of doing to your neighbor as you would your neighbor should do to you—of counting yourself one, and but one, among the millions of mankind, having the rights and privileges of one, not of more than one.   One man, for example, wants but one coat; he has no right to two until every other man has one also, or, at the least, until he has exhausted the means within his power for providing every other man with one.   This Mr. Ruskin proposes, to begin with.   This he maintains to be mere justice.   Generosity, munificence, kindness in any special sense of the term, lie, for him, beyond this; but this at lowest, as the foundation and regulating principle of social morality, he resolutely enforces and demands.   Thus introduced, the following passage will be understood by my readers, and is quoted by me here as essential to a true appreciation of Ruskin in the capacity of philanthropist:

Christian Justice.

You must build upon justice, for this main reason, that you have not, at first, charity to build with.   It is the last reward of good work.   Do justice to your brother (you can do that whether you love him or not), and you will come to love him.   But do injustice to him, because you don't love him, and you will come to hate him.   It is all very fine to think you can build upon charity to begin with; but you will find all you have got to begin with begins at home, and is essentially love of yourself.   You wellto-do people, for instance, who are here to-night will go to "Divine Service" next Sunday, all nice and tidy, and your little children will have their tight little Sunday boots on, and lovely little Sunday feathers in their hats; and you'll think, complacently and piously, how lovely they look! So they do; and you love them heartily, and you like sticking feathers in their hats.   That's all right, that *is* charity; but it is charity beginning at

home. Then you will come to the poor little crossing-sweeper, got up also
—it, in its Sunday dress—the dirtiest rags it has—that it may beg the better; we shall give it a penny, and think how good we are. That's charity
going abroad. But what does Justice say, walking and watching near us?
Christian justice has been strangely mute, and seemingly blind, and, if not
blind, decrepit, this many a day: she keeps her accounts still, however,
quite steadily—doing them at nights, carefully, with her bandage off, and
through acutest spectacles (the only modern scientific invention she cares
about). You must put your ear down ever so close to her lips to hear her
speak; and then you will start at what she first whispers, for it will certainly be, " Why shouldn't that little crossing-sweeper have a feather on
its head as well as your own child?" Then you may ask Justice, in an
amazed manner, "How she can possibly be so foolish as to think children
could sweep crossings with feathers on their heads?" Then you stoop
again, and Justice says—still in her dull, stupid way—"Then, why don't
you, every other Sunday, leave your child to sweep the crossing, and take
the little sweeper to church in a hat and feather?" Mercy on us (you
think), what will she say next? And you answer, of course, that "you
don't, because everybody ought to remain content in the position in which
Providence has placed them." Ah, my friends, that's the gist of the whole
question. *Did* Providence put them in that position, or did *you?* You
knock a man into a ditch, and then you tell him to remain content in the
"position in which Providence has placed him." That's modern Christianity. You say, "*We* did not knock him into the ditch." How do you
know what you have done, or are doing? That's just what we have all
got to know, and what we shall never know, until the question with us,
every morning, is, not how to do the gainful thing, but how to do the just
thing; nor, until we are at least so far on the way to being Christian as
to have understood that maxim of the poor half-way Mohammedan, " One
hour in the execution of justice is worth seventy years of prayer."

Little starving, tatterdemalion crossing-sweeper counts one;
little rosy-faced, well-fed, well-clad English child counts one; in
God's family, in Christ's brotherhood and sisterhood, each, says
Mr. Ruskin, is accurately a unit, and if you adopt the law of
Christian justice, the claim of the one upon you will be the
same as the claim of the other. I am not, be it observed, crit-
icising Mr. Ruskin's opinion, either from the theological or the
politico-economical point of view; I am only trying to enable

my readers to form a precise idea as to what that opinion is, and as to what I mean by saying that Mr. Ruskin's political economy seems to me fundamentally communistic. Let no one infer from this that it has even a remote affinity to the lawless and rebellious projects which are probably associated in the minds of most people with the idea of communism. "If you in the least remember," he said to one of his audiences, "the tone of any of my writings, you must know that they are thought unfit for this age, because they are always insisting on need of government, and speaking with scorn of liberty." He knows that, in a communistic state of society, the absolute condition of even possible success would be subordination to a common authority, submission to a common discipline, loyal and enthusiastic obedience to minute and multitudinous regulations. His system is explicitly communistic. He declines to take into consideration any prospect of social advantage or amelioration that can be shared in by some and not by all. He told the strenuous manufacturers of Lancashire that their "Goddess of Getting on " was no goddess for him, because she was the goddess " not of everybody's getting on, but only of somebody's getting on." The distinction, he said, was " vital, or, rather, death-ful ;" and he set before them a picture of their ideal of life, in order that no mistake might be possible as to what it was that he did *not* approve.

An Englishman's Paradise.

Your ideal of human life is, I think, that it should be passed in a pleasant, undulating world, with iron and coal everywhere underneath it. On each pleasant bank of this world is to be a beautiful mansion, with two wings, and stables and coach-houses; a moderately-sized park; a large garden and hot-houses; and pleasant carriage drives through the shrubberies. In the mansion are to live the favored votaries of the Goddess; the English gentleman, with his gracious wife and his beautiful family; always able to have the boudoir and the jewels for the wife, and the beautiful ball-dresses for the daughters, and hunters for the sons, and a shooting in the Highlands for himself. At the bottom of the bank is to be the mill; not less than a quarter of a mile long, with a steam-engine at each end, and two in the middle, and a chimney three hundred feet high. In this mill are to be in constant employment from eight hundred to a thousand workers, who never drink, never strike, always go to church on Sunday, and always express themselves in respectful language. Is not that, broadly, and in the main features, the kind of thing you propose to yourselves? It is very pretty indeed, seen from above; not at all so pretty, seen from below. For observe, while to one family this deity is, indeed, the Goddess of Getting on, to a thousand families she is the Goddess of *not* Getting on. "Nay," you say, "they have all their chance." Yes; so has every one in a lottery, but there must always be the same number of blanks. "Ah! but in a lottery it is not skill and intelligence which take the lead, but blind chance." What then! do you think the old practice, that "they should take who have the power, and they should keep who can," is less iniquitous, when the power has become power of brains instead of fist? and that, though we may not take advantage of a child's or a woman's weakness, we may of a man's foolishness?

In modern society the distribution of wealth is regulated more by "power of brains" than by anything else, and Mr. Ruskin here pointedly declares that the man who accumulates riches through power of brains is as much a robber as if he took their goods from his neighbors by force. To make assurance doubly sure, he adds, after granting that work must be done, and putting in that caution about "need of government" and "scorn of liberty" which I quoted above, "that there is a wide difference between being captains or governors of work, and taking the profits of it." The manufacturer is to be the captain in an industrial army, and is to make no gain by his captaincy. Mr. Ruskin spoke and published these views more than ten years ago, and therefore he was entirely consistent when, on a recent occasion, having been taken by some rich manufacturer to see the efficiently regulated system of the manufacturer's works, including of course exactitude in payment for labor, he said that it was all very well in its way, but that it could obtain nothing but inexorable condemnation from him as a political economist, inasmuch as it tended to procure estates, luxurious leisure, all that adorns civilized existence, for the masters, and for the masters only. Co-operative enterprises he regards with interest, not because he thinks that they are based upon right social principles, but because he expects them to habituate workmen to the conception that regulation, discipline, loyalty to a common aim and interest, are indispensable in that battle of man with rude nature, that battle of industry in all its departments, by which the earth is compelled to yield up her abundance.

Without question the principle of competition is irreconcilably at variance with Mr. Ruskin's principle of justice. At first glance there may seem to be no profound difference between the principle of "the greatest happiness for the greatest number," which is the principle of competition, and the principle of "the natural, attainable, and just amount of happiness for all," which is the principle of communism; but in point of fact the two are wide as the poles asunder. I am not aware that Mr. Ruskin has ever enunciated those two principles, but it is only in carrying out the latter that his system can be logically and consistently interpreted; and he is logical in believing that modern political economy is dead against him. This, however, does not justify the expressions of unbounded denunciation with which he inveighs against political economists, for they mean well, and if the constitution of society is to remain as at present, they do good. They teach that *if* you are to have competition, a friendly and fair competition is preferable to a narrow, base, and provincial competition. They take it for granted, indeed, that every nation, every man, will seek to profit to the utmost by its or his own strength of brain and hand, but they point out that jealousy and spite, pursuing a policy of "beggar my neighbor," issues practically in a policy of "beggar myself." The Australian Colonies, for example, lying side by side, have—or had recently—their several railway systems arranged, in respect of gauges and otherwise, in such a way as might inflict a maximum of inconvenience upon each other. The political economist, the Adam Smith, or J. S. Mill, undertakes to show, and succeeds in showing, that each of the Colonies would have profited if the system had been calculated to promote the convenience of all. Whether Mr. Ruskin's principle of community, a word which, perhaps, he would prefer to communism, as contrasted with competition, is sound or unsound, this, so far as it goes, is a moral and humane proposition. On no point have I differed so seriously from Mr. Ruskin as in connection with his references to particular economists, his accusation of Mill as a prevaricator, and of Smith as a blasphemer. But his doing so can be accounted for when we reflect that he looks upon them simply as apostles of competition, that he regards competition as the subversion of justice and of Christianity, and, further, that he traces to them and their teaching that destruction of works and scenes of beauty which has been to him an agony for more than forty years. In St. George's Guild Mr. Ruskin proposes to exhibit labor under perfect captaincy, working not for the profit of some, but the good of all. Life under St. George is to be not only economically, but æsthetically a model, and Mr. Ruskin has already designed for his companions an exquisitely beautiful coinage. I look upon the experiment with profound respect and interest, but I cannot add that I am sanguine of its success. Be that as it may, its conception is noble; and Mr. Ruskin has proved, by gifts of superb munificence to Oxford and Cambridge, by devoting the tenth part of all he possessed to purposes of justice and charity, and by delicate and princely generosity to relatives and friends, that it is not only in theories and projects that he can be benevolent. All the charges brought against him by his disparagers, or nearly all, may be reduced to this— that he has made too vehement and constant use of the rhetorical practice of contrast. He could not exalt Turner without spurning contemporary artists, he could not praise the pre-

Raphaelites without using their names as poisoned needles wherewith to transfix and agonize the Academicians; in the white-heat of his enthusiasm for Luini even Turner seems artistically a castaway, and he cannot speak lovingly of mountain pines without bearing false witness—very innocent false wit-'ness—of "lowland trees."

THE END.

VALUABLE AND INTERESTING WORKS

FOR

PUBLIC AND PRIVATE LIBRARIES

PUBLISHED BY HARPER & BROTHERS, NEW YORK.

☞ *For a full List of Books suitable for Libraries, see* HARPER & BROTHERS' TRADE-LIST *and* CATALOGUE, *which may be had gratuitously on application to the Publishers personally, or by letter enclosing Nine Cents in Postage stamps.*

☞ HARPER & BROTHERS *will send their publications by mail, postage prepaid, to any part of the United States, on receipt of the price.*

MACAULAY'S HISTORY OF ENGLAND. The History of England from the Accession of James II. By THOMAS BABINGTON MACAULAY. New and Elegant Edition, from new Electrotype Plates. 5 vols., 8vo, Vellum Cloth with Paper Labels, Uncut Edges and Gilt Tops, $10 00. *Sold only in Sets.* Cheap Edition, 5 vols., 12mo, Cloth, $4 00.

MACAULAY'S LIFE AND LETTERS. The Life and Letters of Lord Macaulay. By his Nephew, G. OTTO TREVELYAN, M.P. With Portrait on Steel. Complete in 2 vols., 8vo, Cloth, Uncut Edges and Gilt Tops, $5 00. Popular Edition, two vols. in one, 12mo, Cloth, $1 75.

HUME'S HISTORY OF ENGLAND. History of England, from the Invasion of Julius Cæsar to the Abdication of James II., 1688. By DAVID HUME. New and Elegant Library Edition, from New Electrotype Plates. 6 vols., 8vo, Vellum Cloth with Paper Labels, Uncut Edges and Gilt Tops, $12 00. *Sold only in Sets.* Cheap Edition, 6 vols., 12mo, Cloth, $4 80.

GIBBON'S ROME. The History of the Decline and Fall of the Roman Empire. By EDWARD GIBBON. With Notes by Rev. H. H. MILMAN and M. GUIZOT. With Index. 6 vols., 12mo, Cloth, $4 80; Sheep, $7 20; Half Calf, $15 30. *New Edition, from new Electrotype Plates, in Press.*

HILDRETH'S UNITED STATES. History of the United States, FIRST SERIES: From the Discovery of the Continent to the Organization of the Government under the Federal Constitution. SECOND SERIES: From the Adoption of the Federal Constitution to the End of the Sixteenth Congress. By RICHARD HILDRETH. 6 vols., 8vo, Cloth, $18 00; Sheep, $21 00; Half Calf, $31 50. *New Edition, from new Electrotype Plates, in Press.*

FIRST CENTURY OF THE REPUBLIC. A Review of American Progress. 8vo, Cloth, $5 00; Sheep, $5 50; Half Morocco, $7 25.

MOTLEY'S DUTCH REPUBLIC. The Rise of the Dutch Republic. A History. By JOHN LOTHROP MOTLEY, LL.D., D.C.L. With a Portrait of William of Orange. 3 vols., 8vo, Cloth, $10 50. A New Cheap Edition. 3 vols., 8vo, Vellum Cloth with Paper Labels, Uncut Edges and Gilt Tops, $6 00. *Sold only in Sets.*

MOTLEY'S UNITED NETHERLANDS. History of the United Netherlands: from the Death of William the Silent to the Twelve-Years' Truce—1609. With a full View of the English-Dutch Struggle against Spain, and of the Origin and Destruction of the Spanish Armada. By JOHN LOTHROP MOTLEY, LL.D., D.C.L. Portraits. 4 vols., 8vo, Cloth, $14 00. A New Cheap Edition. 4 vols., 8vo, Vellum Cloth with Paper Labels, Uncut Edges and Gilt Tops, $8 00. *Sold only in Sets.*

MOTLEY'S LIFE AND DEATH OF JOHN OF BARNEVELD. The Life and Death of John of Barneveld, Advocate of Holland : with a View of the Primary Causes and Movements of "The Thirty-Years' War." By JOHN LOTHROP MOTLEY, LL.D., D.C.L. Illustrated. 2 vols., 8vo, Cloth, $7 00. A New Cheap Edition. 2 vols., 8vo, Vellum Cloth with Paper Labels, Uncut Edges and Gilt Tops, $4 00. *Sold only in Sets.*

PERRY'S HISTORY OF THE CHURCH OF ENGLAND. A History of the English Church, from the Accession of Henry VIII. to the Silencing of Convocation in the Eighteenth Century. By G. G. PERRY, M.A., Canon of Lincoln and Rector of Waddington. With an Appendix containing a Sketch of the History of the Protestant Episcopal Church in the United States of America, by J. A. SPENCER, S.T.D. Crown 8vo, Cloth, $2 50.

HUDSON'S HISTORY OF JOURNALISM. Journalism in the United States, from 1690 to 1872. By FREDERIC HUDSON. 8vo, Cloth, $5 00; Half Calf, $7 25.

JEFFERSON'S DOMESTIC LIFE. The Domestic Life of Thomas Jefferson : Compiled from Family Letters and Reminiscences, by his Great-granddaughter, SARAH N. RANDOLPH. Illustrated. Crown 8vo, Cloth, $2 50.

JOHNSON'S COMPLETE WORKS. The Works of Samuel Johnson, LL.D. With an Essay on his Life and Genius, by ARTHUR MURPHY, Esq. 2 vols., 8vo, Cloth, $4 00; Sheep, $5 00; Half Calf, $8 50.

KINGLAKE'S CRIMEAN WAR. The Invasion of the Crimea: Its Origin, and an Account of its Progress down to the Death of Lord Raglan. By ALEXANDER WILLIAM KINGLAKE. With Maps and Plans. Three Volumes now ready. 12mo, Cloth, $2 00 per vol.; Half Calf, $3 75 per vol.

LAMB'S COMPLETE WORKS. The Works of Charles Lamb. Comprising his Letters, Poems, Essays of Elia, Essays upon Shakespeare, Hogarth, &c., and a Sketch of his Life, with the Final Memorials, by T. NOON TALFOURD. With Portrait. 2 vols., 12mo, Cloth, $3 00; Half Calf, $6 50.

LAWRENCE'S HISTORICAL STUDIES. Historical Studies. By EUGENE LAWRENCE. Containing the following Essays: The Bishops of Rome.—Leo and Luther.—Loyola and the Jesuits.—Ecumenical Councils.—The Vaudois.—The Huguenots.—The Church of Jerusalem. —Dominic and the Inquisition.—The Conquest of Ireland.—The Greek Church. 8vo, Cloth, Uncut Edges and Gilt Tops, $3 00.

MYERS'S REMAINS OF LOST EMPIRES. Remains of Lost Empires: Sketches of the Ruins of Palmyra, Nineveh, Babylon, and Persepolis, with some Notes on India and the Cashmerian Himalayas. By P. V. N. MYERS. Illustrated. 8vo, Cloth, $3 50.

LOSSING'S FIELD-BOOK OF THE REVOLUTION. Pictorial Field-Book of the Revolution: or, Illustrations by Pen and Pencil of the History, Biography, Scenery, Relics, and Traditions of the War for Independence. By BENSON J. LOSSING. 2 vols., 8vo, Cloth, $14 00; Sheep or Roan, $15 00; Half Calf, $18 00.

LOSSING'S FIELD-BOOK OF THE WAR OF 1812. Pictorial Field-Book of the War of 1812: or, Illustrations by Pen and Pencil of the History, Biography, Scenery, Relics, and Traditions of the last War for American Independence. By BENSON J. LOSSING. With several hundred Engravings on Wood by Lossing and Barritt, chiefly from Original Sketches by the Author. 1088 pages, 8vo, Cloth, $7 00; Sheep or Roan, $8 50; Half Calf, $10 00.

FORSTER'S LIFE OF DEAN SWIFT. The Early Life of Jonathan Swift (1667–1711). By JOHN FORSTER. With Portrait. 8vo, Cloth, $2 50.

GREEN'S ENGLISH PEOPLE. History of the English People. By JOHN RICHARD GREEN, M.A. Vols. I., II., and III. ready. 8vo, Cloth, $2 50 per volume.

HALLAM'S MIDDLE AGES. View of the State of Europe during the Middle Ages. By HENRY HALLAM. 8vo, Cloth, $2 00; Sheep, $2 50; Half Calf, $4 25.

HALLAM'S CONSTITUTIONAL HISTORY OF ENGLAND. The Constitutional History of England, from the Accession of Henry VII. to the Death of George II. By HENRY HALLAM. 8vo, Cloth, $2 00; Sheep, $2 50; Half Calf, $4 25.

HALLAM'S LITERATURE. Introduction to the Literature of Europe during the Fifteenth, Sixteenth, and Seventeenth Centuries. By HENRY HALLAM. 2 vols., 8vo, Cloth, $4 00; Sheep, $5 00; Half Calf, $8 50.

SCHWEINFURTH'S HEART OF AFRICA. The Heart of Africa. Three Years' Travels and Adventures in the Unexplored Regions of the Centre of Africa—from 1868 to 1871. By Dr. GEORG SCHWEIN-FURTH. Translated by ELLEN E. FREWER. With an Introduction by WINWOOD READE. Illustrated by about 130 Wood-cuts from Drawings made by the Author, and with two Maps. 2 vols., 8vo, Cloth, $8 00.

M'CLINTOCK & STRONG'S CYCLOPÆDIA. Cyclopædia of Biblical, Theological, and Ecclesiastical Literature. Prepared by the Rev. JOHN M'CLINTOCK, D.D., and JAMES STRONG, S.T.D. *7 vols. now ready.* Royal 8vo. Price per vol., Cloth, $5 00; Sheep, $6 00; Half Morocco, $8 00.

MOHAMMED AND MOHAMMEDANISM : Lectures Delivered at the Royal Institution of Great Britain in February and March, 1874. By R. BOSWORTH SMITH, M.A., Assistant Master in Harrow School; late Fellow of Trinity College, Oxford. With an Appendix containing Emanuel Deutsch's Article on "Islam." 12mo, Cloth, $1 50.

MOSHEIM'S ECCLESIASTICAL HISTORY, Ancient and Modern; in which the Rise, Progress, and Variation of Church Power are considered in their Connection with the State of Learning and Philosophy, and the Political History of Europe during that Period. Translated, with Notes, &c., by A. MACLAINE, D.D. Continued to 1826, by C. COOTE, LL.D. 2 vols., 8vo, Cloth, $4 00; Sheep, $5 00.

HARPER'S NEW CLASSICAL LIBRARY. Literal Translations.

The following Volumes are now ready. 12mo, Cloth, $1 50 each.

CÆSAR. — VIRGIL. — SALLUST. — HORACE. — CICERO'S ORATIONS. — CICERO'S OFFICES, &c.—CICERO ON ORATORY AND ORATORS.— CICERO'S TUSCULAN DISPUTATIONS, &c. — TACITUS (2 vols.). — TERENCE.—SOPHOCLES.—JUVENAL.—XENOPHON.—HOMER'S ILIAD. —HOMER'S ODYSSEY.—HERODOTUS.—DEMOSTHENES (2 vols.).— THUCYDIDES.—ÆSCHYLUS.—EURIPIDES (2 vols.).—LIVY (2 vols.). —PLATO [Select Dialogues].

LIVINGSTONE'S SOUTH AFRICA. Missionary Travels and Researches in South Africa: including a Sketch of Sixteen Years' Residence in the Interior of Africa, and a Journey from the Cape of Good Hope to Loanda on the West Coast; thence across the Continent, down the River Zambesi, to the Eastern Ocean. By DAVID LIVINGSTONE, LL.D., D.C.L. With Portrait, Maps, and Illustrations. 8vo, Cloth. $4 50; Sheep, $5 00; Half Calf, $6 75.

LIVINGSTONE'S ZAMBESI. Narrative of an Expedition to the Zambesi and its Tributaries, and of the Discovery of the Lakes Shirwa and Nyassa, 1858–1864. By DAVID and CHARLES LIVINGSTONE. With Map and Illustrations. 8vo, Cloth, $5 00; Sheep, $5 50; Half Calf, $7 25.

LIVINGSTONE'S LAST JOURNALS. The Last Journals of David Livingstone, in Central Africa, from 1865 to his Death. Continued by a Narrative of his Last Moments and Sufferings, obtained from his Faithful Servants Chuma and Susi. By HORACE WALLER, F.R.G.S., Rector of Twywell, Northampton. With Portrait, Maps, and Illustrations. 8vo, Cloth, $5 00; Sheep, $5 50; Half Calf, $7 25. Cheap Popular Edition, 8vo, Cloth, with Map and Illustrations, $2 50.

GROTE'S HISTORY OF GREECE. 12 vols., 12mo, Cloth, $18 00; Sheep, $22 80; Half Calf, $39 00.

RECLUS'S EARTH.   The Earth: a Descriptive History of the Phenomena of the Life of the Globe. By ÉLISÉE RECLUS. With 234 Maps
and Illustrations, and 23 Page Maps printed in Colors.   8vo, Cloth,
$5 00; Half Calf, $7 25.

RECLUS'S OCEAN.   The Ocean, Atmosphere, and Life.   Being the
Second Series of a Descriptive History of the Life of the Globe.   By
ÉLISÉE RECLUS.   Profusely Illustrated with 250 Maps or Figures, and
27 Maps printed in Colors.   8vo, Cloth, $6 00; Half Calf, $8 25.

NORDHOFF'S COMMUNISTIC SOCIETIES OF THE UNITED
STATES.   The Communistic Societies of the United States, from Personal Visit and Observation; including Detailed Accounts of the Economists, Zoarites, Shakers, the Amana, Oneida, Bethel, Aurora, Icarian,
and other existing Societies.   With Particulars of their Religious Creeds
and Practices, their Social Theories and Life, Numbers, Industries, and
Present Condition.   By CHARLES NORDHOFF.   Illustrations.   8vo,
Cloth, $4 00.

NORDHOFF'S CALIFORNIA.   California: for Health, Pleasure, and
Residence.   A Book for Travellers and Settlers.   Illustrated.   8vo,
Cloth, $2 50.

NORDHOFF'S NORTHERN CALIFORNIA, OREGON, AND THE
SANDWICH ISLANDS.   Northern California, Oregon, and the Sandwich Islands.   By CHARLES NORDHOFF.   Illustrated.   8vo, Cloth,
$2 50.

PARTON'S CARICATURE.   Caricature and Other Comic Art, in All
Times and Many Lands.   By JAMES PARTON.   With 203 Illustrations.
8vo, Cloth, Gilt Tops and uncut edges, $5 00.

*RAWLINSON'S MANUAL OF ANCIENT HISTORY.   A Manual
of Ancient History, from the Earliest Times to the Fall of the Western
Empire.   Comprising the History of Chaldæa, Assyria, Media, Baby-
lonia, Lydia, Phœnicia, Syria, Judæa, Egypt, Carthage, Persia, Greece,
Macedonia, Parthia, and Rome.   By GEORGE RAWLINSON, M.A.,
Camden Professor of Ancient History in the University of Oxford.
12mo, Cloth, $1 46.

NICHOLS'S ART EDUCATION.   Art Education applied to Industry.
By GEORGE WARD NICHOLS, Author of "The Story of the Great
March."   Illustrated.   8vo, Cloth, $4 00.

BAKER'S ISMAILÏA.   Ismailïa: a Narrative of the Expedition to Cen-
tral Africa for the Suppression of the Slave-trade, organized by Ismail,
Khedive of Egypt.   By Sir SAMUEL WHITE BAKER, PASHA, F.R.S.,
F.R.G.S.   With Maps, Portraits, and Illustrations.   8vo, Cloth, $5 00;
Half Calf, $7 25.

BOSWELL'S JOHNSON.   The Life of Samuel Johnson, LL.D., including a Journal of a Tour to the Hebrides.   By JAMES BOSWELL,
Esq.   Edited by JOHN WILSON CROKER, LL.D., F.R.S.   With a Portrait of Boswell.   2 vols., 8vo, Cloth, $4 00; Sheep, $5 00; Half Calf,
$8 50.

VAN-LENNEP'S BIBLE LANDS. Bible Lands: their Modern Customs and Manners Illustrative of Scripture. By the Rev. HENRY J. VAN-LENNEP, D.D. Illustrated with upward of 350 Wood Engravings and two Colored Maps. 838 pp., 8vo, Cloth, $5 00; Sheep, $6 00; Half Morocco, $8 00.

VINCENT'S LAND OF THE WHITE ELEPHANT. The Land of the White Elephant: Sights and Scenes in Southeastern Asia. A Personal Narrative of Travel and Adventure in Farther India, embracing the Countries of Burma, Siam, Cambodia, and Cochin-China (1871-2). By FRANK VINCENT, Jr. Illustrated with Maps, Plans, and Woodcuts. Crown 8vo, Cloth, $3 50.

SHAKSPEARE. The Dramatic Works of William Shakspeare. With Corrections and Notes. Engravings. 6 vols., 12mo, Cloth, $9 00. 2 vols., 8vo, Cloth, $4 00; Sheep, $5 00. In one vol., 8vo, Sheep, $4 00.

SMILES'S HISTORY OF THE HUGUENOTS. The Huguenots: their Settlements, Churches, and Industries in England and Ireland. By SAMUEL SMILES. With an Appendix relating to the Huguenots in America. Crown 8vo, Cloth, $2 00.

SMILES'S HUGUENOTS AFTER THE REVOCATION. The Huguenots in France after the Revocation of the Edict of Nantes; with a Visit to the Country of the Vaudois. By SAMUEL SMILES. Crown 8vo, Cloth, $2 00.

SMILES'S LIFE OF THE STEPHENSONS. The Life of George Stephenson, and of his Son, Robert Stephenson; comprising, also, a History of the Invention and Introduction of the Railway Locomotive. By SAMUEL SMILES. With Steel Portraits and numerous Illustrations. 8vo, Cloth, $3 00.

SQUIER'S PERU. Peru: Incidents of Travel and Exploration in the Land of the Incas. By E. GEORGE SQUIER, M.A., F.S.A., late U. S. Commissioner to Peru, Author of "Nicaragua," "Ancient Monuments of Mississippi Valley," &c., &c. With Illustrations. 8vo, Cloth, $5 00.

STRICKLAND'S (Miss) QUEENS OF SCOTLAND. Lives of the Queens of Scotland and English Princesses connected with the Regal Succession of Great Britain. By AGNES STRICKLAND. 8 vols., 12mo, Cloth, $12 00; Half Calf, $26 00.

THE "CHALLENGER" EXPEDITION. The Atlantic: an Account of the General Results of the Exploring Expedition of H.M.S. "Challenger." By Sir WYVILLE THOMSON, K.C.B., F.R.S. With numerous Illustrations, Colored Maps, and Charts, from Drawings by J. J. Wyld, engraved by J. D. Cooper, and Portrait of the Author, engraved by C. H. Jeens. 2 vols., 8vo, Cloth, $12 00.

BOURNE'S LIFE OF JOHN LOCKE. The Life of John Locke. By H. R. FOX BOURNE. 2 vols., 8vo, Cloth, uncut edges and gilt tops, $5 00.